MEMORY AND IDENTITY
IN ANCIENT JUDAISM AND EARLY CHRISTIANITY

MEMORY AND IDENTITY
IN ANCIENT JUDAISM AND EARLY CHRISTIANITY

A CONVERSATION WITH BARRY SCHWARTZ

Edited by
Tom Thatcher

SBL Press
Atlanta

Library of Congress Cataloging-in-Publication Data

Memory and identity in ancient Judaism and early Christianity : a conversation with Barry
Schwartz / edited by Tom Thatcher.
 p. cm. — (Society of Biblical Literature. Semeia studies ; number 78)
 Includes bibliographical references and indexes.
 Summary: "This volume applies theoretical principles, along with related aspects of
Schwartz's model and the work of other significant memory theorists, to a number
of case studies from ancient Jewish and early Christian history. The contributors to
the present volume ask three questions of specific research problems within their
individual fields of expertise: How can one separate the actual past from commemorative dressing in the extant sources, and what difference does it make to do so?; How
did ancient Jews and early Christians draw upon the past to create a durable sense
of communal identity, often in the face of trauma?; and, What strategies of keying
and framing are evident in the extant sources, and what can these tell us about those
texts and their authors and original audiences? While the contributors to the volume
answer, and nuance, these questions in different ways as they address them to their
respective cases in point, together they serve as the unifying theme of this book"
— Provided by publisher.
 ISBN 978-1-58983-952-6 (paper binding : alk. paper) — ISBN 978-1-58983-954-0
(electronic format) — ISBN 978-1-58983-953-3 (hardcover binding : alk. paper)
 1. Group identity. 2. Collective memory. 3. Church history—Primitive and early
church, ca. 30–600. 4. Judaism—History—Post-exilic period, 586 B.C.–210 A.D. 5. Jews—
Identity. 6. Schwartz, Barry, 1946– I. Thatcher, Tom, 1967– II. Schwartz, Barry, 1946–.
 HM753.M466 2014
 296.09'014—dc23   2014009578

Printed on acid-free, recycled paper conforming to
ANSI/NISO Z39.48–1992 (R1997) and ISO 9706, 1994
standards for paper permanence.

CONTENTS

PART 3: REFLECTIONS ON A COMING CONVERSATION

Abbreviations

1QpHab	Pesher Habakkuk (Dead Sea Scrolls)
AB	Anchor Bible Commentary series
ABRL	Anchor Bible Reference Library
ABD	*Anchor Bible Dictionary* (Doubleday)
AOAT	Alter Orient und Altes Testament series
A.J.	Josephus, *Antiquities of the Jews*
b. Pesah.	Babylonian Talmud tractate Pesahim
b. Roš Haš.	Babylonian Talmud tractate Rosh Hashanah
b. Sanh.	Babylonian Talmud tractate Sanhedrin
b. Suk.	Babylonian Talmud tractate Sukkot
b. Ta'an.	Babylonian Talmud tractate Ta'anit
BECNT	Baker Exegetical Commentary on the New Testament
BETL	Bibliotheca Ephemeridum Theologicarum Lovaniensium
BibInt	*Biblical Interpretation*
B.J.	Josephus, *Jewish War*
BK	*Bibel und Kirche*
BN	*Biblische Notizen*
BR	*Biblical Research*
BTB	*Biblical Theology Bulletin*
BZ	*Biblische Zeitschrift*
BZNW	Beihefte zur Zeitschrift für die neutestamentliche Wissenschaft
C. Ap.	Josephus, *Against Apion*
CBQ	*Catholic Biblical Quarterly*
CBQMS	Catholic Biblical Quarterly Monograph Series
CD	The Damascus Document ("Cairo Damascus," also 4QD, 5QD, 6QD; Dead Sea Scrolls)
Comm. Gal.	Jerome, *Commentary on Galatians*
ConBNT	Coniectanea biblica: New Testament Series
Did.	Didache

DSD	*Dead Sea Discoveries*
Ep.	Augustine, *Epistles*
ESCO	European Studies in Christian Origins
ExpT	*Expository Times*
Flaccus	Philo, *Against Flaccus*
FRLANT	Forschungen zur Religion und Literatur des Alten und Neuen Testaments
Haer.	Irenaeus's *Against Heresies*
Hist. eccl.	Eusebius, *Ecclesiastical History*
Hom. Luc.	Origen, *Homily on Luke*
HTR	*Harvard Theological Review*
Inst.	Quintillian, *Institutes of Rhertoric*
JAOS	*Journal of the American Oriental Society*
JBL	*Journal of Biblical Literature*
JFBT	Jahrbuch für Biblische Theologie
JSHJ	*Journal for the Study of the Historical Jesus*
JSJSup	Journal for the Study of Judaism in the Persian, Hellenistic, and Roman Periods Supplements
JSNT	*Journal for the Study of the New Testament*
JSNTSup	Journal for the Study of the New Testament Supplement Series
JSPSup	Journal for the Study of the Pseudepigrapha Supplement Series
JSOT	*Journal for the Study of the Old Testament*
JSOTSup	Journal for the Study of the Old Testament Supplement Series
JTS	*Journal of Theological Studies*
LCL	Loeb Classical Library
LHJS	Library of Historical Jesus Studies
LNTS	Library of New Testament Studies
LSTS	Library of Second Temple Studies
m. 'Avot	Mishnah tractate 'Avot
m. B. Bat.	Mishnah tractate Bava Batra
m. Mid.	Mishnah tractate Middot
m. Pesah.	Mishnah tractate Pesahim
m. Roš Haš	Mishnah tractate Rosh Hashanah
m. Suk.	Mishnah tractate Sukkot
Mem. rem.	Aristotle, *Memory and Reminiscence*
Midr. Pss	Midrash on Psalms

NICNT	New International Commentary on the New Testament
NICOT	New International Commentary on the Old Testament
NovT	*Novum Testamentum*
NovTSup	Novum Testamentum Supplements
NTOA	Novum Testamentum et Orbis Antiquus
NTS	*New Testament Studies*
NTTSD	New Testament Tools, Studies, and Documents
Orat.	Cicero, *On the Orator*
Phil.	Polycarp, *To the Philippians*
Praescr.	Tertullian, *Prescription against Heretics*
Ps.-Clem.	*Pseudo-Clementine Writings*
RB	*Revue biblique*
RBL	*Review of Biblical Literature*
Rhet. Her.	*Rhetoric ad Herennium*
SacPag	Sacra Pagina series
SBLDS	Society of Biblical Literature Dissertation Series
SBLRBS	Society of Biblical Literature Resources for Biblical Studies
SBLSBL	Society of Biblical Literature Studies in Biblical Literature
SBLSymS	Society of Biblical Literature Symposium Series
SBS	Stuttgarter Bibelstudien
SemeiaSt	Semeia Studies
Sir	Wisdom of Jesus ben Sirach/Ecclesiasticus
SJOT	*Scandinavian Journal of the Old Testament*
SNTSMS	Society for New Testament Studies Monograph Series
STDJ	Studies on the Texts of the Desert of Judah
StPB	Studia post-biblica
STW	Suhrkamp-Taschenbuch Wissenschaft
t. B. Bat.	Tosefta tractate Bava Batra
t. Ta'an.	Tosefta tractate Ta'anit
t. Yoma	Tosefta tractate Yoma
TSAJ	Texte und Studien zum antiken Judentum
TynB	*Tyndale Bulletin*
Vita	Josephus, *Life*
VTSup	Supplements to Vetus Testamentum
WBC	Word Biblical Commentary
WMANT	Wissenschaftliche Monographien zum Alten und Neuen Testamentum
WUNT	Wissenschaftliche Untersuchungen zum Neuen Testament
ZAW	*Zeitschrift für die alttestamentliche Wissenschaft*

ZNW   *Zeitschrift für die neutestamentliche Wissenschaft und die Kunde der älteren Kirche*

PREFACE:
KEYS, FRAMES, AND THE PROBLEM OF THE PAST

Tom Thatcher

Traditionally, volumes of this kind, dedicated to applications of theoretical principles developed by a leading voice in another field, require lengthy introductions that summarize the contribution of the scholar under consideration. In the present case, however, no such introduction is needed, because the individual whose work serves as the platform for these studies on ancient Jewish and Christian collective memory, Barry Schwartz, has himself written an extensive methodological introduction for the book and has also provided a thoughtful response to the remaining studies. Schwartz's contributions here extend a warm and fruitful running dialogue with biblical scholarship that has included participation in several meetings of the Society of Biblical Literature and a number of recent articles on problems in Christian origins (Schwartz 2005a, 2005b, 2011). In the process, Schwartz has become a mentor to many in applications of social/ collective/cultural memory theories to issues in biblical studies, and the present book seeks to continue this conversation through focused reflection on several foundational premises of his theoretical model.

At the risk of overgeneralization, even a cursory review of Schwartz's extensive list of publications on collective memory will reveal that he is an applied theorist: rather than articulating abstract principles and then seeking illustrations to validate his claims, he moves from detailed analyses of historical and contemporary figures and social trends to theoretical reflections on the ways that, and reasons why, groups utilize the past. This approach is readily evident in Schwartz's many detailed studies of iconic figures and events from American history, which typically move from a broad outline of the scholarly consensus on "what actually happened" to close review of the evolving commemoration of individuals and events over time and in different media (art, architecture, literature, holidays, rituals, news outlets, film, etc.). Yet while Schwartz presents himself as a careful social historian, his research is grounded in a number of theoretical assumptions about the relationship between the actual past and collective memory. Several of these assumptions, which together form a solid theoretical foundation, are outlined by Schwartz himself in the introduction to this book, but they may be briefly summarized here by way of preview and to establish a broad conceptual framework for all the chapters to follow.

First, Schwartz's work is characterized by a fierce commitment to the principle that the actual past and its subsequent commemorations are interfluential—interfluential to such an extent that one is never eclipsed by the other in any specific act of memory. While present circumstances determine the form of collective memory, the actual past provides memory's foundational content—memory's limits are fixed, to some degree, by its point of origin. This is not to say, of course, that collective memory can be taken at face value as historical record, nor that the past is immune to manipulation, nor that individuals and societies do not remember and forget selectively. At the same time, Schwartz adamantly rejects constructionist approaches that view memory merely as a mirror of present power relations and instead insists that "the way things are" is a product of "the way things were" and that the actual past is always present, to some degree and in a determinative way, in its subsequent commemorations. This aspect of Schwartz's research puts a fine point on the question of "historicity": When ancient documents are viewed as "sources" for the past, how can one differentiate commemorative dressing from raw historical content, and how would that difference impact the interpretation of those texts?

Second, and building on the first principle, Schwartz consistently emphasizes the normative force of the commemorated past, exploring ways that groups look to past events and individuals as models and patterns. Established exemplars are particularly significant during times of crisis and change, periods when groups face new experiences and circumstances that threaten traditional ways of life and thinking and, sometimes, their very survival. In seasons of trauma, the remembered past provides a sense of continuity and common identity and also offers resources for making sense of present experience. This aspect of Schwartz's research highlights the adaptive nature of the past and the capacity of groups to maintain self-consciousness across generations and in dramatically different circumstances, including circumstances of deep loss and substantive change. Applied to the present discussion, How did ancient Jews and early Christians draw upon the past as a tool for survival in the face of overwhelming challenges to their faith and, in some cases, their communal existence?

Third, and more narrowly, Schwartz has helpfully highlighted two memory techniques, "keying" and "framing," that facilitate the interaction of past and present in ways that support social cohesion. *Keying* is the act of associating, often unconsciously, a present person, event, institution, or experience to a past counterpart; once this connection has been established, the keyed entity and the values associated with it become a *frame* that provides an interpretive context for present experience. In simple terms, memory looks to the past to explain what is happening now, but Schwartz demonstrates that this complex process cannot be conceived simply in terms of drawing analogies or citing historical precedents—keying and framing are mnemonic, not merely rhetorical, strategies, and as such they are generative forces that may manifest themselves in a variety of ways on the surface of texts and other artifacts of group life. Because memory unites the remembered past and its commemorations in a reciprocal cycle of influence, keying becomes a way of drawing the past into the present, and frames become powerful norms for establishing and maintaining social identity. This aspect of Schwartz's work raises important questions about the ways that, and reasons why, ancient Israelites and early Christians remembered as they did. What keys/frames are evident in the available sources, how have these impacted the presentation of both past and present in these documents, why did Jews and Christians draw upon some elements of the past while ignoring others, and what are the interpretive and historical implications of these strategies of remembering and forgetting?

In a general sense, the present volume applies the theoretical principles outlined above, along with related aspects of Schwartz's model and the work of other significant memory theorists, to a number of case studies from ancient Jewish and early Christian history. The contributors to the present volume ask the three questions above of specific research problems within their individual fields of expertise: How can one separate the actual past from commemorative dressing in the extant sources, and what difference does it make to do so? How did ancient Jews and early Christians draw upon the past to create a durable sense of communal identity, often in the face of trauma? What strategies of keying and framing are evident in the extant sources, and what can these tell us about those texts and their authors and original audiences? While the contributors answer, and nuance, these questions in different ways as they address them to their respective cases in point, together they serve as the unifying theme of this book.

Two narrower points relating to the structure and content of the remainder of this collection should be noted before proceeding. First, because questions of history, identity, trauma, cohesion, and mnemonic strategies such as keying/framing are intertwined both in Barry Schwartz's work and in the essays in this volume—and indeed, they must be intertwined, simply because they are inextricable in collective memory itself—the remaining chapters are not organized topically or methodologically. Reflecting the state of current research much more than the state of ancient Judaism and early Christianity, the essays in part 1 explore the works of memory in the world of ancient Israel, while the essays in part 2 focus narrowly on the emerging Christian movement. Effectively, the sequence of chapters follows canonical order, with a view to avoiding the methodological limitations that might be inherent in a more topical arrangement.

Second, and significantly, the authors of these essays have been asked to interact with Schwartz's model in a creative and dialogic fashion, assuming the reader's awareness of the content of Schwartz's introductory essay. As a result, the individual studies engage principles and problems in Schwartz's model but do not offer detailed reviews or critiques of the nuances of his research. Strategically, this approach attempts to imitate the ongoing dialogue between Barry's work and that of biblical scholarship, while at the same time reflecting the origins of the present volume. Schwartz's introduction came to life as a keynote paper in a session of the Society of Biblical Literature, in which leading biblical scholars were asked to reflect on ways that his model might or might not inform their own research. Several of the chapters included here emerged from that session, and the remaining contributors were asked to read and reflect on Barry's keynote address and apply or test his premises to/on a topic within their areas of expertise. Here as in that meeting, Schwartz rounds out the discussion by offering specific remarks in response to each contribution, and readers of the present volume may find it helpful to consult his "Harvest" entry at the end of the book after reading each individual essay to gain a sense of the running dialogue. The present volume is offered in the hope that this conversation will continue for years to come.

Works Cited

Schwartz, Barry. 2005a. Christian Origins: Historical Truth and Social Memory. Pages 43–56 in *Memory, Tradition, and Text: Uses of the Past in Early Christianity*. Edited by Alan Kirk and Tom Thatcher. SemeiaSt 52. Atlanta: Society of Biblical Literature.

——. 2005b. Jesus in First-Century Memory—A Response. Pages 249–61 in *Memory, Tradition, and Text: Uses of the Past in Early Christianity*. Edited by Alan Kirk and Tom Thatcher. SemeiaSt 52. Atlanta: Society of Biblical Literature.

——. 2011. What Difference Does the Medium Make? Pages 225–38 in *The Fourth Gospel in First-Century Media Culture*. Edited byAnthony Le Donne and Tom Thatcher. ESCO/LNTS 426. London: T&T Clark.

Where There's Smoke, There's Fire: Memory and History

Barry Schwartz

Late Second Temple period scholarship is premised on the belief that Jews of the time thought about the past differently from the way we do. Their knowledge was rooted in traditional legends and communal bonds; ours is data-driven, self-critical, and context-free. Both statements—history is subjective and situation-dependent, and history is objective and situation-transcendent—provoke ambivalence because both are partly but not absolutely true. The problem begins when this ambivalence inhibits us from applying the findings of modern research to instances of ancient memory, for these findings often tell us what it means to "remember," help us dissect the complex relation between individual memory and history, and, above all, define the meaning and significance of memory as a *social* phenomenon.

Individuals forget much of their experience—sometimes permanently, sometimes until a cue from the environment awakens it. On the other hand, sometimes individuals experience something they cannot forget. Three examples will help to illustrate this point, which is necessary to the defining of collective memory.

First, few knew much about U.S. President Abraham Lincoln's young adulthood when he was assassinated in 1865. But William Herndon, Lincoln's former law partner, located and interviewed 250 informants, including many former New Salem, Illinois, residents who had known Lincoln while he lived there in the 1830s. Because thirty-five to forty years had passed since these people last saw Lincoln (an interval equal to that separating Mark from the crucifixion of Jesus), Herndon conscientiously weeded out distortions, rumors, and mistakes in order to estimate the truth value of their testimony (Wilson and Davis 1995). He then used this adjusted store of information to publish the most comprehensive biography to date of Lincoln's early life (Herndon and Weik 1889).

In 1895, six years after the release of Herndon's three-volume work and thirty years after Lincoln's death, publisher Samuel S. McClure sent historian Ida Tarbell on a fact-finding tour, during which she conducted scores of face-to-face interviews with Lincoln's former friends and acquaintances (Rice 1998, 57–72). Her requests for information about Lincoln, posted in newspapers throughout the Midwest, yielded many replies—some authentic, some not. Her work resulted in a new interpretation of Lincoln's youth and young adulthood, one that identified his frontier background as an asset rather than a handicap, and she persuasively challenged many of Herndon's negative characterizations of Lincoln. Tarbell is to Herndon, one might say, as John is to Mark, for Tarbell and John both elevated the original portrayal of their subject through a reconfiguration of personal and popular recollections.

As a second case, seventy years after the American Civil War (1861–1865), the Works Progress Administration funded interviews of African Americans who had been born into slave families. This oral-history project covered all slave-holding states and resulted in a vast collection entitled *The American Slave* (Rawick 1977). Based on elderly people's memories of their plantation childhoods, the individual narratives are, in themselves, imperfect sources, but the thick methodological literature (Escott 1979) that has formed around them enhances our overall understanding of the *collective* experience of slave life. *The American Slave* embodies a composite picture that transcends the limitations of any single individual's recollection of his or her personal experience.

For our third example, Katsuichi Honda (1999) interviewed survivors of the December 1937–February 1938 Nanking Massacre. These illiterate victims could not have written their own stories, but their oral retellings, after more than thirty years, substantially enlarged the records of the war-crime tribunals. Here again, the force of individual testimonies emerges from their totality, as the memories of individual survivors converge in a relatively unified portrait.

There can be no objection to defining such works—from Herndon's and Tarbell's books on Lincoln to the final report of the slave narratives to Honda's interviews—as "oral histories," but to do so is to take the viewpoint of the authors alone. In fact, memories of Lincoln, plantation slavery, and the Nanking Massacre were *social* memories, transmitted over time and existing independently of the people whom these authors consulted. The four canonical Gospels embody the same kind of autonomous, *social* memories.

The Gospels are comparable not only to oral and written tradition, which superimposes legend upon reality, but also to historical fiction (with emphasis on the *historical*), as exemplified in the twentieth-century accounts of the historical Abraham Lincoln by Honoré Morrow (1935), Carl Sandburg (1926, 1939), Gore Vidal (1984), and William Safire (1987; see also Fehrenbacher 1987, 228–45). Such works seek to enlarge and vivify the historical plotline by *creating conversations* between Lincoln and others and with himself, conversations that dramatize Lincoln's personality, motives, character, aims, and priorities. The Gospels bring the history of Jesus to life in the same way. No successful historical writer, however, is free to create any conversation he or she likes; the writer must construct talk that readers find plausibly motivated, consistent with the subject's actions, and hence objectively possible.

Memories of Abraham Lincoln, the nineteenth-century "man of sorrows," were passed on orally from one generation to the next, retained long after the people who originally carried them had scattered or died. As these memories were passed on, they were modified, but the essence of the events to which they refer remained unchanged. This essence, and the ways and reasons it is maintained, are the principal subjects of my research into social memory.

What Is Social Memory?

In the social sciences and the humanities, social memory is reputed to be an ambiguous and complex concept (e.g., Olick and Robbins 1998; Olick 2008; Roediger and Wertsch 2008). In fact, no concept is clearer or simpler. Memory is a fundamental property of the mind, an indispensable component of culture, and an essential aspect of tradition. Although individuals alone possess the capacity to remember the past, they never do so singly; they do so with and against others situated in different groups and through the knowledge and symbols that predecessors and contemporaries transmit to them.

A good analogy to social memory is public opinion. Opinions, like memories, can only be held by individuals and can only be assessed by questioning individuals, but when these opinions are aggregated they assume new significance. Collective or *public* opinion affects the way the average person thinks about matters of the day. It renders individuals more or less confident in their own *personal* opinions.[1] Public opinion determines elections, the price of goods, and the morality of given lines of conduct.

---

1. George Herbert Mead formulated the concept of the "generalized other" to

Social memory resembles public opinion but comprises special subject matter. It refers to the *distribution* throughout society of what individuals believe, know, and feel about the *past*, how they judge the *past* morally, how closely they identify with it, and how they commemorate it. The word "distribution" is emphasized above because the key property of a distribution is its variation, which denies the possibility of complete consensus. That every distribution also has a central tendency makes total dissensus equally impossible. Because similar distributions appear in groups of individuals totally unknown to one another, they must be treated as "social facts" (Durkheim 1982, 50–84), *exterior* to the persons who comprise them. Such facts stabilize and link the consciousness of present and past.

Media are memory's vehicles. Premodern memory media included oral presentations, written documents, and commemorative objects, including hagiographic texts, paintings, statues, monuments, shrines, naming practices, oratory, and ritual observances. The latter, ritual observances, are social memory's most general medium. In Judaism, memory flowed through the recital of lectors, often based on written texts and usually occurring within ritual settings (Yerushalmi 1996, 11). As a standardized, repetitive, and symbolic activity that allows participants to define their relation to the past, commemorative ritual fixes in mind the events of the past, a process facilitated by the emotional assembling of the community itself (Durkheim 1965, 414, 433; Kirk 2005b, 7–10). Modern memory media include museums, photographs, cartoons, films, television, and websites. Modern media, prone as they are to suspicion and approbation alike, carry both negative and positive reminiscences: a museum might document atrocities; a text might be damning; a portrait, unflattering; a cartoon, ridiculing; a statue, degrading; a monument, covered with graffiti and uncared for; a shrine, unvisited; ritual observances, with or without oratory, unattended or ridiculed. But most vehicles of social memory convey positive information, positive feelings, and positive judgments. Although frequently violated, a collective pleasure principle seems to be at work. Societies tend to invest more resources in the preservation of positive phases of the past than of negative ones.

To this point, four dimensions of memory have been distinguished: (1) the past as it actually was; (2) "history," which refers to linear repre-

---

explain how aggregated beliefs, sentiments, and moral values enter into the personality of individuals (1967, 152–64).

sentations of the past that take the form of oral and written narratives; (3) "commemoration," whose symbols lift from the historical narrative those parts that best express society's ideals; and (4) social memory—how individuals, in the aggregate, think and feel about the past. From these distinctions arise the problems of how social memories get started and transmitted, how individual memories form the *emergent narratives* that constitute social memory, how social memory is preserved against forces conducive to forgetting and change, how closely the actual past typically corresponds to its historical, social, and commemorative representations, and what makes some historical events more memorable than others.

This chapter orients these theoretical questions to a specific case: the vexing problem of the historical validity of the Gospels, which will be treated here as products of early Christian memory. The remaining chapters in this book will assess my approach by applying it to the broader range of Jewish and Christian texts and historical problems in which the individual contributors specialize.

How Memories Get Started

Those listening to stories about the powers of holy men in the First and Second Temple periods were motivated to remember every word, and we know that the rabbinic tradition, with its admonition to remember (*zakhor*) dominated first-century Jewish culture (Gerhardsson 1961; Yerushalmi 1996, 5–26). On the cognitive underpinning of mnemonic tactics we can always turn to David Rubin (1995), among others, but the more pressing sociological question is why these tactics were employed in the first place. Put another way, where did first-century Jewish memory come from, and why did it assume the form it did?

People who have a stake in a person's or event's memory being maintained (see Lang and Lang 1990; Fine 1996) form the "carrier groups" (Weber 1968, 468–517) that interpret, preserve, and propagate stories about the past. Unrepresented by such groups, the stories important to one generation are forgotten by the next. Sacred history tells us, however, that some stories were unique: remembering them was more than an option, even more than a *personal* duty; it was an obligatory *social role* enacted by religious elites in order to perpetuate consciousness of humanity's debt to God. In fact, these memory virtuosi may have transmitted information almost as accurately as modern news agencies. Sacred events, moreover, were not perpetuated solely by memory elites. Dedicated and potential listeners drew information from eyewitness accounts of men and women *outside* the inner circle of religious followers (see Bauckham 2003). First-century elite testimony remained the gold standard on which other testimonies could be judged, but there was no central control; oral tradition arose unwittingly, from the bottom up, to be later preserved in writing.

Readers of the Torah and its stories were not "cognitive misers" (Fiske and Taylor 1991, 13) trying to simplify the past; they were motivated to remember the past in detail. But how can even inspired and motivated remembering be preserved in societies largely dependent on oral communication? This is a major question in the study of ancient memory. Two communication models may be deployed to explain how social memories were developed and disseminated in an ancient context.

The first model—probably still the dominant model in biblical studies and rabbinics, despite severe limitations that I will soon indicate—is conveniently described by Bart Ehrman (1999). Because a story changes as one person passes it to the next, Ehrman likens its transmission to the game "Telephone." Children play by sitting in a circle. The first child whispers something to the second, who relays it to the third, who tells the next, until the last child hears the final version of what the first one said. This last version invariably turns out to be very different from the original and subject to great hilarity, which is why the game is so popular. The problem with Ehrman's analogy is that ancient stories did not go in circles. They multiplied exponentially: one person told the story to his relatives, friends, and acquaintances, each of whom knew several people and some of whom passed on the story to their own several relatives, friends, and acquaintances. Network theory (Stark 1996) shows that five or six iterations yield thousands of story recipients. Furthermore, this process is not random: it plays out within existing social networks, namely, clusters of people who are likely to share the beliefs and values of the storytellers. Take the early Jesus tradition as an example: if Richard Horsley (1989) is right about ancient Palestine, these social clusters initially consisted of peasants eager to free themselves of the tributes demanded by Roman and Jewish elites. Clustering enhances receptivity to the stories while it limits their variation to a range compatible with recipients' culture and interests.

Networks and clustering point to a second communication model that differs from Ehrman's logic in its conception of memory's origin: a single story may have more than one "original" version. Edmund Leach explains why this is the case in his account of myth transmission.

Let us imagine the situation of an individual A who is trying to get a message to a friend B who is almost out of earshot, and let us suppose that communication is further hampered by various kinds of interference—noise from wind, passing cars, and so on. What will A do? If he is sensible he will not be satisfied with shouting his message just once; he will shout it *several* times, and give a *different* wording to the message each time, supplementing his words with visual signals. At the receiving end B may likely get the meaning of each of the individual messages slightly wrong, but when he puts them together the redundancies and the mutual consistencies and inconsistencies will make it quite clear what is "really" being said. (Leach 1976, 63–64)

Following the logic of this model, the "meaning" of the message is not in any single one of its versions but in all of them taken together. To return to the example noted earlier: Abraham Lincoln's friends did not fall silent when he died; they continued to broadcast his virtues, and they did so convincingly. Eyewitnesses to Lincoln's later life also lived long after his death, and through teaching as well as ordinary social contacts they communicated information about him. Let Lincoln's close friends represent A to K; other eyewitnesses, L to Z. Each witness need not tell the same story in order for a fair estimate of the "real Lincoln" to appear on the "receiving end" of the line (to return to the Telephone analogy). Indeed, the more varied a narrative, the more effectively it is conveyed and remembered. Not every valid story about the past has a single point of origin.

How Individual Memories Become Social Memory

Historical information remains stable when the narrative arising from multiple versions of a famous life story becomes independent of its tellers. Folklore study attests to this aspect of tradition. Late nineteenth- and early twentieth-century French folklorists recorded almost ten thousand popular tales representing stable oral traditions spanning many generations. These anonymous storytellers, according to Robert Darnton, "kept the main elements [of the traditional narratives] intact, using repetitions, rhymes, and other mnemonic devices" (1984, 16; see also Rubin 1995). But why did they go to the trouble? These stories provide a point of entry into the mental world of the French peasant, who passed them on because she found in them a picture of herself and her distress. Folklorists could never reach this entry point had they confined themselves to one version of a story or to fine points of detail, and they felt no need to do so. With thirty-five variations on "Little Red Riding Hood," ninety on "Tom Thumb," and 105 on "Cinderella," there is sufficient redundancy to discern the stem story's theme, style, and tone. This redundancy discloses a social memory that precedes and transcends any specific act of storytelling.

The redundancies in scores of French folk tales are generalizable to other texts, including the Scriptures. Although there are only four partially independent Gospels in the New Testament, they make up in time and topic what they lack in number. They refer to a real historical figure, were written shortly (a few decades) after his death, and remained after their tellers vanished. Such stories, in Emile Durkheim's (1974) words, are "collective representations" that emerge from individual sources.[2] Shortly after Durkheim, Alfred Kroeber expressed a similar understanding. In his words, "there are certain properties of culture—such as transmissibility, high variability, cumulativeness, value standards, influence on individuals—which are difficult to explain strictly in terms of the organic composition of personalities or individuals" (1963, 62). These properties are "superpersonal," which is to say "emergent"—the product of a multiplicity of single interactions.

More recent data demonstrate further the stickiness of emergent narratives. Over a thirteen-year period (1975–1988), historian Michael Frisch instructed his college students to "write down the first ten names that you think of in [relation] to … American history from its beginning through the end of the Civil War." Frisch varied his questionnaire by including and excluding questions about generals, presidents, statesmen, and others. He posed the questions to students with one or no previous college courses in American history and at two different universities in two different states. The student cohorts had no previous communication with one another, used different textbooks, went to different high schools, and had different teachers. Nevertheless, their rank orderings of significant figures in American history were almost identical over the entire thirteen-year time span. Because the same names—Washington, Lincoln, and Jefferson, in that order—occupied the top three presidential ranks for every test group, because these and other rankings were independent of knowledge of American history or differences in regional background, and because the test subjects regularly listed historical figures who are not mentioned in

---

2. "Collective representations," commonly manifested in symbolic and iconic signs, reflect cognitive, affective, and moral states of the "collective consciousness." See here Lukes 1973, 6–8, and also n. 3 below.

standard textbooks (notably Betsy Ross, who, according to popular legend, produced the first American flag), Frisch infers the existence of a collective fixation on origins that the content of history texts alone cannot explain. "[T]he list is not only composed of quasi-mythic figures: as a collective portrait, it has a kind of mythic structure and completeness itself, a character confirmed by its re-creation year after year in nearly identical terms" (Frisch 1989, 1146). Tradition's consistency thus presupposes its autonomy, while autonomy presumes an emergent social memory.

Some (e.g., Megill 2007) have argued that traditions rely on memory only when they are fading, while sound traditions affirm themselves by a canon of authoritative writings, respected institutions, and credible and legitimate leaders. But this is a theoretical, not an empirical, claim, for the opposing logic is equally compelling: far from being a symptom of weakened tradition, memory is strong tradition's main component—the *source* of authoritative writings, respected institutions, and leaders. Edward Shils believed as much, and he went even further. In the study of the Torah, before the Mishnah redaction, written texts were regarded as *auxiliary instruments to aid memory*. Even when technologically unnecessary, therefore, memorization of narratives reinforced tradition—which can only mean that memory's role was ritualistic as well as instrumental, an end in itself. To memorize a narrative, even its broad outlines, was to *internalize* it, to define oneself in its terms (Shils 1981, 92–93).

Preserving Social Memory

The coherence of most historical accounts results not only from the obdurateness of the reality they represent but also because their preservation and transmission processes—keying and framing, oral and written communication, path dependency, sites of memory, and critical life-course periods—are so consequential.

Keying (perhaps most familiar to biblical and rabbinics scholars as an aspect of typology) transforms the meaning of activities understood in terms of one reference frame by comparing them with activities understood in terms of another (Goffman 1974, 40–44, 82). Keying is the action that activates framing. For example, Abraham Lincoln invoked the American Revolution as a frame for the Civil War by keying his Gettysburg Address into it; Carl Sandburg described the liberating power of Franklin Roosevelt's New Deal by keying it to Lincoln's Emancipation Proclamation. Similarly, the Gospels key the activities and fate of Jesus to statements in the Hebrew Scriptures an estimated three hundred times, which affirms both the Gospel writers' mastery of Scripture and their listeners' identification with the history the sacred texts describe.

Keying defines social memory's function, matching the past to the present as (1) a model *of* society, reflecting its needs, interests, fears, and aspirations; (2) a model *for* society, a template for thought, sentiment, morality, and conduct; and, (3) a *frame* within which people find meaning for their experience (Schwartz 2000, 2008; Poole 2008). In these senses, social memory is preserved by and for the functions it performs.

By keying events of the present to a sacred past, communities and their members alike refer to and frame the collective experience. As such, the meaning of a social memory involves "not just the history being commemorated, but the accumulated succession of commemorations" (Olick 2007, 58). Sacred texts are, thus, "path-dependent"—affected not only by their social contexts but also by previous representations of their content. In Georg Simmel's words, "We are free to make the first move, but we are servants of the second" (1977, 92). To the extent that earlier interpretations contributed to the content of later ones, the Gospels possessed an inertia that only significant social change could modify. That 90 percent of the Gospel of Mark appears in Matthew and Luke exemplifies the relevance of path-dependency for memory and tradition.

Scripture obviously plays a major role in maintaining sacred narratives, but its timing, in some cases, has been misunderstood. The failure of Jesus' prophecy that the parousia would occur within the lifetimes of his followers highlights the reasons why the Gospels were not written sooner. The timing of *written* Gospel narratives during the second half of the first century CE reflected not only the dying of a generation of witnesses and a concern to secure their memories, as Jan Assmann (see 2006a; 2006b) famously declared, but also a growing conviction that the end of days was far enough in the future to make time-consuming written accounts worth the effort.

In the Jerusalem temple, also, many Christians and Jews must have seen a concrete link relating their mundane existences to God's larger plan. By destroying the temple, the Roman army destroyed a physical manifestation of God's majesty. What a difference it must have made for this generation! To commemorate God by visiting the place of his presence was one thing; to remember him by listening to lectors' stories in mundane, local contexts, another. Written accounts became sanctified as they replaced the temple as "localizations" (Halbwachs 1992a, 1992b) or "sites" (Nora 1989) of sacred history.

"Critical periods" also play a significant although largely unrecognized role in the preservation of memory. One of the best-established findings of social memory research is that individuals are most likely to remember important events that occur in their late adolescence and early adulthood. The relevance of this critical period to memory was asserted in the writings of Karl Mannheim (1952) but has been verified only recently by Howard Schuman and his associates (Schuman and Scott 1989; Schuman and Corning 2012). Individuals in late adolescence and early adulthood are going through formative years during which a distinctive openness to new points of view, including ideology, religion, politics, and history arises. As late adolescence/early adulthood is the stage in the life cycle when a permanent identity forms (Erikson 1959), the memory of any great person, for his or her admirers or worshipers, fuses with selfhood. As a case in point, those who came to know Jesus during their critical life period would have been more impressed by him, more passionately attached to him, than those born earlier or later. Also, they would have been most receptive to the developing oral tradition in the decades following his death. As a new Christian generation appeared, people exposed to Jesus' teaching and actions during their critical period would have been elderly, roughly fifty to sixty years old. In a society where authority was an entitlement of age and the credibility of a narrative depended on the social status of its transmitter, these individuals would have been effective "opinion leaders" (Katz and Lazarsfeld 1955) as one Gospel succeeded another.

MEMORY AND HISTORY

Memory's carriers are its primary preservers. James Dunn, prominent among historical Jesus scholars, declares that "the quest for the *historical Jesus*" can only be the quest for "Jesus remembered" (2003, 335). In other words, Jesus himself is "unobservable," and the only way we can know him is through his influence on his contemporaries. But how much stock can be placed in their memories? Is it not the destiny of all memory, in fact, to be annihilated by history? Pierre Nora (1989) tells us so, but if we take him uncritically we must not only renounce much of what individual participants have taught us about historical events but also give up all attempts to learn more. That Nora and his likeminded colleagues exaggerate the difference between social memory and history, underestimate their interdependence, misunderstand memory's nature, and vastly understate its validity is the argument to be considered here. At issue is how knowledge of histori-

cal figures, including those for whom little documentation exists, is theoretically possible. Readers will have no trouble identifying implications for
the meaning and authenticity of the Gospels.

Even on its face, belief in the fading of social memory is problematic
because biographers, autobiographers, memoir writers, journalists, novel-
ists, and historians alike are paralyzed without access to it. In recent years,
it is true, a more nuanced perception of the relationship between history
and memory has emerged, but that revision is ambivalent and confusing.
British historian Peter Burke's (1989) oft-cited work remains as good a
sample of this ambivalence as any other. Burke recognizes that "memory
reflects what actually happened and that history reflects memory." But
this traditional view, Burke believes, is no longer valid. "Neither memory
nor history seem objective any longer." Because different historians in different times and places have produced different versions of the past, the
phrase "history as social memory" is simply a "shorthand which sums
up the complex process of selection and interpretation." Burke concedes
that if memory is not distinguished from history, then we fail to recognize
that individuals are influenced by their own experiences of the past. But if
memories are faultlessly embedded in written records, why is there apparently so much discrepancy between written records and the past as it was?

Ambivalence about memory and history actually stems less from
evidence of their discrepancy than from the mentality of contemporary
humanities and social-science scholars, who, being more suspicious of
"knowledge" than was any preceding generation, are more impressed than
ever by proof of memory's imperfections. This new mood has its virtues,
including the protection it affords against naïve realism, but if we do not
recognize it for what it is we lose more than we gain. To say that history and
memory are more "selective" and less "objective" than commonly believed
is to make a useless statement, for partial knowledge is not synonymous
with faulty knowledge. Never in the history of the humanities and sciences
has there been a generation that failed to concentrate on some problems more than others. The question is whether selectivity exposes valid
memory or memory warped for political and ideological reasons. Failure
to resolve this issue is one of the factors concealing the relation between
history and memory.

To trace this problem to its root in social memory research, French
sociologist Maurice Halbwachs proposed the first systematic explanation,
and few scholars today take serious issue with it. Halbwachs was a student
of both Henri Bergson, who emphasized the subjective aspects of time,

thought, and reality, and also of Emile Durkheim, the social realist who taught Halbwachs that society is not reducible to its members' *subjective* states. Society is an *objective* reality, *sui generis* and possessing a "collective consciousness."[3] Halbwachs's work on memory drew more from Bergson than from Durkheim. In *The Legendary Topography of the Gospels*, he declares, "If, as we believe, social memory is essentially a reconstruction of the past, if it adapts the image of ancient facts to the beliefs and spiritual needs of the present, then a knowledge of the origin of these facts must be secondary, if not altogether useless, for the reality *of* the past is no longer *in* the past" (Halbwachs 1992b, 7). After seventy years of subsequent scholarship, this statement seems as if it were made yesterday—which is precisely the problem. No one can doubt that *present* predicaments motivate us to remember different things in different ways, but Halbwachs makes no provision for memory as a route to *past realities*.

Halbwachs's accounts of the Christian memory of Jesus (1992a, 1992b) are stunning because they violate common sense, making the past a hallucination pressed to the service of individual faith and social solidarity. But violations of common sense, although refreshing and stimulating, are often wrong. "The facts are that perception is selective; motivations and needs sensitize us to specific stimuli or sometimes lead to distorted perception.... But these facts should not cause us to ignore the further fact that *reality sets limits to perception*.... No one can live in a real world if we see only what suits us" (Lindesmith, Strauss, and Denzin 1988, 124, emphasis added). Philosopher–social psychologist George Herbert Mead defined "the past as that which *must* have been before it is present in experience as a past" (1929, 238, emphasis added). His point is a special case of Lindesmith, Strauss, and Denzin's premise. Before we can take "the car to be where we are," he adds, "we *must* have first arisen" from sleep (Mead 1929, 238, emphasis added). That previous events *must* have happened in order for their consequences to occur does not mean that all memories are true;

3. Durkheim defines the "collective consciousness" as "the totality of beliefs and sentiments common to the average citizens of the same society [that] forms a determinate system which has its own life.... It is, in effect, independent of the particular conditions in which individuals are placed; they pass on and it remains.... Moreover, it does not change with each generation, but, on the contrary, it connects successive generations with one another. It is, thus, an entirely different thing from particular [consciousnesses], although it be realized only through them" (1965, 79–80). More than one scholar has commented on the convergence between Mead's "generalized other" and Durkheim's "collective consciousness." Collective or social memory is an aspect of both.

it does mean that present conditions can only be the result of past events. Such events have "an implied *objective existence*" and "exist in the present through memory" (Maines, Sugrue, and Katovitch 1983, 164).

While the approach of Mead and his followers is significantly more helpful than Halbwachs's proposal, they fail to go far enough: they mention the reality of the past incidentally, as a *qualification* of their claims about its rootedness in the present. Whether the reality of events is a *primary determinant* of what we remember or mere building material for what present situations require makes a difference. In the first case, memory embodied in the Gospels and elsewhere is a repository of both authentic and inauthentic information; in the latter, a repository of distortions, which, although narrowed by reality, do little more than make the present meaningful.

My reference to "reality" reflects both an epistemological aspect, that some objects of perception exist independently of the mind, and a related metaphysical aspect, that some perceptions exist collectively rather than individually. These observations are hardly new. If a phenomenon reflected no imperceptible but real "thing in itself," declared German philosopher Immanuel Kant (2007), it would have no meaning; reciprocally, the "thing in itself," the *noumenon*, would never transcend what we think of it. On the other hand, references to the past *wie es eigentlich gewesen* are not references to error-free history. Indeed, Leopold von Ranke (1973), author of that famous phrase, knew we can never have at our disposal anything more than residues of events embodied in witness accounts, documents, images, and artifacts. He endeavored to capture the past "as it *essentially* was."[4]

Although history, sacred and secular alike, is malleable and constantly reinterpreted, these variations would not be noticeable if not superimposed upon a stable essence that makes events and individuals recognizable across generations. In many cases, this essence is itself exaggerated, underemphasized, falsified, misrepresented, and misunderstood, but it would be a mistake to take these distortions as social memory's paradigm. Nor may we assume that memories are usually, let alone always, valid. Realism's assumption is more modest: interpretation is more often forced upon the

---

4. Leopold von Ranke was a romantic idealist who never believed the historian's task to be the mere collection of facts. His use of the German adverb *eigentlich*, generally understood by English-language historians to mean "actually," is more accurately translated "essentially"—a term that takes us beneath surface facts. If von Ranke were in fact a narrow empiricist, he would have used the common phrase *wie es eigentlich gewesen ist*. See Novick 1988, 21–23; Iggers and Powell 1990, xix–xx.

observer of an event by its inherent quality than imposed by the observer's worldview and interests. Put another way, *reality counts more than bias in the remembering of most events most of the time.*

Of course, many scholars would reject even this qualified proposition. "To remember," they repeatedly tell us, "is not like pulling files out of a cabinet." But if memories do reflect, to some useful extent, a sequence of happenings, then remembering is indeed comparable to pulling files out of a cabinet. Common sense concedes that people often remember incorrectly, but this same sense tells us that significant distortions of reality are exceptions to normal remembering, which is why we give special names to them: constructions, fabrications, inventions. If human memory were *typically* a creation, it would have no survival value, and we would possess no contact with the past.

Nothing, however, causes more misunderstanding of the history/ memory dynamic than recent concerns about memory's failure among oral cultures. Jack Goody and Ian Watt observe in *Literacy in Traditional Societies* that "societies and groups performing oral tradition censor the past and celebrate only those items of the tradition that are *relevant* to the present situation.... The present takes over; the present *is* the past; fact and fiction merge in an oral symbiosis" (Byrskog 2004, 468–69). But Goody and Watt could not advance such a theory in the first place if they had not already established the content of the essential past: If the past is truly inaccessible, how can we know whether or how it has been taken over by the present? Further, why is it necessary to conclude that present *relevance*, the unexplained something that explains everything else, renders the actual past unknowable? That a historical statement is relevant to the present, or formulated on the basis of present relevance, seems essential if that statement is to be at all comprehensible. But the fact that a historical statement is relevant and comprehensible does not necessarily invalidate it.

The concept of mediation—one of the worst sticking points in social memory scholarship—can be equally misleading. Because events cannot be known to a later generation unless they are remembered and transmitted by predecessors, all knowledge of the past is necessarily vulnerable to the memory lapses of witnesses and the biases of speakers and writers. While this claim is true as far as it goes, it is also exasperating because nothing can be known without mediation. We know about the existence of distant galaxies because powerful but imperfect telescopes mediate the light they emit and thus determine what we see and analyze. Similarly, our expectations affect our perceptions and the conclusions we draw from them, but the correlation between the two is typically far weaker than psychologists lead us to believe (Best 1993; Gross and Leavitt 1994; Ben-Yehuda 1995). History texts and commemorative objects, no less than accounts of the movement of light particles, are at least partly dependent on the reality they represent.

Distortion's Limits

According to the prominent psychologist Daniel L. Schacter (1995), memory by and large reflects reality, "but distortions can arise due to its constructive nature." Schacter's statement, so representative of the present state of social memory scholarship, is symptomatic of century-old disciplinary cultures plagued by excessive, sometimes pathological and often paralyzing cynicism—research cultures so determined to disclose memory's deficiencies that scholars choose for study topics in which only deficiencies are evident. Books and journals typically show memory at its worst because few editors and readers are interested in cases of accurate remembering. Accordingly, investigators tend to design their research with a view to identifying memory's fickleness.

Because constructionism is so evident in the way memory problems are selected and defined, its merits as well as limitations must be acknowledged. "Constructionism" refers to the conviction that social memory depends more on the contingencies of social experience than the qualities inherent in events remembered. Positively, constructionism compels recognition that the past is not always as it now seems on the surface—groups commonly fabricate a past, either wholesale or through selective remembering and forgetting, that is most relevant to their present interests and concerns. The number of examples is limitless. Given the current four-year sesquicentennial of the American Civil War (1861–1865), it is timely to consider how the Civil Rights Movement lessened historians' and the public's interest in Abraham Lincoln as savior of the Union and instead emphasized his role as the Great Emancipator who freed African Americans from slavery, notwithstanding significant historical evidence that would challenge this portrait (Schwartz 2008; Gallagher 2011). Constructionism is provocation, an invitation to interrogate memory by scrutinizing its contexts. Such is its most useful function, for there are no memories that remain the same forever or do not vary among society's regions and groupings. In the world of biblical studies, Rudolph Bultmann and his successors have, in some measure, shown us as much. This is all to the good.

The problem begins, however, when investigators cease to inquire whether a proposition is true or false in itself but instead attempt to understand it solely in terms of the situation within which it has been formed, when they assume that constructions of the past are nothing but constructions, with no real historical core within them, or when they conclude that the actual past is incidental to its subsequent representations and therefore irrelevant as an object of inquiry. If memory cannot be at least partially autonomous, if it must be fully contextualized to be understood, then it ceases to be memory in any real sense of the word and becomes quickly entangled in a web of infinite regress. The situation of the historical observer induces her to interpret a historical event in a particular way, but that observer is rarely an eyewitness of the event she interprets; she is dependent on the representation/testimony of an earlier observer, who in turn saw the event from the standpoint of his own situation, and so forth. History and memory alike become a succession of situations, while the events themselves become secondary.

Equally fruitless is the reduction of social memory and history to their narrative forms. If everything that matters about "history" results from the narrative that conveys it, then the French Revolution consists of no more than the story that gives it meaning. Historian Hayden White (1987) made a career of elevating story structures to this methodological principle, to the consternation of even his admirers. Paul Ricoeur (2004, 21) was right when he warned against colleagues such as White, who approach historical reality solely on the basis of the deficiencies in our store of concrete historical evidence. No one can doubt that every story of every historical event or figure is modified by the way it is told from one generation to the next, but it is equally certain that such a story loses plausibility if it fails to acknowledge the minimal claims of accepted knowledge.

Two cognitive models specify the limits of memory distortion. The first model is exemplified by Frederick Bartlett's (1995) memory experiments in the 1920s. After reading to his subjects a Native American folktale titled "The War of the Ghosts," a story of a mythical battle to the death involving supernatural forces, Bartlett asked them to reproduce the story twenty minutes later. Applying the "repeated reproduction" method, he then asked these subjects to reproduce the story at later times; as they did, the story gradually became shorter and more coherent, with fewer mentions of supernatural powers. The order of events changed. The sacred narrative became mundane—a transformation involving omissions, simplification, and translation of esoteric into familiar detail. Gradually, a Native

American folktale became a story that any Englishman could understand. Bartlett formulated the concept of the "schema" to describe the cognitive dynamic of this transformation. A schema is a framework for the organization of experience without which the capacity to remember is weakened. If two people are asked to watch a soccer game, for example, the person who knows what the game is about—its rules, strategies, player roles—will remember more of its content than the naïve spectator who knows nothing about soccer. The experienced viewer remembers better because his schema provides him a grid on which to locate, then easily recall, the events of the game. Similarly, the gradual transformation of a *Native American* tale may be explained as a translation of the story's elements into mnemonic schemas that were available to Bartlett's *British* subjects.

The problem with Bartlett's experiment, however, which substantially reduces its relevance for understanding the relationship between memory and the actual past, is that its design deprived his subjects of the resources necessary for remembering. Aside from the obvious fact that Bartlett's test narrative could not be relevant to his subject's concerns, he did not warn his respondents that they would be tested, nor did they believe that something of importance might depend on their test performance. Because Bartlett's subjects knew their responses were inconsequential, they relied on the default option, performing as "cognitive misers"—treating the information indifferently and impassively, condensing and simplifying, reducing it to its simplest schematic structure.

Of course, most people must be cognitive misers in order to organize in their minds the vast amount of information to which they are exposed. We simply cannot, and have no need to, remember the myriad of sensory data and bits of information that our brains absorb on a daily basis. But in many situations, including challenges that transcend day-to-day experience, people have a powerful interest in remembering accurately. Detectives, scientists, historians, military air controllers taking messages from besieged soldiers, and many other people of all kinds in specific situations are highly *motivated* to remember, since their success depends on it. Cognitive misers in one situation thus become "motivated tacticians" (Fiske and Taylor 1991, 13) in others. The ignoring or simplifying of information in one realm enables motivated tacticians to remember lengthy and complex details in another. Such has always been the tactician's "motive for history" (Schudson 1992, 213–14).

The main question, then, is not whether one remembers a given text inaccurately but whether one is capable of remembering it *at all* and what kind of incentive induces one to do so. Incentives are not limited to material rewards. On the contrary, "because of his psychological constitution, man cannot live without attachment to some object which transcends and survives him" (Durkheim 1951, 201). If memory promotes such attachment, then Jesus' most enthusiastic admirers, unlike Bartlett's test subjects, must have been intensely inspired motivational tacticians, men and women whose memories were crucial to their lives and self-conceptions. Bartlett's findings, therefore, would be nearly irrelevant to the case of Jewish Christians forming and communicating memories of Jesus during the first century. In the context of widespread belief in the imminence of a day of judgment and the establishment of God's kingdom, those faithful who listened to stories about Jesus must have been desperately motivated to remember every word. Listeners no doubt failed to assimilate everything, but they remembered more than they would have if they had had less of a stake in the message—certainly more than Britons would remember of a random and unfamiliar Native American folktale.

These observations lead to a second model that reveals the limit of memory's weakness, namely, the tendency in experimental accounts to emphasize dissensus rather than consensus, variations rather than similarities. To take one classic example, Elizabeth Loftus (1974) showed test subjects a video of an automobile accident and asked them to estimate the speed of the vehicles on impact. Estimates varied from 30 to 40 miles per hour (50 to 65 km/h), in direct correlation, significantly, to the words the researcher used to describe the impact (e.g., "How fast were the cars moving when they *collided*?" versus "How fast were the cars moving when they *smashed into* one another?"). At first glance, it may give one pause to note that viewers offered such a wide range of estimates, simply on the basis of suggestion, when viewing exactly the same video; on the other hand, no subject estimated the cars to be traveling 10 or 60 miles per hour. Absence of perceptual extremes is also evident in the conformity studies of Asch (1951), where confederates influenced test subjects' estimates of the length of lines, and Sherif's (1935) experiment on perceived movement of a stationary light. In these experimental trials, memory regularly distorts reality to some degree, but does so within a limited range—and this limit confirms reality's constraint on the vulnerability of perception.

To what extent, however, can this principle be applied to historical questions? For example, since the Gospels are the only source of information about Jesus, where are the *external criteria*—comparable to a video of colliding automobiles, a set of premeasured lines, a fixed position of light—against which to test conclusions about their accuracy? How can we be certain we are seeing the world from Jesus' viewpoint when we can only know it from anonymous remembrances captured in the Gospels? The first step toward answering this question is to identify the kinds of events that are most likely to be remembered.

WHAT MAKES EVENTS MEMORABLE?

The concept of "historical significance" generates as much controversy today as ever. Social scientists with even a slightly constructionist bent of mind believe, as did Georg Simmel more than a century ago, that "if something is important, then importance must be '*ascribed*' or '*attached*' to it; in other words, it is important [and memorable] because the historian is interested in it" (1905/1977, 163). Historians who ascribe significance to an event because of its intrinsic importance personify the realist challenge to Simmel's argument. Destructive and order-changing events, such as the bombing of Hiroshima or the attacks of September 11, allow for concrete discussion of this issue. So do creative events, such as the colonization of the New World or the advent of Christianity.

Consider the latter category: creative events. The first step toward determining whether Jesus' significance was ascribed or inherent in his mission is to align it to the worldview of his generation. Most of Jesus' Jewish contemporaries rejected him, but they could not ignore him. To recognize that Jesus challenged many foundational premises of first-century Judaism is to establish context, not causation, let alone Jesus' viewpoint or motives. Yet context is indispensable for estimating viewpoint and motive. Culture, after all, is public, and from the public fact personal attitude is inferred. No one can get into Jesus' mind by imagining herself to be him and envisioning what he thought, but one can analyze the symbolic world—texts, institutional values and practices, religious rituals—for and against which Jesus acted and in terms of which he represented himself. Clifford Geertz (1973) defines this method as "thick description," key to the understanding of any alien thoughtworld.

Researchers who consider Jesus' apocalyptic vision as the basis of his significance draw on multiple sources, and these coexisted with multiple conceptions of the messiah. During the Late Second Temple period different messianic ideas reflected the range of Judaism's variants (see Neusner, Green, and Frerichs 1987). In the first century alone there appeared, besides Jesus, Judas of Galilee, Menachem ben Judah, Theudas, and John of Gischala, all of whom were preceded and followed by other messianic claimants. Why Jesus succeeded while other claimants failed takes us to Jesus' personal appeal and exploits and to the many people with an interest in spreading his story. Jesus' appeal and his disciples' energy would have borne no result if the cultural environment were not conducive to a messiah in the first place. However, there is no strong evidence that Jesus conformed to any one of the messiah ideas that were part of Jewish tradition. When Peter declared Jesus to be the Christ in Mark 8:2, for example, he was uncertain precisely what the title meant. Paul set forth the new messianic idea (MacRae 2007), but Paul's vision cannot be assumed to be *totally* different from that of Jesus himself. To extend Max Weber's famous metaphor, in a society where multiple messianic tracks existed, Jesus was the switchman who determined which one would be followed. Jesus probably recognized his culture's messianic strains, from warrior to prophet, but he seemed to feel an apocalypse coming on; he acted on his feeling, and others followed. Paul's letters invoked comparable images, including the dead literally rising to join Jesus in the clouds (1 Thess 4:13–18). Jesus himself died to rescue humanity (Gal 1:4), but when he returns "every person's work will become manifest, for the day will disclose it, because it will be revealed with fire" (1 Cor 3:15). As Jesus will save us from the "coming wrath…, it is well for a person to remain as he is.… I mean, brethren, the appointed time has grown very short.… The form of the world is passing away" (1 Cor 7:26–31). The Q source, if its proponents are correct, was probably written before Mark and independently of him, but it reveals this same apocalyptic thought world (Gregg 2006). In the words of Ernst Käsemann, "apocalyptic is the mother of all Christian theology" (1969).

Where, then, do we stand on the memorability of Jesus? All ideas and events occur in a context that reduces or amplifies their memorability, but the ideas and events this context must surround, including Jesus' life and death, are fundamentally real. They cannot be defined or interpreted into or out of existence.

CHARISMA AND MIRACLE

Context can provide a framework for interpreting memory's content, but it cannot alone account for that content. If the average person is to be known, we must reach out to him; however, the great person is known because she reaches out to *us* and is therefore more accessible to our understanding (Simmel 1977, 98). But of what does this "reaching out" consist? Contemporary scholars are typically more certain of who Jesus *was* than of any particular thing he *said*. In Max Weber's (1967) view, the prophets' success in promoting the regular study of Torah, which infused everyday conduct with a religious ethos, laid the basis for the moral rationalism of Western civilization. Weber discerned the content of ethics in tradition and law, but he was less concerned with whether or not a particular statement could be ascribed to a given prophet than with the ethos to which that prophet's community conformed. So, too, with Jesus: his place in social memory is defined not by the literal authenticity of his sayings but by the revolutionary ethic he and his followers embraced.[5]

The Late Second Temple period was a "hot" period, a traumatic span of time during which old ways were destroyed and re-created (Levi-Strauss 1966; Shils 1975). It is no simple matter to validate the proposition that no event is intrinsically significant or intrinsically traumatic, that significance and trauma are matters of subjective definition and merely reflections of how the past is perceived and processed (Alexander 2004; Surprenant and Neath 2009). Whether or not individuals choose to *define* events as traumatic, only their objective *consequences* actually make them so. In terms of actual consequences, the early decades of the first century were among history's most pivotal—their events, centered in the Middle East and Mediterranean, challenged and transformed identities as they shifted the course of Western civilization.

During the last century of the Second Temple period, unprecedented conflict over Scripture and its interpretation, surging fear of demons, and anticipation of an apocalypse produced memorable men. Some of these men were "charismatic leaders": they possessed a "gift of grace" and performed extraordinary deeds, including exorcisms and miracles; they aimed to revolutionize their world, to prepare it for a future of holiness and virtue; and they deemed its inhabitants duty-bound to obey their teachings and commands (Weber 1947, 358–63). Jesus was one of these men, and his miraculous accomplishments (no less than twenty-four are described in Mark alone) contributed to his legacy. Indeed, John explains that Jesus made so many miracles that no single story could ever convey them all (20:30; 21:25).

Jesus' miracles can be understood with or without Christian faith. In 1828, Heinrich Paulus, a child of the Enlightenment, avowed Jesus' divin-

---

5. For detail on quotations spuriously attributed to *modern* leaders, see Boller and George 1989, 77–74.

ity while invoking natural causes to explain his miracles. He recognized the power of suggestion and believed Jesus possessed medicines and sedatives to cure physical ailments and exorcise demons. Such claims could not be substantiated, however, until the rise of modern medicine. Under hypnosis, as we now know, "paralyzed" people walk; placebo effects often approach the direct effects of medications measured against them. So certain are we of the mind/body connection that it is difficult *not* to believe that the sick and possessed were healed when Jesus laid his hands upon them. Other miracle stories, particularly those relating to the resurrection, require different kinds of explanation. Given the Jewish practice of burial within three hours of death, Paulus cited frequent failure at the time to establish certain death. He believed Jesus was alive when taken from the cross. Although fear of premature entombment and burial goes back to antiquity, the accumulation of evidence on its *frequency* grew in Europe and America during the late nineteenth and early twentieth centuries (Tebb and Vollum 2011; Wikins 1990). This evidence includes cases of execution, where a person hanged and presumed dead turns out not to be dead at all. Moreover, in the preindustrial world, naïve family members determined whether or not their kin had died, which can only mean the problem might have been even more common than is currently believed. Paulus's statements about miracles, then, are far more plausible today than in the early nineteenth century. In a different but related connection, the frequent sightings of Adolf Hitler and Elvis Presley long after their demise and the denial of Osama bin Laden's death in much of the Middle East illustrate the refusal of the collective consciousness to accept the loss of those who have powerfully influenced it.

Less than a decade after Paulus published his *Life of Jesus,* David Friedrich Strauss (1835) denied Jesus' divinity and declared Paulus's rationalistic accounts of Jesus' miracles less credible than the miracles themselves. Miracle stories were based not on facts but on myths, most of which were conceived before the first written Gospel appeared. The referents of these myths included the yearning for spiritual sustenance (Jesus feeding the multitude) and the need to stand firm against the stormy sea of life (Jesus walking on water). Interpreting miracle stories as statements about the human condition, Strauss negated Paulus's influence as he won enthusiastic acceptance in skeptical circles. As the years passed, his renown grew: George Eliot (Mary Anne Evans) translated his *Life of Jesus* into English; Albert Schweitzer (1926) declared it a turning point in modern biblical scholarship; The Jesus Seminar dedicated its *Five Gospels* to Strauss and continues to recognize scholarly excellence by inducting likeminded researchers into the "Order of D. F. Strauss." Contemporary skeptics embrace Strauss because he denies the miracles that Jesus' followers believed they witnessed. But given the present state of knowledge, one is entitled to ask whether Strauss's accounts were actually more far-fetched than Paulus's and whether Paulus's still untranslated explanations of the Gospels' miracle stories, many of which are admittedly strained, should be at least revisited rather than dismissed out of hand. Paulus's accounts, which recognize the events that Jesus' contemporaries deemed miraculous, are more consistent with the Gospels' accounts than Strauss's, which deny that these events ever happened.

Whatever the merits of the above argument, many scholars who might otherwise accept the Gospels as repositories of memory reject them as soon as the supernatural is invoked. Without miracles, however, what made Jesus distinctive to his generation? If such stories—whether products of supernatural powers, suggestibility, or fictional elaborations of reality—are dismissed entirely from our understanding of Jesus, where are we to find his charisma? And if we cannot find that charisma, how are we to explain Jesus' extraordinary place in his generation's memory? If Jesus did nothing out of the ordinary, why did his contemporaries remember him at all?

Miracle stories are remembered and commemorated not only because they violate the laws of physical nature but also because they have a foundation in human nature. Emile Durkheim (1960), in this regard, believed that human character is double, moved by both personal idiosyncrasies and social imperatives. Miracle stories are parts of the latter; they express the cultural currents personified in those who, against all odds, shape their community's fate. Miracles are in this sense "cultural realities" (Craffert 2009). Above all, the concept of miracle is aligned with beliefs about the holy, which dramatize the universally unbridgeable opposition between the sacred and the profane—a polarity as real today as it was two thousand years ago.

Conclusion

Stated independently of specific cases, theoretical statements are abstract and vacuous. My own statement in this essay has tended toward the abstract, and what it does say about Jesus and his contemporaries adds nothing to what is already known. At issue, however, is whether the weakness in my perspective adds strength to others. This volume's success will therefore hinge not only on the vigor with which its contributors refute, affirm, or qualify my observations on the nature and power of social memory but also whether, in so doing, they advance their own research.

If social memory is to remain stable, it must emerge from its individual sources and be incorporated into a tradition, and that tradition must, in turn, become institutionalized. The memory of all historical figures is institutionalized by rituals, framing, keying, path-dependency, emergent oral tradition, sites of memory, life-course turning points, and, where relevant, Scripture. If these assertions, all constituents of social memory theory, bear any truth, then it is fair to conclude that such theory, in some slight but significant measure, illuminates the biblical texts as pathways to understanding the events and figures described in them. Far from being annihilated by analytic history, as many scholars presently affirm, social memory, properly validated, is history's ultimate foundation.

Most readers will recognize that my application of social memory theory is open to the charge of naïve optimism, an exaggeration of the soundness of what we know about the past and an underestimation of what we do not know. I can only respond to this criticism by pointing out that my approach and this charge represent two competing forms of metaphysical pathos. As defined by Arthur Lovejoy (1948, 11), "metaphysical pathos" refers to the affective climate in which objective propositions reside. The pathos of this chapter is clearly optimistic, while the pathos of much social memory theory is fatalistic—a flaw most evident in the conviction, which survives through conclusions that have nothing to do with evidence, that human memory, individual and social, is *essentially* warped. No worldview, in my judgment, has done more to confound the relation between memory and history, and I have tried to demonstrate its shortcomings. The eminent contributors to this volume must enlarge, modify, and/or refute my assertions.

Works Cited

Alexander, Jeffrey C. 2004. Towards a Theory of Cultural Trauma. Pages 1–30 in *Cultural Trauma and Collective Identity*. Edited by Jeffrey C. Alexander, Ron Eyerman, Bernard Giesen, and Piotr Sztompka. Berkeley: University of California Press.

Asch, Solomon E. 1951. Effects of Group Pressure upon the Modification and Distortion of Judgment. Pages 177–90 in *Groups, Leadership and Men*. Edited by Harold Guetzkow. Pittsburgh: Carnegie.

Assmann, Jan. 2006a. Form as Mnemonic Device: Cultural Texts and Cultural Memory. Pages 67–82 in *Performing the Gospel: Orality, Memory, and Mark*. Edited by Richard A. Horsley, Jonathan Draper, and John Miles Foley. Minneapolis: Fortress.

———. 2006b. *Religion and Cultural Memory: Ten Studies*. Translated by Rodney Livingstone. Stanford, CA: Stanford University Press.

Bartlett, Frederic C. 1995. *Remembering: A Study in Experimental Social Psychology*. Cambridge: Cambridge University Press. [orig. 1932]

Bauckham, Richard, 2003. The Eyewitnesses and the Gospel Traditions. *JSHJ* 1:28–60.

Ben-Yehuda, Nachman. 1995. *The Masada Myth: Collective Memory and Mythmaking in Israel*. Madison: University of Wisconsin Press.

Best, Joel. 1993. But Seriously Folks: The Limitations of the Strict Constructionist Interpretation of Social Problems. Pages 109–27 in *Constructionist Controversies: Issues in Social Problems Theory*. Edited by Gale Miller and James A. Holstein. New York: Aldine de Gruyter.

Boller, Paul F., and John George. 1989. *They Never Said It: A Book of Fake Quotes, Misquotes, and Misleading Attributions*. New York: Oxford University Press.

Burke, Peter. 1989. History as Social Memory. Pages 97–110 in *Memory: History, Culture and the Mind*. Edited by Thomas Butler. Malden, MA: Blackwell.

Byrskog, Samuel. 2004. A New Perspective on the Jesus Tradition: Reflections on James D. G. Dunn's *Jesus Remembered*. *JSNT* 26:459–71.

Craffert, Pieter F. 2009. Jesus' Resurrection in a Social-Scientific Perspective: Is There Anything New to Be Said? *JSHJ* 7:126–51.

Darnton, Robert. 1984. Peasants Tell Tales. Pages 9–72 in *The Great Cat Massacre and Other Episodes in French Cultural History*. New York: Random House.

Dunn, James D. G. 2003. *Jesus Remembered I: Christianity in the Making*. Grand Rapids: Eerdmans.

Durkheim, Emile. 1951. *Suicide: A Study in Sociology*. New York: Free Press. [orig. 1901]

———. 1960. The Dualism of Human Nature and Its Social Conditions. Pages 325–340 in *Essays in Sociology and Philosophy*. Edited by Kurt H. Wolff. New York: Harper & Row. [orig. 1914]

———. 1965. *The Elementary Forms of the Religious Life*. New York: Free Press. [orig. 1915]

———. 1974. Collective Representations. Pages 1–34 in *Sociology and Phi-*

losophy by Emile Durkheim. Edited by Talcott Parsons. New York: Free Press. [orig. 1898]

———. 1982. *Rules of Sociological Method.* Edited by Stephen Lukes. New York: Free Press. [orig. 1895]

Ehrman, Bart. 1999. *Jesus: Apocalyptic Prophet of the New Millennium.* New York: Oxford University Press.

Erikson, Erik H. 1959. *Identity and the Life Cycle.* New York: Norton.

Escott, Paul D. 1979. *Slavery Remembered: A Record of Twentieth-Century Slave Narratives.* Chapel Hill: University of North Carolina Press.

Fehrenbacher, Don E. 1987. The Fictional Lincoln. Pages 228–45 in *Lincoln in Text and Context: Collected Essays.* Stanford, CA: Stanford University Press.

Fine, Gary A. 1996. Reputational Entrepreneurs and the Memory of Incompetence: Melting Supporters, Partisan Warriors, and Images of President Harding. *American Journal of Sociology* 101:1159–93.

Fiske, Susan T., and Shelley E. Taylor. 1991. *Social Cognition.* 2nd ed. New York: McGraw–Hill.

Frisch, Michael. 1989. American History and the Structure of Collective Memory: A Modest Exercise in Empirical Iconography. *Journal of American History* 75:1130–55.

Gallagher, Gary. 2011. *The Union War.* Cambridge, MA: Harvard University Press.

Geertz, Clifford. 1973. *The Interpretation of Cultures: Selected Essays.* New York: Basic Books.

Gerhardsson, Birger. 1961. *Memory and Manuscript: Oral Tradition and Written Transmission in Rabbinic Judaism and Early Christianity.* Lund: Gleerup.

Goffman, Erving. 1974. *Frame Analysis: An Essay on the Organization of Experience.* New York: Harper & Row.

Goody, Jack, and Ian Watt. The Consequences of Literacy. Pages 27–68 in *Literacy in Traditional Societies.* Edited by Jack Goody. Cambridge: Cambridge University Press, 1968.

Gregg, Brian Hahn. 2006. *The Historical Jesus and the Final Judgment Sayings in Q.* WUNT 2/207. Tübingen: Mohr Siebeck.

Gross, Paul R., and Norman Leavitt. 1994. *Higher Superstition: The Academic Left and Its Quarrels with Science.* Baltimore: Johns Hopkins University Press.

Halbwachs, Maurice. 1992a. *Les cadres sociaux de la mémoire.* Travaux de l'année sociologique 9. Paris: Alcan. Translated into English as pages

35–189 in *On Collective Memory*. Edited and translated by Lewis A. Coser. Chicago: University of Chicago Press. [orig. 1925]

———. 1992b. *La topographie légendaire des Évangiles en Terre Sainte: Étude de mémoire collective*. Paris: Presses universitaires de France. Translated into English as pages 193–235 in *On Collective Memory*. Edited and translated by Lewis A. Coser. Chicago: University of Chicago Press. [orig. 1941]

Herndon, William H., and Jesse William Weik. 1889. *Herndon's Lincoln: The True Story of a Great Life*. 3 vols. Chicago: Belford, Clarke.

Honda, Katsuichi. 1999. *Nanjing Massacre: A Japanese Journalist Confronts Japan's National Shame*. Edited by Frank Gibney. Armonk, NY: Sharpe.

Horsley, Richard A. 1989. *Sociology and the Jesus Movement*. New York: Crossroad.

Iggers, Georg, and James M. Powell, eds. 1990. *Leopold von Ranke and the Shaping of the Historical Discipline*. Syracuse, NY: University of Syracuse Press.

Kant, Immanuel. 2007. *Critique of Pure Reason*. New York: Penguin.

Katz, Elihu, and Paul Lazarsfeld. 1955. *Personal Influence: The Part Played by People in the Flow of Mass Communications*. Glencoe, IL: Free Press.

Kirk, Alan. 2005. Social and Cultural Memory. Pages 1–24 in *Memory, Tradition, and Text: Uses of the Past in Early Christianity*. Edited by Alan Kirk and Tom Thatcher. SemeiaSt 52. Atlanta: Society of Biblical Literature.

Kroeber, Alfred L. 1963. *Anthropology: Culture Patterns and Processes*. New York: Harcourt, Brace & World. [orig. 1923]

Lang, Gladys, and Kurt Lang. 1990. *Etched in Memory: The Building and Survival of Artistic Reputation*. Chapel Hill: University of North Carolina Press.

Leach, Edmund. 1976. The Structure of Myth. Pages 57–91 in *Claude Levi-Strauss*. New York: Penguin Books.

Levi-Strauss, Claude. 1966. *The Savage Mind*. Chicago: University of Chicago Press.

Lindesmith, Alfred R., Anselm L. Strauss, and Norman K. Denzin. 1988. *Social Psychology*. Englewood Cliffs, NJ: Prentice Hall.

Loftus, Elizabeth F. 1974. Reconstruction of Automobile Destruction: An Example of the Interaction between Language and Memory. *Journal of Verbal Learning and Verbal Behavior* 13:585–89.

Lovejoy, Arthur. 1948. *Essays in the History of Ideas*. Baltimore: Johns Hopkins University Press.

Lukes, Steven. 1973. *Emile Durkheim: His Life and Work*. New York: Penguin Books.

Macrae, George W. 2007. *Studies in the New Testament and Gnosticism*. Edited by Daniel J. Harrington and Stanley B. Marrow. Eugene, OR: Wipf & Stock. [orig. 1987]

Maines, D., N. M. Sugrue, and M. A. Katovitch. 1983. The Sociological Import of G. H. Mead's Theory of the Past. *American Sociological Review* 48:161–73.

Mannheim, Karl. 1952. The Sociological Problem of Generations. Pages 286–320 in *Essays on the Sociology of Knowledge*. Edited by Paul Kecskemeti. London: Routledge & Kegan Paul. [orig. 1928]

Mead, George Herbert. 1929. The Nature of the Past. Pages 235–42 in *Essays in Honor of John Dewey*. Edited by J. Coss. New York: Henry Holt.

———. 1967. *Mind, Self, and Society From the Standpoint of a Social Behaviorist*. Edited by Charles Morris. Chicago: University of Chicago Press. [orig. 1934]

Megill, Allan. 2007. *Historical Knowledge, Historical Practice: A Contemporary Guide to Practice*. Chicago: University of Chicago Press.

Morrow, Honoré. 1935. *Great Captain: Three 'Lincoln' Novels*. New York: William Morrow.

Neusner, Jacob, William Scott Green, and Ernest S. Frerichs, eds. 1987. *Judaisms and Their Messiahs at the Turn of the Christian Era*. Cambridge: Cambridge University Press.

Nora, Pierre. 1989. Between Memory and History: Les Lieux de Mémoire. *Representations* 26:7–24.

Novick, Peter. 1988. *That Noble Dream: The "Objectivity" Question and the American Historial Profession*. Ideas in Context. Cambridge: Cambridge University Press.

Olick, Jeffrey K. 2007. *The Politics of Regret: On Collective Memory and Historical Responsibility*. New York: Routledge.

———. 2008. Collective Memory: A Memoir and Prospect. *Memory Studies* 1:19–25.

Olick, Jeffrey, and Joyce Robbins. 1998. Social Memory Studies From Collective Memory to the Historical Sociology of Mnemonic Practices. *Annual Review of Sociology* 24:105–40.

Paulus, Heinrich Eberhard Gottlob. 1828. *Das Leben Jesu als Grundlage einer reinen Geschichte des Urchristentums*. 2 vols. Heidelberg: Winter.

Poole, Ross. 2008. Memory, History and the Claims of the Past. *Memory Studies* 1:149–66.

Ranke, Leopold von. 1973. *Theory and Practice of History.* Edited by Georg G. Iggers and Konrad von Molke. Indianapolis: Bobbs-Merrill.

Rawick, George P. ed. 1977. *The American Slave.* 17 vols. Prepared by the Federal Writers Project of the Works Progress Administration. Westport, CT: Greenwood.

Rice, Judith R. 1998. Ida M. Tarbell: A Progressive Look at Lincoln. *Journal of the Abraham Lincoln Association* 19:57–72.

Ricoeur, Paul. 2004. *Memory, History, Forgetting.* Translated by Kathleen Blamey and David Pellauer. Chicago: University of Chicago Press.

Roediger, Henry L., and James V. Wertsch. 2008. Creating a New Discipline of Memory Studies. *Memory Studies* 1:9–22.

Rubin, David. 1995. *Memory in Oral Traditions: The Cognitive Psychology of Epic, Ballads, and Counting-Out Rhymes.* New York: Oxford University Press.

Safire, William. 1987. *Freedom: A Novel of Abraham Lincoln and the Civil War.* New York: Avon.

Sandburg, Carl. 1926. *Abraham Lincoln: The Prairie Years.* 2 vols. New York: Harcourt, Brace.

———. 1934. Lincoln-Roosevelt. *Today.* February 10, no. 5.

———. 1939. *Abraham Lincoln: The War Years.* 4 vols. New York: Harcourt, Brace.

Schacter, Daniel L., ed. 1995. *Memory Distortion: How Minds, Brains and Societies Reconstruct the Past.* Cambridge: Harvard University Press.

Schudson, Michael. 1992. *Watergate in American Memory: How We Remember, Forget, and Reconstruct the Past.* New York: Basic Books.

Schuman, Howard, and Jacqueline Scott. 1989. Generations and Collective Memories. *American Sociological Review* 54:359–81.

Schuman, Howard, and Amy Corning. 2012. Generational Memory and the Critical Period: Evidence for National and World Events. *Public Opinion Quarterly* 76:1–31.

Schwartz, Barry. 2000. *Abraham Lincoln and the Forge of American Memory.* Chicago: University of Chicago Press.

———. 2008. *Abraham Lincoln in the Post-heroic Era: History and Memory in the Late Twentieth Century.* Chicago: University of Chicago Press.

Schweitzer, Albert. 1926. *The Quest of the Historical Jesus.* Translated by W. Montgomery. London: Black. [German orig. 1906]

Sherif, Muzafir. 1935. A Study of Some Social Factors in Perception. *Archives of Psychology* 27, no. 187.

Shils, Edward A. 1975. Charisma, Order, and Status. Pages 256–75 in *Cen-*

ter and Periphery: Essays in Macrosociology. Chicago: University of Chicago Press.

———. 1981. *Tradition.* Chicago: University of Chicago Press.

Simmel, Georg. 1977. *The Problems of the Philosophy of History: An Epistemological Essay.* Translated and edited by Guy Oakes. New York: Free Press. [orig. 1905]

Stark, Rodney. 1996. *The Rise of Christianity: A Sociologist Reconsiders History.* Princeton: Princeton University Press.

Strauss, David Friedrich. 1973. *The Life of Jesus Critically Examined.* Edited by Peter C. Hodgson. Translated by George Eliot. London: SCM. [orig. 1835]

Surprenant, Aimée M., and Ian Neath. 2009. *Principles of Memory: Essays in Cognitive Psychology.* London: Taylor & Francis.

Tebb, William, and Edward P. Vollum. 2011. *Premature Burial and How It May be Prevented: With Special Reference to Catalepsy, Trance, and Other Forms of Suspended Animation.* Toronto: University of Toronto Libraries. [orig. 1905]

Vidal, Gore. 1984. *Lincoln: A Novel.* New York: Ballantine Books.

Weber, Max. 1947. Charismatic Authority. Pages 358–63 in *The Theory of Social and Economic Organization.* Edited by Talcott Parsons. New York: Free Press. [orig. 1921]

———. 1967. *Ancient Judaism.* Edited and translated by Hans Gerth and Don Martindale. New York: Free Press. [orig. 1952]

———. 1968. *Economy and Society.* Berkeley: University of California Press.

White, Hayden. 1987. *The Content of the Form: Narrative Discourse and Historical Representation.* Baltimore: Johns Hopkins University Press.

Wikins, Robert A. 1990. *Death: A History of Man's Obsessions and Fears.* New York: Barnes & Noble.

Wilson, Douglas, and Rodney O. Davis. 1998. *Herndon's Informants: Letters, Interviews, and Statements about Abraham Lincoln.* Urbana: University of Illinois Press.

Yerushalmi, Yosef. 1996. *Zakhor: Jewish History and Jewish Memory.* Seattle: University of Washington Press. [orig. 1982]

PART 1
REMEMBERING IN JEWISH ANTIQUITY

Selective Recall and Ghost Memories: Two Aspects of Cultural Memory in the Hebrew Bible

Carol A. Newsom

Biblical studies has long been concerned with aspects of what is now called "cultural memory," especially in the form of a preoccupation with tradition history.[1] Yet even though the major theorists of tradition history were active at the same time that Maurice Halbwachs and Aby Warburg were developing their ideas about cultural memory in society and art, there is no evidence of intellectual cross-fertilization. More recently, the debates over historiography in biblical studies in the 1990s raised in an acute fashion issues relating to the preservation of reliable data in the historical narratives of the Bible versus the invention of traditions that were strategically passed off as historical memories for political purposes (on the latter, see, e.g., Davies 1992; Lemche 1993; Whitelam 1996; Thompson 1999). Initially these debates, too, were carried on without dialogue with the emerging field of cultural memory studies, but in the last decade the engagement with this field has led to more sophisticated explorations of the nature of historical memory (see, e.g., Brettler 2001; Smith 2004; Hendel 2005; Carstens, Hasselbalch, and Lemche 2012). Yet while biblical studies has only recently come to recognize the importance of cultural memory, the reverse has not been the case. One of the important works by Halbwachs (1992 [1941]) was a study of the reception of biblical traditions in the legendary topography of Christian Palestine. Similarly, biblical figures and mnemonic practices embedded in biblical literature have been of central importance in Jan Assmann's seminal writings (1997, 2000, 2006, 2011). Both fields will likely benefit from more intentional mutual engagement.

As a step toward furthering this potentially fruitful dialogue, this essay will revisit two biblical phenomena relevant to the topic of cultural memory that I first explored without reference to that field of study. Bringing those earlier investigations into conversation with the insights of cultural

---

1. See the recent survey and case study by Knight (2009) and his earlier study (2006). One might also note the focus on memory in biblical theology in Childs 1962.

memory studies, and particularly of Barry Schwartz's conceptualization of the relationship between the past and its textual commemorations, may open up aspects of the issues I did not previously perceive. I hope these case studies may also illumine aspects of cultural memory that are worthy of further exploration in other contexts. As Astrid Erll points out, memory studies may have different emphases. Some emphasize "cultural *memory*," some "performative acts of cultural *remembering*," and others "amnesia, oblivion and social *forgetting*" (Erll 2011, 8, emphasis original). The case studies I examine here touch on all three aspects.

Historical Résumés and Cultural Memory: The Strategic Uses of Selective Recall[2]

In addition to the great works of historical memory that dominate the Hebrew Bible—the Primary History of Genesis–2 Kings and the Secondary History of Chronicles, Ezra, and Nehemiah—there are a surprisingly large number of historical résumés that succinctly recount the major events of Israelite and Judean history. These brief retellings can be found in a variety of different types of literature, including Deuteronomistic prose (Josh 24; 1 Sam 12), prophetic texts (Jer 32:16–24; Ezek 20), prayers (Neh 9), and psalms (Pss 78; 105; 106; 135; 136). They also occur in nonbiblical narrative fiction (e.g., Achior's recitation of Israelite history in Jdt 5), in Jewish Hellenistic historiography (e.g., Josephus's speech before the walls of Jerusalem in *B.J.* 5.377–419), and in early Christian narrative (e.g., Stephen's speech in Acts 7). In apocalyptic literature they feature as *vaticinia ex eventu* (e.g., the Animal Apocalypse in 1 En. 85–90; the Apocalypse of Weeks in 1 En. 93:1–10; 91:11–17; the Cloud Vision in 2 Bar. 53–74). The widespread incidence of the historical résumé and the fact that many of its literary settings represent the résumé as a speech or public prayer strongly suggest that it was also an oral performance genre.

Although the various résumés differ considerably in scope, in level of detail, in the choice of beginning and ending points, in ideological stance, and in the way the materials are configured, they all recognizably tell the *same* story.[3] They are all performances of a master narrative. The concept of the master narrative is important for cultural memory studies because

---

2. My earlier exploration of this material was framed in relation to cognitive studies (Newsom 2006).

3. The historical résumés in Dan 2, 7, 8, and 11 differ in that they trace the history of sovereignty rather than being shaped by the history of Israel or of the righteous.

it identifies a culturally authoritative narrative account of a common history.[4] It encodes the cultural memories that are agreed to be of definitive importance. But where does the master narrative *exist*? It cannot simply be identified with any of the particular performances or instantiations of it, for its existence is the precondition that makes all performances possible as effective communicative acts. At the same time, the master narrative does not have the transcendent status of a platonic ideal. It is rather a body of tacit knowledge organized by a basic chronology of key episodes that is shared by a community and that can be activated and engaged by a particular performance. That is to say, the recitation of a historical résumé does not serve to communicate information. It is first of all an exercise in shared remembering. This tacit knowledge allows the audience to recognize and approve (or reject as false) any particular performance of the master narrative. This tacit knowledge, however, is always more extensive and more heterogeneous than any particular performance. That is to say, more is always known than is ever told. Many variant narratives can be constructed from the same body of cultural memory. Thus any particular performance of the master narrative is not only an exercise in shared remembering but is also a rhetorical attempt to construct and convey significance for particular purposes.

Here the insights of Paul Ricoeur (1984–1988) into the nature of narrative and its relation to temporality are particularly helpful (see also Erll 2011, 152–57). Ricoeur notes that narrative involves two types of temporality. One is simple chronology, the succession of events one after the other. For the most part, the Israelite master narrative has an assumed chronology from which one could not deviate. At some point, of course, it would likely not yet have been generally agreed how the traditions about the patriarchs were to be related to one another and how that complex of narratives was to be coordinated with the traditions of the exodus and conquest. But at some point before the composition of the historical résumés listed above the chronology appears to have been established, though not all make reference to the patriarchal traditions.

---

4. The concept was popularized by Jean-François Lyotard (1984) and has been widely influential, though many disagree with Lyotard's claim that the postmodern world treats master narratives with incredulity. Historian Allan Megill (2007, 167) helpfully distinguishes master narrative ("the authoritative account of some particular segment of history") from grand narrative ("the authoritative account of history generally") and from metanarrative (a "belief in God or in a rationality somehow inherent in the world, which serves to justify the grand narrative").

Chronology itself, however, provides only minimal coherence, producing something more like a chronicle than a narrative. Only as the events are emplotted, organized "into an intelligible whole," do they become a story. Ricoeur refers to this act as "configuration," which happens as emplotment "extracts a figure from a succession" (1984–1988, 1:66). Configuration may be established in many ways. The choice of beginning and ending points is often critical. Episodes may be related causally or as elements of a journey. Alternatively, they may constitute repeated historical instantiations of a theme. Configuration is what permits the events to be experienced not simply as a series but to be "grasped together" in "the unity of one temporal whole" (1:66). Thus, configuration is not atemporal so much as it is the bending of time, so that in place of a sense that things could go on forever, "the plot imposes the 'sense of an ending' . . . on the indefinite succession of incidents." When the story is a well-known one, emplotment permits one to invert the natural order of time, so that one can "read the ending in the beginning and the beginning in the ending" (1:67).

Bringing together Ricoeur's understanding of the two temporalities of narrative with the notion of the master narrative described above allows one to account for the fact that the historical résumés of the Hebrew Bible and related literature can differ not only in details but, in some cases, to such degree that they could be seen as nearly contradictory understandings of the common tradition. Configuration is what establishes the criteria of relevance as one selects episodes and details from the body of cultural memory. Which of the things that everyone knows belong in the story, and which do not? If the configuration is successful and the emplotment establishes coherence, then what is left out will not be perceived as an omission that threatens credibility but rather simply as details that, while true, are not relevant to the story being told. The configured plot is a filter that eliminates the static that might be produced by irrelevant information, even as it organizes the relevant material into a meaningful pattern.

An example of the effects of such configuration can be seen in the radically different narrations of Israelite history preserved in Pss 105 and 106. These two compositions differ stylistically in such ways that it is unlikely they were originally composed as a set, but their juxtaposition in the psalter appears intentionally designed to call attention to their contrasting accounts of history. Psalm 105 tells a story of providential protection, beginning with Abraham and the promise of the land of Canaan (105:8–11) and ending with the gift of the promised land enacted (105:42–45).

Its intervening episodes illustrate protection against oppression in Canaan (105:12–15), against famine in the land (105:16–23), against oppression in Egypt (105:24–38), and from dangers in the wilderness (105:39–41). It is emplotted as a journey: to Canaan, from Canaan to Egypt, from Egypt back to Canaan. The sense of an ending is provided by the fulfillment of the promise, which is also the final arrival at the destination. This strong closure does not invite one to think how the story might continue after "he gave them the lands of nations . . . that they might keep His laws and observe His teachings" (105:44–45; NJPS). Nor is it clear how far from these events the speaker and audience stand. Instead, the rhetorical purpose appears to be to merge the audience's time with the time of the fulfillment of the promise, including the keeping of the laws and teachings. Here recollection serves as normative prescription.

Psalm 106, by contrast, establishes its criterion of relevance by means of confession (106:6: "We have sinned like our ancestors; we have gone astray, we have acted wickedly"; 106:6, trans. mine). In contrast to the configuration of promise and journey in Ps 105, here the structure is highly repetitious, as every incident recalled is shaped to illustrate the theme of rebellion. Indeed, one might say that only one thing happens over and over. The time period framed is also different, beginning with the rebellion at the Sea of Reeds and concluding with the speaker's present in exile and diaspora. The author's emplotment, however, allows him to distort natural temporality. Some twenty-seven verses, including all of the episodes described with specific detail, concern the exodus and wilderness period, while the subsequent centuries-long period from the entry into the land until the exile is narrated in ten very general verses. It would seem that the strong paradigm of the wilderness rebellion exhausts the very possibility of history, since seemingly nothing new can happen, yet the rhetorical purpose of the psalm includes the construction of a hopeful future. The final act of narration includes God's perception of the people's distress and hearing of their cry, with the result that God is reminded of his covenant and relents (106:44–45). The language evokes Exod 2:23–25 and opens up the possibility of a new deliverance—of a new and different story. As their captors show them mercy (Ps 106:46) instead of the oppression shown by the Egyptians, so perhaps the people might not be like their ancestors who "did not remember your abundant love" (106:7) but will instead "confess your holy name" (106:47).

The Psalter's juxtaposition of these two psalms suggests that the notion of a master narrative should not be oversimplified. It is not a single, fixed story but a set of cultural memories that offers both constraint and the possibility to tell and retell the tale in an inexhaustible variety of ways. Perhaps certain categories developed by Aleida Assmann can be of help in grasping its flexibility. Assmann distinguishes between "stored memory" and "functional memory," or "archival" and "working" memory. Stored or archival memory "contains that which has become unusable, obsolete, or foreign; the neutral, identity-abstract factual knowledge; but also the repertoire of missed opportunities, alternative options, and unused chances." But it can also be a "reservoir for future functional memories," a "resource for the renewal of cultural knowledge," and a "condition for the possibility of cultural change" (both quotes A. Assmann 1999, 140). It is rather difficult to identify this stored memory unless it is in fact pulled out of cold storage and put to use. One example from the Hebrew Bible might be the changing role of the story of "the sons of God and the daughters of men" from Gen 6:1–4. In the Primeval History it is a marginal narrative, obsolete, and perhaps with a foreign feel. In the hands of the tradents of the Enochic traditions, however, it is dusted off and made into the paradigmatic episode that gives meaning to the grand narrative of history itself (1 En. 85–90).

Assmann contrasts such archived memories with functional or working memory, which she characterizes as "an acquired memory, which emerges from a process of choosing, connecting, and constituting meaning. Unstructured, disconnected elements enter the functional memory composed, constructed, and connected. Meaning emerges from this constructive act, a quality which the stored memory fundamentally lacks" (A. Assmann 1999, 137; trans. Erll 2011, 35). While acknowledging Assmann's distinction, I would suggest that functional/working memory actually has something of the storehouse as well. Or, perhaps a better analogy would be that of the clothes closet. There are, to be sure, items pushed to the remote sides or stored on high shelves of which one is dimly aware but that are truly not part of one's functional wardrobe, though they might at some future date be retrieved. But for the rest there exist a large number of items that have indeed been chosen but that can be combined and recombined into a variety of different ensembles. Moreover, some clothes are more suitable for one season than another and so are chosen or left according to one's immediate needs. What I have described in this analogy is similar to the way in which I have distinguished between the tacit knowledge that constitutes the master narrative and particular performances of it, which may be tailored for particular purposes.

To this point, I have spoken as though the master narrative sets the limits of the sayable, except where an act of retrieval from stored memory recasts it. But that is not entirely the case, as the odd historical résumé in Ezek 20 illustrates. Ezekiel's account is often referred to as a "revisionist" history of Israel, though that description minimizes its discrepancy from other accounts. Although it is not impossible that Ezekiel genuinely draws on divergent traditions, it is more likely that he is deliberately inventing an alternative history. Most strikingly, Ezekiel traces Israel's apostasy back to an otherwise unattested worship of Egyptian idols (20:8). In the account of the wilderness period he refers to violations of Sabbaths and other laws (20:13) that have no basis in otherwise-known traditions (Block 1997, 633). Nor is it likely, in my opinion, that the distinction between the two sets of laws, one that gives life and another, punitive set of "not good laws" that leads to death, is based in received tradition (contra, e.g., Hahn and Bergsma 2004, who identify the "not good laws" with Deuteronomy). All of these innovations are rather part of Ezekiel's attempt to do grotesque historiography, as he does also in the allegorical histories in chapters 16 and 23.

Why would Ezekiel construct a history that is so much at odds with the master narrative that both he and his audience could scarcely fail to interpret it as contradiction of common cultural memory? The answer may be found in a statement by the philosopher of history R. G. Collingwood: "every present has a past of its own, and any imaginative reconstruction of the past aims at reconstructing the past of *this* present" (1946, 247). Since Ezekiel considered the present of his people to be one of radical apostasy, he constructs the only past that he judges can rightly account for it, one in which the sins of the contemporary period are present from the very beginning (see Greenberg 1983, 383). The force of Ezekiel's rhetoric thus depends upon his audience's recognizing his deliberate distortion of cultural memory.

While there is much more that might be explored in relation to the way cultural memory is engaged in the construction of these capsule histories of Israelite history, there is a quite different point of engagement with cultural memory studies that I wish to take up in the second part of this essay. This is the phenomenon of "ghost memories," that is to say, memories that remain recognizably intact even as they are transferred from one character to another.

GHOST MEMORIES OF NABONIDUS AND THE RECONSTRUCTION OF THE
MEMORY OF NEBUCHADNEZZAR[5]

Nabonidus, the last king of the Neo-Babylonian Empire, occupied an important place in history, but he did not fare so well in cultural memory. Although mentioned in a number of later cuneiform documents and discussed by Berossus, the Hellenistic-era Babylonian historian, Nabonidus was largely forgotten by Greek and Jewish writers. Herodotus (*Hist.* 1.188–189) probably refers to him in a garbled way as "Labynetus." When Xenophon describes Cyrus's conquest of Babylon (*Cyr.* 7.5.1–36), he does not mention the name of the last king of Babylon, probably because he did not know it. Moreover, he reports that the king was killed, which scholars now think was not the case.[6] Even though Josephus had access to the reasonably accurate account of Berossus, he was clearly puzzled by what he read, since his own cultural memory was shaped by the account of Dan 5 about the fall of the Babylonian kingdom under Belshazzar. He resolved the contradiction by saying that the Babylonian kingdom "passed to Baltasares, who was called Naboandelos by the Babylonians. It was against him that Cyrus, king of Persia and Darius, king of Media, took the field" (*A.J.* 10.231–232).

Historical information about Nabonidus was only recovered in the late nineteenth century, when the emerging field of Assyriology discovered historical and literary documents concerning him. What scholars quickly recognized was that biblical writings had, in fact, preserved memories of Nabonidus, though these traditions were attached to the name of Nebuchadnezzar. Already in articles published at the turn of the twentieth century, Riessler (1899, 43) and Hommel (1902, 145–50) had argued that the narrative about Nebuchadnezzar in Dan 4 was actually based on traditions about Nabonidus (see also the review of early scholarship in Dommershausen 1964, 31–40). The discovery of the Jewish Prayer of Nabonidus in Qumran Cave 4 proved definitively that Jews had written compositions about Nabonidus. Subsequently, the recovery of Nabonidus's own inscription from Harran in 1956 allowed scholars to see how literary

---

5. As with my earlier study on the historical résumés, my initial study of Nabonidus traditions was conducted in conversation with cognitive studies (Newsom 2010). Concurrently with the present essay, I have been reworking my understanding of the Nabonidus traditions in relation to cultural memory studies.

6. Berossus and the Dynastic Prophecy report that Nabonidus was spared by Cyrus and made governor of a remote province. For Berossus, see Josephus, *C. Ap.* 1.152–153; for the Dynastic Prophecy, see Grayson 2000, 33.

and content features from that very inscription were utilized, independently, in Dan 4 and the Prayer of Nabonidus (Koch 1993, 89–98; Newsom 2010, 70, 77–79). Indeed, as von Soden (1935) had already argued, traditions about Nabonidus may also have influenced Dan 2, 3, and 5.

The evidence for the presence of Nabonidus traditions in Dan 2 is the most indirect, though it is not insignificant. Of all the Neo-Babylonian kings, only Nabonidus had a particular interest in revelatory and ominous dreams, to which he made reference in several of his inscriptions (Beaulieu 1989, 218).[7] Indeed, his claims to revelatory dreams were ridiculed in the hostile Verse Account of Nabonidus (Schaudig 2001, 569, 576). It is not simply the fact that an ominous dream occurs in Dan 2 that suggests a possible allusion to Nabonidus. If that were all, then one might more likely attribute the presence of the dream to the similarities between Dan 2 and the story of Joseph and Pharaoh in Gen 41. But other details point toward Nabonidus. In Dan 2 the dream occurs in the second year of the king's reign and gives him cause for severe anxiety, presumably about his security on the throne. The interpretation of the dream brings the king relief, and he rewards Daniel, the interpreter. The dream as preserved in Dan 2 is no earlier than the Seleucid period and has an eschatological conclusion (see 2:36–45), but since it is widely agreed that the narrative itself originated earlier, it is likely that the present version of the dream either represents a modification of or a substitution for the original dream, though opinions differ as to what might have stood in its place in an earlier version (see, e.g., Kratz 1991, 134–38; Collins 1993, 162–70).

Nabonidus, a usurper of nonroyal blood, was known to be anxious about the legitimacy of his kingship. In an inscription from his first regnal year he reports a dream in which he saw a conjunction of the moon (Sin) and the great star (Marduk). A "young man" reassures him that "the conjunction does not involve evil portents"; to the contrary, later in the dream Marduk explicitly legitimizes his kingship (Beaulieu 1989, 111; Schaudig 2001, 514–19, 525). Though the evidence for Nabonidus traditions in Dan 2 is not conclusive, the similarities between the dream motifs are intriguing, especially in light of stronger evidence for other chapters.

Daniel 3 is thought by many scholars to preserve a parodic echo of Nabonidus's cultic reforms, in which he championed the veneration of the

---

7. For the texts, see Schaudig 2001.These include the Ehulhul Cylinder I.15–26 (416–417, 436); Harran Inscription I.11; III.1–2 (488, 496, 493, 498); the Babylon Stela VI–VII (519–520, 525–526); and an inscribed bead (545).

moon god Sin. He expressed his devotion by installing a new and non-traditional cult statue of Sin in Harran and asserting that the Esagil temple in Babylon actually belonged to Sin because of the lunar crescent iconography found there (Beaulieu 2007, 139). Moreover, the motif of the fiery furnace has recently been argued to derive from a literary topos that was part of the school curriculum in Neo-Babylonia (Beaulieu 2009). These two elements suggest that the origins of Dan 3 derive from the sixth century and preserve memories of Nabonidus.

The strongest case for influence can be made for Dan 4. Even before the discovery of the Harran inscriptions of Nabonidus, scholars had noted that, of the Neo-Babylonian monarchs, only Nabonidus had an extended period of absence from Babylon. Moreover, though the anti-Nabonidus Verse Account does not explicitly call him mad, it depicts him as irrational. The Harran inscriptions, however, show such close similarities with Dan 4 (and aspects of the Prayer of Nabonidus) that it appears that the Jewish authors of these texts had some direct or indirect knowledge of the contents and style of the inscriptions, probably through the mechanism of public reading and oral transmission (see further Newsom 2010, 77–79).

Daniel 5 is clearly related to Nabonidus traditions, since Belshazzar was the son and co-regent of Nabonidus. The account of a great feast occurring on the night that Babylon fell has the marks of legend, though it appears to be an early one, since both Herodotus (*Hist.* 1.191) and Xenophon (*Cyr.* 7.5.25) preserve versions of it. Recently, however, scholars have argued that there may be a recollection of a historical event in the traditions, perhaps reflecting an *akitu* festival in honor of Sin (Beaulieu 1989, 228). The actual fate of Belshazzar is not known.

Taken together, there is evidence of a substantial cultural memory of Nabonidus in the narratives of Daniel, yet it is a ghost memory, for Nabonidus haunts the stories without ever being mentioned explicitly. The textual data raise two theoretical questions. First, what were the conditions under which Nabonidus was first the subject of Jewish interest and then of Jewish forgetting? Second, what was the effect of repurposing Nabonidus stories to engage the cultural memory of Nebuchadnezzar?

Nabonidus would have been a figure of significance to the Babylonian Jewish community and to Jewish soldiers in his army during the time of his reign.[8] It is likely that the tensions within the city between supporters and

---

8. Meyer (1989, 99–101) suggests that Jewish troops may have been part of Nabonidus's army at Teima. In my opinion, the more likely source of the court tales

opponents of Nabonidus during the final years of his reign also affected the Jewish community, with the prophet responsible for Isa 40–55 publicly supporting the imminent victory of Cyrus the Persian (Isa 45:1–8). This would be the context in which stories about Nabonidus would most likely be composed, though one may debate exactly what stance the narratives take toward him. While the narratives burlesque the king and make him a somewhat ridiculous figure, the narratives in Dan 2–4 all end with the king's confession of the power of the God of the Jews. The Prayer of Nabonidus similarly represents him as a king who came to see the error of idolatry. In my opinion, though the narratives do make fun of the king, they ultimately show him to be a worthy ruler and, as Dan 4 indicates, one chosen by God to exercise sovereignty. Thus, they may have functioned as part of a Jewish defense of him against the rival claims of Second Isaiah for Cyrus (Newsom 2010). Although the memory of Nabonidus played a role in the Babylonian revolt against the Persians in 522 BCE, when Nidintu-Bel claimed to be the son of Nabonidus, memory of him is likely to have quickly receded as the Persians completed the consolidation of their empire (Briant 2002, 115–21).

While it is fairly easy to see why Nabonidus faded from Jewish memory after 538 BCE, this act of cultural forgetting could have happened by the simple neglect of the stories in which he figured. But the social issues that the stories negotiated, namely, how to relate Jewish loyalty to the Most High God with service to a gentile king, remained important issues during the Persian period. Indeed, new stories of a similar type were composed. Although Dan 6 now refers to a legendary king called Darius the Mede, it is likely that the story was originally told about the Persian Darius I (Collins 1993, 264). Moreover, other narratives were composed concerning Cyrus, including the stories of Bel and the Dragon. But the Nabonidus narratives were not simply transferred forward to one of the reigning Persian monarchs; they were also transferred backward to recast the memory of an earlier figure, Nebuchadnezzar. This requires further explanation.

The earliest Jewish construction of the memory of Nebuchadnezzar is conflicted. As Matthias Henze (2009, 112) has shown, the Deuteronomistic History graphically depicts Nebuchadnezzar's conquest of Judah and Jerusalem, including his acts of cruelty toward Zedekiah (2 Kgs 25), yet

---

is the Jewish scribes of Babylon itself, perhaps those associated with the Judean royal family, who were clients of Nabonidus.

Nebuchadnezzar is viewed as acting with the approval of the God of Israel. The same interpretation is found in Ezekiel (17:11–21; 26:7) and Jeremiah (21:7; 22:25), where Nebuchadnezzar is merely the instrument of God's judgment against Judah. The developing textual tradition of Jer 27:5–7 goes somewhat further. Although LXX Jer 34:5 (= MT Jer 27:5) indicates that the God of Judah gives dominion to Nebuchadnezzar, the later MT refers to him as "my servant, King Nebuchadnezzar" and has a more elaborate description of the bestowal of sovereignty upon him. Even here, however, there is no indication that Nebuchadnezzar has self-awareness of this relationship with the Judean God—his state of mind is of no interest to the tradents of MT Jeremiah. These texts, and in particular the prophetic ones, were formed as part of an inner-Judean debate about the intentions of their God and, in consequence of that, the aptness of a policy of submission or resistance to Babylonian forces. Thus, Nebuchadnezzar's authorization as instrument or even as delegated ruler was shaped by this context. Alongside this justification of the actions of Nebuchadnezzar, however, was also a tradition of pure rage against Babylon and its king for the cruel destruction of Jerusalem, a tradition preserved in Jer 49–51.

While the texts discussed here were all likely produced by the generation that experienced the traumatic events of 587 BCE, the fall of Judah and the destruction of the temple by Nebuchadnezzar created a traumatic memory that haunted Judaism for centuries. The later cipher of "Babylon" for "Rome" is evidence of that. How traumatic memory is dealt with depends in part on the nearness or distance from the events in question, as well as the circumstances of the community to whom the memory belongs. If narratives like that of Dan 1–4, which depict the religious transformation of Nebuchadnezzar, had been composed by the generation that experienced the destruction of Jerusalem, then one might well judge them to be ethically repugnant, a betrayal of the suffering of the Judeans killed and exiled. With the passage of time, however, a certain freedom to use fictive play to deal with traumatic memory may be useful (see the similar conclusion on the book of Judith's representation of Nebuchadnezzar in Henze 2009, 119). The Nabonidus stories, with their concluding praise of the God Most High by the king, provided to later generations a useful vehicle for detoxifying the memory of Nebuchadnezzar. To tell a story about a king whose actions were traumatically inscribed onto Jewish memory and to represent him as a king who himself traumatically came to recognize the power of the God of the Jews is to exert agency in the symbolic realm to heal a wound of memory.

At the same time, the narratives of Daniel show some hesitancy about probing that wound too deeply. Daniel 1 does not describe the events of 587 BCE but instead draws on 2 Chr 36:5–7 for the tradition of a campaign by Nebuchadnezzar against Jehoiakim, otherwise unattested. The destruction of Jerusalem and the burning of the temple are absent from Daniel's storyworld (only the OG of Dan 4:19 refers to the temple's desolation). In the "Nebuchadnezzar redaction," these are distinctly diaspora tales, and the critical issues revolve not around the fate of Jerusalem but rather the concerns of a minority population whose religious self-understanding is at odds with the claims of a gentile empire. Thus Nebuchadnezzar, as the one initially responsible for the large eastern diaspora of Jews, can serve as a figure who condenses all of the subsequent gentile monarchs under whom the Jews must live. The confessions of the Most High that conclude chapters 2, 3, and 4 can be seen as comparable to the construction of the memory of Cyrus as one who also acknowledged that "the Lord God of Heaven has given me all the kingdoms of the earth" (2 Chr 36:23). Whether or not the Persians ever used such rhetoric in their dealings with the small nations of their empire cannot be determined. But the existence of that text, together with the adaptation of the Nabonidus narratives for the towering figure of Nebuchadnezzar, are an indication of how important it was for the Jews to construct a cultural memory in which their God was recognized by these powerful monarchs as the source of their own sovereign power—whether these monarchs were involved in the destruction or the restoration of the temple and its community.

The two small case studies presented here only begin to touch on the many ways in which cultural memory studies and biblical studies can mutually inform one another. Whether Israelite and Judean scribes were using inherited traditions about their own origins and experience or whether they were attempting to master experiences thrust upon them by the events of international powers, the work of producing usable cultural memory was a critical task.

Works Cited

Assmann, Aleida. 1999. *Erinnerungsräume: Formen und Wandlungen des kulturellen Gedächtnisses.* Munich: Beck.

Assmann, Jan. 1997. *Moses the Egyptian: The Memory of Egypt in Western Monotheism.* Cambridge: Harvard University Press.

———. 2000. *Religion und kulturelles Gedächtnis.* 3rd ed. Münich: Beck.

———. 2006. Form as Mnemonic Device: Cultural Texts and Cultural Memory. Pages 67–82 in *Performing the Gospel: Orality, Memory, and Mark*. Edited by Richard A. Horsley, Jonathan Draper, and John Miles Foley. Minneapolis: Fortress.

———. 2011. Israel and the Invention of Religion. Pages 175–205 in *Cultural Memory and Early Civilization: Writing, Remembrance, and Political Imagination*. Cambridge: Cambridge University Press.

Beaulieu, Paul-Alain. 1989. *The Reign of Nabonidus, King of Babylon, 556–539 B.C.* New Haven: Yale University Press.

———. 2007. Nabonidus the Mad King: A Reconsideration of His Steles from Harran and Babylon. Pages 137–68 in *Representations of Political Power: Case Histories from Times of Change and Dissolving Order in the Ancient Near East*. Edited by Marlies Heinz and Marian H. Feldman. Winona Lake, IN: Eisenbrauns.

———. 2009. The Babylonian Backround of the Motif of the Fiery Furnace in Daniel 3. *JBL* 128:272–90.

Block, Daniel I. 1997. *The Book of Ezekiel: Chapters 1–24*. NICOT. Grand Rapids: Eerdmans.

Brettler, Marc Z. 2001. Memory in Ancient Israel. Pages 1–17 in *Memory and History in Christianity and Judaism*. Edited by Michael Signer. Notre Dame, IN: University of Notre Dame Press.

Briant, Pierre. 2002. *From Cyrus to Alexander: A History of the Persian Empire*. Translated by Peter Daniels. Winona Lake, IN: Eisenbrauns.

Carstens, Pernille, Trine Hasselbalch, and Niels Peter Lemche, eds. 2012. *Cultural Memory in Biblical Exegesis*. Perspectives on Hebrew Scriptures and Its Contexts 17. Piscataway, NJ: Gorgias.

Childs, Brevard. 1962. *Memory and Tradition in Israel*. London: SCM.

Collingwood, R. G. 1946. *The Idea of History*. New York: Oxford University Press.

Collins, John J. 1993. *Daniel: A Commentary on the Book of Daniel*. Hermeneia. Minneapolis: Fortress.

Davies, Philip R. 1992. *In Search of Ancient Israel: A Study of Biblical Origins*. JSOTSup 148. Sheffield: Sheffield Academic Press.

Dommershausen, Werner. 1964. *Nabonid im Buche Daniel*. Mainz: Matthias Grünewald.

Erll, Astrid. 2011. *Memory in Culture*. Translated by Sara Young. New York: Palgrave Macmillan.

Grayson, Albert Kirk. 2000. *Assyrian and Babylonian Chronicles*. Texts from Cuneiform Sources. Winona Lake, IN: Eisenbrauns.

Greenberg, Moshe. 1983. *Ezekiel 1–20*. AB 22. Garden City, NY: Doubleday.

Hahn, Scott Walker, and John Seitze Bergsma. 2004. What Laws Were "Not Good"? A Canonical Approach to the Theological Problem of Ezekiel 20:25–26. *JBL* 123:201–18.

Halbwachs, Maurice. 1992. *La topographie légendaire des Évangiles en Terre Sainte: Étude de mémoire collective*. Paris: Presses universitaires de France. Translated into English as pages 193–235 in *On Collective Memory*. Edited and translated by Lewis A. Coser. Chicago: University of Chicago Press. [orig. 1941]

Hendel, Ronald. 2005. *Remembering Abraham: Culture, Memory, and History in the Hebrew Bible*. New York: Oxford University Press.

Henze, Matthias. 2009. Babylon Remembered: Nebuchadnezzar in the Collective Memory of Ancient Israel. Pages 108–20 in *With Wisdom as a Robe: Qumran and Other Jewish Studies in Honour of Ida Frölich*. Edited by Károly Dániel Dobos and Miklós Kozeghy. Hebrew Bible Monographs 21. Sheffield: Sheffield Phoenix Press.

Hommel, Fritz. 1902. Die Abfassungszeit des Buches Daniel und der Wahnsinn Nabonids. *Theologisches Literaturblatt* 23:145–50.

Knight, Douglas A. 2006. *Rediscovering the Traditions of Israel*. 3rd ed. SBLSBL 16. Atlanta: Society of Biblical Literature.

———. 2009. Traditio-Historical Criticism: The Development of the Covenant Code. Pages 97–116 in *Method Matters: Essays on the Interpretation of the Hebrew Bible in Honor of David L. Petersen*. Edited by Joel M. LeMon and Kent Harold Richards. SBLRBS 56. Atlanta: Society of Biblical Literature.

Koch, Klaus. 1993. Gottes Herrschaft über das Reich des Menschen: Daniel 4 im Licht neuer Funde. Pages 77–119 in *The Book of Daniel in the Light of New Findings*. Edited by A. S. van der Woude. BETL 106. Leuven: Leuven University Press.

Kratz, Reinhard G. 1991. *Translatio Imperii: Untersuchungen zu den aramäischen Danielerzählungen und ihrem theologiegeschichtlichen Umfeld*. WMANT 63. Neukirchen-Vluyn: Neukirchener.

Lemche, Niels Peter. 1993. The Old Testament—A Hellenistic Book? *SJOT* 7:163–93.

Lyotard, Jean-François. 1984. *The Postmodern Condition: A Report on Knowledge*. Translated by Geoff Bennington and Brian Massumi. Theory and History of Literature 10. Minneapolis: University of Minnesota Press.

Megill, Allan. 2007. *Historical Knowledge, Historical Practice: A Contempo-

rary Guide to Practice. Chicago: University of Chicago Press.

Meyer, Rudolf W. 1989. *Zur Geschichte und Theologie des Judentums in hellenistisch-römischer Zeit.* Edited by Waltraut Bernhardt. Neukirchen-Vluyn: Neukirchener.

Newsom, Carol A. 2006. Rhyme and Reason: The Historical Résumé in Israelite and Early Jewish Thought. Pages 215–33 in *Congress Volume: Leiden, 2004.* Edited by André Lemaire. VTSup 109. Leiden: Brill.

———. 2010. Why Nabonidus? Excavating Traditions from Qumran, the Hebrew Bible, and Neo-Babylonian Traditions. Pages 57–80 in *The Dead Sea Scrolls: Transmission of Traditions and Production of Texts.* Edited by Sariana Metso, Hindy Najman, and Eileen Shuller. STDJ 92. Leiden: Brill.

Ricoeur, Paul. 1984–1988. *Time and Narrative.* 3 vols. Translated by Kathleen McLaughlin and David Pellauer. Chicago: University of Chicago Press.

Riessler, Paul. 1899. *Das Buch Daniel.* Kurzgefasster wissenschaftlicher Kommentar zu den Heiligen Schriften des alten Testaments 3.3.2. Stuttgart: Roth.

Schaudig, Hanspeter. 2001. *Die Inschriften Nabonids von Babylon and Kyrus' des Grossen samt den in ihrem Umfeld entstandenen Tendenzschriften.* AOAT 256. Münster: Ugarit-Verlag.

Smith, Mark S. 2004. *The Memoirs of God: History, Memory, and the Experience of the Divine in Ancient Israel.* Minneapolis: Fortress.

Soden, Wolfgang von. 1935. Eine babylonische Volksüberlieferung von Nabonid in den Danielerzählungen. *ZAW* 53:81–89.

Thompson, Thomas L. 1999. *The Mythic Past: Biblical Archaeology and the Myth of Israel.* New York: Basic Books.

Whitelam, Keith W. 1996. *The Invention of Ancient Israel: The Silencing of Palestinian History.* London: Routledge.

Old Memories, New Identities: Traumatic Memory, Exile, and Identity Formation in the Damascus Document and Pesher Habakkuk

Tim Langille

As communities continue to shape and reshape their collective memories, new events and information are constantly combined and integrated with previous knowledge to form flexible mental schemas. Representation of trauma and construction of collective identity are facilitated by these flexible, preexisting schemas. Memories of events run back and forth in time, from past to present and vice-versa, as more recent events and figures are associated with earlier ones (Schwartz 1991, 222, 233–34; van der Kolk and van der Hart 1995, 171; Yerushalmi 1996). The shattering and disruptive experiences of trauma are processed and represented through already-existing mnemonic and narrative structures (Caruth 1995, 153; Schwartz 1996; van der Kolk and van der Hart 1995, 170–76). For instance, the analogy between the exodus from Egypt and the return from the Babylonian exile established in Jeremiah (16:14–15 = 23:7–8), Isaiah (48:20; 51:9–11; 52:4; see Japhet 2006, 502), and Ezra-Nehemiah was appropriated by later mnemonic communities, such as those that produced the Damascus Document (CD) and Pesher Habakkuk (1QpHab).[1]

This paper explores ways in which CD and 1QpHab revisit the traumatic memories of the destruction of Jerusalem and the Babylonian exile in the formation of exclusivist collective identities. More specifically, I argue that revisiting and reshaping these sites of memory contributes to the creation of boundaries between the elect and the traitors or the pure and the impure. In the process, I discuss the ways in which CD and 1QpHab attempt to restore what they narrativize as the loss of an original preexilic identity.

---

1. In using the term "mnemonic communities," I follow Eviatar Zerubavel, who uses it simply to refer to a community of memory (Zerubavel 2003, 4; see also Schwartz 1991, 222).

Following Dominick LaCapra's discussion of the ways that groups convert absence (something that never was) into loss (specific historical events), a strategy that creates the perception of an original unity or identity that has been polluted or contaminated, I look at the ways in which CD and 1QpHab represent the restoration of an idealized preexilic identity through the elimination of polluters and contaminators of the collective self, culminating in an eschatological return to Jerusalem and the temple (see Zeph 3:11). In other words, I examine the ways in which these texts represent restoration and recovery from destruction and exile as processes of cleansing or eliminating impure elements from the collective self (cf. Ezra-Nehemiah). In representing restoration, the producers of CD and 1QpHab mask structural trauma (the transhistorical absence represented as the loss of an original unity or purity) in its representation of historical trauma (the destruction of the temple and the Babylonian exile).[2]

After outlining my theoretical framework in conversation with several concepts introduced by Barry Schwartz—intergenerational memory, sites of memory, ritual and memory, keying, schemas, memorable events, and trauma—this essay will address (1) the ways in which the repetitive temporality of traumatic memory creates a bifurcation of the collective self and collapses the distinctions between the past and present so that the desires of the present are imposed on the past through keying into earlier sites of memory to authorize the discourse of the text;[3] (2) the roles of the discourse of exile and temporal rupture and continuity in separating the elect from the traitors; and (3) how the strategic keying of collective

---

2. According to LaCapra, "[t]he traumatizing events in historical trauma can be determined (for example, the events of the Shoah), while structural trauma (like absence) is not an event but an anxiety-producing condition of possibility related to the potential for historical traumatisation. When structural trauma is reduced to, or figured as, an event, one has the genesis of myth wherein trauma is enacted in a story or narrative from which later traumas seem to derive (as in Freud's primal crime or in the case of original sin attendant upon the Fall from Eden)" (2001, 82).

3. Pierre Nora defines a "site of memory" (*lieu de mémoire*) as "any significant entity, whether material or non-material in nature, which by dint of human will or the work of time has become a symbolic element of the memorial heritage of any community" (1996, xvii). Following Nora's definition, Ehud Ben Zvi (2012, 141) uses "site of memory" to refer to "any constructed space, place, event, figure, text or the like—whether it exists 'materially' or only in the mind of members of a social group—whose presence in the relevant cultural milieu evokes or was meant to evoke core images or aspects of images of the past held by the particular social group who lives in that cultural milieu." Following this paradigm, sites of memory relevant to the present study would include the wilderness, Jerusalem, the exodus, the exile, Moses, and Torah.

memories of revelation in the wilderness, exile, and return connect these mnemonic communities to an idealized past in imagining the desired end of a restored Jerusalem, temple, and original unity.

COLLECTIVE TRAUMA, COLLECTIVE MEMORY: THE HAUNTING EFFECTS OF POSTMEMORY

The reaction to, and reception of, traumatic events can be inter/transgenerational. Marianne Hirsch defines this process as "postmemory," "the relationship of the second generation to powerful, often traumatic, experiences that preceded their births but that were nevertheless transmitted to them so deeply as to seem to constitute memories in their own right" (2008, 103).[4] According to Hirsch, postmemory illumines the problem of mnemonic transmission through ruptures, when cultural archives and institutions are threatened or destroyed: "the structure of postmemory clarifies how the multiple ruptures and radical breaks introduced by trauma and catastrophe inflect intra-, inter- and trans-generational inheritance" (2008, 111). Postmemory reactivates earlier, more distant archival/cultural/collective memories "by reinvesting them with resonant individual and familial forms of mediation and aesthetic expression" (2008, 111; see Schwartz 1996). As a result, "less-directly affected participants" engage in the postmemorial work that allows memories of events that occurred before their birth to persist, even long after those individuals more directly affected by the events have long passed (Hirsch 2008, 111). For Hirsch, memory is "an affective link to the past" and "an embodied living connection" that is symptomatic of "a need for inclusion in a collective membrane forged by a shared inheritance of multiple traumatic histories and the individual and social responsibility we feel toward a persistent and traumatic past"

---

4. Hirsch's concept of postmemory connotes a historicity that is absent in antiquity, as memory functions differently in modernity than it did in antiquity. Hirsch applies postmemory to Holocaust survivor accounts and memories of a series of catastrophic events that contain a historicity (i.e., we know that the Holocaust happened) that is not applicable to the ancient events discussed in this paper. Her work focuses on the ways in which the traumatic memories of Holocaust survivors are transferred to and represented in second-generation fiction, art, memoir, and testimony. With that said, I find Hirsch's concept of postmemory, and her work on inter/transgenerational memory in general, to be a valuable heuristic device in analyzing the intergenerational transmission of trauma. Because Hirsch's work is read in various ways, postmemory has turned out to be a fruitful and malleable concept. Thus, I use this concept with an awareness of the potentially anachronistic implications of doing so.

(2008, 111; see Schwartz 1996). In what follows, I extend Hirsch's concept of postmemory beyond the second generation to subsequent generations, here the mnemonic communities of the first century BCE who produced CD and 1QpHab and keyed into memories of the Babylonian exile in the sixth century BCE.

Hirsch's work participates in an ongoing and developing theoretical discussion in Holocaust studies and other fields on trauma, memory, and intergenerational acts of transfer (Hirsch 2008, 104). Eva Hoffman calls the intergenerational dimensions of traumatic memory "the transmission of trauma" (2010, 408). She describes the haunting presence of trauma and loss as one that continues "to overwhelm and overshadow the present," as the process of mourning never lifts (2010, 411). The transmission and presence of trauma that continues to haunt the present are dimensions I will highlight throughout my textual analyses below.

Importantly, discussions of the transmission of trauma—which have proliferated and become increasingly pressing with the numerous genocides and collective catastrophes that have marked the twentieth and early twenty-first centuries—focus on the "affective impact of trauma and its aftermath, the ways in which trauma can recall, or reactivate, the effects of another, exceed the bounds of traditional historical archives and methodologies" (Hirsch 2008, 104; see Schwartz 1996, 908–9, 920–25). Hirsch describes the process of postmemory and the affective impact on the descendants of survivors as one in which later generations "remember" via stories and images that are transmitted "so deeply and affectively as to seem to constitute memories in their own right." Thus, the connection of postmemory to the past is not facilitated by "recall" but rather by imagination, projection, and creation. The affective force of postmemory may even displace the memories of later generations as the past haunts the present (Hirsch 2008, 106–7). Some of the points raised by Hirsch are applicable to the central concerns of this essay: the symbolic and affective force of memories of exodus and exile in the collective memories of CD and 1QpHab; the reactivation of earlier sites of sites of memory by later traumatic events, to the point that the earlier ones displace contemporary experiences and stories; the haunting effects of past trauma in the present.

The transmission of real or imagined events can be reactivated and reshaped to such an extent that distinctions between past and present collapse. For instance, when mnemonic communities conflate and/or blur the distinction between historical trauma (e.g., the loss of Jerusalem and the temple) with structural trauma (e.g., the transhistorical absence of an original unity or purity), these communities are haunted by the past by reliving and reshaping it constantly and collapsing the distinction between past and present (LaCapra 2001, 42–47). The reliving of the past and collapsing of past and present are trademarks of postmemory.

LaCapra posits that sites of memory often are sites of trauma, "and the extent to which it remains invested with trauma marks the extent to which memory has not been effective in coming to terms with it, notably through modes of mourning" (1998, 10). LaCapra's statement resonates with Michael Knibb's observation that some Second Temple literature presents Israel in a state of exile that continued well into the Second Temple period, an exile that would not be overcome until divine intervention reinstituted God's rule in the land (Knibb 1976, 272). In other words, for some mnemonic communities, the exile was not overcome during the Second Temple period and was revisited and reactivated as a site of trauma by later Second Temple communities (see Blenkinsopp 2005, 19).

As I will show in my textual analysis below, CD and 1QpHab mourn the absence of a pure preexilic identity by conflating absence and loss. In other words, these texts produce discourses based in absence. As LaCapra argues, the narrativization of absence often includes elements of sin or fault that are overcome through eschatology or salvation in the end (2001, 51). This point also speaks to Knibb's work on the ongoing corrupt state of an indefinite exile—in which only the community responsible for producing the text is the exception—that is finally overcome through an eschatological resolution (Knibb 1976). In CD and 1QpHab, the absence of a pure and intact preexilic identity continues to haunt the mnemonic community to the point that the exile is represented as continuing well into the Second Temple period. Following LaCapra, I argue that this coveted preexilic identity is "regained in some hoped-for, apocalyptic future or sublimely blank utopia that, through a kind of creation *ex nihilo*, will bring total renewal, salvation or redemption" (2001, 57).

Mnemonic Rupture and Continuity, Restoration, and Purification

With a focus on a troubled and ruptured past and as a structure that transmits traumatic memory, postmemory oscillates between rupture and continuity (Hirsch 2008, 106; see Schwartz 1991, 222). Michael Pickering and Emily Keightley discuss the ways in which mnemonic communities create a sense of difference generationally "not by making a complete break with inherited pasts, but through the dialectical relationships between continuity and rupture, intimate knowing and irreducible difference that occur vertically through time in genealogical relationships" (2013, 126). The oscillations and dialectics between rupture and continuity are a central feature of this essay as I explore the ways in which reactivating and reliving past collective trauma allows CD and 1QpHab to separate themselves from the impurities of the past and their present, mark the beginnings of a new purified era, and reconnect with an idealized past, which they mimic and emulate. In other words, this essay explores the spaces between discourses of destruction and restoration, exile and return, absence and presence, and rupture and continuity (see Pickering and Keightley 2013, 124).

New collective identities emerge out of ruptures or cultural crises (Eyerman 2004, 160), more specifically through memories and representations of ruptures or cultural crises. A rupture or cultural crisis provides an opportunity to create both continuity and discontinuity with the past, as older traditions are used for new purposes in new social conditions (Hobsbawm 1992, 5; Schwartz 1996; 1991, 221). In many cases, events or memories of events that threaten to tear the social fabric or eliminate social institutions are represented as ruptures or watershed events, which are venues for identity formation and construction (Zerubavel 2003, 83–85). LaCapra calls these ruptures or watershed events "founding traumas" because they become the basis for collective identity. He argues that shattering, destructive, or disorienting experiences of violence or persecution that become reference points for founding traumas are typical of myths of origins. According to LaCapra, these events may become "the valorized or intensely cathected basis for identity for a group rather than pose the problematic questions of identity" (2001, 23; see further Schwartz 1996). Following LaCapra, I examine how the language in CD and 1QpHab is consistent with processes of identity formation in which a trauma is construed as a founding, generative, and integrative identity marker (in the sense that it integrates or brings together several other identity markers).

Founding traumas are inter/transgenerational sites of memory that may be revisited and appropriated by new groups with new causes (Winter 2010, 317; see further Schwartz 1996). In other words, sites of traumatic memory can be revisited and reoccupied (LaCapra 1994). The intimately related and intertwined phenomena of collective trauma, collective memory, and collective identity have the potential to unite or divide (Smelser 2004, 44; Erikson 1994, 231–42). In instances of division, fault lines in collectivities are revealed in the contested spaces of sites of memory. In such cases, traumatic experiences and memories can open up fault lines that previously ran silently through the macrostructure of a collectivity and fragment that group. These fault lines create a bifurcation of a collectivity that separates the pure from impure contaminants (Erikson 1994, 236). For some mnemonic communities, restoration and recovery from traumatic events require processes of cleansing or eliminating outsiders or impurities from the social group.

Discourses of cleansing impure elements of a group in response to founding traumas produce notions of pure beginnings, collective intactness, and imagined consensus that exclude identifiable outsiders from a uniform way of life (see LaCapra 2001, 43–85; Zerubavel 2003, 82–83). In instances of mnemonically and discursively restoring a lost unity, identity formation makes ideological use of traumatic events in foundational ways "in terms of the concept of a chosen people or a belief in one's privileged status as victim" (LaCapra 2001, 81). Founding events are represented as watersheds that mark the transition from one distinct chapter to the next because mnemonic communities represent them as times of significant identity transformation (Zerubavel 2003, 82). However, as LaCapra argues, notions of simple continuity or discontinuity with the past are deceptive because continuity "involves not pure identity over time but some mode of repetition, and change is not a totally discrete process even in extreme forms of trauma" (1994, 174).

With the above in mind, it is important to recognize that notions of pure beginnings and original unity are illusory (see Latour 1993). According to LaCapra, the conversion of absence (something that never existed in the first place) into loss (a historic loss that is to be worked through by mourning) results in perceptions of an original unity or identity that has been polluted or contaminated by others; this lost unity is restored through eliminating those who are identified as social contaminants. In some instances these contaminants are part of the collective self, or "that sinful other in oneself" (LaCapra 2001, 58), leading to a bifurcation of the collective self that corresponds to the pure or the elect being separated from and seeking to eliminate or cleanse the impure traitors. However, the works of both Hirsch and Michael Rothberg reveal problems in linear notions of memory and identity, whether postmemory or multidirectional memory, as memory and identity are malleable, mutable, fluid, and shared by strange bedfellows (see Hirsch 2008; Rothberg 2009; Pickering and Keightley 2013, 120–21; J. Assmann 2006, 29). Rothberg's model of multidirectional memory outlines the ways in which memory and identity are fuzzy concepts, not zero-sum games with mnemonic winners and vanquished losers (Rothberg 2009, 1–12).[5]

Applied to the present case, although CD and 1QpHab construct identity through discourses of exile and separation, their mnemonic communities share memories and identities with those whom they represent as the impure other, including the Hasmonean high priests. As Carol Newsom has shown, Second Temple texts in general are part of a community of discourse that was shaped by dialogical relationships with the larger mnemonic and discursive worlds of Second Temple Judaism (2004, 1–21). Thus, mnemonic communities that opposed each other on some ideological level and represented the other as impure or impious nevertheless participated in dialogical relationships (see Bakhtin 1981, 281) and shared sites of memories. Not surprisingly, the memories invoked and represented in CD and 1QpHab concerning the state and legitimacy of Jerusalem, the temple, and the high priesthood are in a dialogical relationship with the memories of those whom their authors may have considered impure, namely, the Hasmoneans.

Reshaping Traumatic Memories through Schemas and Keying

The schematization of memory involves adapting, appropriating, reusing, and resynthesizing past experiences—both our own and others—to forge new identities and conceptions of ourselves and others, including proximate others (Pickering and Keightley 2013, 121). Barry Schwartz describes the mnemonic mechanism behind this process as "keying," which "transforms memory into a cultural system not because it consists of invisible mental operations, but because it matches publicly accessible (i.e., symbolic) models of the past … to the experiences of the present. Keying arranges cultural symbols into a publicly visible discourse that flows through the organizations and institutions of the social world" (Schwartz 1996, 911). Schwartz goes on to note that keying "connects otherwise separate realms

---

5. As Rothberg argues, "[o]ur relationship to the past does partially determine who we are in the present, but never straightforwardly and directly, and never without unexpected or even unwanted consequences that bind us to those who we consider other" (2009, 5). The multidirectionality of collective memory emerges out of "a malleable discursive space in which groups do not simply articulate established positions but actually come into being through their dialogical interactions with others; both the subjects and spaces of the public are open to continual reconstruction" (Rothberg 2009, 5).

of history" (1996, 911). In other words, keying creates a mnemonic frame that connects and matches the past and the present.

Keying and mnemonic, cultural schemas are most instrumental in the transmission of postmemory and multidirectional memory. Hirsch discusses the aesthetic, symbolic, and institutional structures and tropes that facilitate and transmit postmemory (2008, 107; see also Schwartz 1996). For her, "pre-established forms" are the "impersonal building blocks of affiliative postmemory" (Hirsch 2008, 120). In other words, the generations of affiliative postmemory rely on tropes and schemas for the shaping and negotiation of the past and the present, as well as individual and collective identity (Hirsch 2008, 124–25; see Schwartz 1996). These mnemonic tropes and images, imprinted on our brains as we bring them from the present to the past "hoping to find them there and to have our questions answered, may be screen memories—screens on which we project present our timeless needs and desires and which thus mask other images and other concerns" (Hirsch 2008, 120).

These screen memories, according to Rothberg, are related to and part of multidirectional memory. Screen memories, in the most general sense, are directly relevant to the representation of memories in CD and 1QpHab: collective memories of the exodus stand in for the exile; the destruction and exile of 587 BCE stand in for the persecution of their own respective communities, which see themselves in exile during the Hasmonean period. Evidence of mnemonic substitution and displacement may be found throughout CD and 1QpHab. Rothberg views screen memories as a phenomenon of individual memory and multidirectional memory as its collective equivalent. Although both screen memories and multidirectional memories illustrate the inevitable displacement and substitution in mnemonic processes, Rothberg differentiates between screen memory and multidirectional memory not only in terms of individual versus collective recall but also because screen memory often replaces a disturbing memory with a more comforting one, whereas multidirectional memory substitutes two or more traumatic memories (2009, 13).

The schematization, replacement, substitution, and multidirectionality of traumatic memories were not uncommon during the Second Temple period. As Schwartz notes in the introduction to the present volume, this was a "hot" period, "a traumatic span of time during which old ways were destroyed and re-created" (p. 28). What is most important here is the role that imagination plays in these mnemonic processes and the re-creation of cultural archives. Rothberg calls imaginative links "the substance of multidirectional memory" (2009, 18). Pickering and Keightley describe the relationship between memory and imagination as one of productive tension that is integral for the transmission of postmemory. They suggest that neither memory nor imagination is sufficient alone in illumining "the complex interplay of experienced and inherited pasts: the ways in which they are performed and revised continually in a constantly changing present, and the ways in which they extend their reach into the realm of the possible" (2013, 122). Imagination is what makes mnemonic communities inheritors and transmitters of memory as it combines "the inherited past, the experienced past, and the present moment of telling" (2013, 125). As Schwartz notes, "[t]he presence of inherited memories in the midst of invented memories is not an anomaly requiring reconciliation" (1991, 234). Mnemonic imagination is what helps negotiate and facilitate the oscillations and tensions between rupture and continuity (Pickering and Keightley 2013, 127–28).

Traumatic Memory in the Damascus Document and Pesher Habakkuk: Establishing the Elect and the Traitors

Before beginning my analysis, I will make some preliminary comments about the texts under investigation. Two medieval copies of the CD were discovered at the end of the nineteenth century in an Old Cairo synagogue storeroom (the Cairo Genizah). The abbreviation CD stands for Cairo Damascus, with CD-A referring to manuscript A and CD-B referring to manuscript B. Manuscript A is the longer of the two and dates to the tenth century CE, whereas manuscript B dates to the twelfth century. In the 1940s, ten fragments of CD were discovered in Caves 4, 5, and 6 at Qumran, which are known as 4QD, 5QD, and 6QD, with Cave 4 yielding the most manuscripts, eight. All ten Qumran manuscripts date from the beginning of the first century BCE to the middle of the first century CE. CD is divided cleanly into two parts: the Admonition (CD 1–8; 19–20) and the Laws (CD 9–16; Hempel 2000, 15–24). My discussion here focuses on the Admonition of CD-A, which is regarded as a composite work with a coherent and discernible plot and structure (see Davies 1983, 48–55, 202; Grossman 2002, 15–24, 37–41).

1QpHab is a pesher, or commentary, text. The Hebrew term *pesher* (פשר; plural: pesharim) means "interpretation." Maurya Horgan (1979) lists fifteen texts (with the possibility of three additional texts) that constitute the pesharim corpus from Qumran. Shani Berrin defines pesher as "a form of biblical interpretation peculiar to Qumran, in which biblical poetic/prophetic texts are applied to postbiblical historical/eschatological settings through various literary techniques in order to substantiate a theological conviction pertaining to divine reward and punishment" (2005, 110). 1QpHab and the pesharim from Qumran in general understand earlier events, even those of the distant past, to be relevant to the present and the imminent end time in the immediate future—a future that has already begun (Berrin 2005, 116–17). The distinctive formal feature of pesharim is the citation of an authoritative/biblical text (the "lemma") followed by the pesher ("Its interpretation concerns…") that reads the past into the present and/or near future by applying the content of the lemma to a contemporaneous context (i.e., the sociohistorical context of the mnemonic community; see Berrin 2005, 111). 1QpHab, which was among the original seven scrolls recovered from Qumran Cave 1, is a pesher of the book of Habakkuk, keying Habakkuk's prophecies of the Chaldean destruction of a sinful Judah (Hab 1–2) to its own time. Given that 1QpHab interprets the Chaldeans to be the "Kittim," most likely referring to the Romans, the text can be dated to the second half of the first century BCE, in either the late Hasmonean or early Roman period.

I proceed from the premise that CD and 1QpHab likely were produced by different communities, neither of which I will refer to as "the Qumran community" or "Qumran Judaism." Collins (2009) outlines the problems with attempting to correlate the site of Qumran with the texts discovered there in constructing the identity of one hypothetical community, which both inhabited the site and produced the texts. With that caveat, it is evident that the mnemonic communities that produced CD and 1QpHab drew on similar sites of memory, employed familiar cultural frameworks and schemas, and shared some common worldviews and linguistic tropes. Furthermore, both CD and 1QpHab share features and family resemblances with other texts discovered at Qumran, especially those commonly classified as "sectarian" (Wittgenstein 2003, 27–28; see further Fowler 1982, 40–41; Swales 1990, 49–51; Ryan 1981, 118). Some of the strong family resemblances discussed below that are shared by CD, 1QpHab, and other "sectarian texts" include separation of and/or dualism between the righteous and impious (1QM, 1QS, 4QMMT, 4Q171, 4Q174, 4Q177, 4Q387, 11QMelch), exilic discourse and wilderness identity (1QM, 1QS, 4QMMT, 4Q161, 4Q177, 4Q390, 4Q403; see Abegg 1997; Najman 2006; Talmon 1966), and eschatological worldviews (1QM, 1QS, 4QMMT, 4Q174, 4Q177, 11QMelch; see Collins 1997). However, I agree with Florentino García Martínez that Dead Sea Scrolls scholarship "should not only go beyond the 'canonical divide' but also beyond the 'sectarian divide,' and we should consider each composition of the whole collection on its own and on the basis of the partial and accidental evidence which has reached us, we should decide in each case the authority each single book may have had for the group that put the collection together" (2010, 244). Following García Martínez, CD and 1QpHab will be approached here as individual texts, each of which should be considered on its own, that share family resemblances and sites of memory with not only other sectarian texts discovered at Qumran but also many other authoritative texts from the Second Temple period (e.g., Ezra-Nehemiah, Daniel, Enoch, Jubilees, 1–2 Maccabees).

A prominent and persistent shared feature in Second Temple literature is the revisiting and reshaping of memories of the destruction of Jerusalem and the Babylonian exile. As discussed above, collective memories of trauma serve as inter/transgenerational sites of memory that may be reactivated and reshaped by later groups that bring the past into the present (Winter 2010, 317). Memories of 587 BCE and the Babylonia exile are exemplary of the presence of, and tension between, rupture and continuity, as mnemonic communities connect the prophetic remnant of exile with the founders and origins of a new covenant community. Davies describes the rupture and continuity, as well as the construction of an exclusive collective identity, in CD's revisiting and reshaping memories of the Babylonian exile and return as follows: "The community 'remembers' itself as the real Israel, the legitimate continuity of the old one, the real chosen people, but also in one sense *not* Israel—not the old Israel, and not the 'Israel' from which it is now segregated" (2010, 36). Once again, the tensions between rupture and continuity are overcome by the imagination of representation (see Pickering and Keightley 2013, 127–28), in this case, memories and discourses of a prophetic remnant.

The fact that multiple mnemonic communities were fixated on and reproduced memories of 587 BCE and the Babylonian exile speaks to LaCapra's assertion that some sites of trauma are revisited because groups have not come to terms with that trauma through mourning (1998, 10). In other words, the past persists via postmemory as it intrudes and shapes the present, which itself shapes and reshapes the remembered past. Here one need think only of the ways in which Hoffman describes the transmission of trauma as haunting and overwhelming the present (2010, 411). Again, notions of a past haunting the present correspond to Knibb's position that some Second Temple literature presents Israel in a continuous state of exile that was not overcome. CD and 1QpHab represent full restoration as occurring at the *eschaton*, when only members of their respective communities are restored (Knibb 1976, 272).

The inter/transgenerational sites of trauma of the destruction of 587 BCE and the exile become the foundation for identity construction in CD and 1QpHab. In fact, in these texts the Chaldean campaign against Jerusalem is not only an earlier site of trauma to be revisited and virtually, but still experientially, relived, even if through acts of imagination, but also one that embodies in itself the answer to a present-day, pressing question for the community: Who will possess the land in the future? The repetitive temporality and haunting effects of traumatic postmemory collapse distinctions between past, present, and future in these texts. The presence of this process in 1QpHab should not come as a surprise, since by definition pesharim fuse together past, present, and future. These texts are haunted by the past, and the exile is never overcome because absence is the object of mourning (i.e., an original and idealized preexilic identity). The mourning of the absence of a pure preexilic identity in CD and 1QpHab leads to eschatological worldviews and narratives of restoration and renewal that seek to eliminate pollutants and impurities in the social body.

In mourning the absence of this idealized preexilic identity, CD and 1QpHab reshape earlier sites of trauma—the destruction of 587 BCE and the exile—to position their respective communities in the present and establish an eschatological future, at which time the elect will possess the land and return to Jerusalem. Both texts begin by invoking violent imagery in establishing the origins of their respective communities: CD refers to Israel being delivered to the sword (CD-A 1.3–5), and 1QpHab complains of violence in the land that marks the beginning of the generation (1QpHab 1.2–8; see further Jassen 2010). CD and 1QpHab then revisit the memory of the Chaldean destruction of Jerusalem while distinguishing between the elect and the traitors, or the pure and impure (CD-A 1.6–21; 1QpHab 2–3). Importantly, in both texts the impure traitors reside in Jerusalem, defiling its temple.

In CD, the elect are represented as the pure remnant that survived the destruction of Jerusalem in 587 BCE.

> For when they were unfaithful in forsaking him, he hid his face from Israel and the sanctuary and delivered them up to the sword. But when he remembered the covenant with the forefathers, he saved a remnant

for Israel and did not deliver them up to destruction. And at the period of wrath, three hundred and ninety years after having delivered them into the hand of Nebuchadnezzar, king of Babylon, he visited them and caused to sprout from Israel and from Aaron a shoot of planting, in order to possess his land and to become fat with the good things of his soil. (CD-A 1.3–8)[6]

When God turned away from those who had forsaken him and delivered them up to the sword, he remembered the covenant with the ancestors and saved a remnant for Israel (השאיר שארית לישראל, CD-A 1.4–5), which is the foundation of the true Israel and new covenant community in CD. The new covenant community, which is juxtaposed with the congregation of traitors (בעדת בוגדים, CD-A 1.12), is a shoot from Israel and Aaron that is to possess the land in the future (ויצמח מישראל ומאהרן שורש מטעת לירוש את ארצו, CD-A 1.3–8; 2.11). The producer(s) of CD show the malleability of a site of trauma through mnemonic obliteration and telescoping time (see Henige 1974) in creating continuity between past, present, and future. CD telescopes the 390 years between Nebuchadnezzar's destruction and the emergence of the pure remnant of the new covenant community (see Ezek 4:5). In the process, CD effaces the memory of the return from Babylon, subsequent history, and any other identities (see Davies 2010, 36; CD-A 1.6–8), as the exile continued throughout the Second Temple period until the emergence of this pure remnant. Instead, the new covenant community in CD are the exiles who will return to the land. The producer(s) of CD self-identify as those who (alone) remained pure and faithful in exile (Blenkinsopp 2005, 19).

In 1QpHab, the elect, who are led by the persecuted Teacher of Righteousness (מורה הצדק), are separated from three enemies: (1) the wicked, who are Judeans; (2) the Kittim, who are associated with the Chaldeans of the past and the Romans in the present and future; and (3) the traitors (בוגדים), who are violators of the covenant (Jokiranta 2005, 30–31).[7]

> [... The interpretation of the word concerns] the traitors with the Man of the Lie, since they do not [believe in the words of] the Teacher of Righteousness from the mouth of God; and (it concerns) the traito[rs of the]

---

6. All translations are from García Martínez and Tigchelaar 2000.

7. The designation "Teacher of Righteousness" occurs at least seventeen times in Dead Sea Scrolls, including 1QpHab 1.13; 2.2; 5.10; 7.4; 8.3; 9.9–10; 11.5; CD-A 1.11; 6.11 ("the one who teaches righteousness"; see Stuckenbruck 2010, 26–27). The Teacher of Righteousness is also mentioned in 1QpMic and 4QpPs.

new [covenant] si[n]ce they did not believe in the covenant of God [and dishonoured] his holy na[me]. Likewise: *Blank* The interpretation of the word [concerns the trai]tors in the last days. They are the violator[s of the coven]ant who will not believe when they hear all that is going [to happen t]o the final generation, from the mouth of the Priest whom God has placed wi[thin the Commun]ity, to foretell the fulfillment of the words of his servants, the prophets, [by] means of whom God has declared all that is going to happen to his people Is[rael]. *Hab 1:6* For see, I will mobilize the Chaldeans, a cruel [and deter]mined people. *Blank* Its interpretation concerns the Kittim, wh[o ar]e swift and powerful in battle, to slay many [...] in the kingdom of the Kittim; they will take possession [of many countries] and will not believe in the precepts of [Go]d [... *Hab 1:6* They go across the earth] to [take possession of dwellings, not theirs. Its interpretation ...] and they will advance over the plain, to destroy and pillage the cities of the country. (1QpHab 2.1–3.1)

All three enemies will be divinely punished for their transgressions, which include forsaking the precepts of God (1QpHab 2.14–15; 8.10), robbing the nations (3.1–2; 9.5), acting with hubris (4.2–3; 10.13), performing illicit cultic activities (4.13; 6.4–5; 12.8–9), and persecuting the vulnerable (6.11–12; 12.1–3; Jokiranta 2013, 115). 1QpHab represents the traitors of its own people who occupy the Jerusalem temple to be more wicked than the plundering and marauding armies of the Kittim (Jokiranta 2013, 163; 2005, 30–31). In fact, the Kittim merely act as agents delivering divine retribution in the eschatological future against the Wicked Priest (הכוהן הרשע) of the Jerusalem temple, who has acted wickedly against the elect.[8]

> And what it says: *Hab 2:8a* «Since you pillaged many peoples all the rest of the nations will pillage you». Its interpretation concerns the last priests of Jerusalem, who will accumulate riches and loot from plunder-

---

8. The identities of the Teacher of Righteousness and the Wicked Priest are topics of much scholarly discussion. For a brief discussion and survey of scholarship, see Davies 1983, 14–20; Charlesworth 2002, 80–118. Although most scholars believe that the Wicked Priest was a Hasmonean ruler who opposed the Teacher of Righteousness, I agree with Davies's assessment that "[t]he methods and assumptions attending this process of reasoning are ill-founded and precarious, nor indeed can they say be said to have produced any unaninimity" (1983, 15). In a more recent publication he states that "[t]he central figures of sectarian history all have sobriquets, nicknames. This usage serves to underline the typological or symbolic nature of the events and persons being alluded to; the individual identity of the characters is simply not as important as their roles in a preordained divine plan. The only real historical agent is God himself" (Davies 2010, 31).

ing the nations. However, in the last days their riches and their loot will be given in to the hands of the army of the Kittim. *Blank* For they are *Hab 2:8a* «the rest of the nations». *Hab 2:8b* For the human blood (spilt) and the violence (done) to the country, the city and all/who dwell/in it. Its interpretation concerns the [Wi]cked Priest, whom, for the wickedness against the Teacher of Righteousness and the members of his council, God delivered into the hands of the enemies to disgrace him with a punishment, to destroy him with bitterness of soul for having acted wickedly against his elect. (1QpHab 9.2–12)

In 1QpHab, the destruction of the traitors of the covenant in the last days makes the return of the elect to Jerusalem possible. Revisiting memories of the Chaldean destruction of Jerusalem and having the Kittim destroy the impure priests in Jerusalem signals the beginning of the process of restoration and return in the last days, when the wicked will be removed from the earth (1QpHab 13.2).

Revisiting and reshaping the trauma of 587 BCE and the exile is an effective means of producing new collective identities by establishing it as a founding trauma. The language in CD and 1QpHab is a prime example of processes of identity formation in which a trauma is represented as a founding, generative, and integrative identity marker. According to Newsom, designations such as "the elect" or "the remnant for Israel" are an "intense rhetorical attempt to create new communities of discourse that could provide the basis for new social formations" (Newsom 2004, 10). Maxine Grossman sees the dualistic language that frames the memories of these events to be indicative of intracommunal conflicts (Grossman 2002, 135–36, 156–57). Thus, we can see evidence of the interweaving of the inherited past and the experienced past. The exclusivist and divisive language used in CD and 1QpHab is not surprising in that sites of trauma have the potential to unite or divide groups, especially in instances of postmemory when absence and loss have been conflated. According to LaCapra, "the conflation of absence and loss would facilitate the appropriation of particular traumas by those who did not experience them, typically in a movement of identity formation which makes invidious and ideological use of traumatic series of events in foundational ways or as symbolic capital" (2001, 65). For the communities responsible for CD and 1QpHab, the process of restoration after destruction and exile is what separates their communities from a sinful Second Temple period and includes eliminating the impure part of Second Temple Judea (see LaCapra 2001, 43–85). In other words, the pure and impure in CD and 1QpHab are established through revisiting and reshaping the catastrophic events of the destruction of the First Temple and Babylonian exile.

Both CD and 1QpHab mourn the absence of an original preexilic identity, thereby producing notions of a continuous state of exile and impurities in the social body that can be overcome only through physical or discursive separation from these impurities before the ultimate restoration of an eschatological end, which will cleanse and restore Jerusalem and the temple to a pure state. In doing so, CD and 1QpHab build temporal bridges to an idealized past through keying into memories of the wilderness, exile, and return. The memories and discourse of the wilderness and exile provide the necessary discursive separation from impurities in the present before an eschatological end.

Exile and Separation

The result of restoration is twofold: not only do social groups try to remove themselves mnemonically and discursively from perceived impurities; they also create a bond or common culture with those with whom they identify (see Erikson 1994, 236–37). Reflecting this principle, the communities that produced CD and 1QpHab avoid contamination by discursively establishing an exilic identity—whether in Damascus,[9] the wilderness, or some other real or imagined location (see Grossman 2002, 196–200; Lied 2005)—that both functions as a common culture or kinship and makes them the legitimate recipients of revelation. This pure exilic identity in CD and 1QpHab is juxtaposed with the impure and polluted people of Jerusalem.

In both CD and 1QpHab, the elect are located in exile outside of Jerusalem. Although exile initially is a result of punishment and persecution, it becomes a necessary reality for revelation, covenant-making, purification, and restoration (see Talmon 1966, 62–63). Jerusalem is a site of impurity, whereas exile in the wilderness is a liminal space in which the new covenant and the identity of the elect are established (see Lied 2005, 121). Exile and restoration are as interrelated as memory and identity, so it is

---

8. Damascus/the land of Damascus is mentioned five times in CD-A (6.5, 19; 7.14–15, 18–19; 8.21), twice in CD-B (19.34 = CD-A 8.21; 20.12), and once in 4QCD (3; 3.20 = CD-A 7.19), all of which are found in the Admonition (Lied 2005, 110–11). The meaning, location, and interpretation of "Damascus" have been a topic of much scholarly debate, with some arguing that Damascus is a metaphor for Babylon (Murphy O'Connor 1974) and others Qumran (Knibb 1994). For a survey of scholarship on these issues, see Davies 1996, 95–11; 1983, 16–17; Knibb 1983; and Lied 2005.

not surprising that the discourse of exile plays such a central role in the process of restoration and the establishment of identity in these two documents. Memories of periodic exile followed by return are fertile ground for the seeds of an exclusive identity of a restored Israel to flourish, as the discourse of exile provides geographic separation from the contaminants and pollutants in Jerusalem.

Memories of exile and return appear throughout authoritative texts of the Second Temple period, encompassing heroes of the faith from Adam and Eve to Cain and Abel, Abraham, Jacob, Joseph, Moses and Joshua, and Ezra and Nehemiah (Carroll 1998, 63; Talmon 2001). Shemaryahu Talmon notes that preexilic conceptions of exile were mainly negative, whereas views of the homeland were positive, but that these traditional connotations of exile and homeland undergo a "contextual conversion" in narratives of restoration from the Second Temple period (2001, 132). Similarly, Hindy Najman outlines the transformation of the wilderness, which once signified exile and punishment, into a space of purification and revelation during the Second Temple period (2006, 100–101). In reference to the Second Temple and talmudic periods, Isaiah Gafni shows how exile can be seen as punishment or blessing, as well as ways in which attributes of the homeland—such as Davidic leadership and remnants of the temple—can be applied to life outside the homeland (1997, 98–116). Finally, Liv Lied, in her discussion of Gafni, identifies Jer 24:1–10; 38:2 and Ezek 17:1–10 as precursors for positive evaluations of exile (2005, 124).

Both CD and 1QpHab read the past through the present by mapping their own discourses of exile and persecution onto earlier sites of memories of sojourns in wilderness. Whether in actual or imaginative/metaphorical exile (see Grossman 2002, 196–200), memories of exile and the wilderness in CD and 1QpHab are examples of the hybrid representation of the experienced past and inherited past of postmemory. In both texts, exile becomes the prototypical Israelite experience in wilderness, one of transformation and purification in a liminal space. Here exile in the wilderness is associated with purification and the homeland becomes a place of impurity and punishment in the present (cf. Ezra–Nehemiah; cf. 1QS 8.12–14; see Lied 2005, 115). However, the texts suggest that the process of restoration has begun and that Jerusalem will be returned to a purified state in the near future. Both texts key into the Isaianic concept of a remnant emerging out of exile for a future return to Jerusalem (see Blenkinsopp 2005, 226).

Reminiscent of Ezra-Nehemiah, the discourse of exile allows CD to dissociate the new covenant community from those in the land, namely, "the house of Judah" (בית יהודה), which likely refers to Jerusalem and its immediate environs (see Lied 2005, 106–7; Knibb 1983, 108). The return-ees/converts of Israel (שבי ישראל) left the land of Judah and dwelt in Damascus (CD-A 4.3; 6.5; cf. Amos 5.27), where they established the new covenant (CD-A 6.19; 19.33–34; 20.12). Removal from the geographical space of the impure Other, or the impure part of the collective self (CD-A 6.14–18), creates the space necessary for identity dissociation and con-struction. CD-A 4.15–18 refers to the corruption and impurities of Jerusa-lem when Israel is ensnared by the three nets of Belial: fornication, wealth, and polluting the temple. In sum, the producer(s) of CD construct the identity of the new covenant community in exile against that of the house of Judah (see Bergsma 2008).

In 1QpHab, the Wicked Priest is the figurehead of the traitors and character foil of the Teacher of Righteousness. According to 1QpHab, the Wicked Priest is responsible for chasing the Teacher of Righteousness away from a polluted Jerusalem and pursuing him to his house of exile (אבית גלותו) on Yom Kippur (1QpHab 11.4–8). Although this was initially an act of punishment and persecution, the "house of exile" provides geographic separation from a polluted Jerusalem. Thus, as in CD, 1QpHab engages in the discourse of righteous exiles (see Jokiranta 2013, 115). Loren Stuck-enbruck notes that the liturgical commemoration associated with the memory of the persecution and exile of the Teacher of Righteousness, who is a figure of the past, is significant because the community would not have been able to observe Yom Kippur without invoking and reliving the memory of this persecution and exile.[10]

> The association between the Wicked Priest's persecution of the Teacher and the Day of Atonement thus means that the *pesharist* not only retells a past event, but also stresses its timing at a festival that was no doubt being observed by the *pesharist's* own community, which could not mark the event without recalling what had happened to the Teacher. Here the analogy between the Teacher and the later community emerges: the pas-

---

10. According to Gabrielle Spiegel, the fundamental goal of liturgical commemo-ration "is to make it [the remembered event] live again in the present, to fuse past and present, chanter and hearer, into a single collective entity. History, in the sense that we understand it to consist of unique events unfolding within the irreversible linear time, is absorbed into cyclical, liturgical memory" (2002, 149). Liturgical memory reincar-nates, resurrects, and recycles the past to bring it to life in the present so that the past does not remain in the past but gazes forward from the living present to the imagined future (Spiegel 2002, 162).

sage refers to the observance of Yom Kippur, a festival at which the high
priest in the Jerusalem Temple officiated. The Teacher and his group,
however, are said to have been pursued to their "House of Exile," that
is, away from Jerusalem. Therefore, the memory of the event, when the
Teacher was unjustly pursued by the Wicked Priest, would have functioned to reinforce the community's self-perception that its observance
of the Torah—*away from the Jerusalem cult* where an erring calendrical system remained in use—was correct. Thus a ritual "site of memory"
would have provided a rally point for the *pesharist's* community. (Stuckenbruck 2010, 41–42)

In other words, Yom Kippur reinforced the collective memory and discourse of exile outside of Jerusalem, which is a locus for revelation and
proper observance of Torah. Once again, the experienced past and the
inherited past are interwoven in the transmission and hybrid representation of postmemory.

In the next column of 1QpHab, the Wicked Priest is blamed for the
pollution and defilement of Jerusalem (Grossman 2002, 200).

Hab 2:17 «Owing to the blood of the city and the violence (done to) the
country». Its interpretation: the city is Jerusalem in which the /Wicked/
Priest performed repulsive acts and defiled the Sanctuary of God. The
violence (done to) the country are the cities of Judah which he plundered
of the possessions of the poor. (1QpHab 12.6–10)

The literary proximity between the house of exile of the Teacher of Righteousness and the polluted Jerusalem of the Wicked Priest is no coincidence,
as it emphasizes the juxtaposition between the two sites. Similarly, in contrast to the Teacher of Righteousness and his house of exile, the "Spreader
of the Lie" is accused of misdirecting many and "building a useless city
with blood and erecting a community with deceit for his own glory, wearing out many by useless work and teaching them a[c]ts of deceit, so that
their labours are for nothing; so that those who derided and insulted God's
chosen will go to the punishment of the fire" (1QpHab 10.9–13). Finally,
1QpHab outlines the punishment of the Wicked Priest for the injustices he
has committed against Jerusalem: "«will appall you, owing to the human
blood and violence (done to) the country, the city and all who dwell there.»
The interpretation of the word concerns the Wicked Priest, to pay him the
reward for what he did to the poor.... God will sentence him to destruction" (1QpHab 12.1–5).

REVELATION IN THE WILDERNESS AND THE RETURN TO JERUSALEM

In addition to the discursive separation from the impurities of Jerusalem, exile in the wilderness invokes memories of the Sinai experience (see Najman 2003; Grossman 2002, 162–67). CD authorizes itself through what Najman calls "Mosaic Discourse"; indeed, "[t]he only passable roads to textual authority led through the past. Mosaic Discourse was one such route" (2003, 15). Thus, the revelation at Sinai is an occasion of liturgical and repetitive temporality, "not a one-time event, but rather an event that can be re-presented, even in exile" (2003, 36). Revelation and proper interpretation and observance of Torah does not take place in Jerusalem, but in the wilderness of exile, where it is inscribed back to Sinai, Moses, and Mosaic Torah. In CD, the Teacher of Righteousness is the true interpreter of Torah and the recipient of revelation, as he is "to direct them in the path of his heart" and make known to the last generations "what he had done for the last generation, the congregation of traitors" (CD-A 1.11–12; see Hacham 2010, 10–11). According to Talmon, the images of the Teacher of Righteousness and Interpreter of the Law were patterned on that of Moses (Talmon 1966, 58).[11] As Davies observes of the Interpreter of the Law, "we will presumably never know if there was a *dwrš htwrh*, or, if there was, who he was, or if the authors of these passages knew his identity. It is his *function* that matters; typologically he is to be seen as the second Moses, just as for other Jewish groups Ezra was. The entire simple memory, in fact, is typological in form and function" (2010, 36; see CD-A 7.14–21). In CD, Mosaic law and a second Moses figure link the past, present, and future through an unbroken chain of transmission, from creation down to the new covenant established with the pure remnant of Israel. This process, again, is facilitated by imagination and the familiar cultural typologies of postmemory. Proper interpretation and observation of Torah separates

---

11. According to Loren Stuckenbruck, "[e]ven if, strictly speaking, neither the Interpreter nor the eschatological one teaching righteousness can be identified with the Teacher of Righteousness, the passage strongly connects membership in the community with faithfulness to and observance of the Torah, with respect to which the Teacher was seen to have played an indispensible role" (Stuckenbruck 2010, 35). Davies notes the similarity between the Interpreter of the Law and the Teacher of Righteousness but outlines the important distinctions between the two figures as follows: "the arrival of the 'Teacher' is placed well after the formation of the 'root' and even further from the survival of the remnant, while the 'Interpreter' is placed at the very origins of the remnant community. The 'Interpreter of the Law' in CD is a past figure; the 'one who teaches righteousness' of VI,11 is a future figure" (1983, 123–24).

members from nonmembers of the covenant community in CD-A 1.16–18; 4.9–12; 20.25–28.

CD outlines the way in which the Watchers and the sons of Noah and their families did not heed the precepts of God and were subsequently cut off (CD-A 2.16–3.1). But Abraham, Isaac, and Jacob were friends of God and subsequently became eternal members of the covenant (ויכתבו אוהבים לאל ובעלי ברית לעולם, CD-A 3.3–4). However, Jacob's sons broke the covenant and were punished accordingly, and their sons were cut off in the wilderness (CD-A 3.4–7). After possessing the land, the covenant was broken again, and the Israelite kings in Jerusalem were cut off and the land was laid to waste (CD-A 3.7–10).

> For many have gone astray due to these [sinful desires against the coven-ant]; brave heroes stumbled on account of them, from ancient times until now. For having walked in the stubbornness of their hearts the Watchers of the heavens fell; on account of it they were caught, for they did not heed the precepts of God. And their sons, whose height was like that of cedars and whose bodies were like mountains, fell. All flesh which there was on the dry earth expired and they became as if it had never been, because they had realized their desires and had failed to keep their cre-ator's precepts, until his wrath flared up against them. Through it, the sons of Noah and their families strayed, through it, they were cut off. Abraham did not walk in it, and was counted as a friend for keeping God's precepts and not following the desire of his spirits. And he passed (them) on to Isaac and to Jacob, they kept (them) and were written up as friends of God and as members of the covenant for ever. *Blank.* Jacob's sons strayed but were punished in accordance with their mistakes. And in Egypt their sons walked in the stubbornness of their hearts, plotting against God's precepts and each one of them were cut off in the wilder-ness. <And He spoke> to them in Qadesh: *Deut 9:23* «Go and posses the land». But they preferred the desire> of their spirit, and did not listen to the voice of the creator, the precepts he had taught them, and murmured in their tents. And the wrath of God flared up against their congregation. And their sons died through it, and through it their kings were cut off, and through it their warriors perished, and through it their land was laid waste. (CD-A 2.16–3.10)

Significantly, of the eighteen lines in CD-A 2.16–3.11, sixteen are devoted to the periods leading up to and including Moses. Thus, only two lines are allocated to the periods of Israelite history between Moses and the emergence of the new covenant community from exile 390 years after the

Israelite kings were cut off and the land was laid to waste by Nebuchad-nezzar (see CD-A 1.3–8; Anderson 1994, 16). This is another instance of CD telescoping time and using literary-chronological proximity to link the new covenant community to a foundational moment in the Israelite past.

The chain of transmission from Sinai to the new covenant community in exile is outlined in CD-A 6.2–7.

> But God remembered the covenant of the forefathers. *Blank* and he raised from Aaron men of knowledge and from Israel wise men, and made them listen. And they dug a well: *Num 21:18* «A well which the princes dug, which the nobles of the people delved with the staff». The well is the law. And those who dug it *Blank* are the converts of Israel, who left the land of Judah and lived in the land of Damascus, all of whom God called princes, for they sought him, and their renown has not been repudiated in any-one's mouth. And the staff is the Interpreter of the Law....

This passage connects the covenant and Torah of the wilderness genera-tion to those of the converts of Israel that were established while in exile in Damascus (cf. CD-A 7.14–21). Once again a mnemonic connection is established between exodus and exile (see Grossman 2002, 91, 124–25). In other words, the members of the new covenant community are the wise men from Israel and the converts from Israel who emerged from Aaron and are the legitimate inheritors and interpreters of Torah. In addition to the Interpreter of the Law, the Teacher of Righteousness is also an authori-tative voice for the proper interpretation of Torah (CD-B 20.27–28, 32–33; see García Martínez 2010, 23–33).

Also connecting the new covenant community to Moses and Sinai is the organization of the community in camps of tens, fifties, hundreds, and thousands (CD-A 13.1–2), figures corresponding to preexilic Israel's organization in the desert in Exod 18:21–25 (Hempel 2000, 40). Noting the numerous biblical spatial tropes and paradigms invoked in CD, Lied concludes that

> the description of the camps, the references to the presence of God and of the Laws as central forces among the remnant group operating inde-pendent of the institutions of Palestine all point to the flexible and mobile spatial patterns characteristic of the Exodus story. By recalling the camps of the Exodus CD-A brings a powerful set of paradigmatic events into play as central arguments for the redemption of the remnant group. Just as the first Exodus once saved Israel, a similar set of events will again save the remnant. (2005, 118; CD-A 5.19).

Thus, to use Schwartz's term, the producer(s) of CD key into the memory of the exodus in representing the community's sojourns in the wilderness—literally or metaphorically—so that the community's life mirrors the experiences of the generation of Moses, thereby making it a liminal space between the reception of the covenant and the entry into the promised land (Davies 2000, 32). According to CD, the law has been revealed to the multitude of the camp (CD-A 15.13–14). The past, present, and future are connected when members pass the new covenant on to their children. On the day when their children speak to the "Inspector of the Many" (המבפר אשר לירבים), the members are to enroll their children with "the oath of the covenant which Moses established with Israel, the covenant to rev[ert to] to the law of Moses (תורה משה) with the whole heart and [with] the who[le] soul" (CD-A 15.8–10).

As noted earlier, 1QpHab asserts that proper observation and interpretation of Torah occurs in exile with the Teacher of Righteousness and his later community, not in Jerusalem with the Wicked Priest. The Teacher of Righteousness is remembered and represented as the interpreter par excellence of Torah and the prophets (Stuckenbruck 2010, 31). According to García Martínez, the Teacher of Righteousness "is clearly presented as the expected 'prophet like Moses' in Deut 18:15" (2010, 240–41). The Teacher of Righteousness receives revelation and interprets all the mysteries of the words of God's servants and prophets (כול רזי דברי עבדיו הנבאים, 1QpHab 2.8–9; 7.4–5; see Stuckenbruck 2010, 32). The Teacher of Righteousness not only understands the hidden meanings of these authoritative texts but also infuses his own interpretations and subsequent new writings with equal authority (García Martínez 2010, 241–42). Those who do not adhere to his interpretations are called traitors (הבוגדים, 1QpHab 2.5) and violators of the covenant (עריצי הברית, 2.6). The men of truth (אנשי האמת) who properly observe the law (עושי התורה) follow the interpretations of the Teacher of Righteousness (1QpHab 7.10–11). In fact, 1QpHab's interpretation of Hab 2:4b ("But the righteous will live because of their loyalty to him") concerns "all observing the Law in the House of Judah, whom God will free from the house of judgment on the account of their toil and of their loyalty to the Teacher of Righteousness" (8.1–3). Juxtaposed with the Teacher of Righteousness and his authoritative interpretations of Torah in exile are the priests in Jerusalem who reject Torah. For instance, the "Man of the Lie" is accused of rejecting Torah (איש הכזב אשר מאס את התורה, 1QpHab 5.11–12; cf. 2.1–4). 1QpHab connects the past, present, and eschatological future through the Teacher of Righteousness and his interpretations that extend to the final age and beyond.

> Its interpretation concerns the Teacher of Righteousness, to whom God has made known all the mysteries of the words of his servants, the prophets. *Hab 2:3* For the vision has an appointed time, it will have an end and not fail. Its interpretation: the final age will be extended and go beyond all that the prophets say, because the mysteries of God are wonderful. *Hab 2:3b* Though it may tarry, wait for it; it definitely has to come and will not delay. Its interpretation concerns the men of truth, those who obey the Law, whose hands will not desert the service of truth when the final age is extended beyond them, because all the ages of God will come at the right time, as he established for them in the mysteries of his prudence. (1QpHab 7.4–14)

As García Martínez notes, the Teacher of Righteousness is a figure of the past to whom God made known all the mysteries, but his revelations remain permanently present within the community (2010, 241). In other words, the Teacher of Righteousness and his interpretations do the work of post-memory as he both inherits the mysteries of the words of the prophets and transmits them in the present and into the future until the end times, creating an inter/transgenerational mnemonic chain that connects figures from the idealized past to himself and his own community and those of the future.

Conclusions

CD and 1QpHab revisit and relive the destruction of 587 BCE until an eschatological end that finally overcomes a continuous state of exile. I have argued that the mourning over the absence of a pure preexilic identity led to reliving the condition and to an inability to overcome exile. The process of mourning creates, in turn, a social bond that reinforces the hope that this preexilic identity will be restored through an eschatological end that cleanses the impurities in Jerusalem. Again, converting absence into loss and then mourning that absence creates misplaced nostalgia and imagined utopias in the quest for a new unity (LaCapra 2001, 46). Moreover, the discourse of absence produces notions of a collective sin that is overcome only by the possibility of eschatology (LaCapra 2001, 51). This framework of collective sin to be overcome through the purification of eschatology corresponds to Knibb's model of continuously sinful and exilic Second Temple Judea that is purified at the eschaton.

Both CD and 1QpHab are future-oriented and look ahead to this eschatological future, when the traitors will be punished and the elect will return to
Jerusalem. In doing so, CD and 1QpHab reactivate the same site of trauma,
the destruction of Jerusalem in 587 BCE, to initiate the process of destruction, purification, and restoration. This being said, CD looks to the past and
telescopes the 390 years between Nebuchadnezzar's destruction and the
emergence of the pure remnant of the new covenant community who will
return to Jerusalem. In other words, the destruction has occurred, and the
community is the elect preparing to return. 1QpHab, on the other hand,
simultaneously gazes at the past and the future: the earlier site of memory
of the Chaldean destruction is revisited and relived, but the destruction that
will establish the community as the pure remnant has yet to happen. The
eschatological future is imminent as the community is living in the final
generation, when the Kittim will destroy the wicked and impure in Jerusalem and the elect will return from exile as the pure remnant. Both texts
write the past in the present by participating in the hybridization process
of postmemory that combines the experienced past and inherited past in
imaging a future temporality. The imagination of representation helps navigate the bumpy terrain, tensions, and oscillations of rupture and continuity.
CD and 1QpHab create continuity between their respective communities
(the elect in the present) and the remote idealized past of Moses and the
wilderness generation at Sinai, as well as that of the ancient prophets, while
they simultaneously separate themselves through the discourse of exile from
impurities of the past and present (the defiled Jerusalem and the indefinite
state of exile that envelopes Second Temple Judea).

The discourse of exile and the reestablishment of the covenant and the
authority of Torah are means to the desired end of a restoration of Jerusalem, the temple, and an idealized past identity. Much of the language
of normativity of Torah in CD and 1QpHab is directed against those who
defiled the Jerusalem temple (CD-A 4.18; 1QpHab 12:8–11). These are
texts that establish the authority of the true Israel in exile but are oriented
toward Jerusalem (Brooke 2008; cf. Talmon 1966, 61–66). For instance, the
producer(s) of CD hoped for a return to the land and a restoration of the
true Israel: "he visited them and caused to sprout from Israel and Aaron a
shoot of the planting, in order to posses the land and to become fat with the
good things of his soil" (פקדם ויצמח מישראל ומאהרן שורש מטעת לירוש
את ארצו ולדשן בטוב אדמתו; CD-A 1.7–8).

According to George Brooke, the community or communities who
envisioned themselves in the wilderness express identity as an intermediate

state: emerging from exile but not yet back in Jerusalem; in the promised land but not yet out of the wilderness. Moreover, if we were to situate either text in a community or communities somewhere in the Judean Desert, it would have been located between Sinai and Jerusalem, between the wilderness of the ancient Israelites and the site of the purified sanctuary, between exile and complete return. The memories and typologies of Sinai provide models of community organization for a community in a betwixt state. The communities responsible for CD and 1QpHab imagined themselves in the wilderness, whether psychologically or physically, as the new covenant community, interpreters of Torah, and recipients of revelation. The chain of revelation connected the past (Sinai) with the present (the wilderness) and the future (Jerusalem). Revelation and proper understanding of the Torah paved the road from the revelatory past to the future return to Jerusalem (Brooke 2008, 85; cf. Talmon 1966, 61–66) as these communities of postmemory imagined themselves as both inheritors and transmitters of memory, tradition, and revelation.

WORKS CITED

Abegg, Martin. 1997. Exile and the Dead Sea Scrolls. Pages 11–25 in *Exile: Old Testament, Jewish, and Christian Conceptions*. Edited by James M. Scott. JSJSup 56. Leiden: Brill.

Anderson, G.A. 1994. The Status of the Torah before Sinai: The Retelling of the Bible in Damascus Covenant and the Book of Jubilees. *DSD* 1:1–29.

Assmann, Jan. 2006. *Religion and Cultural Memory: Ten Studies*. Translated by Rodney Livingstone. Stanford, CA: Stanford University Press.

Bakhtin, Mikhail. 1981. *The Dialogic Imagination: Four Essays*. Edited by Michael Holmquist. Translated by Caryl Emerson and Michael Holmquist. University of Texas Press Slavic Series 1. Austin: University of Texas Press.

Ben Zvi, Ehud. 2012. The Study of Forgetting and the Forgotten in Ancient Israelite Discourse/s: Observations and Test Cases. Pages 155–74 in *Cultural Memory in Biblical Exegesis*. Edited by Pernille Carstens, Trine Bjørnung Hasselbalch, and Niels Peter Lemche. Piscataway, NJ: Gorgias.

Bergsma, John S. 2008. Qumran Self-Identity: 'Israel' or 'Judah'? *DSD* 15:172–89.

Berrin, Shani. 2005. Qumran Pesharim. Pages 110–33 in *Biblical Interpre-*

tation at Qumran. Edited by Matthias Henze. Studies in the Dead Sea Scrolls and Related Literature. Grand Rapids: Eerdmans.

Blenkinsopp, Joseph. 2005. The Qumran Sect in the Context of Second Temple Sectarianism. Pages 10–25 in *New Directions in Qumran Studies: Proceedings of the Bristol Colloquium on the Dead Sea Scrolls, 8–10 September 2003*. Edited by Jonathan G. Campbell, William John Lyons, and Lloyd K Pietersen. LSTS 52. London: T&T Clark.

Brooke, George J. 2008. Moving Mountains: From Sinai to Jerusalem. Pages 73–90 in *The Significance of Sinai: Traditions about Sinai and Divine Revelation in Judaism and Christianity*. Edited by George J. Brooke, Hindy Najman, and Loren.T. Stuckenbruck. Themes in Biblical Narrative 12. Leiden: Brill.

Carroll, Robert P. 1998. Exile! What Exile? Deportation and the Discourses of Diaspora. Pages 62–79 in *Leading Captivity Captive: "The Exile" as History and Ideology*. Edited by Lester L. Grabbe. JSOTSup 278. Sheffield: Sheffield Academic Press.

Caruth, Cathy. 1995. Introduction. Pages 151–57 in *Trauma: Explorations in Memory*. Edited by Cathy Caruth. Baltimore: Johns Hopkins University Press.

Charlesworth, James H. 2002. *The Pesharim and Qumran History: Chaos or Consensus?* Grand Rapids: Eerdmans.

Collins, John J. 1997. *Apocalypticism in The Dead Sea Scrolls*. Literature of the Dead Sea Scrolls. New York: Routledge.

———. 2009. Beyond the Qumran Community: Social Organization in the Dead Sea Scrolls. *DSD* 16:351–69.

Davies, Philip R. 1983. *The Damascus Covenant: An Interpretation of the Damascus Document*. JSOTSup 25. Sheffield: JSOT Press.

———. 2000. The Judaism(s) of the Damascus Document. Pages 27–43 in *The Damascus Document: A Centennial of Discovery. Proceedings of the Third International Symposium of the Orion Center for the Study of the Dead Sea Scrolls and Associated Literature, 4–8 February 1998*. Edited by Joseph M. Baumgarten, Esther G. Chazon, and Avital Pinnick. STDJ 34. Leiden: Brill.

———. 2010. What History Can We Get from the Scrolls, and How? Pages 31–46 in *The Dead Sea Scrolls: Texts and Contexts*. Edited by Charlotte Hempel. STDJ 90. Leiden: Brill.

Erikson, Kai. 1994. *A New Species of Trouble: Explorations in Disaster, Trauma, and Community*. New York: Norton.

———. 1995. Notes on Trauma and Community. Pages 183–99 in *Trauma:*

Explorations in Memory. Edited by Cathy Caruth. Baltimore: Johns Hopkins University Press.

Eyerman, Ron. 2004. The Past in the Present: Culture and the Transmission of Memory. *Acta Sociologica* 47:159–69.

Fowler, Alastair. 1982. *Kinds of Literature: An Introduction to the Theory of Genre and Modes*. Cambridge: Cambridge University Press.

Gafni, Isaiah. 1997. *Land, Center and Diaspora: Jewish Constructs in Late Antiquity*. JSPSup 21. Sheffield: Sheffield Academic Press.

García Martínez, Florentino. 2010. Beyond the Sectarian Divide: The "Voice of the Teacher" as an Authority-Conferring Strategy in Some Qumran Texts. Pages 227–44 in *The Dead Sea Scrolls: Transmission of Traditions and Production of Texts*. Edited by Sarianna Metso, Hindy Najman, and Eileen Schuller. STDJ 92. Leiden: Brill.

García Martínez, Florentino, and Eibert J. C. Tigchelaar. 2000. *The Dead Sea Scrolls Study Edition*. 2 vols. Leiden: Brill.

Grossman, Maxine L. 2002. *Reading for History in the Damascus Document: A Methodological Study*. STDJ 45. Leiden: Brill.

Hacham, Noah. 2010. Exile and Self-Identity in the Qumran Sect and in Hellenistic Judaism. Pages 3–21 in *New Perspectives on Old Texts: Proceedings of the Tenth International Symposium of the Orion Center for the Study of the Dead Sea Scrolls and Associated Literature, 9–11 January, 2005*. Edited by Esther G. Chazon and Betsy Halpern-Amaru. STDJ 88. Leiden: Brill.

Hempel, Charlotte. 2000. *The Damascus Texts*. Sheffield: Sheffield Academic Press.

Henige, David. 1974. *The Chronology of Oral Tradition: Quest for a Chimera*. Oxford Studies in African Affairs. Oxford: Clarendon.

Hirsch, Marianne. 2008. The Generation of Postmemory. *Poetics Today* 29.1:103–28.

Hobsbawm, Eric. 1992. Introduction: Inventing Tradition. Pages 1–14 in *The Invention of Tradition*. Edited by Eric Hobsbawm and Terence Ranger. Cambridge: Cambridge University Press.

Hoffman, Eva. 2010. The Long Afterlife of Loss. Pages 406–15 in *Memory: Histories, Theories, Debates*. Edited by Susannah Radstone and Bill Schwartz. New York: Fordham University Press.

Horgan, Maurya P. 1979. *Pesharim: Qumran Interpretation of Biblical Books*. CBQMS 8. Washington, DC: Catholic Biblical Association of America.

Japhet, Sara. 2006. Periodization between History and Ideology II: Chronology and Ideology in Ezra-Nehemiah. Pages 491–508 in *Judah and the Judeans in the Persian Period*. Edited by Oded Lipschits and Manfred Oeming. Winona Lake, IN: Eisenbrauns.

Jassen, Alex P. 2010. The Dead Sea Scrolls and Violence: Sectarian Formation and Eschatological Imagination. Pages 13–44 in *Violence, Scripture, and Textual Practice in Early Judaism and Christianity*. Edited by Ra'anan S. Boustan, Alex P. Jassen, and Calvin J. Roetzel. Leiden: Brill.

Jokiranta, Jutta. 2005. Pesharim: A Mirror of Self-Understanding. Pages 23–34 in *Reading the Present in the Qumran Library: The Perception of the Contemporary by Means of Scriptural Interpretations*. Edited by Kristin De Troyer and Armin Lange. SBLSymS 30. Atlanta: Society of Biblical Literature.

———. 2013. *Social Identity and Sectarianism in the Qumran Movement*. STDJ 105. Leiden: Brill.

Knibb, Michael A. 1976. The Exile in the Literature of the Intertestamental Period. *Heythrop Journal* 17:253–72.

———. 1983. Exile in the Damascus Document. *JSOT* 25:99–117.

Kolk, Bessel A. van der, and Onno van der Hart. 1995. The Intrusive Past: The Flexibility of Memory and the Engraving of Trauma. Pages 158–82 in *Trauma: Explorations in Memory*. Edited by Cathy Caruth. Baltimore: Johns Hopkins University Press.

LaCapra, Dominick. 1994. *Representing the Holocaust: History, Theory, Trauma*. Ithaca, N.Y.: Cornell University Press.

———. 1998. *History and Memory after Auschwitz*. Ithaca, NY: Cornell University Press.

———. 2001. *Writing History, Writing Trauma*. Baltimore: Johns Hopkins University Press.

Latour, Bruno. 1993. *We Have Never Been Modern*. Translated by Catherine Porter. Cambridge: Harvard University Press.

Lied, Liv. 2005. Another Look at the Land of Damascus: The Spaces of the *Damascus Document* in Light of Edward Soja's Thirdspace Approach. Pages 101–25 in *New Directions in Qumran Studies: Proceedings of the Bristol Colloquium on the Dead Sea Scrolls, 8–10 September 2003*. Edited by Jonathan G. Campbell, William John Lyons, and Lloyd K. Pietersen. LSTS 52. New York: T&T Clark.

Murphy O'Connor, Jerome. 1974. The Essenes and Their History. *RB* 81:215–44.

Najman, Hindy. 2003. *Seconding Sinai: The Development of Mosaic Discourse in Second Temple Judaism*. JSJSup 77. Leiden: Brill.

————. 2006. Towards a Study of the Uses of the Concept of Wilderness in Ancient Judaism. *DSD* 13:99–113.

Newsom, Carol A. 2004. *The Self as Symbolic Space: Constructing Identity and Community at Qumran.* STDJ 52. Leiden: Brill.

Nora, Pierre. 1996. *Realms of Memory.* Edited by Lawrence D. Dritzman. 3 vols. New York: Columbia University Press.

Pickering, Michael, and Emily Keightley. 2013. Communities of Memory and the Problem of Transmission. *European Journal of Cultural Studies* 16.1:115–31.

Rothberg, Michael. 2009. *Multidirectional Memory: Remembering the Holocaust in the Age of Decolonization.* Stanford, CA: Stanford University Press.

Ryan, Marie-Laure. 1981. Introduction: On the Why, What, and How of Generic Taxonomy. *Poetics* 10:109–26.

Schwartz, Barry. 1991. Social Change and Collective Memory: The Democratization of George Washington. *American Sociological Review* 56.2:221–26.

————. 1996. Memory as a Cultural System: Abraham Lincoln in World War II. *American Sociological Review* 61.5:908–27.

Smelser, Neil J. 2004. Psychological Trauma and Cultural Trauma. Pages 43–75 in *Cultural Trauma and Collective Identity.* Edited by Jeffery C. Alexander, Ron Eyerman, Bernhard Giesen, Neil Smelser, and Piotr Sztompka. Berkeley: University of California Press.

Spiegel, Gabrielle M. 2002. Memory and History: Liturgical Time and Historical Time. *History and Theory* 41:149–62.

Stuckenbruck, Loren T. 2010. The Legacy of the Teacher of Righteousness in the Dead Sea Scrolls. Pages 23–49 in *New Perspectives on Old Texts: Proceedings of the Tenth International Symposium of the Orion Center for the Study of the Dead Sea Scrolls and Associated Literature, 9–11 January, 2005.* Edited by Esther G. Chazon and Betsy Halpern-Amaru. STDJ 88. Leiden: Brill.

Swales, John M. 1990. *Genre Analysis.* Cambridge: Cambridge University Press.

Talmon, Shemaryahu. 1966. The Desert Motif. Pages 31–63 in *Biblical Motifs: Origins and Transformations.* Edited by Alexander Altmann. Cambridge: Harvard University Press.

————. 2001. "Exile" and "Restoration" in the Conceptual World of Ancient Judaism. Pages 107–46 in *Restoration: Old Testament, Jewish and Christian Perspectives.* Edited by James M. Scott. JSJSup 72. Leiden: Brill.

Winter, Jay. 2010. Sites of Memory. Pages 312–24 in *Memory: Histories, Theories, Debates*. Edited by Susannah Radstone and Bill Schwartz. New York: Fordham University Press.

Wittgenstein, Ludwig. 2003. *Philosophical Investigations*. 3rd ed. Translated by G. E. M. Anscombe. Malden, MA: Blackwell.

Yerushalmi, Yosef. 1996. *Zakhor: Jewish History and Jewish Memory*. Seattle, WA: University of Washington Press. [orig. 1982]

Zerubavel, Eviatar. 2003. *Time Maps: Collective Memory and the Social Shape of the Past*. Chicago: Chicago University Press.

Cult's Death in Scripture: The Destruction of Jerusalem's Temple Remembered by Josephus and Mark[*]

Gabriella Gelardini

> By destroying the temple, the Roman army destroyed a physical mani-
> festation of God's majesty. What a difference it must have made for this
> generation! (Schwartz, p. 16)

To build on the words of Barry Schwartz, the destruction of the temple in 70 CE definitely "made a difference" for Flavius Josephus, who witnessed its eradication and recorded his memories shortly thereafter in Rome. Though his account of the conflict in *Jewish War* (*Bellum judaicum*) was intended to set the Roman campaigns, especially those of the Flavians Vespasian and Titus, into the desired perspective, he focuses on the temple's destruction, giving close attention to the matter of responsibility and thus weighing the question of war guilt. Josephus's well-known answer to this problem is unambiguous: the Roman commanders were not responsible for the temple's ruin, but rather their Jewish counterparts. First, the Jewish commanders had waged an unjust war, directed against their own countrymen; second, they had defiled the temple by misusing it as a military camp and battlefield; and, third, by interrupting God's accustomed daily sacrifice, they had deprived God of continuous worship and irrevocably antagonized him. Keying these offenses to earlier acts of covenant breaking, Josephus asserts repeatedly that God had to leave his house and bring the Romans to purge both the city and the temple with fire. Yet while this interpretation may have helped the Flavians at the inception of their reign, its subversive tone cannot be missed. Because victory had been granted by the God of the Jews rather than by a Roman god, it came to the Flavians with term limits, so to speak, with a specific time-bound purpose. This reading of Josephus does not exclude a possible reconciliation in the (near) future.

Recent biblical scholarship has argued that Mark also recalled the same war and its destruction of the temple. According to this view, Mark,

---

[*] I am grateful to Dr. Mark Kyburz and Dr. John Peck for proofreading this essay.

like Josephus, set down his memories in Rome at the beginning of the Fla-vian reign, partly in reaction to other accounts, not least that of Josephus. Hence, Mark notably keys the life of Jesus to the Flavian triumph and also to the obloquy of the Jews. Mark transcends Josephus, however, by por-traying Jesus as one whose death made amends for the three main offenses of the Jewish rebels, thereby instituting a path for God's covenant renewal and subsequent return, which Christ will anticipate as the risen one. In the process, Jesus sets Israel free as the legitimate messianic ruler and becomes himself the "cornerstone" of God's new dwelling (Mark 12:10).

While neither Josephus nor Mark, both of whom presumably wrote in the presence of the temple spoils, may have intended to replace the Jerusa-lem temple with their constructions, Mark's text may have achieved exactly that in the end, since political realities on the ground did not develop according to hope. Mark's depiction of Jesus as one who restored a path to God's presence and benevolence, something that under normal cir-cumstances only cult sites could provide, in the long run may have proven sufficient for audiences both then and in future.

The present essay seeks to demonstrate three points, in dialogue with Barry Schwartz's remarks in the introduction to this volume and else-where. First, both Josephus's war account and Mark's Gospel represent social memories related to a traumatic experience. Second, both authors apply keying to preserve their contesting memories. Third, both resulting representations of the past, albeit varying, serve pragmatic purposes that seek to subversively destabilize the Roman perspective on the one hand and to stabilize the Judean perspective on the other.

JOSEPHUS ON THE JEWISH WAR AND THE DEATH OF JERUSALEM

> Most impious wretch, should anyone deprive you of your daily food, you would consider him an enemy; and do you hope to have God, whom you have bereft of His everlasting worship, for your Ally in this war? And do you impute your [own] sins to the Romans, who, to this day, are con-cerned for our laws and are trying to force you to restore to God those sacrifices which *you* have interrupted? (*B.J.* 6.100–101)[1]

Josephus portrays himself uttering the above words, shouting from outside the temple precinct to John of Gischala, one of the two leading Judean

---

1. All citations of Josephus's *Jewish War* are from the Loeb edition, trans. H. St. J. Thackeray. Emphasis above original in Thackeray's translation.

insurgents, who during the revolt tried to defend his position in the temple to the very end. The setting is summer, 70 CE; outside Jerusalem, Titus camps with four legions and as many auxiliary forces. The first, second, and third walls of the city have already been secured, and even the fortress Antonia, situated at the northwest corner and towering over the temple area, has been captured. Well aware that Roman intrusion into the temple precincts would set the seal on the city's capture, the rebels do their utmost to confine the Gentiles to the Antonia. They succeed, for the moment at least, but for lack of men they cease daily offerings on 17 Tammuz (June–July). When Titus learns of this, he commands Josephus to convey to John the same message that he had sent earlier: if he wishes to fight, he may come out with as many men as he wishes, at no risk to either the city or temple (*B.J.* 6.95). John counters by casting reproaches and imprecations upon Josephus, finally adding that Jerusalem will never fall because it is God's own city (*B.J.* 6.98). Josephus's reply is quoted above: by stopping the daily sacrifices, John has deprived God of his "daily food," that is, his "everlasting worship." How can one hope to have God as an ally, Josephus asks, and at the same time impute those sins to the Romans, who have taken care to have Jewish laws observed, nearly compelling these sacrifices to go on being offered to God, while John has interrupted them? Who cannot lament the amazing change made in the city, Josephus asks, when the enemy now corrects John's impiety, so that a Jew formed by the Jewish code becomes the greater enemy (*B.J.* 6.101–102)? Josephus proceeds to remind John of an oracle in the prophets, which he believes to be fulfilled upon the miserable city just now, which foretold that Jerusalem would fall when a Jew began the slaughter of his own countrymen. With the city and the entire temple now filled with Jewish dead, God himself will purge both with fire, ridding it of John's pollution by means of the Romans (*B.J.* 6.109–110).

As the rebels reply derisively to two further messages, Titus resumes operations and fulfills Josephus's prophecy. By means of night attacks and ramps up the walls of the temple complex, the Romans promptly force their way into the temple forecourt, succeed in pushing the rebels back into the temple's inner court, and finally put them to flight as Roman solders torch the temple, allegedly against the will of Titus. But before the temple is engulfed by flames on 10 Av, Titus, the victorious general, profanes the temple—for the last time—by entering the holy of holies with his commanders (*B.J.* 6.260), a place forbidden to foreigners under penalty of death (*B.J.* 5.194; 6.124–126; *A.J.* 15.417). With the temple and its adjacent buildings aflame and the rebels withdrawn to the upper city, the Romans bring their ensigns into the holy precinct, set them near its eastern gate (the one toward the Mount of Olives and the only one used liturgically; see m. Mid. 1.3), and make sacrifices while proclaiming Titus their emperor with joyous acclamation (*B.J.* 6.316). Soon the upper city is taken. Prevented from fleeing by the siege and weakened by famine, many rebels surrender, including their commanders John of Gischala and Simon ben Giora (*B.J.* 6.433). Titus orders the city to be plundered and burned, according to the laws of war; collects prisoners in the temple's inner court, where he deals with them summarily (*B.J.* 6.414–419); and finally orders that the city and temple be razed (*B.J.* 7.1). Thus, only five months after the beginning of the siege, in the second year of Vespasian's reign (late September 70 CE), Titus claims victory for Rome and himself over the Jewish insurgents (*B.J.* 6.435).

After Vespasian and Titus return to a splendid welcome in Rome (*B.J.* 7.63–119), the Senate grants the victors their customary honors, including a triumph, which father and son celebrate jointly in 71 CE (*B.J.* 7.121). During that procession the populace of Rome see with their own eyes the evidence of ignominious Jewish defeat and definitive loss of sovereignty (*B.J.* 7.122), as the temple spoils are displayed and the Jewish commander Simon ben Giora, whom the Romans deemed chief culprit, is executed (*B.J.* 7.148, 154).

JOSEPHUS AS SOCIAL REMEMBRANCER

The particulars of Josephus's report, summarized above, are recollections, the work of a memory whose prowess Josephus took great pride in (*Vita* 8). These memories must have emanated for the most part from internal snapshots (Halbwachs 1925, 373) of experiences related to the Flavian campaign, which Josephus witnessed from the very beginning—first in Galilee as enemy and prisoner of the Romans, later as their advisor and possibly even friend. Accordingly, Josephus was sent from Alexandria to accompany Titus before the walls of Jerusalem, assisting him throughout the entire siege (*B.J.* 1.3; *Vita* 416; *C. Ap.* 1.47–48) and afterward traveling with the emperor to Rome (*Vita* 422).

But Josephus is no stand-alone memoirist. Instead, his recollections are set against those of other witnesses and situated among different groups (Schwartz, p. 9 above). Accordingly, he begins his war narrative by dissociating himself from other eyewitness reports, which he condemns as "false," and also from hearsay accounts, which he regards as "contradictory" (*B.J.* 1.1–2). His preface also blames the Greek historians for not attending to their duty to write about events of their own time, instead wasting energy by composing inferior versions of past histories. Like a war reporter today, Josephus praises the "undertaking to preserve the memory [μνήμη]of what has not been before recorded, and to represent the affairs of one's own time to those that come afterwards" (*B.J.* 1.15). He himself aspires to make good for past neglect and distortion by presenting to Greeks as well as Romans a "memorial [μνήμη] of great actions" by both war parties, a "history" (ἱστορία) that is not only impartial but also, he asserts, accurate and true (*B.J.* 1.9, 12, 15, 16, 30; 7.454–455; *A.J.* 1.1–4; *Vita* 361–367; *C. Ap.* 1.52).

Yet Josephus's account goes beyond his own individual observations, notes, and recollections. He openly admits to having used additional sources, including testimonies from Jewish deserters—whom only he was able to understand—and later Vespasian's commentaries, Vespasian and Titus's recollections, and the testimonies of Romans and Jews, such as Agrippa II, who had taken part in the war (*B.J.* 1.16; *Vita* 342; 358; *C. Ap.* 1.49–52, 56). Josephus's account is a collective representation and a construction of social memory that, he assures us, will satisfy those who want the truth rather than simply a good read (*B.J.* 1.30). Nonetheless, Josephus also indulges in fictionalizing, such as when his interpretation of facts is turned into the dialogue between himself and John of Gischala quoted above.

Josephus is no dispassionate reporter. On the contrary, in his preface he asks readers to indulge his laments on the miseries of his people, even if that infringes on the genre of history writing (*B.J.* 1.9, 11–12), because emotions play such an important role in Josephus's account. In his case, one may speak with Jan Assmann of a "communicative memory" (2007, 13). Josephus bewails the destruction of his fatherland and with it the annihilation of the temple, a symbol for the loss of national sovereignty (*B.J.* 1.10; *Vita* 418). Yet more movingly, Josephus also bewails the personal catastrophe visited on him and his family by the war. Josephus reports having found himself frequently in danger of death, even after his imprisonment, as Jews and Romans alike accused him of treachery (*Vita* 416). During Jerusalem's siege, his wife and his father, along with his mother—to whom apparently he was deeply attached—were imprisoned by rebels inside the city. Since there is no mention of them in the context of Titus's release orders—the list of the "tyrant's" prisoners—one must assume that they died either by their own hand or from pestilence or famine (*B.J.* 5.419, 533, 544–546; 6.412, 421). Moreover, Josephus found many of his relatives, friends, and acquaintances imprisoned and even crucified by the Romans after the conquest of Jerusalem, although luckily Titus acceded to Josephus's pleas for clemency for no fewer than 244 individuals (*Vita* 419–421). When Josephus chose as his second wife a Jewish "virgin" among the captives from Caesarea, matters may have been complicated not only by halakic concerns (as a prisoner she could have been defiled by a Roman and thus could not marry Josephus, since he was a priest; see Lev 21:7; *C. Ap.* 1.35), but also because she would have been deeply affected by the unparalleled massacre at Caesarea under the last Roman procurator Gessius Florus, which unleashed the Jewish uprising against the Romans (*B.J.* 2.457). Unsurprisingly, she left Josephus soon thereafter (*Vita* 414–415). As a young man, Josephus not only lived through a traumatic epoch but also, judging from his own statements, saw himself, understandably, as traumatized (*Vita* 418).

After Josephus had prepared and ordered all his materials in Rome and finally found time to write his history, aided by assistants who knew Greek (*B.J.* 1.19–30; *C. Ap.* 1.50; see Fentress and Wickham 1992, 73), he set up shop in Vespasian's former house, where he was granted lodgings (*Vita* 423). Beyond this gesture of patronage, he was accorded further honors in the form of allowances, land in Judea, Roman citizenship, and the family name "Flavius." Finally, when various parties tried to defame him, all three Flavian emperors held their protecting hand over Josephus (*Vita* 422–425, 428–429). Yet notwithstanding the lucky turn of fortune in his domestic and public affairs, his book apparently found a ready market among not only Romans but also his own people (*C. Ap.* 1.51). Josephus's account remains not only a signal instance of reportage growing out of war trauma but also and in his view a contemporary history that takes up the narrative thread where the historical and prophetic books of the Bible end (*B.J.* 1.17–18).

KEYING TRAUMA

By indicating his intention to continue the Jewish historical account where Scripture had left off, Josephus establishes, to use Schwartz's language, a particular interpretive "frame," in this case a frame that is not unexpected from someone who claimed descent from priests, for Jews a badge of a "family's splendor" (*Vita* 1–2). It is emphatically the case that the priest

Josephus remembers the past "through the knowledge and symbols that predecessors" have transmitted to him (Schwartz, p. 9 above), keying his own experiences and memories to Scripture. But Josephus is not only a profound expert on the content of the biblical texts, the laws and history contained in them; he also lays claim to the gift of augury through the interpretation of biblical oracles and dreams (*B.J.* 1.3; 3.351–354, 399–407; 4.626–629; *Vita* 9). As an expert on Scripture and its interpretation, Josephus is not only well acquainted with the cultic function of Jerusalem's temple but also intimately familiar with its role in times of war. God's dwelling on earth secures not only the temple's existence; the presence of God in the midst of his people also protects individual life and safeguards the survival of the entire nation. In Scripture, therefore, God's presence is considered the central factor of national security.

Reflecting this perspective, Josephus paraphrases Solomon's prayer after God's descent into the newly completed First Temple, evidence that YHWH had chosen it as his habitation, as follows.

> But I have built this Temple to Thy name so that from it we may, *when sacrificing* and seeking good omens, send up our prayers into the air, to Thee, and may even be persuaded that Thou art present and not far removed. For, as Thou seest all things and hearest all things, Thou dost not even when dwelling here where is Thy rightful place, leave off being very near to all men, but rather art present with everyone who asks for guidance, both by night and by day. (*A.J.* 8.108–109, emphasis added; see 1 Kgs 8; 2 Chr 6)[2]

Josephus's Solomon suggests that God's presence requires sacrifices. Sacrifices alone, however, do not suffice, since God's presence also demands righteousness from everyone and faithfulness toward the admonitions of the fathers and covenant laws. This theme emerges clearly in God's reply to Solomon in a dream, informing him that his prayer has been heard and that God will be true to his word under the following conditions.

> [H]e would preserve the Temple and would abide in it forever, if his [Solomon's] descendants and *all the people acted righteously*; as for the king himself, God said that *if he abided by his father's counsels*, He would first raise him to a height and greatness of happiness beyond measure, and

---

2. All citations of Josephus's *Jewish Antiquities* (*Antiquitates judaicae*) are from the Loeb edition, translated by H. St. J. Thackeray and Ralph Marcus.

that those of his own line should forever rule the country and the tribe of Judah. If, however, he should be faithless to his task and forget it and turn to the worship of foreign gods, He would cut him off root and branch and would not suffer any of their line to survive nor allow the people of Israel to go unharmed, but would utterly destroy them with wars and countless afflictions and, after driving them out of the land which He had given to their fathers, would make them aliens in a strange land, and the Temple, which had only now been built, He would give over to their enemies to burn down and sack, and would also raze their city to the ground by the hand of their enemies. (*A.J.* 8.126–128; see 2 Chr 7)

Aside from sacrifice and righteousness, God's presence is contingent on a third stipulation: holiness, the cultic purity of his temple. The universal ancient conception of a separation between the profane and the sacred is spelled out in three rare descriptions of the Herodian Temple based on Josephus's personal and Mishnaic recollections (see m. Middot). While the later of Josephus's accounts (*A.J.* 15.380–423) presents Herod's magnificent renovation and amplification of the Second Temple in the context of his impressive building program, the earlier (*B.J.* 5.184–247) serves to describe the battleground in the context of Titus's siege. All three descriptions agree that the temple precincts consist of areas of varying degrees of holiness: an outer (or first) temple court accessible also to non-Jews, and an inner (or second) temple court accessible only to pure Jews (*A.J.* 8.96 adds "observant of the law"). The inner court was in turn divided into three areas to which increasing degrees of holiness were ascribed: the court to the east, the so-called women's court, accessible to Jewish women and men; the middle, or men's, court, accessible only to Jewish men; the court to the west, the so-called priests' court, accessible only to priests. Priests were permitted access to the front part or first room, the sanctum, of the temple, but the rear part or second room of the temple, the so-called holy of holies, was restricted to the high priest only, and this only once a year during Yom Kippur, as it was considered to be the room in which God was enthroned (*B.J.* 5.193, 199; *A.J.* 15.417–419; see m. Mid. 2). The care taken to preserve the sanctity of these various areas was rigorous, for the temple itself was built by priests only, and Herod, although the patron of the complex, never entered either the priests' court or the temple, as he was not of sacerdotal descent (*A.J.* 15.390, 420). Moreover, the most important feast in Jewish liturgy, Yom Kippur, was dedicated to the annual purification not only of the people but also, and particularly, of the temple itself (see Lev 16).

According to Josephus, the disregard of the three prerequisites to God's presence—the cessation of daily sacrifices, injustice (against fellow countrymen), and defilement of the temple with blood and corpses—by the rebels, especially John of Gischala, necessarily brought God's verdict into play, activating the covenant curses. Supporting this interpretation is Josephus's apt digression, immediately following the passage where Titus profanes the temple, in which he recalls that four years earlier, on a night during the feast of Pentecost, the priests performing their rites heard a sound as of a great multitude announcing the exodus of God, an unambiguous sign of covenant breaking (*B.J.* 6.300; see also 5.412–413).

Josephus enlarges his keying of Titus's conquest of the temple and Jerusalem to covenant breaking when he, like the earlier canonical prophets, links it to former conquests of the city, which become a frame for interpretation (see Mason 2003, 20–21). Titus, like earlier conquerors in their military, political, and economic calculus, had captured both city and temple, looting and profaning or even destroying them: the Egyptian Shishak (*A.J.* 8.258–259), the Babylonian Nebuchadnezzar (*A.J.* 10.144–150), the Syrian Antiochus IV (*B.J.* 1.32; *A.J.* 12.248–256), and the Roman Pompey (*B.J.* 1.152–153; *A.J.* 14.74). Titus's duplication of the past in the present meant that defeat had to be interpreted, in the context of Scripture, as the expression of Jewish failure and guilt (see Assmann 2007, 72). But by the same token, this mnemonic strategy had the advantage of ascribing neither Jewish defeat nor the enemy's victory to foreign gods. Framed by Scripture, Josephus could portray defeat as a product of Israel's sins, with God leaving his temple and bringing down just punishment. Apart from the historical problems Josephus's interpretation may pose, the ethical and corrective function of his mnemonic strategy is obvious.

Stabilizing and Destabilizing Memory

Josephus reconstructed the past not only with the knowledge and symbols transmitted to him by his predecessors but also with resources supplied by his contemporaries, particularly the Romans. It is no surprise that Romans in general and the Flavians in particular could identify with Josephus's account of the war (*Vita* 363). The possibility of looking at the war from both sides, for Josephus, was enhanced by several factors, among them the circumstance that the Flavians probably treated him both badly and well, sparing and saving his life at the same time. These complex conditions forced him to craft a narrative that would please and serve the emperors.

In his own self-interest, and to assure self-protection, Josephus devised a medium that would stabilize their power, which they owed solely to the popular acclaim surrounding their victory over the Jews.

Titus's essential, and effective, strategy had been to conquer the temple via the Antonia Fortress and then, via the temple, to take the entire city (*B.J.* 5.356). Although Josephus repeatedly assures readers that Titus intended to save the temple (e.g., *B.J.* 6.241), he also presents substantial evidence that would contradict his own claim. The Roman officers were well aware that "the Jews would never cease from rebellion while the temple remained as the focus for concourse from every quarter" (*B.J.* 6.239). The profanation of the temple, the Roman sacrifices in the temple precincts, and the acclamation of Titus as emperor there must have served to demonstrate that Jupiter, to whom each Roman general sacrificed near the Capitolium at the beginning and end of his military campaign, was greater than the Jewish God (Mason 2003, 22). The removal of the temple spoils, apparently a point of pride for Vespasian, and the deposit in his palace of the law of the Jews (symbol of God's word) along with the temple veils (symbol of access to God), would point to the same conclusion (*B.J.* 7.158–162). Similarly, the penalty tax introduced by Vespasian, the *fiscus Iudaicus*, which rededicated the tax owed to the Jerusalem temple by adult Jews (only males) to Jupiter Optimus Maximus (including Jewish women), supplied welcome reparation funds for the rebuilding of Jupiter's main temple in Rome, the Capitolium (*B.J.* 7.218), which had been destroyed only one year before the fall of Jerusalem during the civil war between Vitellius and Vespasian. Notably, Vespasian concluded his campaign against the Jewish God by closing the Jewish temple in Heliopolis (*B.J.* 7.420–436).

Contrary to Josephus's representation, then, and consistent with the basic data he records, it was very much in the interests of Titus and Vespasian to raze Jerusalem's temple (see Schwier 1989, 1–3, 308–37; Goodman 2007). The victory of Jupiter over YHWH may have been a crucial propaganda move in Rome, for it obscured the perceived guilt of the Flavians for having destroyed the capitol—the warrantor of Rome's state security—during their own struggle for power.[3] Such guilt called into question the claim to power authenticated through Jupiter—a property indispensable for any aspirant to the imperial throne. Their likely accentuation of Jupiter's victory over the Jewish God—without sinning against YHWH, as Josephus

---

3. By contrast, Cassius Dio charges Vitellius's soldiers with having torched the capitol (*Hist.* 64.17.3).

stresses (*B.J.* 1.12)—equipped them with a counternarrative, one in which the Flavians, although unable to claim divine ancestry, had provided Jupiter with a victory. That victory in turn rendered them eligible for divine legitimation through their chief god or, more bluntly, demanded that Jupiter offer the Flavians divine legitimation in exchange for military success.

In line with these considerations, it seems that Josephus must have submitted his war narrative to Vespasian and Titus relatively early, "when the facts were almost under men's eyes" (*Vita* 361; *C. Ap.* 1.51): between 75 CE (the *terminus a quo*, as the completion of temples is mentioned) and 79 CE (the year of Vespasian's death). If this dating is correct, the conquest of the Masada fortress by Flavius Silva in 74 CE, and with it the complete subjugation of Judea, preceded the first draft of *Bellum judaicum* by only one year (*B.J.* 7.252–406). Also in 75 CE, Vespasian rebuilt the capitol and completed a temple for the goddess of peace, in which "he laid up the vessels of gold from the Temple of the Jews, on which he prided himself" (*B.J.* 7.158–161). Just as the temple was the emperor's material ensign of his glory, so Josephus's account was its literary counterpart, both completed simultaneously in order to serve the liturgical calendar of a new leadership that had finally attained its uncontested place of power (see Connerton 1989, 41).

With his account, Josephus may have supported not only a Roman agenda but also the pro–Roman views current among some Jews and possibly also among Jewish or non-Jewish Christians (Mason 2009b). The factors pointing to this conclusion include not only the aforementioned popularity of his book among Jews but also his admonitions to co-religionists "who may be tempted to revolt" (*B.J.* 3.108), for example, Jews beyond the Euphrates, in Egypt (particularly Alexandria), and in Cyrene (*B.J.* 1.3, 6; 7.407–419, 437–453).

Here again, however, readings that define Josephus's agenda entirely in terms of his pro-Roman perspective overlook the subversive aspects of his portrayal of the war within the frame of covenant theology. This is evident above all in the explicit and repeated exposition of his view that the Jewish God, not Jupiter, helped the Romans achieve victory (see, e.g., *B.J.* 5.367, 412; 7.360; Mason 2003, 69). Further, the God of the Jews granted Rome victory for the exclusive purpose of purifying his defiled temple and city (*B.J.* 4.323; 5.19; 6.110). But this punishment ends where penitence begins, a change of heart invoked in vain from the rebels (*B.J.* 5.415; 6.103: μετανοέω). If penitence has the potential to alter a people's fate, one may infer that the subsequent activation of covenant blessings, and with it the recovery of Jewish national sovereignty, lies in the future, to begin, as it did after the Babylonian exile, with the reconstruction of the temple and the subsequent return of God to the midst of his people. As a priest and former advocate of war against Rome (*B.J.* 1.3), Josephus does not explicitly promote the rebuilding of Jerusalem's temple nor the return of the temple spoils. Nevertheless, he may have hoped for it, in the face of the rebuilding of Rome's Capitolium.

MARK'S MEMORY OF JESUS AND EMPIRE

> While they were eating, he took a loaf of bread, and after blessing it he broke it, gave it to them, and said, "Take; this is my body." (Mark 14:22; NRSV)

While the proximity of Josephus's *Bellum judaicum* to Jewish/Roman strife is obvious, that of the Gospel of Mark is less so. Nevertheless, supported by Mark's explicit references to war (e.g., Mark 13) and also by its semantic references to military struggle (e.g., "Legion" in Mark 5), the reception history of the oldest Gospel has traditionally placed Mark's account in temporal proximity to the Jewish revolt, and more recent scholarship has related its composition directly to the first Jewish–Roman war (see Hengel 1984; Theissen 1989; Marcus 1992; Yarbro Collins 2006). A growing number of interpreters reads the Markan text as both social memory and reaction literature, containing reminiscences of this disastrous war informed not only by the knowledge and symbols of predecessors and contemporaries—particularly Josephus—but also remembered both with and against other groups and individuals (see Schwartz pp. 7–8, 12–13, 26–27, above; Mason 2003, 2). Such readings locate both Mark and his audience in Rome after the Flavian triumph in 71 CE and assume that Mark was familiar with Josephus's war account, or at least with those books that Josephus had "previously composed in my vernacular tongue [Aramaic]" and later translated into Greek for presentation to the emperor (*B.J.* 1.3). These readings are generally informed by a theoretical perspective that is political in its thrust, viewing Mark as counterimperial or empire-critical. Early proposals in this vein include the groundbreaking studies of Gerd Theissen (1999) and Richard Horsley (2001), who both read Mark as an "anti-Gospel," the "politically subversive underground literature" of subjugated subjects. According to Theissen, these subjects may have reacted in this way to their damaged messianic hopes, specifically to Josephus's transfer of those hopes from the vanquished Jews to the new Roman dynasty, in line with the propaganda of these *homines novi*. In contrast to Josephus's memory project, Mark portrayed Jesus as a counterimage to Rome's imperial claims, an anticipated "ruler and monarch" who would bring deliverance from oppression.

More recently, Martin Ebner (2000, 2003, 2008, 2009, 2011) and Brian Incigneri (2003) have extended this approach and its implications. Ebner stresses the significance of the genre of the Markan text, which he sees as the oldest portrayal of Jesus' life (2004). Ebner reads Mark as a *vita* that proclaims the "beginning of the gospel of God's kingdom" (Mark 1:1), a kingdom that opposes the "gospels of Vespasian's ascension to power" portrayed by Josephus (*B.J.* 4.618, 656; Ebner 2008, 170–72; 2009, 14–16). Accordingly, Ebner contends that numerous aspects of Mark's Gospel parallel or contrast the themes of Flavian ascension. In much the same spirit, Incigneri identifies "matches" (2003, 363) that, in his view, must have been very important to Mark's traumatized audience, who may have been existentially affected by them. Tat-siong Benny Liew also identifies literary resistance in Mark's Gospel (1999), yet against colonialism, and thus exemplifies how its author is committed to its presuppositions. In Liew's view, Mark not only drew a counterimage of Roman governance but resisted it by mimicking it (2006). Feminist approaches to Mark (see, e.g., Fander 2005) and contextual approaches (see, e.g., Tamez 2011) point in a similar direction. Interpreters who situate Mark's Gospel in the context of Jewish–Roman strife have repeatedly drawn on the theoretical model of James C. Scott, who distinguishes between the "public" and "hidden" transcripts that define patterns of life and communication between ruler and ruled, oppressor and oppressed, lord and slaves (1990, esp. 1–16). As political power in antiquity was established and sustained by the military, a facet largely disregarded in the contextualizing interpretations noted above, the analysis to follow examines both political aspects and military themes and semantics in Mark's presentation.

If it is arguable that Mark, who situated his *vita* of Jesus in the 30s of the first century, reacted to events that took place from the mid 60s to the early 70s, then his reference points are necessarily multiple. Josephus's contemporary, most likely a Jew like himself, reacts on the one hand to a triumphal Roman view, co-fashioned by Josephus, and on the other hand to a desolate Judean view, which must have affected Jewish daily life, through the mnemonic lens of Jesus' life. Hence, two moods seem to be present. Rather than interpreting Mark's text only on the basis of either a triumphal or a desolate perspective, Theissen—in my view rightly—opted for acknowledging both, a *theologia gloriae* as well as a *theologia crucis* (1999, 393). While the triumphal mood seems to point to Liew's aforementioned mimicry of colonial rulers, the inscription "king of the Jews" on Jesus' cross explicitly points to the Roman charge of attempted insurgency (Mark 15:26).

If Mark relates the Flavian triumph to Jesus' triumph and the Judean defeat to Jesus' death, it remains to be considered what he may have intended to convey through Jesus' resurrection. In my view, this aspect plays a key role within his narrative plot and brings the discussion back to the temple and its cult.

Keying Jesus to the Jewish War

Among the obvious ways that Mark keys the life of Jesus to the triumphant Flavians is through the use of the term εὐαγγέλιον, with which Mark prominently opens his *vita* (Mark 1:1). Although dispute remains over whether εὐαγγέλιον names the subsequent portrayal of Jesus' life, the word's semantic imprint in the context of Flavian imperial propaganda supports the view that Mark wanted to have his book framed by the ruler's perspective, that is, against expectations of accomplished or forthcoming deeds, heroic and victorious actions, which in retrospect portray the attainment of power as well-deserved and desired by God. Accordingly, the "ruler" Jesus is portrayed as God's Son; as the "anointed one," the Christ, who deservedly finds God's pleasure; and as the messianic representative of God's kingdom, who legitimately represents him on earth—unlike Vespasian and later Titus (Mark 1:1, 11; 9:7). This will of God is announced to Jesus, who seems to foreknow it, and also to his contemporaries, through the "messenger" John the Baptist, just as Vespasian and Titus found their herald in Josephus (Mark 1:2; *B.J.* 3.400: ἄγγελος).

Because Herod's and his sons' territory was owned by Rome, Judea had been incorporated in phases into the imperial province of Syria, with the Syrian legate holding supreme military command over Judea. Accordingly, when the Judean insurgence erupted in 66 CE, it was Cestius, Syria's legate, who marched against the Judean rebels from the north by crossing into Galilee. But when Cestius was ignominiously defeated by the rebels, Nero transferred command of Syria's troops to Vespasian (*B.J.* 3.7), who likewise crossed the border into seditious territory from the north, that is, Galilee (*B.J.* 2.503; 3.127). The conquest of Galilee gave Vespasian a good deal of trouble, despite the support he received from the citizens of Sepphoris, the strategically important former capital of Galilee, especially the well-fortified cities of Jotopata, under Josephus's command, and Gamla. But once Vespasian, supported by Titus, succeeded in capturing Taricheae (Magdala) and Gischala, the whole of Galilee could be subdued (*B.J.* 4.120). During the Galilean campaign, Josephus reports that Vespasian twice entered the Gaulanitis, first when he accepted an invitation from his ally Agrippa II to his capital Caesarea Philippi and later when he besieged Gamla, which also belonged to Agrippa (*B.J.* 3.443; 4.11). Afterward Vespasian went into the Syrian Decapolis to join the forces that Titus had led from Caesarea to Scythopolis (*B.J.* 3.446–447).

In a similar geographical progression, the Markan Jesus' path begins in Galilee (1:14–15), where he, like the Roman generals, enjoys success. Thus Jesus confronts a large group of demons (Mark 5:1–20) whose name (Legion) and host (swine) recall the *Legio X Fretensis*, the Roman legion most involved in the war (*B.J.* 2.500; 3.65; 5.41; 7.5, 164; see Marcus 2000–2009, 1:351; Ebner 2009, 57–60).[4] Near Magdala (Taricheae), Jesus comes to the aid of his followers who are straining against an adverse wind on the lake (Mark 6:47–52), the same place where Titus would later ride through the water to mount a surprise attack against the renegade city (*B.J.* 3.497). In Nazareth, Jesus encounters resistance (Mark 6:1–6), a circumstance that may be explained by the fact that his hometown belonged to the catchment area of Sepphoris, the city that Herod Antipas expanded and made his capital in honor of Augustus after the latter had appointed him tetrarch over Galilee and Perea (*A.J.* 18.27). Like Vespasian, Jesus disrupts his "campaign" of liberating the whole of Galilee from demons (Mark 1:38–39), first with two forays into Gaulanitis—one to the country of the Gerasenes (which I take to be Gergesa) and another to Caesarea Philippi (5:1; 8:22), in Jesus' time the capital of Herod's son Philippus—followed by a visit to the Decapolis (7:31). In Caesarea Philippi Jesus is acclaimed by his followers as the anointed king, the Christ (8:29; 14:61–62; 15:2), a narrative strategy that allows Mark to portray Jesus proleptically laying claim to the Herodian kingdom, whose last representative was King Agrippa II, Vespasian's ally. It may not be accidental that Caesarea Philippi has strong associations with the other Caesarea, where, according to Josephus, Vespasian was acclaimed emperor and future king.

---

4. Portions of the Tenth Legion served Cestius and later Vespasian and Titus against the Judean rebellion. When Titus returned to Rome, the Tenth Legion stayed behind to guard Jerusalem and finally supported Flavius Silva in the capture of Masada.

In the ensuing campaign, Vespasian subjected Perea and then Judea, an operation he concluded in Jericho (*B.J.* 4.439, 450, 455), proceeding to seize all the neighborhoods surrounding Jerusalem (*B.J.* 4.588). But when Vespasian learned of Nero's death (*B.J.* 4.491), he postponed his expedition to await word on the transfer of power (*B.J.* 4.497). Hearing that Galba had been made emperor, Vespasian sent Titus to Rome to receive instructions for the war against the Jews (*B.J.* 4.498). But before Titus could reach Rome, Galba was slain and Otho seized power (69 CE), whereupon Titus returned to Caesarea (*B.J.* 4.501). According to Josephus, when Vespasian's indignant troops then learned that Vitellius had become emperor, they quickly acclaimed their general emperor in Caesarea (Maritima), believing that his military successes warranted it and that they themselves were the best of the legions (*B.J.* 4.601).

After returning to Syria, Vespasian took a detour through Alexandria so as to bring this Egyptian province rich in corn onto his side. Although Vespasian apparently was lacking in "prestige" (*auctoritas*) and "divinity" (*maiestas*), both were given to him in Alexandria by means of two miraculous healings, one of a blind man and another of a man with a crippled hand. These were interpreted as signs of divine favor, particularly by Serapis, and were subsequently broadcast widely as evidence of divine legitimation of Vespasian's power by the Egyptian deity (Tacitus, *Hist.* 4.81; Suetonius, *Vesp.* 7.2). When Vespasian received notice that his troops in Rome had dispossessed Vitellius, he hastily returned to Rome in 70 CE, sending Titus with a select part of his army to destroy Jerusalem (*B.J.* 4.655–658). Titus arrived before the city gates around Pesach (May), when Jerusalem was full of pilgrims (*B.J.* 6.421), seized and profaned the temple around Tisha B'Av (August), and conquered the city around Yom Kippur (September), while his father was being enthusiastically welcomed in Rome.

Similarly, Jesus, after a detour into Syria (Mark 7:24–31), returns to his capital, the political and cultural center of Judea. Just as he did in the capitals of Antipas's and Philip's territories, he reinforces his claim to power in Jerusalem vis-à-vis the local elites and indirectly vis-à-vis Rome, although here more explicitly than in the tetrarchies. By the time Jesus arrives in Jerusalem, he has already provided abundant proof of his prestige and divinity, along with marks of divine favor, including more than one restoration of sight to the blind (Mark 8:22–26) and healing of a crippled hand (3:1–5). In correspondence with Vespasian's *adventus*, Jesus likewise arrives in Jerusalem with a great entourage (10:32) and is similarly hailed as the new and legitimate (= messianic) offspring of David's house (11:8–

10). Also like Titus, after Jesus gains access to the city he goes immediately into the temple, "looks around at everything" (Mark 11:11), and follows this exploratory scouting with rhetorical sparring matches, taking on all the domestic elites: chief priests, scribes, and elders (11:27), Pharisees and Herodians (12:13), and, finally, even the Sadducees (12:18). These encounters, which take place right before Passover (14:1), are so successful that "no one dared to ask him any question" (Mark 12:34).

But before Jesus can prove his worth, his well-deserved reign is abruptly cut short by treachery. At this turn, Mark's keying of Jesus' life to the vanquished and desolate Jewish commanders reveals one of the most obvious parallels between Jesus' and the commanders' allegiances, inner dispute, and civil war, as Josephus repeatedly stresses (e.g., *B.J.* 4.131). Josephus was among the first to experience directly the destructive impact of the contest among the Judean generals. According to him, John of Gischala contended against his own command over Galilee (*B.J.* 2.590), resourcefully developing strategies in order to bring about Josephus's downfall (e.g., spreading defamations against him that resulted in the dispatch of a delegation from Jerusalem to question his authority, *B.J.* 2.626–628). Josephus was also disparaged among locals, leading to the apostasy not only of domestic militia but also and repeatedly of entire cities, such as Sepphoris or Tiberias (e.g., *B.J.* 2.615). In the context of these inner conflicts, both the sanctification and profanation of the Sabbath were in various situations applied as a stratagem (e.g., *Vita* 275). Finally, when Josephus's hideout in Jotopata was revealed to the Romans, he surrendered voluntarily and thus was spared, calling God to witness that he had not gone over to the Romans "as a deserter of the Jews, but as a minister" from God in order to announce to the future emperors their destiny (*B.J.* 3.355).

Jesus also experiences antagonism and mortal danger from local elites in Galilee: the Pharisees and Herodians in Capernaum, who saw him as profaning the Sabbath by healing someone on that day (Mark 3:1–6). Likewise, one can interpret the "unfaithfulness" (6:6: ἀπιστία) that Jesus encounters in Nazareth—and implicitly in Sepphoris—as analogous to the disloyalty of the Galilean cities with which Josephus repeatedly struggled. Further, just as with Josephus, a delegation from Jerusalem tries to discredit Jesus by purporting that his power is granted not by divine but by satanic will (3:22–30), prompting Jesus to say that a kingdom or a house divided against itself cannot stand (3:23–25). But unlike Josephus, Mark's Jesus is a man prepared to die, particularly after his followers acclaim him as Christ, the messianic king. No less than three times, Jesus explicitly announces his impending death on the way to Jerusalem (Mark 8:31; 9:31; 10:32–34), making it clear that it "must be" (8:31: δεῖ), that it is decreed by God.

Civil strife raged not only in Galilee but even more so in Jerusalem, initially between the legitimately appointed general of Jerusalem, the high priest Ananus, and the Zealots, and later between John of Gischala and Simon ben Giora. Ananus succumbed to the Zealots because John betrayed him; subsequently, the high priest was caught and murdered, along with 8,500 of his militia, in the temple precincts. According to Josephus, this incident marked the beginning of the capital's end, not only because of this hideous slaughter and defilement of the temple precincts but also because Ananus seemed the only Judean general capable of entering into treaties with the Romans to save the city (B.J. 4.318–321). Therefore, in Josephus's view, God must have tolerated Ananus's death because he had doomed the polluted city to destruction and resolved to purge the sanctuary by fire (B.J. 4.323). Not by accident, then, did learned scribes interpret the incident on Pentecost 66 CE, when the eastern gate of the inner court "was seen opened of its own accord about the sixth hour of the night," as evidence that the "security of their holy house was dissolved … and that the gate was opened for the advantage of their enemies" (B.J. 6.293–295). Four years later, Titus marched against Jerusalem, and although he came to fulfill omens similar to those mentioned above, he himself was not spared threats to his life, twice in particularly hazardous ways on the Mount of Olives (B.J. 5.47–97).

Eventual defeats always announced themselves by way of antecedent desertions and defections to the Romans, by either citizens or militias. In Galilee, Josephus experienced this firsthand when nearly all his men "dispersed themselves and fled, not only before they came to a battle, but before the enemy ever came in sight" (B.J. 3.129). The same was true in Jerusalem, where, however, flight was more dangerous because it was severely avenged by John and Simon. After the city was captured, Titus ordered the famished survivors brought into the inner court of the temple, where they were sentenced either to death on the cross or in the arena or sold into slavery (B.J. 6.414–419). Among these prisoners were the messianic pretenders John and Simon (B.J. 7.29), who chose not to take their own lives, as they so often had demanded from their followers, but voluntarily gave themselves over to the Romans, John to be perpetually imprisoned and Simon to be slain during the triumphal procession in Rome (B.J. 6.433–434).

Like Josephus and Ananus, Jesus falls into the enemy's hands through betrayal (Mark 14:10–11). But before that, he also announces the destruction of the defiled temple (11:15–19; 13:1–2) and coming wars and famines, all things that "must take place" (13:7–8). Jesus is arrested in Gethsemane, on the Mount of Olives (14:43–54), where he suffers mortal anguish, as Titus would later (14:32–42). Like the Jewish generals, Jesus is abandoned by his followers at the critical hour (14:27, 50). Once captured, Jesus is immediately brought to the chief priest, where the Sanhedrin also convenes (14:53). The exact location of this meeting is not indicated in the text, but according to the Mishnah the office of the high priest was in the courtyard south of the temple in the "chamber of wood" next to the "chamber of hewn stone" where the great Sanhedrin usually met (m. Mid. 5.4). Theoretically, then, Jesus may have received his trial at about the same place as Titus's prisoners. From there Jesus is passed on to Pilate, who hands him over to be crucified, as were many prisoners of war (Mark 15:15). Pilate's Roman soldiers grant Jesus a triumph, though not in order to dignify him like Vespasian but in order to humiliate him (15:16–20). Like Simon, Jesus dies at the hands of the Romans (15:21–39). At the very moment of his death, God leaves the temple, as insinuated by Jesus' cry, "My God, my God, wherefore have you forsaken me?" (15:34), rending as he departs the temple "curtain," most likely that of the inner sanctum (15:38; see *B.J.* 5.219).

STABILIZING AND DESTABILIZING MEMORY

While Mark's keying of Christ's *vita* to the Flavian ascension may have implied divine pleasure to some audiences, contemporary readers may have wondered what purpose the keying of Jesus' death to Judean ignominy could have served, apart from perhaps promoting a sense of empathy for the conquered Jews and raising ethical implications about their treatment (see Kirk 2005, 204–6). In what way could Jesus' death have been viewed as an achievement?

The Roman triumph honored the victorious general but was also a ritual celebrating the conclusion of a military campaign (Rüpke 1990, 223–34). A triumph was granted to generals whose war was considered just, a *bellum iustum*. These processions ended in front of the most august temple in ancient Rome, that dedicated to Jupiter Optimus Maximus on the Capitoline Hill, which must have lain in ruins when the Flavian victories were celebrated. Capped and gowned in regalia resembling the costume of Jupiter, Vespasian and the entire procession waited "until the execution of the enemy's general was announced" (*B.J.* 7.153). When Vespasian was told that Simon ben Giora had died, he and Titus offered to Jupiter the sacrifices they had consecrated (*B.J.* 7.155), most likely in the same place that every general offered mandatory sacrifices at the end of a campaign to purify himself and the country from war guilt. Symbolically, Jupiter's acceptance of the sacrifice meant also a merging of the victor with the deity, the royal son with the godfather, and also granted divine legitimacy for regency by the Roman chief deity.

In keying Jesus' death to the Roman triumph, Mark makes his protagonist play both roles, at once the Roman victor and the Jewish general to be slain. Against this background, Jesus' death purifies the guilt of the Judean generals for waging an unjust, unholy war (*B.J.* 5.375–419). Mark shows Jesus interpreting his death as a "ransom for many," perhaps a proleptic ransom for the many war victims among his people (Mark 10:45). Following the logic of the Roman triumph, the author may even have intended to portray Jesus' death as the sacrifice owed to the chief God to cleanse the defiled city and temple. It may be no coincidence that Mark has Jesus describe himself as "sitting at the right hand of God" in the near future (12:36; 14:62; see also 16:19), the place in the celestial holy of holies, God's throne room, where he withdrew after leaving his earthly sanctuary right beneath. The fact that Jesus sees himself seated there attests to his certainty that God will accept his sacrifice and render him the restorer of sacrifices that had ceased in the temple. That Jesus refers to his body as "bread" (Mark 14:22) invites associations with his perceived role in the narrative as the one who gives back to God the "food" of which the rebels had deprived him. In Jewish cult, access to the holy of holies was allowed only on Yom Kippur, the day the city fell to Titus; it served mainly the purpose of purifying God's people and God's temple (Lev 16). Purification, in turn, was necessary in order to celebrate covenant renewal, which was and still is intimately related with this festival (see Gelardini 2011). This is perhaps why Mark identifies not only Jesus' body with sacrifice but also his blood with covenant renewal (Mark 14:24).

According to the Judean perspective, then, the "triumph" of Mark's Jesus brings the Judean war to a conclusion, undoing two of the transgressions Josephus charges to the Jewish generals. On the one hand, like the Flavians, Jesus cleanses the state of war guilt (caused by an unjust war) and defilement (caused by temple profanation); on the other, he restores God's interrupted sacrifice. These two accomplishments are the outstanding achievements of Jesus' death and are prerequisites to appeasing God and reintroducing access to the deity in the context of covenant renewal.

While God's acceptance of Jesus' sacrifice, like Jupiter's acceptance of the Flavian sacrifice, results in a merging of messianic king with God and of Son with Father, still Jesus' reign on earth, in contrast to that of Rome, is not apparent. Yet Mark announces it repeatedly. Mark seems to see resurrection not as Jesus' apotheosis but rather as his return, similar to John the Baptist's return as Elijah *redivivus* (see Mark 8:31; 9:9, 31; 10:34; 14:27; 16:6). It is a return in great "power" (13:26: δύναμις)—in Josephus a synonym for "army"—and according to Mark's Jesus a powerful return in the "glory of his father," similar to Titus's return with his father's legions (8:38; 13:26; 14:62). It will be a return at the starting point of Vespasian's successful Galilean campaign, and from there it will move all the way to Jerusalem's gates (13:28–37). Under the premise of a renewed covenant, it will be a return to fight a *bellum iustum*, a holy war in which God himself will put the enemies "under his [Christ's] feet" (12:36), an aspect that redeems the third charge of the Judean generals, namely, to have waged an unjust war. But a holy war and an expulsion of the enemy would result, just as in Rome, in a physical return of God to his capital, his new temple (see Mark 13:34–35). The passage in which Jesus as the rejected stone has become the cornerstone may then have been meant to construe Jesus as the cornerstone of a new temple (12:10; see Isa 28:16), similar to the cornerstone of Vespasian's rebuilt Capitolium (Tacitus, *Hist.* 4.53; Rüpke 2006, 557). In the context of a calendric liturgy (Connerton 1989, 41), Jesus became so on Pesach, a feast whose related "metanarrative" in biblical and related literature long has served as a "mnemonic frame" for liberation from oppressive powers. This narrative prospect, along with the centurion's statement after Jesus' death, "This man was God's Son!" (Mark 15:39), may or may not have destabilized Rome's memory. However, the Roman officer's insight that Jesus was of divine nature is an acknowledgment of his, and implicitly of Judean, power, a power that potentially could prove threatening or disturbing to the empire. Could it be that Mark on a literary basis helped to facilitate further resistance, which only a little later erupted in the insurgency of Alexandria in 115–117 CE and in the Bar Kokhba revolt in 132–135 CE?

CONCLUSION

Building on Barry Schwartz's theoretical apparatus, the interpretation of Jesus' death as, inter alia, the cleansing and reintroduced sacrifice and of his resurrection as the beginning of God's powerful and liberating return into the midst of his people, set against the background of multiple interpretive frames, both Roman and Judean, may explain why the memory of resurrection and transformation in the first century, and later the patristic motif of the *Christus* and *ecclesia militans*, were popular and handed down in memory to future generations (Schwartz 2005, 258).

As shown, I do not think Josephus or Mark believed he had replaced the temple with a memorial construction; quite the contrary. Nevertheless, it may be that Mark's text in particular, when the hoped-for rebuilding of Jerusalem's temple proved to be a long time coming, in a certain sense replaced the lost sacred site. Viewed in this light, the proclaimed reinstituted access to God provided by Jesus may have been considered sufficient (see Heb 4:14–16; 10:19–22). In that sense, then, Jan Assmann's contention becomes more persuasive, that the destruction of the temple was preceded and accompanied by the death of the cult in Scripture (2007, 164).

WORKS CITED

Assmann, Jan. 2007. *Religion und das kulturelles Gedächtnis: Zehn Studien.* Beck'sche Reihe 1375. 3rd ed. Munich: Beck.

Connerton, Paul. 1989. *How Societies Remember.* Themes in the Social Sciences. Cambridge: Cambridge University Press.

Ebner, Martin. 2000. Im Schatten der Großen: Kleine Erzählfiguren im Markusevangelium. *BZ* 44:56–76.

———. 2003. Evangelium contra Evangelium: Das Markusevangelium und der Aufstieg der Flavier. *BN* 116:28–42.

———. 2008. Das Markusevangelium. Pages 154–83 in *Einleitung in das Neue Testament.* Edited by Martin Ebner and Stefan Schreiber. Kohlhammer Studienbücher Theologie 6. Stuttgart: Kohlhammer.

———. 2009. *Das Markusevangelium: Neu übersetzt und kommentiert.* Stuttgart: Katholisches Bibelwerk.

———. 2011. Das Markusevangelium und der Aufstieg der Flavier: Eine politische Lektüre des ältesten "Evangeliums." *BK* 66.2:64–69.

Fander, Monika. 2005. "Mein Gott, mein Gott, warum hast du mich verlassen?" (Mk 15,34): (Kriegs-)Traumatisierung als Thema des Markusevangeliums. Pages 116–56 in *Christologie im Lebensbezug.* Edited by Elisabeth Moltmann-Wendel and Renate Kirchhoff. Göttingen: Vandenhoeck & Ruprecht.

Fentress, James, and Chris Wickham. 1992. *Social Memory: New Perspectives on the Past.* Oxford: Blackwell.

Goodman, Martin. 2007. *Rome and Jerusalem: The Clash of Ancient Civilizations.* New York: Knopf.

Halbwachs, Maurice. 1925. *Les cadres sociaux de la mémoire*. Travaux de l'année sociologique 9. Paris: Alcan.

Hengel, Martin. 1984. Entstehungszeit und Situation des Markusevangeliums. Pages 1–47 in *Markus-Philologie: Historische, literargeschichtliche und stilistische Untersuchungen zum zweiten Evangelium*. Edited by Hubert Cancik. WUNT 33. Tübingen: Mohr.

Horsley, Richard A. 2001. *Hearing the Whole Story: The Politics of Plot in Mark's Gospel*. Louisville: Westminster John Knox.

Incigneri, Brian J. 2003. *The Gospel to the Romans: The Setting and Rhetoric of Mark's Gospel*. Biblical Interpretation Series 65. Leiden: Brill.

Josephus. 1961. *Jewish War*. Translated by H. St. J. Thackeray. LCL. Cambridge: Harvard University Press.

———. 1963. *Antiquites of the Jews*. Translated by Ralph Marcus and Allen Wikgren. LCL. Cambridge: Harvard University Press.

———. 1966. *Against Apion*. Translated by H. St. J. Thackeray. LCL. Cambridge: Harvard University Press.

Kirk, Alan. 2005. The Memory of Violence and the Death of Jesus in Q. Pages 191–206 in *Memory, Tradition, and Text: Uses of the Past in Early Christianity*. Edited by Alan Kirk and Tom Thatcher. SemeiaSt 52. Atlanta: Society of Biblical Literature.

Liew, Tat-siong Benny. 1999. *Politics of Parousia: Reading Mark Inter(con)textually*. Biblical Interpretation Series 42. Leiden: Brill.

———. 2006. Tyranny, Boundary, and Might: Colonial Mimicry in Mark's Gospel. Pages 206–23 in *The Postcolonial Biblical Reader*. Edited by R. S. Sugirtharajah. Oxford: Blackwell.

Marcus, Joel. 1992. The Jewish War and the Sitz im Leben of Mark. *JBL* 111:441–62.

———. 2000–2009. *Mark: A New Translation with Introduction and Commentary*. 2 vols. AB 27–27A. New York: Doubleday.

Mason, Steve. 2003. *Josephus and the New Testament*. 2nd ed. Peabody, MA: Hendrickson.

———. 2009. Of Audience and Meaning: Reading Josephus's *Judean War* in the Context of a Flavian Audience. Pages 45–67 in *Josephus, Judea, and Christian Origins: Methods and Categories*. Peabody, MA: Hendrickson.

Rüpke, Jörg. 1990. *Domi militiae: Die religiöse Konstruktion des Krieges in Rom*. Stuttgart: Steiner.

———. 2006. Tempel, Daten, Rituale—Die Götter als Langzeitgedächtnis der Gesellschaft. Pages 554–569 in *Erinnerungsorte der Antike: Die römische Welt*. Edited by Elke Stein-Hölkeskamp and Karl-Joachim Hölkeskamp. Munich: Beck.

Schwartz, Barry. 2005. Jesus in First-Century Memory—A Response. Pages 249–61 in *Memory, Tradition, and Text: Uses of the Past in Early Christianity*. Edited by Alan Kirk and Tom Thatcher. SemeiaSt 52. Atlanta: Society of Biblical Literature.

Schwier, Helmut. 1989. *Tempel und Tempelzerstörung: Untersuchungen zu den theologischen und ideologischen Faktoren im ersten jüdisch-römischen Krieg (66–74 n.Chr.)*. NTOA 11. Göttingen: Vandenhoeck & Ruprecht.

Scott, James C. 1990. *Domination and the Arts of Resistance: Hidden Transcripts*. New Haven: Yale University Press.

Tamez, Elsa. 2011. The Conflict in Mark: A Reading from the Armed Conflict in Colombia. Pages 101–25 in *Mark*. Edited by Nicole Wilkinson Duran, Teresa Okure, and Daniel M. Patte. Translated by Leticia Guardiola-Sáenz. Texts @ Contexts. Minneapolis: Fortress.

Theissen, Gerd. 1989. *Lokalkolorit und Zeitgeschichte in den Evangelien: Ein Beitrag zur Geschichte der synoptischen Tradition*. NTOA 8. Göttingen: Vandenhoeck & Ruprecht.

———. 1999. Evangelienschreibung und Gemeindeleitung: Pragmatische Motive bei der Abfassung des Markusevangeliums. Pages 389–414 in *Antikes Judentum und Frühes Christentum: Festschrift für Hartmut Stegemann zum 65. Geburtstag*. Edited by Bernd Kollmann, Wolfgang Reinbold, and Annette Steudel. BZNW 97. Berlin: de Gruyter.

Yarbro Collins, Adela. 2006. Christian Messianism and the First Jewish War with Rome. Pages 333–43 in *Biblical Traditions in Transmission: Essays in Honour of Michael A. Knibb*. Edited by Charlotte Hempel and Judith M Lieu. JSJSup 111. Leiden: Brill, 2006.

Memory and Loss in Early Rabbinic Text and Ritual[*]

Steven D. Fraade

In memory of Dorothy S. Fraade, 1923–2011

Early rabbinic literature poses special challenges to social memory theory and its application that are in some ways very different from those posed by the New Testament and the search for the "historical Jesus." Conversely, early rabbinic literature provides exceptional opportunities for examining the relation between the practice and theory of collective memory in relation to the formation and maintenance of social identity. In what follows I will attend to both these challenges and opportunities (typically the flip side of one another) through the analysis of specific rabbinic texts that both thematize and practice collective memory in the face of profound collective loss.

The "challenges" noted above are highlighted when read against the backdrop of Schwartz's analysis of the sources for Jesus' career in the introduction to this volume and elsewhere. First, there is no central coherent narrative of the origins of rabbinic Judaism nor any extant continuous biographical narratives, even if fictitious, of its "founding figures" (e.g., Hillel, Rabban Yohanan ben Zakkai, Rabbi Akiva). All we have are scattered narrative fragments or anecdotes that are adduced for entirely nonbiographical/historiographical purposes, nothing like the New Testament Gospels. Second, at least as recorded in early rabbinic literature, if these "founding figures" were portrayed in any sense as "charismatic," it was not due primarily to their supernatural or miraculous fetes nor to their apocalyptic pronouncements or eschatological roles but rather to their memorized control of received scriptural and oral traditions and their interpretive acuity in teaching, applying, and exemplifying those traditions. Third, early rabbinic corpora do not establish their authority (such as it is) through attribution to named authors, whether pseudepigraphical or historical, even though indi-

---

* I wish to acknowledge the sage interventions of Vered Noam in reading an earlier version of this essay.

vidual pronouncements may be attributed to, or anecdotal narratives might have as their subjects, named sages, whom we may presume at the very least to have lived. Rather, they are composite anthologies, often structured as commentaries to antecedent texts, whether scriptural or rabbinic, with an implied claim to *collective* authorship and authority (see Fraade 2011). Dating the composite collections is hard enough; dating their contained traditions, whether legal or narrative, is even more difficult, rendering their employment for historicist narrative reconstruction difficult at best. Fourth and finally, since early rabbinic teaching comes under the rubric of "oral Torah" (תורה שבעל פה) or "oral teaching" (משנה) as distinct from "written Torah" (תורה שבכתב) or "read Scripture" (מקרא), great premium is placed on memorization, and many rabbinic texts express fears of forgetting what has been learned and provide techniques for the "art of memory" (see Naeh 2001, 2005; Fraade 2007). Thus, as a laboratory for the examination of the workings of collective memory, rabbinic literature is unusual for both its insistence on the orality of its teachings and for their packaging as collective (anonymously anthologized) teaching.

With these general considerations of limitations and opportunities in mind, we may direct our attention more narrowly to the topic at hand. Memory, both individual and collective, is, by definition, principally (but not solely) about the past. Similarly, we might presume that the past, by definition, is no longer present, that is, is lost. Memory is the means by which we seek to retrieve the past, to recover it so as to restore it, as it were, to the present by a process of re-presentation. Conversely, memory is a means of entering and reliving, as it were, the past, if only briefly. To the extent to which memory is collectively shared, it must be ritually embodied.

But what is the nature of that recovery when what is remembered is loss itself, that is, something that cannot be restored, at least not in the near future? For early rabbinic Judaism, the defining loss (among others, e.g., prophecy) is that of the Second Temple and its sacrificial worship at the hands of the Romans in 70 CE. The central figures in the recovery from the destruction of the temple, according to both rabbinic tradition and modern historiography, are Rabban Yohanan ben Zakkai and his students, who flourished in the Land of Israel during the mid- to late first century CE. We will focus in what follows on a few specific textual embodiments of that tradition, with particular attention to their incorporation of memory and commemoration (for earlier and broader treatments, see, e.g., Neusner 1970; Kister 1998; Cohn 2012).

Rabban Yohanan ben Zakkai's Edicts of Ritual Commemoration

The following passage, from the earliest extant rabbinic text, the Mishnah (ca. 200 CE), gives legal and ritual expression to the challenges of adapting Judaism and Jewish society to the radically altered conditions following the destruction of the Second Temple and the combined needs of collective Israel (however broad or narrow) both to preserve the memory of what was lost and to compensate for that loss.

יום טוב של ראש השנה שחל להיות בשבת במקדש היו תוקעים אבל לא
במדינה. משחרב בית המקדש התקין רבן יוחנן בן זכאי שיהו תוקעין בכל
מקום שיש בו בית דין. אמר רבי אלעזר, «לא התקין רבן יוחנן בן זכאי אלא
ביבנה בלבד». אמרו לו, «אחד יבנה ואחד כל מקום שיש בו בית דין». ועוד
זאת היתה ירושלם יתירה על יבנה שכל עיר שהיא רואה ושומעת וקרובה
ויכולה לבא תוקעין וביבנה לא היו תוקעין אלא בבית דין בלבד.

(m. Roš Haš. 4.1–2)

The festival day of the New Year that coincided with the Sabbath—in the temple they would sound the shofar, but not in the provinces. When the temple was destroyed, Rabban Yohanan ben Zakkai made the rule that they should sound the shofar in every locale in which there was a court. Said R. Eleazar, "Rabban Yohanan ben Zakkai made that rule only in the case of Yavneh alone." They said to him, "All the same are Yavneh and every locale in which there is a court." And in this regard also was Jerusalem ahead of Yavneh: in every town that is within sight and sound [of Jerusalem], and nearby and able to come up to Jerusalem, they sound the shofar. But as to Yavneh, they sound the shofar only in the court alone.

בראשונה היה הלולב ניטל במקדש שבעה ובמדינה יום אחד. משחרב בית
המקדש התקין רבן יוחנן בן זכאי שיהא לולב ניטל במדינה שבעה זכר
למקדש ושיהא יום הנף כולו אסור.

(m. Roš Haš. 4.3; see also m. Suk. 3.12)

In olden times the *lulav* was taken up in the temple for seven days, and in the provinces for one day. When the temple was destroyed, Rabban Yohanan ben Zakkai made the rule that in the provinces the *lulav* should be taken up for seven days, as a memorial to the temple, and that the day [16 Nisan] on which the *omer* is waved should be wholly prohibited [in regard to the eating of new produce].[1]

---

1. Both translations above are slightly modified from Neusner 1988, 305.

The two sources cited above are legal narratives that describe rulings of Rabban Yohanan ben Zakkai in the aftermath of the destruction of the Second Temple, which had been the center of Jewish worship, principally sacrificial. At issue is whether certain ritual practices that had been restricted to the Jerusalem temple (blowing the shofar on Rosh Hashanah when coinciding with Shabbat; taking the *lulav* for all seven days of Sukkot; see also m. Roš Haš. 4.4 with respect to calendrical matters) should be allowed in local communities once sacrificial worship in the temple was no longer possible. Whether these narratives are historically representative, that is, whether Yohanan ben Zakkai actually made these rulings as described (and, if so, whether they were followed by anyone other than his disciples), or whether they are rhetorical retrojections from a later time (but prior to the Mishnah's redaction around 200 CE) cannot be ascertained from either internal or external evidence. Of interest in our present context are aspects of the stories relating to memory and loss.

According to the first source above (m. Roš Haš. 4.1–2), at some point, presumably after Yohanan ben Zakkai's death, his successors differed in their memory of what precisely he had ruled. Was the prerogative of Jerusalem before the temple was destroyed transferred thereafter only to Yavneh (to which Yohanan ben Zakkai relocated shortly before the temple was destroyed) by virtue of its (presumably rabbinic) court, or did it extend to any town that contained a (presumably rabbinic) court?[2] In other words, what was the extent of the compensatory displacement of Jerusalem's status once the temple was gone? This disagreement presumes that Yohanan ben Zakkai's ruling had not been committed to writing but to memory, resulting in two different versions of what he had ruled.

Even so, Jerusalem, as the Jewish "metropolis" (literally, "mother city," to borrow Philo's term; see *Flaccus* 46), enjoyed a status that was unequaled by any other city or town, even Yavneh, with that status extending beyond its central temple/court to the city as a whole, including, as it were, its suburbs.[3] Thus, at the same time that centralized ritual and worship is decentralized, and what had once been Jerusalem's special status (by virtue of its temple) is, in the aftermath of the destruction of the temple, distributed to other towns by virtue of their (presumably rabbinic) courts, at least

---

2. For another example of the transfer of (judicial) authority from the Temple Mount in Jerusalem to Yavneh, see *Sipre Deut.* 153–154 (Finkelstein 1969, 206–7) and discussion in Fraade 1991, 83–87.

3. A similar attitude toward the expanded "temple city" can be seen in the Temple Scroll from Qumran (e.g., 11QT^a 45.11–12); see also Eliav 2005.

one aspect of Jerusalem's exceptionalism is preserved—that is, remains in the past while being remembered in the present, both through textual and ritual practice.

According to the second source above (m. Roš Haš. 4.3), Yohanan ben Zakkai is said to have made a similar ruling that distributed another of Jerusalem's sole ritual prerogatives while the temple stood to other towns in the aftermath of its destruction. The taking of the *lulav* for all seven days of Sukkot, previously the prerogative of the temple alone, is termed a "memorial to (reminder of) the temple."[4] Thus, in distributing Jerusalem's special status to the other towns after the destruction of the temple, the temple is not to be forgotten, as if superseded, but emphatically remembered, perhaps with a hint of hope in its eventual rebuilding. In performing the ritual of taking the *lulav*, formerly associated with the temple, outside of Jerusalem after its destruction, the association with the temple is not reduced but accentuated. Thus, we see here a similar dialectic as we saw in the previous *mishnayot* of displacement and preservation of the temple's privileged status after its loss, its very displacement being the occasion for its ritualized commemoration, with the performative effect of linking the worshiper to past loss while keeping alive the hope for eventual restoration.[5] Here as elsewhere, memory points simultaneously backward and forward in time.

Turning to our earliest running commentary on the book of Leviticus, the Sifra, we observe the same tradition as found in the Mishnah, but now formulated exegetically as an interpretation of Lev 23:40.

«ולקחתם לכם ביום הראשון [...] ושמחתם לפני ה' אלהיכם שבעת ימים»
(ויקרא כ"ג מ'), ולא בגבולים כל שבעה. ומשחרב בית המקדש התקין רבן
יוחנן בן זכאי שיהיה לולב ניטל במדינה שבעה זכר למקדש, ושיהיה יום
הנף כולו אסור.

(Sifra Emor 16.9; ed. Weiss 1862, 102d)

---

4. The phrase זכר למקדש is found in tannaitic collections only here and in parallels: m. Suk. 3.12; Sifra Emor 16.9 (ed. Weiss 1862, 102d); and t. Yoma 1.9, in a case of unapproved memorializing. The expression זכר לירושלים ("in memory of Jerusalem") appears three times in a toseftan passage that will be treated below (and another three times in a close parallel).

5. Compare the phrase זכר למקדש כהלל ("in memory of the temple as Hillel [did in temple times]") in b. Pesaḥ. 115a and the Passover Haggadah (immediately preceding the meal), which evinces memory of what has been lost (the Passover sacrifice), ritual reenactment of its performance as if continually present (but without its central sacrificial ingredient), and a hope for its restoration.

"[On the first day you shall take ...], and you shall rejoice before the Lord your God seven days" (Lev. 23:40): but not outside [of Jerusalem] all seven [days]. When the temple was destroyed, Rabban Yohanan ben Zakkai made a rule that in the provinces the *lulav* should be taken for seven days, as a memorial to the temple, and that the day on which the *omer* is waved should be wholly prohibited [in regard to the eating of new produce]. (my translation)

From this we can see the exegetical underpinnings of the tradition that, so long as the temple stood, rejoicing with the *lulav* for seven days was to be performed "before the Lord your God," in God's presence—that is, within the temple. With the destruction of the temple, Yohanan ben Zakkai might have decided that the condition of "before the Lord your God" could no longer be fulfilled and that the *lulav* should only be taken on the first day of the festival in fulfillment of the beginning of the verse, "On the first day you shall take...." Instead, he is said to have ruled that in the aftermath of the destruction of the temple one should take the *lulav* for all seven days anywhere, not so much as a biblical ritual obligation in its own right but in memory of the destroyed temple. That is, so long as one did so in commemoration of the destroyed temple, "before the Lord your God" could apply "in the provinces." In effect, one should perform the ritual as if in Jerusalem while the temple was standing ("before the Lord your God") while recognizing that it is not. Implicitly, the central locus of the presence of God has been decentralized, even as the loss of center is acknowledged.

It should be noted that centuries later, in the iconography of the synagogue, the *etrog* and *lulav* commonly appear with ritual objects associated with the temple: holy ark, menorah, shofar, and incense shovel (see Hachlili 2001, 211–27, esp. 216–18). The association of the *lulav* with the temple did not cease with the latter's destruction but rather continued, with the visual representation of the *lulav* (among other ritual objects) preserving the memory and symbolic presence of the temple among synagogue worshipers, wherever they might be. We should not ignore the role of visualization, alongside orality and aurality, in collective memory (see Fraade 2009). However, with time the association of the *etrog* and *lulav* with the Jerusalem temple per se may have been somewhat weakened, at least in common perception, as the ritual performance of their being "taken" was associated more immediately with the locus of the synagogue. Alternatively, the ritual of the *etrog* and *lulav* may be viewed as one of many media by which the synagogue was itself experienced as זכר למקדש (see Fine 1997, who appears to overlook this aspect).

Finally, the conclusion of the mishnah (m. Roš Haš. 4.3) and its associated midrash (Sifra Emor 16.9) draws a distinction between the time
of the temple, when new produce could be eaten on the 16th of Nisan as
soon as the *omer* (barley sheaf) had been waved in the temple, and the
time after its destruction, when, according to a ruling of Yohanan ben
Zakkai, the *omer* could no longer be waved and new produce could not
be eaten on that whole day. Here again, the sense of loss (of the "day of
waving") is dialectically juxtaposed with a sense of overcoming of loss
(by taking the *lulav*), discontinuity with the (temple) past and continuity
with it, notwithstanding the temple's loss. In the case of the shofar, loss is
overcome (while still recalled), whereas in the case of the "day of waving"
an unbridgeable gap between present and past is affirmed implicitly, only
to be bridged with the future rebuilding of the temple (explicitly in the
Babylonian Talmud's commentary ad loc., b. Suk. 41a; b. Roš Haš. 30a, at
מהרה יבנה בית המקדש).

Narratives of Reaction to the Loss of the Temple

We turn now to a relatively late collection of narrative traditions that portray immediate rabbinic reactions to the destruction of the Second Temple.
In this case, the memories of that event appear to be inconsistent.

[א] שמעון הצדיק היה משירי אנשי כנסת הגדולה הוא היה אומר: על
שלשה דברים העולם עומד על התורה ועל העבודה ועל גמילות חסדים.

.....

[ב] ותלמוד תורה חביבה לפני המקום מעולות....מכאן לחכם שיושב ודורש
בקהל שמעלה עליו הכתוב כאלו הקריב חלב ודם לגבי מזבח.

.....

[ג] הא למדת שאין עבודה שהיא חביבה לפני הקדוש ברוך הוא יותר
מעבודת בית המקדש.

.....

[ד] פעם אחת היה רבן יוחנן בן זכאי יוצא מירושלים והיה ר' יהושע הולך
אחריו וראה בית המקדש חרב אמר ר' יהושע, »אוי לנו על זה שהוא חרב
מקום שמכפרים בו עונותיהם של ישראל«. א"ל, »בני אל ירע לך. יש לנו
כפרה אחת שהיא כמותה ואיזה זה גמילות חסדים שנאמר ›כי חסד חפצתי
ולא זבח‹ (הושע ו' ו')«.

.....

[ה] באותה שעה שנלכדה ירושלים והיה רבן יוחנן בן זכאי יושב ומצפה וחרד
כדרך שהיה עלי יושב ומצפה שנאמר »והנה עלי יושב על הכסא יד דרך
מצפה כי היה לבו חרד על ארון האלהים« (שמואל א' ד' י"ג). כיון ששמע

רבן יוחנן בן זכאי שהחריב את ירושלים ושרף את בית המקדש באש קרע
בגדיו וקרעו תלמידיו את בגדיהם והיו בוכין וצועקין וסופדין.

(*Abot de Rabbi Nathan* A4; ed. Schechter, 18–24)

[A] Simeon the Righteous was among the last of the men of the Great
Assembly. He used to say: On three things the world stands: on the [study
of] Torah, on the [temple] service, and on acts of lovingkindness.
......
[B] But the study of Torah is more beloved by God than burnt offerings....
Hence, when a sage sits and expounds to the congregation, Scripture
accounts it to him as though he had offered up fat and blood on the altar.
......
[C] Thus you learn that there is no service more beloved of the Holy One,
blessed be He, than the temple service.
......
[D] Once as Rabban Yohanan ben Zakkai was coming forth from Jerusalem, Rabbi Joshua followed after him and beheld the temple in ruins.
"Woe unto us," Rabbi Joshua cried, "that this, the place where the iniqui-
ties of Israel were atoned for, is laid waste!"

"My son," Rabban Yohanan said to him, "be not grieved; we have
another atonement as effective as this. And what is it? It is acts of lovingkindness, as it is said, 'For I desire mercy and not sacrifice' (Hos. 6:6)."
......
[E] It was then that Jerusalem was destroyed. Meanwhile Rabban
Yohanan ben Zakkai sat and waited trembling, the way Eli had sat and
waited; as it is said, "Lo, Eli sat upon his seat by the wayside watching,
for his heart trembled for the ark of God" [1 Sam 4:13]. When Rabban
Yohanan ben Zakkai heard that Jerusalem was destroyed and the temple
was up in flames, he tore his clothing and his disciples tore their clothing,
and they wept, crying aloud and mourning.[6]

This late collection, The Fathers according to Rabbi Nathan, which
has incorporated what can be presumed to be earlier traditions, narra-
tively depicts two seemingly contradictory reactions of Rabban Yohanan
ben Zakkai to the destruction of the Second Temple. The overall passage
is structured as a commentary on m. 'Avot 1.2 (section A), in which the
high priest Simon the Righteous (ca. 200 BCE) enumerates the three things
upon which the "world stands." Such a tripod suggests that if any one of
the legs were to be removed, the world would topple. When the statement
would have been made (or was imagined to have been made), the temple

---

6. Translation slightly modified from Goldin 1955, 32–37.

still functioned; when it was rabbinically commented upon, the temple service had long ceased to exist. The only way for the world to survive this loss would be for the remaining two legs to assume the burden formerly born by the now-missing leg, or for "(temple) service" (עבודה) to be reinterpreted as referring to other kinds of service/worship, services no longer requiring the temple with its sacrificial worship and continuing in its absence.

It is with respect to this very question of how to regard and respond to the temple's loss that our commentary appears to be contradictory. On the one hand, section B suggests that God prefers Torah study to sacrificial worship and that Torah teaching is accounted by God as a divinely sanctioned substitute for temple worship. In other words, the loss of temple worship could easily, and preferably, be replaced. On the other hand, section C insists at length (note that the quote above is an abbreviated citation) that the world depends on the temple service for its very maintenance and that it is God's most beloved form of worship.[7] Further, this contradiction is directly ascribed to Rabban Yohanan ben Zakkai himself, who thereby exemplifies two very different responses to the destruction of the temple. On the one hand (section D), he comforts his student, Rabbi Joshua (ben Hananyah), relying on a prophetic prooftext to prove that God prefers acts of lovingkindness to temple sacrifices. On the other hand, Yohanan ben Zakkai is portrayed (section E), again with the assistance of a scriptural prooftext, as being in a state of abject mourning for the destroyed temple, with no hint of possible consolation or substitution. There is no way to know which, if either, of these scenes represents the "actual" reaction of the great sage to the destruction of the temple—it would be futile to ask which picture better portrays the "historical" Yohanan ben Zakkai.

Of course, one might try to harmonize the two representations of Yohanan ben Zakkai, suggesting that perhaps they represent different responses at different times or under different circumstances, for example, one to a student and one while alone. However, the fact that the same contradictory expressions are directly juxtaposed by the anonymous anthologizer and independently of Yohanan ben Zakkai (sections B and C), with each providing scriptural warrants, suggests that the inclusion of seemingly

---

7. For a similar, but less dramatic, redactional juxtaposition of seemingly contradictory views of Temple worship as being both lost but replaced, and continually present and important, see *Sipre Deut* 41 (ed. Finkelstein, 87–88) and discussion in Fraade 1991, 89–92, 241 n. 81.

opposite responses sheds less light on the "historical" Yohanan ben Zakkai than on the composite nature of the redacted text, whose reader/auditor would encounter therein two very different emotional perspectives on the destruction of the temple. These cannot be reductively harmonized without distorting the redacted text as a whole: as it stands, the destruction of the temple represents a rupture of a fundamental, irreparable nature, calling for acts of mourning; *and also*, the destruction of the temple is a loss for which divinely *preferred* substitutes (Torah study, acts of lovingkindness, prayer) are readily available, thereby calling for compensatory rehabilitation. Was the editor simply unable to choose between these options, or did "he" not choose between them because they are both "true," even though in sharp dialectical tension with one another? These are not two versions of a single historical event, between which *we* must choose which to remember or which *we* need to condense into a single synoptic narrative. They represent two recognizable and understandable but irreconcilable ways of re-presenting and responding to the *loss of past* and a *past of loss*. To quote Barry Schwartz's introduction to the present volume, "the 'meaning' of the message is not in any single one of its versions, but in all of them taken together" (p. 13 above).

As much as works of collective memory might seek to be socially unifying, they also can serve to divide a larger society into social subsets that seek to respond to common loss in divisively contested manners, as is further illustrated by the following passage from the Tosefta.

[11] משחרב הבית האחרון[8] רבו פרושין בישראל שלא היו אוכלין בשר ולא שותין יין. ניטפל להן ר' יהושע. אמ' להן, «בניי, מפני מה אין אתם אוכלין בשר?» אמרו לו, «נאכל בשר שבכל יום היה תמיד קרב לגבי מזבח ועכשיו בטל?» אמ' להן, «לא נאכל. ומפני מה אין אתם שותין יין?» אמרו לו, «יין נשתה שבכל יום היה מתנסך על גבי המזבח ועכשיו בטל?» אמ' להם, «לא נשתה.» אמ' להם, «אם כן לחם לא נאכל שממנו היו מביאין שתי הלחם ולחם הפנים. מים לא נשתה שמהן היו מנסכין מים בחג. תאנים וענבים לא נאכל שמהם היו מביאין בכורים בעצרת.» שתקו.

[12] אמ' להם, «בניי, להתאבל יותר מדיי אי איפשר ושלא להתאבל אי איפשר. אלא כך אמרו חכמים: סד אדם את ביתו בסיד ומשייר דבר מועט זכר לירושלם.»

[13] עושה אדם צרכי סעודה ומשייר דבר מועט, זכר לירושלם.

---

8. The Erfurt manuscript reads בית המקדש ("temple").

[14] עושה אשה תכשיטין ומשיירת דבר מועט, זכר לירושלם שנ' «אם
אשכחך ירושלם תשכח ימיני תדבק לשוני לחכי אם לא אזכרכי» (תהלים
קל"ז ה'-ו) וגו'.

[15] וכל המתאבלים עליה בעולם הזה שמחים עמה לעולם הבא שנ'
«שמחו את ירושלם וגילו בה כל אוהביה» (ישעיה צ"ו י) וגו'.

(t. Soṭ. 15.11–15; ed. Lieberman 1973, 243–44)[9]

[11] After the last temple was destroyed, abstainers [pĕrûšîn] became
many in Israel, who would not eat meat or drink wine. R. Joshua engaged
with them, saying to them, "My children, on what account do you not eat
meat?" They said to him, "Shall we eat meat, for every day a continual
burnt offering [of meat] was offered on the altar, and now it is no more?"
He said to them, "Then let us not eat it. And then why are you not drinking wine?" They said to him, "Shall we drink wine, for every day wine
was poured out as a drink offering on the altar, and now it is no more?"
He said to them, "Then let us not drink it." He said to them, "But if so, we
also should not eat bread, for from it did they bring the two loaves and
the showbread. We also should not drink water, for they did pour out a
water offering on the Festival. We also should not eat figs and grapes, for
they would bring them as firstfruits on the festival of Aseret [Shabu'ot]."
They fell silent.

[12] He said to them, "My children, to mourn too much is not possible
and not to mourn is not possible. But thus have the sages said: A man
puts on plaster on his house but leaves open a small area, as a memorial
[זכר] to Jerusalem.

[13] "A man prepares what is needed for a meal but leaves out some small
things, as a memorial to Jerusalem.

[14] "A woman prepares her ornaments but leaves out some small thing,
as a memorial to Jerusalem, since it is said, 'If I forget you, O Jerusalem,
let my right hand wither! Let my tongue cleave to the roof of my mouth, if
I do not remember you, if I do not set Jerusalem above my highest joy!'"
(Ps 137:5–6)

[15] And whoever mourns for her in this world will rejoice with her in
the world to come, as it is said, "Rejoice with Jerusalem and be glad for

9. See t. B. Bat. 2.17; t. Ta'an. 3.14; b. B. Bat. 60b; b. Ta'an. 30b; Midr. Pss. 137:6. See
also Lieberman 1973, 772–74.

her, all you who love her; rejoice with her in joy, all you who mourn over her." [Isa 66:10][10]

Here again, for purposes of the present discussion, the question of the historicity of the portrayed dialogue between the "abstainers" (see Fraade 1988, 269–72) and Rabbi Joshua ben Hananyah is immaterial. Viewed as an artifact of memory, the toseftan passage reflects two approaches to collective loss and its commemoration: one of ongoing self-denial, one of symbolic omission. The dietary self-denials of the "abstainers" are explained as acts of sympathy (mourning) for the loss of the temple, the daily rituals of which prominently featured meat and wine. According to this view, it would be inappropriate to derive pleasure from foods that are associated with the destroyed temple and its lost rituals. Rabbi Joshua replies with a *reductio ad absurdum*, arguing that such thinking would lead to self-denial of virtually all types of food and drink, and seeks a middle ground between excessive mourning and no mourning at all, a universal dilemma (see Sir 38:16–23). This middle ground is reached by invoking three rabbinic responses that are less abstinent than symbolic, common social practices in which something small but noticeable is "left out" as a "memorial/reminder of Jerusalem." The spatial loss of the holy temple is mirrored, as it were, in the seemingly mundane spaces left in the plaster of one's house, the arrangement of one's meal, and the ornamentation of one's self (or one's wife).

Whereas the position of the "abstainers" might be assumed to reflect the supererogatory practices of a separatist group (*pĕrûšîn*) rather than Jewish society overall,[11] the prescriptions of the sages (phrased as the recommended practices for any "man" or "woman") would have been intended for wide social adoption. These "memorials/reminders of Jerusalem" would have a chance of long-lasting and broadly collective concrete practice. Such symbolic but tangible and visible practices would ensure long-lasting *collective* memory of Jerusalem (and its temple), thereby fulfilling the evocative words of the psalmist, "If I forget you, O Jerusalem...."

---

10. Translation slightly modified from Neusner 1979, 209. Note that Neusner fails to translate the latter half of the first sentence in 15.12.

11. This is stated explicitly in the preceding section of the Tosefta (15.10; ed. Lieberman, 243): אמ' ר' ישמעאל: מיום שחרב בית המקדש דין הוא שלא לאכל בשר ושלא לשתות יין. אלא שאין בית דין גוזרין על הצבור דברים שאין יכולין לעמוד בהן ("Said R. Ishmael, 'From the day on which the Temple was destroyed, it would have been reasonable not to eat meat and not to drink wine. But a court does not make a decree for the community concerning things which the community simply cannot bear'" [trans. Neusner 1979, 208]).

Lest, however, we think of the memory of Jerusalem as only past-directed and present-enacted, the passage ends with a midrashic reading of Isa 66:10 that evokes the fulfillment and completion of present mourning for past loss in future (eschatological) rejoicing.

Conclusion: Memory, Ritual, and History

The seemingly contradictory, but more likely dialectical, ways that rabbinic textual and ritual collective memory re-presents the loss of the temple might be compared to the ways that private individuals respond to the loss of a loved one: we grieve as if nothing can fill the void, even as we learn to compensate through substitution for our loss; we seek to remain connected to and mournful of a loved one whose loss cannot be restored, even as we draw meaning from his or her life and its loss that enables us to move forward with our own lives. Social memory, especially its textualization and ritualization as commemoration, facilitates both, continually connecting to a shared past, whether glorious or tragic, which we can never fully retrieve and to which there is no return, while at the same time enabling us to transcend (but not efface) the loss of past so as to face and embrace the future through constant reengagement with a past of loss. The writing of history, whether sacred or critical, enables us to experience the very same "dialectic of alternity" between experiencing time as both continuity and rupture, זכר למקדש—the recalling of a receding holiness/wholeness that is ever yet before us as we pursue both completion and restoration.

The acknowledged difficulties of reconstructing a coherent and continuous historical narrative from the works of collective memory that we have examined renders those works of memory no less historical in their own rights as textual/social practices of profound historical response.

Works Cited

Cohn, Naftali S. 2012. *The Memory of the Temple and the Making of the Rabbis*. Divinations: Rereading Late Ancient Religion. Philadelphia: University of Pennsylvanian Press.

Eliav, Yaron Z. 2005. *God's Mountain: The Temple Mount in Time, Place, and Memory*. Baltimore: Johns Hopkins University Press.

Fine, Steven. 1997. *This Holy Place: On the Sanctity of the Synagogue During the Greco-Roman Period*. Notre Dame, IN: Notre Dame University Press.

Finkelstein, Louis. 1969. *Sifre on Deuteronomy*. New York: Jewish Theological Seminary of America.

Fraade, Steven D. 1988. "Ascetical Aspects of Ancient Judaism." Pages 253–88 in *Jewish Spirituality: From the Bible through the Middle Ages*. Edited by Arthur Green. World Spirituality 13. New York: Crossroad.

———. 1991. *From Tradition to Commentary: Torah and Its Interpretation in the Midrash Sifre to Deuteronomy*. Jewish Hermeneutics, Mysticism, and Religion Series. Albany: State University of New York Press.

———. 2007. "Rabbinic Polysemy and Pluralism Revisited: Between Praxis and Thematization." *AJS Review* 31:1–40.

———. 2009. "The Temple as a Marker of Jewish Identity before and after 70 CE: The Role of the Holy Vessels in Rabbinic Memory and Imagination." Pages 237–65 in *Jewish Identities in Antiquity: Studies in Memory of Menahem Stern*. Edited by Lee I. Levine and Daniel R. Schwartz. TSAJ 130. Tübingen: Mohr Siebeck, 2009.

———. 2011. "Anonymity and Redaction in Legal Midrash: A Preliminary Probe." Pages 9–29 in *Malekhet Maḥshevet: Studies in the Redaction and Development of Talmudic Literature*. Edited by Aaron Amit and Aharon Shemesh. Ramat-Gan: Bar-Ilan University Press.

Goldin, Judah, trans. 1955. *The Fathers according to Rabbi Nathan*. New Haven: Yale University Press.

Hachlili, Rachel. 2001. *The Menorah: The Ancient Seven-Armed Candelabrum: Origin, Form and Significance*. JSJSup 68. Leiden: Brill.

Kister, Menahem. 1998. "Legends of the Destruction of the Second Temple in Avot De-Rabbi Nathan" [Hebrew]. *Tarbiz* 67:483–529.

Lieberman, Saul. 1973. *Tosefta Ki-Fshuṭaḥ: A Comprehensive Commentary on the Tosefta, Part 8: Order Nashim* [Hebrew]. New York: Jewish Theological Seminary of America.

Naeh, Shlomo. 2001. "עשה לבך חדרי חדרים: עיון נוסף בדברי חז"ל על המחלוקת." Pages 851–75 in *Renewing Jewish Commitment: The Work and Thought of David Hartman*. Edited by A. Sagi and Z. Zohar. Tel-Aviv: Hakibbutz Hameuchad.

———. 2005. "אומנות הזיכרון: מבנים של זיכרון ותבניות של טכסט בספרות חז"ל." Pages 543–89 in *Meḥqerei Talmud III: Talmudic Studies Dedicated to the Memory of Professor Ephraim E. Urbach*. Edited by Yaakov Sussmann and David Rosenthal. Jerusalem: Magnes.

Neusner, Jacob. 1970. *Development of a Legend; Studies on the Traditions concerning Yohanan ben Zakkai*. StPB 16. Leiden: Brill.

———. 1979. *The Tosefta Translated from the Hebrew, Third Division, Nashim (The Order of Women)*. New York: Ktav.

———. 1988. *The Mishnah: A New Translation*. New Haven: Yale University Press.

Weiss, Isaac Hirsch. 1862. *Sifra*. Vienna: Shlosberg.

PART 2
REMEMBERING IN EMERGING CHRISTIANITY

The Memory–Tradition Nexus in the Synoptic Tradition: Memory, Media, and Symbolic Representation[*]

Alan Kirk

Tradition and memory are distinct yet somehow cognate phenomena, and Synoptic scholarship going back to the form critics has struggled with how properly to construe their relationship. The work of Barry Schwartz and Jan Assmann on social and cultural aspects of memory, and of experimental psychologists on its cognitive aspects, provides a framework for reconceptualizing and potentially resolving the vexed problem of the memory–tradition nexus. But the exploitation of memory research in Gospels scholarship has been scattershot and fragmentary, often ill-informed or selectively employed in special pleading. In English-language scholarship the discussion seems to have settled out into stagnating and, in my view, irrelevant disputes over the reliability of eyewitness recollection. Reading through current research on the topic, one often finds only perfunctory attention given to the core problem of where and how memory and tradition intersect and, similarly, a curious tendency to look at memory in complete isolation from the complex media phenomenon of tradition.

To a significant extent, this impasse reflects the fact that certain assumptions the form critics made about the tradition–memory nexus are still taken for granted. After clarifying the older form-critical model, this essay will review recent contributions to the debate from Richard Bauckham, Rob McIver, Alexander Wedderburn, Dale Allison, Samuel Byrskog, James Dunn, and Markus Bockmuehl. I will argue that the conceptual models advanced in these newer studies still do not deal satisfactorily, or in some cases not fully, with the problem of the *tension* and *nexus* between memory and tradition. The question then arises of how the memory–tradition relationship might be conceived with greater precision. Drawing upon a number of authorities, and with particular reference to Barry Schwartz's

* I am grateful to Samuel Byrskog, Zeba Crook, Chris Keith, Tom Thatcher, and Ritva Williams, all of whom read earlier drafts of this essay and provided invaluable critical feedback.

"Collective Forgetting and the Symbolic Power of Oneness: The Strange Apotheosis of Rosa Parks" (2009), I will argue that tradition is a product of cultural practices of *commemoration*; more precisely, that tradition is a media-based artifact that not only emerges but is also transmitted at the interface of the cognitive, social, and cultural operations of memory. While the discussion will move mostly at the theoretical level, keeping in view tradition as a cultural phenomenon, I will conclude by indicating lines of application to the Synoptic tradition.

TRADITION AND MEMORY IN FORM CRITICISM

The widespread (if not uncontested) institutional confidence the classical form-critical account of the Synoptic tradition enjoyed in the middle decades of the twentieth century eventually gave way to increasing uncertainty. However, with no consensus forming around any alternative approach, important aspects of the form-critical model have continued to supply the default premises for the great analytical enterprises for which a working theory for the historical development of the early Jesus tradition is indispensable: historical Jesus research, Synoptic source and redaction criticism, tradition histories, and the like.

The form-critical account was predicated on a strong distinction between "memory" and "tradition." In this scheme, memory was peripheral to the tradition, and for all practical purposes the form critics and their followers eliminated memory as a factor in the history of the tradition. For the most part, by "memory" they understood the individual faculty of personal recollection, or "reminiscence." While memory traces of this sort lay at the origins of the tradition, they were a residuum, mostly inert with respect to developments in the tradition itself. Though far from denying continuity between history and developments in the tradition (in fact, affirming it), Rudolf Bultmann located the sources of the tradition in recurrent settings in the life of the early Christian communities. Correlating form to social function, and holding that the eschatological communities lacked a constitutive orientation to the past, Bultmann inferred that contemporary social and theological interests were the leading factors generating the tradition, the expansion of which was also driven by innate laws of development and *religionsgeschichtliche* forces (see Bultmann 1975, 37–39).[2] The gospel

---

2. According to Amos Wilder, the "naïve eschatological immediacy" of primitive Christianity "exclude[s] conscious concern with mnemonics, catechetical purpose

tradition was a bifurcated entity: a growing mass of tradition coming to overlay diminishing residues of memory.

Dennis Nineham expressed this approach with particular clarity in a two-part article published in 1958 and 1960. For Nineham, memory and tradition are distinct, even incommensurable, entities. He associates memory with individual eyewitness testimony such as might be given in court and thus characterizes it as "knowledge of the particular, inclusion of the merely memorable, as opposed to the edifying" and as possessing "exact biographical and topographical precision and the like" (Nineham 1958, 13). These traits are conspicuous by their absence from the Synoptic tradition, which is formal, stereotyped, restrained in descriptive detail, edifying, and thus, Nineham concludes, the product not of memory but "the impersonal needs and forces of the community" (1958, 13). Nineham acknowledges that some early interface with memory was likely; this would account for traces in the tradition of some authentic recollections of Jesus. But since this "initial stage" the tradition has followed an autonomous course of development, for otherwise individual eyewitness testimony with its distinguishing properties should be visible within it as foreign matter; indeed, "if the Gospel material derives from *two very different types of source* we should expect it to show signs of its *double origin*" (Nineham 1958, 17, emphasis added). As Nineham's comments illustrate, form-critical analysis disconnected memory from the developing tradition. Compensating for the weak agency accorded to memory—its inert, trace-like existence and marginalization vis-à-vis other forces acting within and upon the tradition—were creative communities and the large-scale incorporation of inauthentic materials into the tradition.

The categories "authentic" and "inauthentic" are entailed by the form-critical model, according to which the tradition is an admixture of mutually alien elements, a dualism expressed with particular sharpness in Funk and Hoover's manichaean characterization of "the authentic words of Jesus" as "traces that cry out for recognition and liberation from the firm grip of those whose faith overpowered their memories" (Funk and Hoover 1993, 4). Funk and Hoover conceive memory as individual eyewitness recollection such as might be given in court or passed along chains of individuals in the form of "hearsay evidence." Since the standard against which eyewitness testimony is measured is its exactness of correspondence to original occur-

---

or halakic procedure" and "require[s] radical disallowance of existing culture and its forms" (1962, 8, 13).

rences, and since eyewitness testimony is demonstrably inefficient in this regard (a problem exacerbated by second-hand transmission), Funk and Hoover's estimation of the quality of the memory element of the tradition is not high. As with eyewitness testimony in court, the tradition must therefore be filtered through forensic "rules of evidence" to identify materials useful for historical reconstruction (Funk and Hoover 1993, 16).[3] The corollary mode in which they regard memory affecting the history of the tradition is likewise in a weak retentive capacity: the probability of authenticity will be higher for *short* sayings and stories (Funk and Hoover 1993, 289).

In reflecting upon these approaches influenced by form criticism (see also below on Wedderburn and Allison), it is noteworthy that, while memory is regarded as a residual ingredient in the tradition, when it comes to actual analysis memory is not treated as ontologically different from the tradition. Rather, what is "memory" in the tradition is identified over against fabricated material through application of criteria of historical criticism. The merits of the historiographical method aside, this indicates that the form-critical model is certainly deficient as an account of the memory-tradition nexus and of how memory is mediated in the tradition.

It is important to emphasize that major features of form criticism are of enduring significance. The form critics—and Bultmann in particular—understood that the history of the tradition is inseparable from the historical situatedness of the tradent communities—in other words, that present realities affect appropriations of the past. The form critics thereby anticipated key aspects of social and cultural memory analysis. In giving attention to recurring forms, they recognized that tradition is a media-based entity.[4] In the same vein, they were impressed by and sought to account for the autonomy of the tradition. But the form critics did not have an adequate working conception of memory, and so looked elsewhere for the forces driving the tradition's formation and development.

---

3. Bart Ehrman also construes memory in its relation to the tradition on the model of individual recollection that becomes increasingly corrupt as the multiple links in its second-hand transmission down serial chains of individuals increase in distance from the original eyewitness versions of stories. Thus he likens the transmission of the tradition to the children's game "Telephone" (Ehrman 1999, 51–52; 2004, 48–53).

4. On this point see Ruben Zimmermann: "Erinnerung vollzieht sich immer medial, nicht nur sprachgebunden, sondern auch formgebunden, was die alte formgeschichtliche Forschung jenseits ihrer falschen Schlussfolgerungen zur Recht erkannte" ["The act of remembering is always mediated, not only by language but also by form—something that classical form-criticism despite its faulty inferences correctly recognized"] (2008, 104; 2010, 137–38, 143).

The Memory–Tradition Nexus in Recent Scholarship

The problem of memory and the Synoptic tradition has received renewed attention in recent New Testament scholarship. A review of several leading voices in the discussion will analyze how each conceives the tradition–memory nexus.

Richard Bauckham

Richard Bauckham inverts the form-critical configuration of memory and tradition, assigning the dominant role to eyewitness memory: the agents in the formation and transmission of the Synoptic tradition were the eyewitnesses. Moreover, the forms of the Synoptic tradition can be understood as immediate formations of eyewitness memory, for scientific research shows that memory formation occurs through cognitive activities of selection, condensation, narrative scripting, and schematic representation in culturally appropriate forms (Bauckham 2006, 331–55).[5] To get around the difficulty that the phenomenological profile of eyewitness recollection actually corresponds poorly to the profile of the Jesus tradition, Bauckham proposes that the eyewitnesses further refined their memory products into "manageable units of tradition that could be passed on to others"—in other words, the eyewitnesses were also the ones who shaped the tradition (2006, 343). Its subsequent transmission also occurred under their formal control (2006, 228–29, 240, 314; 2008, 231).

Bauckham resists, as an unnecessary concession to form criticism, giving vaguely conceived communities any significant role in the formation of the tradition beyond receiving it from the eyewitnesses. But he strains to contain the tradition within these eyewitness boundaries. The schemata and narrative scripts used in the cognitive formation of memory are culturally available communicative genres, and the subsuming of shared memory in these forms occurs through social rehearsal. Though Bauckham argues that these factors are only "the necessarily social context of an individual's remembering" (2006, 337),[6] their effect is the formation of a body of publicly available tradition untethered from the individual memory of any specific eyewitness. This would draw the tradition into the

---

5. Bauckham justly complains that the critical response to his book overlooked this element of his argument (2008, 252).

6. His claim is belied by the fact that he must posit an institutionalized role for the Twelve in the formation and transmission of the tradition.

ambit of social and cultural memory forces. To escape this predicament, Bauckham asserts the autonomy of individual "recollective" memory over against "collective" memory and proceeds to contend that the formal role accorded the eyewitnesses in primitive Christianity ensured the privileging of individual eyewitness memory in the tradition and therefore the tradition's isolation from social memory forces (2006, 33–34, 315–18). This buffers the tradition from external forces in the crucial first phase of its formulation and transmission. But having reduced the tradition so completely to the eyewitness testimony of a limited circle of individuals, Bauckham has difficulty giving a satisfactory explanation of the patterns of variation and agreement in the Synoptic tradition. The problem is that the eyewitness testimony paradigm is a model of static memory transmission that by definition puts the premium on exactness of correspondence with experienced events. This is difficult to square with the evident dynamism of the tradition. The causes of variation that Bauckham proposes accord with his individualistic, stasis model for the tradition: translation variants; different original versions of sayings; formulations by different eyewitnesses; interpretative interventions by eyewitnesses; and necessary literary modifications by the Evangelists (2006, 285–87; 2008, 229–40).[7]

The difficulties for this account continue to mount. In Bauckham's scenario the tradition is directly formulated by eyewitnesses, indeed, precipitated virtually right out of eyewitness memory, but as a thereby externalized artifact it exists distinct from eyewitness memory, and as such it is susceptible of autonomous development. Hence he must bring the transmission of the tradition under the external, institutionalized control of eyewitness memory until it makes its way into the written Gospels. The tradition is the direct product of eyewitness memory, transmitted "*as the eyewitnesses' testimony*" (2006, 293, emphasis original), reaching the Evangelists, therefore, "not [as] oral tradition but eyewitness testimony" (2006, 8). But under the influence of the Papias fragment, Bauckham then depicts the Evangelists treating their materials as "tradition," construed as an entity distinct from and inferior to personal eyewitness memory, for like Papias they seek out direct eyewitness verification of their received traditions, preferring the voice of living eyewitnesses over the received tradition (2006, 19–34, 292).

---

7. Bauckham appeals here to the Greek historians' practice of varying the wording of their sources (2006, 237), but the historians strove for a homogeneous stylistic variation quite unlike the heterogeneous Synoptic patterns.

This incoherent account of the tradition is mirrored in Bauckham's attribution of conflicting procedures to the Evangelists. On the one hand they are tradents who consolidate a tradition formed and transmitted by eyewitnesses, adjusting it skillfully to narrative contexts. On the other they are oral historians who prefer the living voice of eyewitness memory over mere tradition, who seek out "named informants," going "either to eyewitnesses or to the most reliable sources that had direct personal links with the eyewitnesses" and for whom "[c]ollective tradition as such would not have been their preferred source" (2006, 34; see also 479). To square this circle, Bauckham adduces the hypothesis that in the named individuals in the tradition the Evangelists obliquely identify their eyewitness sources. Ironically, he ends up in the company of Funk and Hoover, depreciating a tradition transmitted through a "chain of informants" and depicting the Evangelists as Jesus-questers in the Funk and Hoover mold, "cross-examin[ing] their witnesses in a way somewhat similar to legal practice in a court" (2006, 479).

Rob McIver

Drawing upon numerous empirical psychological studies, McIver mounts a robust defense of the reliability of eyewitness testimony. But to an even greater extent than Bauckham, he tries to associate characteristic features of the Synoptic tradition directly with the phenomenological profile of individual memory as the latter is described in the experimental studies he cites. This leads him, like Nineham, to look through the tradition for survivals and outcroppings of personal episodic memory (McIver 2011, 123). The results are meager (for all practical purposes the same as Nineham's), and McIver ends up making the modest claim that the Synoptic materials are "consistent with eyewitness accounts," though they "are not presently formulated as direct eyewitness reports" (130, 147). He therefore locates the contribution of eyewitness memory at the initial formation of the tradition and falls back, like Bauckham, on the expedient that eyewitness memory, institutionalized in the Twelve, acted as an external control on the formation and transmission of the tradition. Nevertheless, he continues to experiment with superimposing the functional profile of individual recollection upon the Synoptic tradition. He weighs the effects on the transmission of the tradition of the "forgetting curve" for earlier-acquired but seldom-rehearsed knowledge (for example, of a foreign language studied in high school), and he argues that much Synoptic variation arises from memory's experimentally verified inefficiency in the recollection of details. Inconsistencies such as whether there were one or two Gerasene demoniacs or one or two blind men outside Jericho "are precisely the type of variations one might expect of various eyewitness reports of the same event" (2011, 156).[8]

As noted, McIver acknowledges that the phenomenological profiles of eyewitness recollection and the Synoptic tradition actually do not match up very well, but further questions may be raised about the relevance of much of the experimental research on individual recollection that he adduces. As Schwartz observes in his introduction to the present collection, most of these psychological studies feature randomly selected, isolated subjects recollecting unrehearsed information of no or, at best, transitory significance to their lives. This is hardly analogous to commemorative practices in a community. Research on the cognitive operations of memory has much to contribute to our understanding of the formation and transmission of tradition, but the complex media profile and cultural history of tradition cannot be transposed onto graphs of individual memory functionality. This cuts both ways, of course. It is not uncommon for critics more skeptical of the tradition also to make simple correlations between eyewitness testimony (emphasizing its limitations) and the tradition.[9]

ALEXANDER WEDDERBURN AND DALE ALLISON

Alexander Wedderburn and Dale Allison's interest is in assessing the significance of memory research for work on the historical Jesus. Both understand their task, as critical historians, as being to distinguish in the tradition a body of secure historical facts about Jesus, and they come at the memory–tradition problematic from that angle.

For Wedderburn, it is a matter of sound historical method that the materials most useful for historical reconstruction are the recollections of

---

8. Armin D. Baum also proposes that the experimentally verified error range in reproduction of information in individual recollection helps explain Synoptic patterns of variation (2008, 268–69). But Baum's interest is not the eyewitness testimony–tradition problematic but rather memory as the transmission and enactment medium for oral tradition and how this might contribute to a solution to the Synoptic problem.

9. Judith Redman, for example, in her critique of Bauckham associates features of the variation profile of the Synoptic tradition directly with "the eyewitness effect," that is, with experimentally documented inefficiencies of eyewitness recollection (2010, 193 et passim).

eyewitnesses. Eyewitnesses' memories of Jesus, however, were distorted, owing to the inefficiency and situational contingency of individual recollection (Wedderburn 2010, 217). Memory, insofar as it is of use for historical reconstruction, equates to this personal episodic memory, and is thereby inherently unique to the individual eyewitnesses. The wider circles of believers to whom the latter recounted their memories therefore cannot truly be said to be "remembering" the events of Jesus' life (2010, 200–204). "[W]hat they remember," Wedderburn states, "are no longer the events of Jesus' life but the recitation of traditions about them" (2010, 201).[10] Memory and tradition thus are separate in kind and sequence: the existence of the tradition depends upon memory, but as a secondary effect. Tradition is successor to memory; it appears when living memory is not extant owing to the absence or death of eyewitnesses. Tradition roughly corresponds to the derivative memories of the wider circles of believers, those who received their accounts second-hand from the eyewitnesses (2010, 223).[11] It certainly retains an imprint left by the eyewitnesses' memories, but it is susceptible to all the formative, post-Easter interests at work in the communities. Wedderburn does not explain how the perceptible media forms of the tradition emerged from these derivative memories—perhaps because, in his view, what is relevant for a critical history is the testimony of eyewitness informants, traces of which can be tentatively recovered through applying criteria of historical criticism to the tradition. But the same analytical gap appears in the first part of his account as well: he does not consider the question of how the personal memories of eyewitnesses were *mediated*.

Allison's concern is the precision with which the deliverances of memory correspond to original occurrences. To this end, he has immersed himself in scientific research on memory but, like McIver, predominantly

---

10. This corresponds to the distinction cognitive psychologists draw between personal episodic memory (personally experienced) and semantic (acquired) memory. But Wedderburn overdraws the distinction. Gerald Echterhoff notes that "semantische und episodische Gedächtnisleistungen keineswegs völlig unabhängig voneinander sind, sondern ebenfalls auf vielfältige Weise miteinander interagieren" ["semantic and episodic memory, far from functioning independently of each other, actually interact with one another in many ways"] (2004, 72). Similarly David Manier and William Hirst: "Many semantic memories begin as episodic memories. But the episodic memory often fades, leaving behind only the semantic memory of what was learned" (2010, 254).

11. "A later generation or a wider circle might have no personal memories of Jesus themselves and be wholly dependent on what others had imparted to them; here to speak of 'Jesus traditions' may be more fitting" (Wedderburn 2010, 200).

in the experimental studies on individual recollection. This has a similarly warping effect upon his view of the relationship between memory and tradition, an effect connected, moreover, with his adoption of widespread but inadequately examined assumptions about how memory is mediated in tradition. Because experimental studies show that individual memory is inefficient when it comes to exactness of recall over intervals, Allison's characterization of memory in the Synoptic tradition has a strikingly gloomy tone, with frequent references to "the sins of memory" and "the sins of ecclesiastical recall" (e.g., Allison 2010, 23, 27, 164). Like McIver, Allison correlates the inefficiencies of individual recollection directly to patterns of variation in the Synoptic tradition: discrepancies in the particulars of the equipment instructions to the disciples, for example, are of the sort that occur in different eyewitness reports of an event (Allison 2010, 12–13). In his view, the tradition likely had its beginnings in eyewitnesses recalling their memories, but "those memories must have been subject to all the failures and biases that modern science has so helpfully if disturbingly exposed" (2010, 30). Yet Allison offers no account of how the forms of the tradition emerged from these activities of recollection; he simply takes over the form-critical model, according to which reminiscences are present in the tradition like traces of an alien substance.[12]

Samuel Byrskog

Samuel Byrskog seeks to correct form criticism's one-sidedly homeostatic, collectivist conception of the tradition, replacing it instead with an account grounded in verifiable mnemonic practices of the ancient world, one that moreover restores to individual remembering its essential place within social processes of memory.[13] In this connection, he analyzes Gos-

---

12. E.g.: "recollections must be mixed with much else" (Allison 2010, 10); "reminiscence lies within a text" (436); "previous chapters have mined the Jesus tradition for memory" (435). The historiography of Jesus research, which is grounded in form-critical assumptions about the tradition, classifies these traces as the "authentic" elements of the tradition. Allison's scientifically informed knowledge of the inefficiencies of individual recollection has affected his opinion of even these materials: "Even where the Gospels *preserve* memories, those memories cannot be miraculously pristine; rather, they must often be dim or muddled or just plain wrong" (2010, 9, emphasis added).

13. A "homeostatic" theory of tradition reduces, and thus allegorizes, the elements of a tradition at each moment in its history to contemporary community conditions (see Byrskog 2007, 11).

pel origins in the light of ancient oral history practices, taking additional cues from Paul Thompson's theoretical work on oral history (Byrskog 2000; see Thompson 2000). Oral history as practiced by ancient historians was a characteristic combination of *history* (investigation) and *narrative* (interpretation). This approach gives Byrskog leverage on the analogous problem of the interaction of past with present, of *history* with *story*, in the Synoptic tradition (Byrskog 2000, 44–45, 254–65; 2008a, 158). Consonant with oral history methods, ancient historians put a premium on eyewitness informants; accordingly, Byrskog argues that the testimony of eyewitness informants is a form of memory practice pertinent to the Synoptic tradition and the work of the Evangelists (2000, 18–28). Circles of Jesus' followers likely would have formed "a decisive body of eyewitnesses and informants, to be questioned and interrogated as the gospel tradition eventually took shape and developed" (2000, 69). But Byrskog judiciously rejects the positivist understanding of eyewitness recollection so pervasive in scholarship, namely, that it is direct factual recall (either more or less reliable or hopelessly flawed, depending on the critic). Rather, oral history research indicates that eyewitness memory and oral tradition share important features: the informants' remembering of Jesus was subjectively filtered; it was a reconfiguring act of interpretation by persons living in the existential tension of past with present; it was their *story* proclaimed to others (2000, 28, 106–7, 254–55; 2004, 463; 2008a, 159; 2009b, 42–43; 2012, 19).

Of particular interest here is Byrskog's account of how and where the oral histories of eyewitnesses, and the work of the Evangelists as oral historians, intersect with the tradition—its origins and transmission. On this point Byrskog leaves an explanatory gap, albeit a small one, between oral histories on the one hand and the formation and transmission of tradition on the other—between ancient historiographical, authorial practices and practices associated with cultivation of tradition, more often than not by anonymous tradents (the Gospel writers being a case in point). While taking the view that eyewitness oral histories share important properties with oral tradition, on occasion Byrskog speaks as though eyewitness memory and tradition have different modes of transmission: on the one hand, oral histories of eyewitnesses transmitted to other individuals on the pattern of Peter to Mark, Polycarp to Irenaeus; on the other hand, communally rehearsed tradition (2000, 106, 288; 2004, 466–67). Oral history transmission, he suggests, is living and interpretive, whereas tradition is the preserve of official tradents whose activity, though not excluding interpretive work, is the faithful transmission of materials in which the "visions and experiences of the eyewitnesses have ... become stylized into fixed patterns of tradition" (2000, 157; see also 1994).

Byrskog depicts the Evangelists as oral historians who in accordance with ancient practices seek out material from informant testimony and—where access to this living memory fails—from tradition (Byrskog 2000, 267–74, 288).[14] Living memory is the preferred channel, for eyewitness voices are susceptible of being buried in traditioning processes, of being heard "only vaguely and indirectly" in the tradition (2000, 267–68, 272). But Byrskog also argues unequivocally that tradition *mediates* memory. In the passion narrative "[o]ral history had been narrativized already in the tradition; it was mediated to the evangelist through a narrating text" (2000, 272). Oral tradition is the communications medium for memory; "[t]he observation of an eyewitness becomes, in a sense, tradition as soon as it is communicated from one person to another" (2009b, 42). In the Markan *chreia* genre one finds the narrativizing impulse of memory fine-tuned for performance and transmission (2010, 17–20; 2009b, 50). The convergence of memory and tradition is already entailed in the teacher-disciple relationship in the discipleship circle (2010, 5; 2011, 1477–78). Byrskog's recent essays on the *Sitz im Leben* construe the tradition itself as the primary mnemonic entity and its cultivation as a memory event, a "negotiation between the two temporal horizons" of past and present (2006, 323, 335–36; 2007, 22; 2008b, 43–44). The transmission of tradition is not a matter of "passive reproduction and copying" but of "oral and re-oralized moments of remembrance" (2012, 21). Correspondingly, the tradents themselves are the active memory agents.

JAMES DUNN

James Dunn posits a direct causal connection between memory and tradition but prescinds from any detailed analysis of this nexus.[15] Without an account of the transformation of shared memories into the media of the tradition, Dunn ends up coupling memory and tradition together through

---

14. Byrskog argues that Papias's procedures, including Papias's preference for the "living voice," are relevant for understanding the work of the Evangelists.

15. "That, for me, was self-evidently how the memories of the first disciples worked. I did not see a need to provide a theoretical model of how memory works.... The synoptic tradition was for me ... the evidence and proof of how the first disciples' memories worked" (Dunn 2010, 291).

vague terms such as "impact" and "impression": "the impacting word or event *became* the tradition of that word or event" (Dunn 2003, 239, emphasis original); "that *impact-expressed-in-verbal-formulation* was itself the beginning of the Jesus tradition" (2003, 883, emphasis original); from the "put[ting] of memories into words" during gatherings of the disciples, "the oral tradition ... would thus begin to take shape" (2011, 198). One gathers that Dunn conceives tradition as verbal formulations generated by the direct "imprint," or "impression," of memory, for its part a medium that bears the "impression" of the "impact" made by Jesus on individual disciples (2008, 290). Variation in the tradition is partly traceable to differential "impacts" of Jesus on different disciples (2007, 191; 2011, 198).

Dunn rejects the positivistic notion that in isolating memories in the tradition one is in touch with a historical reality unfiltered by perception and interpretation; in fact, he uses the term "impact" in recognition of reception factors in remembering (2003, 130–33). But as critics have noted, his model does not adequately account for the complexity of the relationship between the empirical realities and memory, on the one hand, or between memory and tradition, on the other (Byrskog 2004, 462–63; Häfner 2007, 107). The notion of memory as a static entity—an imprint— carries into Dunn's tendency to locate the "remembering" of Jesus in the stable, "core" elements of a tradition and, conversely, to regard its variant elements (those not owing to differential originating "impacts" or to plural original formulations) as embroidery, as superficial performance variants—"superficial" in the sense that they do not substantively impact the core of the tradition (Dunn 2003, 203, 233–34, 240, 246). Thus, while the form critics looked for authentic memory elements beneath layers of tradition, Dunn seeks the original form of the tradition by distinguishing stable from variant elements. It is therefore unsurprising that he regards social and cultural memory approaches, which see in patterns of Synoptic variation a manifestation of the present/past dialectic of memory, to be a "challenge" to his thesis (2007, 181).

To be sure, Dunn's reading in memory theory is perfunctory, and therefore his understanding of social and cultural memory is a "presentist" caricature, one that exaggerates the impact of the present upon conceptions of the past (2007, 180). Nevertheless, a line of analysis that takes memory as an active rather than static presence in the tradition cuts across Dunn's approach. Dunn concedes that memory forces of this sort are evident in the Gospel of Thomas, the Gospel of John, and to an extent the Gospel of Matthew. He therefore adopts Bauckham's strategy and argues ad hoc that the Synoptic tradition, at least at its formation and during the first two generations of its transmission, was insulated from these forces by countervailing constraints that "operated to maintain the impact and character of the original remembering of Jesus" (2007, 192). The irony is that Dunn's dismissal of social and cultural memory analysis prevents him from recognizing important ways that the tradition actually sustains vital connections to the past.

Markus Bockmuehl

Markus Bockmuehl associates memory with individual eyewitness recollection but gives particular weight to the phenomenon of the three-generation lifespan of "living memory." This span of living memory lasts about 150 years: it begins with the apostolic eyewitnesses and ends with the passing of the generation able to claim direct acquaintance with those who were disciples of the apostles. It equates to "an unbroken ... chain of *personal recollection* reaching back to the apostles themselves," and its corresponding mode of transmission is the passing of individual memories from master to disciple (Bockmuehl 2006, 184, emphasis original).

The generational memory framework Bockmuehl seizes upon here is significant, and its importance has been recognized in other cultural history inquiries (e.g., Assmann 1992, 50–56, 218–21; Welzer, Moller, and Tschuggnall 2002).[16] It is well grounded in demographic and social realities: according to Bas van Os, the survival of numbers of eyewitnesses, including Jesus' family members, into the late first century is, statistically speaking, highly probable (2011, 57, 83). Moreover, this living memory framework is a topos found in early Christian traditions that connect Mark to Peter, Irenaeus to John through Polycarp, Valentinus to Paul through Theudas, in Papias's enquiries after the "living voice," and the like (Bockmuehl 2006, 178–84). But the difficulty is that Bockmuehl's account fails to connect this generational memory framework with the Synoptic (and Johannine) tradition; he treats it as a stand-alone transmission of personal memories from individual to individual down the three-generation span. And though he assumes, in connection with Justin's reference to

---

16. As Bockmuehl points out, people who as children had extensive contact with their grandparents will be familiar with this inter-generational memory span—had I ever bothered to ask her, my grandmother, who was born and grew up just south of Ottawa, likely could have related childhood memories of Sir John A. MacDonald (first prime minister of Canada, d. 1891).

the "memoirs of the apostles," that "personal memory" has been transmitted in the Gospels (2006, 185), his interest lies more in the post-200 CE shape of memories transmitted down the generational chain (that is, after the latter's life span) than in the memory–tradition nexus in the Gospels (2006, 179).[17]

Commemoration, Tradition, and Symbolic Representation

All the accounts above, including that of the form critics, posit or at least assume a nexus of some sort between memory and tradition, but each runs up against the problem of correlating memory with the distinctive phenomenology of tradition. Notably, most view "memory" as something uniquely individual—"personal recollection," "reminiscence," "eyewitness testimony," "informant testimony," and the like. Accordingly, the tendency (though not for all) is to take fullness of correspondence as the standard against which to grade memory's functionality from case to case. There is something intuitively appealing about conceiving memory this way. We experience memory as the quintessential individual faculty, as an interior mental reality and cognitive reflex that connects us reliably to our past experiences. This is what gives rise to the memory–tradition problematic, for "tradition" seems to be something quite different: an aggregate of cultural genres publicly cultivated in various media and apt to follow its own autonomous, often highly kinetic, course of development. Yet, like memory, tradition is representational of past events, at least ostensibly. Moreover, it comprises materials passed down from the past, often through the instrumentality of memory, which is often also instrumental in its enactment. In the scholarship surveyed above, the term "tradition" is often little more than a vague placeholder; with some exceptions (among whom were the form critics), there is little consideration given to tradition as a cultural medium with a distinctive phenomenology. In what follows, it will be shown that tradition is in fact the "form of memory" (Assmann 2006, 72), an artifact of commemorative processes. Tradition is realized in specific media forms that come into existence and are transmitted at the interface of the cognitive, social, and cultural operations of memory (see further Kirk 2010b, 821–28; 2010a; 2009, 166–72).

---

17. Bockmuehl does suggest that the generational memory framework would have acted as an external control upon the tradition (2006, 172).

Experimental studies on the cognitive formation of memory show that memory is not so much a faculty of passive recall as an active faculty that condenses and compounds elements selected from the diffuse flux of experience into economical scripts (articulated in a neurologically encoded information network called an "engram"). This is a practical matter of achieving mnemonic efficiency and functionality—shedding the surfeits of detail that under conditions of exact recall would induce cognitive paralysis. But it is more than that: out of experiences memory abstracts patterns and concepts, and out of similar events it compounds generic memories with representational, emblematic functions, fashioning cognitive scripts that give individuals and the groups to which they belong dispositional orientation to the world (Squire and Kandel 1999, 46, 206; Bartlett 1995, 53–54, 63, 83, 126–27; Bonanno 1990, 177; Rubin 1995, 7; Straub 2010, 221; Schwartz 2009, 139). "Those who remember everything," notes Jan Assmann, "are unable to orient themselves in time and society in the same way as those who notice everything are unable to orient themselves in space. Orientation requires selection. The function of memory is orientation" (2006, 68).

An important cognitive operation in this large-scale reduction in complexity is the shaping of memories to formulaic types drawn from the cultural repertoire of genres and narrative schemata. Here we see the intersection of neural with cultural processes, so that, as Ruben Zimmermann puts it, memory and remembering are *mediengebunden* (2008a, 106). The formation of memories by encoding in formulaic types and schemata that possess cultural resonance has a large mnemonic pay-off: it stabilizes memories, gives them simplicity and coherence, and makes them capable of classification, all of which facilitates their recollection. At the same time, it renders memories intelligible and communicable, for genres and narrative schemas are not ideal abstractions but pragmatic media for communication (see further Zimmermann 2008a, 106; 2008b, 155; Le Donne 2007, 169). But the effect is not only to model memories to these representational types (and vice versa). Because these forms and narrative scripts are interpretative schemas, the effect is to summon up in the recollection of a memory its existential and moral significance for the rememberer (see Rubin 1995, 280–81; Straub 2010, 216; LeDonne 2007, 169; 2009, 72–80). Memory-encoding therefore entails some distancing, or better, abstracting, from originating occurrences. It must be stressed that this very distancing is a mnemonic strategy: the outcome of these complex cognitive syntheses are memory artifacts, *representations* of the past that exchange exact recall for enormous mnemonic advantage.

The connection that exists between memory formation and a cultural repertoire of genres and narrative scripts indicates that human memory is not simply a neurobiological matter; rather, memory forms at the interface of cognitive processes with culture. The neural processes of the human brain are "enculturated"—"wired," we might say—into the vast external matrix of a cultural tradition that comprises the symbolic resources of a culture. In all their media complexity, these resources constitute the accumulated cultural memory of a society, the "external memory field" indispensable for the brain's formation of memory in its conceptual and symbolic fullness (Donald 2001, 150, 311; Markowitsch 2010, 280). Jürgen Straub writes that memory and recollection "depend on cultural resources, tools, and templates. In this way, they represent cultural psychic structures" (Straub 2010, 222). Sherry Ortner points out that cultural symbols provide the coordinates for cognitive and affective orientation, supplying normative ordering categories that enable thought and make experience intelligible. Without a field of orienting cultural symbols, basic concept formation and meaningful action would not be possible (Ortner 1973). Merlin Donald aptly describes the external cultural symbol network, wired into the processes of the human brain, as "a distributed cognitive system" (Donald 2001, 318).

Applied to the concerns of the present discussion: it is at this cognitive-cultural interface that "tradition" takes shape. "Gattungen haben als Erinnerungsmedien," states Zimmermann, "also eine traditionsstiftende Funktion."[18] Memory is coextensively articulated in culturally preformed genres and narrative scripts, expressed in various media, that give it not merely an external formal structure in tradition but at the same time a refinement and enrichment that tap into the deep symbolic resources of the cultural memory. "[W]e are dealing here," notes Straub, "not with 'media' as variable instances of *transmission*, but with *constitutive* symbolic forms without which memory and recollection would be unthinkable" (Straub 2010, 220). And to touch here briefly on the Synoptic tradition, tradition formation at the cognitive-cultural interface is not a solely post hoc operation upon the raw, amorphous matter of experience. Jesus' words drew upon cultural forms and meanings and his significant actions enacted cultural scripts before these ever took their commemorated form in the tradition.

---

18. Zimmermann 2008a, 109: "Cultural genres, as the media of memory, are essential to the formation of tradition"; see also 2008b, 144.

The shaping of memory along the lineaments of cultural genres and scripts renders it communicable, and it is in the course of sharing and rehearsing memories in the groups for which they hold pertinence—that is, in commemoration—that they come into sharper relief as standardized forms of a shared tradition bearing the shared meanings and norms of a community. The anthropologist Liisa Malkki observed this occurring in "real time" in refugee camps in Tanzania, among Hutu who had just fled from the genocide in Burundi.

> Accounts of these key events [experiences in, and flight from, the Burundi genocide] very quickly circulated among the refugees, and, often, in a matter of days, acquired what can be characterized as "standard versions" in the telling and retelling.... [T]hey were accounts which, while becoming increasingly formulaic, also became more didactic and progressively more implicated in, and indicative of, something beyond them.... [T]he "standard versions" acted as diagnostic and mnemonic allegories connecting events of everyday life with wider historical processes impinging on the Hutu refugees. (Malkki 1995, 106)[19]

Malkki notes that these became "moral ordering stories" in the formation of the postgenocide moral universe of the refugees (1995, 244). Loveday Alexander finds a similar line of development in the ἀπομνημονεύματα traditions of Xenophon and Lynceus: "At the heart of this process is the formalized oral activity of ἀπομνημόνευσις, 'recounting' or 'commemoration,' in which personal memories are shaped and processed (μελετᾶν) into ἀπομνημονεύματα, 'reminiscences.' ... These are the basic building blocks of oral tradition, which can become relatively stable within a short time and can then survive transmission across many generations" (Alexander 2009, 143). Notably, these externalized entities come to operate as the cognitive basis for memory even for contemporaries of the persons and events commemorated. "Xenophon," Alexander writes, "could justly claim to be writing on the basis of his own personal recollection of Socrates. But a glance at Xenophon's work makes it clear ... that even within one generation, memory, however personal in origin, is already molded by the literary forms and expectations of the larger society" (2009, 121).[20] The tradition that thus

---

19. Jan Vansina writes, "[G]roup traditions can be created quite rapidly after the events and acquire a form which strikingly makes such a tradition part of a complex of traditions" (1985, 20).

20. On the *chreia* and *apophthegma* as narrative memory media, see Byrskog 2009a, 48.

forms is not a complete cultural *novum*. Memory's enabling cultural repertoire of genres and narrative interpretive schemas is by definition already a
tradition, the media of the more ancient cultural memory (Zimmermann
2008b, 145). An emergent tradition thus always forms within an encompassing cultural tradition; a tradition that is not semiotically tuned to the
defining narratives, persons, texts, and motifs of the epic past would not be
intelligible, memorable, or historical (see Schwartz 1998).

Thus far I have proposed that memory formation occurs where cognition meets culture and that memory formation and tradition formation
exist on a continuum. But of course, not all memory formation results in
a normative body of tradition.[21] The conditions for the emergence of the
latter may be explored by returning to the discussion above on the cognitive operation of condensation, the massive reduction of detail that goes
into memory formation. As noted, selectivity and simplification is a functional matter of achieving mnemonic efficiency, that is, of turning what
seem to be memory's cognitive deficits into advantages. But selectivity
and simplification has a value-added side: it is simultaneously a distilla-
tion of the meaning, the significance, of events for the rememberer(s),
the effect of which is to give memories normative and affective density
(Squire and Kandel 1999, 78; Bruner and Feldman 1996, 291–93). In other
words, memory formation is *symbolic representation*. In Sapir's definition,
symbols are "condensations" of meaning (1949, 564), or, in Geertz's fuller
formulation, "vehicles for a conception … abstractions from experience
fixed in perceptible forms, concrete embodiments of ideas, attitudes, judgments, longings, or beliefs" (1973, 91). Here we find ourselves again at the
boundary with cultural memory, where under certain conditions the cognitive processes of condensation, selection, and schematization have the
potential to be taken up into wider cultural and moral-formation projects
and their various media. Barry Schwartz, in his study of historical simplification and selectivity in the commemoration of the civil rights heroine
Rosa Parks,[22] expresses this principle succinctly: "Cognitive deficit … rein-

---

21. Though even here the distinction should not be overdrawn. A person's store of
individual memories functions as a sort of constitutive personal tradition, and family
memories are a cultivated tradition.

22. Rosa Parks (1913–2005) was an African American seamstress who lived in
Montgomery, Alabama. In December 1955 she was arrested for refusing to give up
her bus seat to a white passenger. Her act of civil disobedience was a catalyzing factor
leading to the Montgomery bus boycott, a milestone in the American civil rights
movement.

forces rather than creates society's need to represent its ideals with unique symbols" (Schwartz 2009, 139).

More precisely, it is through social processes of *commemoration* that memory is transmuted into bodies of normative tradition. "[C]ommemoration," Schwartz observes, "is the lifting from the historical record of events that best symbolize society's ideals.... [C]ommemoration ... is selective, highlighting an event's most significant moral feature" (2009, 132; see also Vansina 1985, 105–6). Tradition as a form- and media-based entity is the outcome of this memorializing drive. Jan Assmann observes that, as with material artifacts, the formal aspects of tradition are "devices of stabilization meant to render permanent the volatile words in the flow of time ... [to] render ... a text definable in space and time" (2006, 72).[23] Moreover, the form-giving genres and abstracting narrative schemas—in the case of Rosa Parks that of the "wronged innocent"—are themselves bearers of intrinsic meaning that, together with their powerful mnemonic effects, contribute to the symbolizing operations of tradition (Schwartz 2009, 136).[24] As Echterhoff puts it, the "kognitive oder neuronale Repräsentationssysteme" take corresponding expression in external systems of cultural memory representation, as information encoded tangibly in texts, monuments, songs, ritual practices, and other media (2004, 65). Casey aptly characterizes commemoration, in the diverse external media in which it is realized, as "*intensified* remembering" (emphasis original).

> One way to intensify something is to give it a thicker consistency so as to help it last or to remain more substantively. Such thickening is surely the point of any memorialization, whether it be ceremonial, sculptural, scriptural, or psychical. Every kind of commemoration can be considered an effort to create a lasting "remanence" for what we wish to honor in memory—where "remanence" signifies a perduring remainder or residuum (as in the literally thick stone of war memorials or grave markers). (Casey 1987, 273)

---

23. Historical Jesus scholarship, not sufficiently recognizing the extent to which the tradition is the artifact of commemorative processes, often approaches the Gospels as garden-variety archival materials, for example, regarding them in their relative brevity as very incomplete records preserving just traces of events rather than being symbolically concentrated mediations of the aggregate of events.

24. Zimmermann refers to this as a convergence of "Medium und Botschaft" ["medium and message"] (2008b, 165; see also 156–57; 2008a, 110–11).

In her analysis of the ἀπομνημόνευμα genre Alexander observes the continuity of development from "remembering" to media-based "memorializing" of exemplary individuals (the memorializing of Socrates, Demonax, and Epicurus by Xenophon, Lucian, and the Epicureans, respectively), noting, moreover, that μνημονεύω and its cognates ἀπομνημονεύω and διαμνημονεύω cover, in her words, "the full range of 'remembering' as a mental act, through 'making mention' as a verbal act, to 'memorial' as a physical or textual record" (Alexander 2009, 188; see also 140–42).

We are now in a position to account for the *autonomy* of tradition vis-à-vis the historical events and occurrences that are its grounds. As noted earlier, memory work is neither concerned for nor cognitively capable of exact, mechanical redescription. Rather, it amounts to the abstraction of salient elements and patterns of meaning from the flux of experience and the configuration of these elements and patterns in mnemonically efficient, symbolically concentrated memory scripts that are mediated in various genres and schemas. The effect, as Terrence Deacon puts it, is an "increasingly indirect linkage between symbolic mental representation and its grounds of reference" (1997, 424). The autonomy of tradition, in other words, is owing to the reality that, as with any symbolic, commemorative artifact, tradition stands in a representational relationship to the foundational past. The mnemonic pay-off of this representational relationship is considerable. The Rosa Parks commemorative narrative again illustrates the point: "People who cannot remember the [thirteen-month, historically multifarious Montgomery] bus boycott as a whole can retrieve the [Rosa Parks] schema in which its elements are stored." The Rosa Parks narrative is at the same time a concentrated mnemonic script of, and frame for, the ideals and moral norms driving the civil rights movement, moreover one that aligns the Montgomery protests "with the classical stories of oppressed people's struggle for justice" (both quotes Schwartz 2009, 136).

In fact, a community is able to remember, inculcate, and transmit its formative past only to the extent that that past has been mnemonically consolidated in the schematic forms of a tradition. Tradition artifacts are media-borne symbolic entities that objectify, or as Jan Assmann expresses it, make "visible … permanent, and transmittable" (and, we should add, replicable) the defining elements of a community's moral universe (2006, 70; also Geertz 1973, 95–97, 363–67). Much like language itself, tradition operates as a "superordinate" system of normative symbols, a versatile cognitive system, the elements of which are capable of being brought into new configurations and applications and mobilized to meet new challenges that arise with shifts in a community's historical and social horizons (Deacon 1997, 87–99, 451; also Bartlett 1995, 225–27; Casey 1987, 286). Tradition fulfills these vital functions in virtue of its autonomy—its abstraction from, and thus representational relationship to, foundational historical events that are its grounds. But this is the autonomy of a symbol: a symbol's existence is a function of the realities it represents. What Casey says of memory can be said of tradition: it remains "enmeshed in its origins even when it seems to be functioning independently of them" (Casey 1997, 280). It is an autonomy, moreover, largely expressed through the internal resources and symbolic potential of the tradition itself.[25]

This active memory function of tradition helps explain the multiformity of tradition (its property of variability). Tradition—the significant past—is refracted through the contemporary realities of a tradent community, but the converse is also true: a community refracts and thereby cognitively apprehends its contemporary realities through the lens of its tradition. To borrow Schwartz's words, tradition is "an expressive symbol—a language, as it were, for articulating present predicaments," but it is also "an orienting symbol—a map that gets us through these predicaments by relating where we are to where we have been" (Schwartz 1996, 910; see also Vansina 1985, xii; Byrskog 2010, 27–28). By means of this "intrinsic double aspect" of tradition the normative force of the past is continuously brought to bear upon present exigencies and crises (Geertz 1973, 93).[26] This accounts (though certainly not wholly) for a tradition's characteristic multiformity, its transformation in different contexts as a tradent community anchors itself to its core identity and norms in changing circumstances and in the face of new challenges. As with any cultural object, tradition in its various media realizations leads a cultural life of its own as it reacts with the historical contingencies of its

---

25. In reference to the Synoptic tradition this principle is articulated by Gerhardsson 1979, 57–58; 1991, 89; in reference to the Hebrew Bible tradition, see Fishbane 1985, 86–87.

26. See also Zimmermann's discussion of the "Vergangenheitsbezug und Gegenwartswirkung" ["referentiality to the past and effects upon the present"] of the parables as "Gedächtnisgattungen" ["memory-genres"] (2008a, 119). "Vor dem Hintergrund einer literarischen (und umso mehr auch oralen) Gedächtniskultur spieglen abweichende Überlieferungen gerade die erinnernde Bewahrung früherer Überlieferungsformen bei gleichzeitigem Bemühen um gegenwartsbezogene Vermittlung" ["Seen against the backdrop of a literary, and to an even greater degree oral, memory culture, divergent traditions reflect a memorializing conservation of earlier forms of the tradition through a contemporizing enactment of those traditions"] (2008a, 113–14).

tradent communities. In this regard, the profoundly existential aspect of memory also carries over into the enactment of tradition. So powerful and concentrated are its representational effects that tradition seems to participate in, even mediate tangibility and reality to, what it represents, while drawing the participants into that reality such that it forms them at a deep level. Schwartz observes that the Rosa Parks narrative "represent[s] morally and emotionally what the civil rights movement meant to its beneficiaries"; it "promot[es] attachment" and "encourage[s] commitment" (Schwartz 2009, 133; see also Zimmermann 2008a, 110; Sapir 1949, 10–11; Donald 2001, 153–56). We can refer to this as the "sacramental" dimension of tradition, and it is the effect of tradition's memory function.

Conclusion

Though the model for memory and tradition sketched out above attempts a broad description of cultural processes of tradition formation and cultivation, it is of course intended to contribute to work on the history of the Synoptic (and Johannine) tradition. But it is important to keep in mind that it adduces research and ideas in other disciplines, where as biblical scholars we can quickly get out of our depth. Sweeping deductive claims about the origins and history of the Jesus tradition are therefore not advisable; the model's usefulness is best assessed in piecemeal analyses of the tradition, in application to source-critical and other classic research problems in Synoptic and Johannine scholarship. It needs to be emphasized that this approach is structured upon the achievements of form criticism—small forms and genres as the core media of the tradition; recognition of the tradition's autonomy; correlation of the history of the tradition to the history of the tradent communities—while also moving memory, understood here as the primary culture-formative force, from a peripheral to a central role in the development of the tradition.

As such, the model proposed here has potential to further clarify prominent aspects of the Synoptic tradition. These include not only that tradition's deep tincturing by the older biblical tradition but also its pronounced normative complexion, visible in its density in dominical sayings and pronouncement stories, in which nonnormative elements have receded almost to a vanishing point. Patterns of agreement and variation in the Synoptic tradition can be analyzed with reference to the memory function of tradition and source-critical questions reevaluated in light of the work of scribal tradents as cultivators of a memory-based tradition who worked at the boundary of orality and literacy. As an approach attuned to ancient media realities, it has the potential to address problems in the history of the tradition having to do with the shift from oral to written media or with how canonization trajectories might be latent in the memory function of tradition. Finally, it has obvious relevance for historical Jesus research, raising the question of what sort of historiography is required to deal with tradition—a media-based artifact with a commemorative and representational relationship to historical realities.

Works Cited

Alexander, Loveday. 2009. Memory and Tradition in the Hellenistic Schools. Pages 113–53 in *Jesus in Memory: Traditions in Oral and Scribal Perspectives*. Edited by Werner H. Kelber and Samuel Byrskog. Baylor, TX: Baylor University Press.

Allison, Dale C., Jr. 2010. *Constructing Jesus: Memory, Imagination, and History*. Grand Rapids: Baker Academic.

Assmann, Jan. 1992. *Das kulturelle Gedächtnis: Schrift, Erinnerung und politische Identitiät in frühen Hochkulturen*. Munich: Beck.

———. 2006. Form as Mnemonic Device: Cultural Texts and Cultural Memory. Pages 67–82 in *Performing the Gospel: Orality, Memory, and Mark*. Edited by Richard A. Horsley, Jonathan Draper, and John Miles Foley. Minneapolis: Fortress.

Bartlett, Frederic C. 1995. *Remembering: A Study in Experimental Social Psychology*. Cambridge: Cambridge University Press. [orig. 1932]

Bauckham, Richard. 2006. *Jesus and the Eyewitnesses: The Gospels as Eyewitness Testimony*. Grand Rapids: Eerdmans.

———. 2008. In Response to My Respondents: *Jesus and the Eyewitnesses* in Review. *JSHJ* 6:225–53.

Baum, Armin D. 2008. *Der mündliche Faktor und seine Bedeutung für die synoptische Frage*. Tübingen: Franke.

Bockmuehl, Markus. 2006. *Seeing the Word: Refocusing New Testament Study*. Grand Rapids: Baker Academic.

Bonanno, George A. 1990. Remembering and Psychotherapy. *Psychotherapy* 27:175–86.

Bruner, Jerome, and Carol Fleisher Feldman. 1996. Group Narrative as a Cultural Context of Autobiography. Pages 291–317 in *Remembering Our Past: Studies in Autobiographical Memory*. Edited by David C. Rubin. Cambridge: Cambridge University Press.

Bultmann, Rudolf. 1975. *The Presence of Eternity: History and Eschatology.* Westport, CT: Greenwood.

Byrskog, Samuel. 1994. *Jesus the Only Teacher: Didactic Authority and Transmission in Ancient Israel, Ancient Judaism, and the Matthean Community.* ConBNT 24. Stockholm: Almqvist & Wiksell.

———. 2000. *Story as History—History as Story: The Gospel Tradition in the Context of Ancient Oral History.* WUNT 123. Tübingen: Mohr Siebeck.

———. 2004. A New Perspective on the Jesus Tradition: Reflections on James D. G. Dunn's *Jesus Remembered. JSNT* 26:459–71.

———. 2006. A New Quest for the *Sitz im Leben*: Social Memory, the Jesus Tradition, and the Gospel of Matthew. *NTS* 52:319–36.

———. 2007. A Century with the *Sitz im Leben*: From Form-Critical Setting to Gospel Community and Beyond. *ZNW* 98:1–27.

———. 2008a. The Eyewitnesses as Interpreters of the Past: Reflections on Richard Bauckham's *Jesus and the Eyewitnesses. JSHJ* 6:157–68.

———. 2008b. Memory and Identity in the Gospels: A New Perspective. Pages 33–57 in *Exploring Early Christian Identity.* Edited by Bengt Holmberg. WUNT 226. Tübingen: Mohr Siebeck.

———. 2009a. Introduction. Pages 1–20 in *Jesus in Memory: Traditions in Oral and Scribal Perspectives.* Edited by Werner H. Kelber and Samuel Byrskog. Waco, TX: Baylor University Press.

———. 2009b. When Eyewitness Testimony and Oral Tradition Become Written Text. *Svensk exegetisk årsbok* 74:41–53.

———. 2010. The Transmission of the Jesus Tradition: Old and New Insights. *Early Christianity* 1:1–28.

———. 2011. The Transmission of the Jesus Tradition. Pages 1465–94 in volume 2 of *Handbook for the Study of the Historical Jesus.* Edited by Tom Holmén and Stanley E. Porter. Leiden: Brill.

———. 2012. From Memory to Memoirs: Tracing the Background of a Literary Genre. Pages 1–21 in *The Making of Christianity: Conflicts, Contacts, and Constructions: Essays in Honor of Bengt Holmberg.* Edited by Magnus Zetterholm and Samuel Byrskog. ConBNT 47. Winona Lake, IN: Eisenbrauns.

Casey, Edward S. 1987. *Remembering: A Phenomenological Study.* Bloomington: Indiana University Press.

Deacon, Terrence W. 1997. *The Symbolic Species: The Co-evolution of Language and the Brain.* New York: Norton.

Donald, Merlin. 2001. *A Mind So Rare: The Evolution of Human Consciousness.* New York: Norton.

Dunn, James D. G. 2003. *Jesus Remembered I. Christianity in the Making.* Grand Rapids: Eerdmans.

———. 2007. Social Memory and the Oral Jesus Tradition. Pages 179–94 in *Memory in the Bible and Antiquity.* Edited by Stephen C. Barton, Loren T. Stuckenbruck, and Benjamin G. Wold. WUNT 212. Tübingen: Mohr Siebeck.

———. 2008. Eyewitnesses and the Oral Jesus Tradition. *JSHJ* 6:85–105.

———. 2010. In Grateful Dialogue: A Response to My Interlocutors. Pages 287–323 in *Memories of Jesus: A Critical Appraisal of James D. G. Dunn's* Jesus Remembered. Edited by Robert B. Stewart and Gary R. Habermas. Nashville: Broadman & Holman.

———. 2011. Remembering Jesus: How the Quest for the Historical Jesus Lost Its Way. Pages 183–205 in volume 2 of *Handbook for the Study of the Historical Jesus.* Edited by Tom Holmén and Stanley E. Porter. Leiden: Brill.

Echterhoff, Gerald. 2004. Das Außen des Erinnerns: Was vermittelt individuelles und kollektives Gedächtnis? Pages 61–82 in *Medien des kollektiven Gedächtnisses: Konstruktivität—Historizität—Kulturspezifität.* Edited by Astrid Erll and Ansgar Nünning. New York: de Gruyter.

Ehrman, Bart. 1999. *Jesus: Apocalyptic Prophet of the New Millenium.* Oxford: Oxford University Press.

———. 2004. *The New Testament: A Historical Introduction to the Early Christian Writings.* 3rd ed. Oxford: Oxford University Press.

Fishbane, Michael. 1985. *Biblical Interpretation in Ancient Israel.* Oxford: Clarendon.

Funk, Robert W., and Roy W. Hoover. 1993. *The Five Gospels: The Search for the Authentic Words of Jesus.* New York: Macmillan.

Geertz, Clifford. 1973. *The Interpretation of Cultures: Selected Essays.* New York: Basic.

Gerhardsson, Birger. 1979. *The Origins of the Gospel Traditions.* Philadelphia: Fortress.

Häfner, Gerd. 2007. Das Ende der Kriterien? Jesusforschung angesichts der geschichtstheoretischen Diskussion. Pages 97–130 in Knut Backhaus and Gerd Häfner, *Historiographie und fiktionales Erzählen: Zur Konstruktivität in Geschichtstheorie und Exegese.* Neukirchen-Vluyn: Neukirchener.

Kirk, Alan. 2005a. The Memory of Violence and the Death of Jesus in Q. Pages 191–206 in *Memory, Tradition, and Text: Uses of the Past in Early*

Christianity. Edited by Alan Kirk and Tom Thatcher. SemeiaSt 52. Atlanta: Society of Biblical Literature.

———. 2005b. Social and Cultural Memory. Pages 1–24 in *Memory, Tradition, and Text: Uses of the Past in Early Christianity*. Edited by Alan Kirk and Tom Thatcher. SemeiaSt 52. Atlanta: Society of Biblical Literature.

———. 2008. Manuscript Tradition as a *tertium quid*: Orality and Memory in Scribal Practices. Pages 215–34 in *Jesus, the Voice, and the Text: Beyond The Oral and the Written Gospel*. Edited by Tom Thatcher. Waco, TX: Baylor University Press.

———. 2009. Memory. Pages 155–72 in *Jesus in Memory: Traditions in Oral and Scribal Perspectives*. Edited by Werner H. Kelber and Samuel Byrskog. Waco, TX: Baylor University Press.

———. 2010a. Memory Theory: Cultural and Cognitive Approaches to the Gospel Tradition. Pages 57–67 in *Understanding the Social World of the New Testament*. Edited by Dietmar Neufeld and Richard E. DeMaris. New York: Routledge.

———. 2010b. Memory Theory and Jesus Research. Pages 809–42 in volume 1 of *Handbook for the Study of the Historical Jesus*. Edited by Tom Holmén and Stanley E. Porter. Leiden: Brill.

Le Donne, Anthony. 2007. Theological Memory Distortion in the Jesus Tradition: A Study in Social Memory Theory. Pages 162–77 in *Memory in the Bible and Antiquity*. Edited by Stephen C. Barton, Loren T. Stuckenbruck, and Benjamin G. Wold. WUNT 221. Tübingen: Mohr Siebeck.

———. 2009. *The Historiographical Jesus: Memory, Typology, and the Son of David*. Waco, TX: Baylor University Press.

Malkki, Liisa H. 1995. *Purity and Exile: Violence, Memory, and National Cosmology among Hutu Refugees in Tanzania*. Chicago: University of Chicago Press.

Manier, David, and William Hirst. 2010. A Cognitive Taxonomy of Collective Memories. Pages 253–61 in *A Companion to Cultural Memory Studies*. Edited by Astrid Erll and Ansgar Nünning. New York: de Gruyter.

Markowitsch, Hans J. 2010. Cultural Memory and the Neurosciences. Pages 275–83 in *A Companion to Cultural Memory Studies*. Edited by Astrid Erll and Ansgar Nünning. New York: de Gruyter.

McIver, Robert K. 2011. *Memory, Jesus, and the Synoptic Gospels*. SBLRBS 59. Atlanta: Society of Biblical Literature.

Nineham, D. E. 1958. Eyewitness Testimony and the Gospel Tradition. *JTS* NS 9:13–25, 243–52.

———. 1960. Eyewitness Testimony and the Gospel Tradition. *JTS* NS 11:253–64.

Ortner, Sherry B. 1973. On Key Symbols. *American Anthropologist* 75:1338–46.

Os, Bas van. 2011. *Psychological Analyses and the Historical Jesus: New Ways to Explore Christian Origins.* LNTS 432. London: T&T Clark.

Redman, Judith. 2010. How Accurate Are Eyewitnesses? Bauckham and the Eyewitnesses in the Light of Psychological Research. *JBL* 129:177–97.

Rubin, David. 1995. *Memory in Oral Traditions: The Cognitive Psychology of Epic, Ballads, and Counting-Out Rhymes.* New York: Oxford University Press.

Sapir, Edward. 1949. *Selected Writings of Edward Sapir.* Edited by David G. Mandelbaum. Berkeley: University of California Press.

Schwartz, Barry. 1996. Memory as a Cultural System: Abraham Lincoln in World War II. *American Sociological Review* 61:908–27.

———. 1998. Frame Image: Toward a Semiotics of Collective Memory. *Semiotica* 121:1–38.

———. 2009. Collective Forgetting and the Symbolic Power of Oneness: The Strange Apotheosis of Rosa Parks. *Social Psychology Quarterly* 72:123–42.

Squire, Larry R., and Eric R. Kandel. 1999. *Memory: From Mind to Molecules.* New York: Scientific American Library.

Straub, Jürgen. 2010. Psychology, Narrative, and Cultural Memory: Past and Present. Pages 215–28 in *A Companion to Cultural Memory Studies.* Edited by Astrid Erll and Ansgar Nünning. New York: de Gruyter.

Thompson, Paul. 2000. *Voices of the Past: Oral History.* 3rd ed. Oxford: Oxford University Press.

Vansina, Jan. 1985. *Oral Tradition as History.* Madison: University of Wisconsin Press.

Wedderburn, Alexander J. M. 2010. *Jesus and the Historians.* WUNT 269. Tübingen: Mohr Siebeck.

Welzer, Harald, Sabine Moller, and Karoline Tschuggnall. 2002. *Opa war kein Nazi: Nationalsozialismus und Holocaust im Familiengedächtnis.* Die Zeit des Nationalsozialismus. Frankfurt: Fischer.

Wilder, Amos. 1962. Form History and the Oldest Tradition. Pages 3–13 in *Neotestamentica et Patristica: Eine Freundesgabe, Herrn Professor Dr. Oscar Cullmann zu seinem 60. Geburtstag überreicht.* Edited by W. C.

van Unnik. NovTSup 6. Leiden: Brill.

Zimmermann, Ruben. 2008a. Gleichnisse als Medien der Jesuserinnerung: Die Historizität der Jesusparablen im Horizont der Gedächtnisforschung. Pages 87–121 in *Hermeneutik der Gleichnisse Jesu: Methodische Neuansätze zum Verstehen urchristlicher Parabeltexte.* Edited by Ruben Zimmermann. WUNT 231. Tübingen: Mohr Siebeck.

———. 2008b. Formen und Gattungen als Medien der Jesus-Erinnerung: Zur Rückgewinnung der Diachronie in der Formgeschichte des Neuen Testament. Pages 131–67 in *Die Macht der Erinnerung.* Edited by Ottmar Fuchs and Bernd Janowski. JFBT 22. Neukirchen-Vluyn: Neukirchener.

———. 2010. Memory and Form Criticism: The Typicality of Memory as a Bridge between Orality and Literality in the Early Christian Remembering Process. Pages 130–43 in *The Interface of Orality and Writing: Speaking, Seeing, Writing in the Shaping of New Genres.* WUNT 260. Edited by Annette Weissenrieder and Robert B. Coote. Tübingen: Mohr Siebeck.

Prolegomena on the Textualization of Mark's Gospel: Manuscript Culture, the Extended Situation, and the Emergence of the Written Gospel[*][1]

Chris Keith

> It is important, in my opinion, to approach the description of mnemonic phenomena from the standpoint of the *capacities*, of which they are the "happy" realization. (Ricoeur 2004, 21, emphasis original)

One of the defining characteristics of Barry Schwartz's substantial contributions to social memory studies is his consistent insistence that researchers should avoid being more skeptical about the connections between the past and the present than is warranted (inter alia, Schwartz 1982, 395–96; Zhang and Schwartz 1997, 189–91, 196–97, 205–8). This theme has also featured prominently in Schwartz's interdisciplinary contributions to biblical studies. In one of his early contributions, he argued against overly cynical skepticism in Gospels scholarship (Schwartz 2005, 47–54; see also 2011, 225–26, 230–34), and his introductory essay to this volume continues in this vein. Schwartz asserts, for example, that lived experience sometimes leads directly to mnemonic forms (that is, sometimes the past creates rather than is created) and that "history texts and commemorative objects … are at least partly dependent on the reality they represent" (p. 22).

Schwartz is aware that the past is malleable, indeed, exceedingly malleable at times, but the above quotation reveals his conviction that there is nevertheless an organic relationship between originating events and their subsequent commemorations. There is no such thing as a wholesale fabrication, because even polemical twistings of the past do not foist their fabrications upon a tabula rasa. In this sense, any hermeneutical (re)shaping of the past is, in one form or another, a reaction that is dependent simultaneously upon the actual past and past interpretations of the past.

* I am grateful to Karl Galinsky and the Memoria Romana project for a grant that funded a large portion of this research in spring 2012.

There are, therefore, constraints and limitations upon the interpretive trajectory that emerges from past events. Schwartz refers to this hermeneutical indebtedness as "path dependency" and observes that "sacred texts are … 'path-dependent'—affected not only by their social contexts but also by previous representations of their content" (p. 16, above). In light of path-dependency, according to Schwartz, scholars are warranted to speculate about the nature of a(n inaccessible) past event in light of its (accessible) subsequent commemorations and impacts. To take the title of his introductory essay to this volume, when one sees smoke, one is sometimes justified to conclude that there is a fire—or at least, something very much like fire.

Thus far Schwartz has primarily applied these insights to questions of historicity in the Gospels, self-consciously speaking from the standpoint of an outsider to the discipline. His approach finds parallels in biblical studies, however, particularly in similar applications of a *Wirkungsgeschichte* approach to historical Jesus research (e.g., Theissen and Winter 2002, 173–74; Keith 2011a, 124–88; Le Donne 2009, 72–75; Schröter 2002, 163–212) and hermeneutics (e.g., Bockmuehl 2006, 66–68; Knight 2010, 137–46; see also Thiselton 1992, 327; 2009, 219–20). Despite differences in scope and topic, these approaches hold in common a concern to include the aftermath of an initiating cause (text, interpretation, historical event, etc.) in scholarly understandings, interpretations, and reconstructions of that cause.

The current essay argues for the appropriateness of applying a path-dependency or *Wirkungsgeschichte* perspective to a critical problem relating to media studies: Mark's textualization of the oral gospel tradition.[2] This essay will lay the groundwork for a fresh approach to the textualization of Mark's Gospel, wherein scholarly assessment of the possible reasons for, and significance of, Mark's transition of the Jesus tradition from the oral medium to the written medium must account for the aftermath of that decision. In particular, future assessments must account for the explosion of Gospel literature in early Christianity and the new genre's prominent role in the formation and maintenance of early Christian identity in subsequent centuries. As I will detail further below, this proposal stands in stark contrast to (but ultimately complements) the majority of prior assessments

---

2. My focus here is specifically on Mark's transition of the Jesus tradition from the oral to the written medium in the form of a narrativized manuscript. There were, of course, important precursors to Mark's work in early Christian manuscript culture, for example the veneration and collection of the Pauline Epistles or possibly *testimonia* or Q. Space prohibits discussion of these cases in the present essay.

of Mark's textualization of the Jesus tradition, which exhibit what I here term the "oral-preference perspective" on Mark's actions. The contribution of this essay is therefore to provide a base for understanding Mark's written Gospel not just in terms of what it purportedly brought to an end in oral tradition but also in terms of what it commenced in textual tradition. If Mark's Gospel was anything in the ancient Christian media world, it was not the oral tradition's Grim Reaper but rather the catalyst for a new genre that harnessed the technology of writing and manuscripts in, at times, unprecedented ways.[3]

Along these lines, I must underscore that what follows will offer methodological prolegomena for this new approach to Mark's textualization of the Jesus tradition, with a full assessment of the aftermath of Mark's act deferred in view of space limits. This concentration on the underlying methodology is necessary because the issues, and thus the history of research, are complex, as was Mark's media environment. Therefore, in the first half of this essay I will articulate the oral-preference perspective, which dominates the *status quaestionis*, as the legacy of Werner Kelber's highly influential *The Oral and the Written Gospel* (1983). I will then introduce Jan Assmann's concept of the *zerdehnte Situation* ("extended situation") as an appropriate corrective to the oral-preference perspective. By way of preview, I will argue that, in addition to observing the possibility that any number of historical contexts could have prompted the writing of Mark's Gospel, one can confidently affirm that Mark placed the Jesus tradition in a manuscript in order to escape the limitations of oral transmission.

THE LONG, TALL SHADOW OF WERNER KELBER

More than any other study, Werner Kelber's landmark *The Oral and the Written Gospel* (1983) still looms large over the question of orality in early Christianity and the specific question of the textualization of Mark.[4] It is no overstatement to say that the answers scholars today seek in New Tes-

---

3. Thus, Zimmermann: "The written texts were simultaneously aural texts that did not finalize a memory culture so much as set it in motion" (2010, 140).

4. The question of Mark's occasion for writing a Gospel is distinct from the question of why he chose the manuscript medium to address that occasion. In view of the obvious overlap between them, however, it is perhaps surprising that recent monographs on the purpose of Mark's writing ignore *The Oral and the Written Gospel* altogether (e.g., Roskam 2004) or discuss it in a single footnote (e.g., Winn 2008, 23 n. 61).

tament media studies are to questions that originated with Kelber. Fortunately, there is no need to rehearse in great detail Kelber's theory, criticisms of it, or the subsequent discussion that it generated; two recent volumes on Kelber and his work (Horsley et al. 2006; Thatcher 2008a), as well as a related collection of essays (Weissenrieder and Coote 2010), amply accomplish these tasks (see also Dewey 1995, esp. 139–212). Here I will focus on Kelber's framing of the question and the manner in which his approach privileged the oral aspects of the composition of Mark's Gospel over the textual aspects of that phenomenon.

Kelber and the Form Critics: Framing the Question

Kelber persuasively exposed the serious flaw in the form-critical paradigm, and he did so in terms of the sociohistorical contexts of early Christianity. For the form critics, the move from oral gospel tradition to written gospel tradition was significant insofar as it was the symbolic threshold between the two great eras of early Christianity that their model assumed as its foundation: early Palestinian Christianity and later Hellenistic Christianity.[5] The move from oral to written tradition was, however, insignificant for the form critics from a media-critical perspective, since they saw no substantive difference between the oral medium and the written medium. As Kelber perceptively noted, the form-critical model of tradition treated the written Gospels like a gravitational pole toward which the oral tradition was inevitably moving and always had been moving—textuality was simply the logical telos for orality. This perspective is evident, for example, in Bultmann's claim that the composition of the Gospels "involves nothing in principle new, but only completes what was begun in the oral tradition" (1963, 20, also 163, 331; Dibelius 1934, 3).[6] The written Gospels, under such

---

5. Bultmann refers to the distinction between Palestinian Christianity and Hellenistic Christianity as "an essential part of my inquiry" (1963, 5). In *From Tradition to Gospel*, Dibelius argues that the literary origins of the Greek, textualized, narrativized, gospel tradition cannot be located in Aramaic-speaking Palestinian Christianity due to its illiteracy and general lack of familiarity with literary culture (1934, 5, 9, 39, 234).

6. Before Kelber's critique, the lingering effects of this approach to the composition of the Gospels is illustrated in the following quote by Robinson: "But if we have learnt anything over the past fifty years [i.e., the reign of the form critics from the 1920s to the 1970s] it is sure that whereas epistles were written for specific occasions…, gospels were essentially for continuous use in the preaching, teaching, apologetic and liturgical life of the Christian communities. They *grew out of* and with the needs" (1976, 94, original emphasis altered to current emphasis; see also 96).

a paradigm, lack all novelty and are the mere "completion" of the transmission forces of the oral tradition.[7] Although Dibelius attributes some degree of significance to the writing of the tradition, seeing the text as an effort to corral an oral tradition "that had grown 'wild' and had been consciously corrected," he nevertheless refers to "the work of the evangelists" as a "further development" of what had already happened in the development of the oral forms (1934, 4).

Kelber's major accomplishment was to demonstrate that the assumed inevitable and organic nature of this transition was incongruent with a predominantly oral early Christian culture. Although Kelber's alternate proposal was multifaceted and more nuanced than often portrayed, two of his foundational points are particularly important for the present discussion. First, oral tradition and written tradition are different: they have different dynamics of transmission and different social contexts in which they operate, differences perhaps best highlighted for Kelber by the performative nature of oral tradition (1983, 91–92). *The Oral and the Written Gospel* draws heavily upon the works of Milman Parry, Albert Lord, and Walter Ong to demonstrate the dynamics of oral tradition and their considerable differences with the dynamics of textuality (Kelber 1983, esp. 44–89). On this basis, Kelber concludes that "the written Gospel cannot be properly perceived as the logical outcome of oral proclivities and forces inherent in orality" (1983, 90). While I and others have argued that Kelber overstated the differences between orality and textuality (see Achtemeier 1990, 15 n. 87, 27 n. 156; Keith 2011b, 49–69; Kirk 2008, 215–18), there can be little doubt that these differences require scholars not to overlook the significance of the transition between the two media.

Second, in his criticism of Birger Gerhardsson's alternative to the standard form-critical model, Kelber (1983, 14–25) highlights an important issue that the form critics assumed but did not address sufficiently: If most early Christians were illiterate, what need had they of a written text? "Plainly,

---

7. Dibelius, explaining the need to "inquire ... as to the law" by which the fixation of the gospel tradition occurred, reasons that, "If there is no such law, then the writing of the Gospels implies not an organic development of the process by means of collecting, trimming, and binding together, but the beginning of a new and purely literary development. If there was no such motive, then it is quite impossible to understand how men who made no pretentions to literature could create a tradition which constituted the first steps of the literary production which was then coming into being" (1934, 11). Implicit in this statement is the proposition of both Kelber and the current essay: if one does not assume an inherent move toward textuality, Mark's textualization of the tradition cries out for explanation.

the taking of notes and the cultivation of writing was a world apart from the life style of these prophetic transmitters of Jesus' sayings. They had no aids in writing" (Kelber 1983, 25). In this way, Kelber again drew attention to the fact that the writing of a Gospel was far from inevitable or common-sensical, a point that Stanton had earlier made (1975, 15). Since 1983, the studies of Harris (1989) and Hezser (2001) have subsequently confirmed the predominantly illiterate nature of the social contexts in which early Christianity emerged (see also Keith 2009, 53–94; 2011a, 71–123).

In drawing attention to the differences between orality and textual-ity, on the one hand, and the illiterate/oral nature of early Christianity, on the other hand, Kelber framed in an enduring fashion the essential ques-tion: "Why did Mark write a Gospel?" Why did a written text emerge in an illiterate culture that had functioned well with the Jesus stories in an oral medium? What necessitated the medium transition?

Kelber's own initial answer to the above questions has been less endur-ing than his substantial impact on the field of enquiry.[8] *The Oral and the Written Gospel* focused almost obsessively on the rupture between the oral tradition and the written tradition that occurred at Mark's hands. Kelber consistently refers to the differences between "fluid" oral tradition and "fixed" written tradition (1983, 32, 62, 63, 91, 94, 146, 158, 202, 209, 217), offering negative qualitative assessments of the media transition: Mark's work was "disruptive," "disjunctive," "destructive," a "disorientation"; "The text ... has brought about a freezing of oral life into textual still life.... Mark's writing manifests a transmutation more than mere transmission, which results in a veritable upheaval of hermeneutical, cognitive reali-ties" (1983, 91, 92, 94, 169, 172, 207, main quote 91). Ultimately Kelber asserts that Mark assaulted the oral medium as a means of assaulting the Christology of the oral Jesus tradition, which focused upon Christ's living presence in the community. Kelber locates this composition (which, for him, means both the narrativization and textualization of the tradition) sociohistorically in post-70 CE Christianity, a time when the trauma of the "death of Jerusalem" forced early Christians to face fully the crucifixion of Jesus, since both events made Jesus' absence painfully clear (1983, 211). In this context Mark employed the technology of writing in order to shift the locus of Christian authority from a present-focused Christology of the

---

8. So Thatcher: "Time has shown that the book [*The Oral and the Written Gospel*] was a milestone in biblical studies, significant less for the answers it gave than for the questions it raised" (2008a, 2).

living Lord to a past-focused text that recounted his life and death (Kelber 1983, 93, 184–226). Mark's text was thus the salve for the wounds of the crucifixion and destruction of Jerusalem and simultaneously brought death to the oral tradition.

Like the form critics against whom he argued, then, Kelber saw the transition from orality to textuality as the threshold between two early Christian epochs and as a significant marker between two Christologies. Unlike the form critics, he saw the transition from orality to textuality as a cataclysmic explosion demanding explanation rather than casual dismissal as the logical outcome of oral-transmission processes.

KELBER'S ORAL-PREFERENCE PERSPECTIVE

In light of the predominantly oral/illiterate nature of early Christianity, Kelber is entirely correct that the writing of Mark demands an explanation, even though his own original explanation does not enjoy wide acceptance. I suggest here, however, that Kelber's original proposal has proven unpersuasive partly because it ignored almost entirely the textual and artifactual dynamics of Mark's act. This point raises a crucial but overlooked aspect of Kelber's seminal proposal and its effect on subsequent discussion. When Kelber assessed Mark's transition of the Jesus tradition from the oral to the written medium, he stood firmly on the oral side of that transaction: his foci were the nature of orality, the oral nature of early Christianity, the ways in which textuality supposedly brings those dynamics to a grinding halt, and yet also the ways in which Mark's Gospel (as text) continues to reflect its oral heritage. Entirely absent from *The Oral and the Written Gospel* is any sustained discussion of the book culture into which Mark moved the tradition and the functions of textuality *as* textuality, rather than as simply the residue of orality.[9] In light of this seeming preference to approach Mark's media transition in terms of orality, I refer to Kelber's position as "the oral-preference perspective."

This wide-angle perspective rooted in orality led Kelber to fail to consider at least two important matters: what a manuscript contributes to the transmission process; and the explosion of "Gospel" literature that came in the wake of Mark's Gospel. As noted earlier, I will here concentrate on the

---

9. Thus Kelber speaks consistently throughout chapter 3 of "Mark's oral legacy" (also the chapter title), and in chapter 4 ("Mark as Textuality") he describes his approach by noting that "[t]his chapter is concerned with Markan textuality *and the nature of its relation to the oral legacy*" (1983, 90, emphasis added).

former issue and leave the latter for a later treatment. At least three developments in research since the *The Oral and the Written Gospel* have brought
these two issues to the fore: the fall of the so-called "great divide" between
orality and textuality;[10] an emphasis upon tradition transmission as identity marking and/or constructing;[11] and the enlarging role of "memory" as
an analytical category in conceptions of transmission processes. Each of
these theoretical developments has forced scholars to reconsider transmission practices in terms of continuity in addition to degrees of discontinuity.
Significantly, Kelber himself has often led the charge in reconsideration
and further development of his own prior ideas (1988, 31–42; 1995, 139–
67; 2005, 221–48; 2007; 2008, 235–62; 2009, 173–85, 201–6; 2010, 70–99),
to such an extent that one could now justly refer to the early Kelber and the
later Kelber. As a particular example, and one to which I will return shortly,
in a 2005 essay, while discussing again the composition of Mark's Gospel,
but this time in light of cultural memory theory, Kelber shifts the accent
from Mark's *destructive* act upon oral Christology to his *constructive* act of
"solidifying" Christian identity (2005, 244).

Despite the progress of the discussion, however, scholars (including Kelber) still routinely overlook the significance of Mark's Gospel as a
physical artifact, preferring instead to focus upon texts' effects upon oral
tradition or the manners in which texts still function like oral tradition.
For example, in a 2008 essay tellingly entitled, "The Gospel of Mark as
Oral Hermeneutic," Joanna Dewey describes her approach to Mark in precisely this manner: "I think that the Gospel of Mark is basically an *oral*
narrative built on *oral* storytelling, employing an *oral* style, and plotted

---

10. On the fall of the "Great Divide," see Keith 2011b, 54–61. Kelber has claimed
in multiple locations that the term "Great Divide" was imposed on his work by others
(1997, xxi; Kelber and Thatcher 2008a, 29). On the one hand, Kelber doth protest too
much: he himself uses the phrase "great divide" (1983, 203), and his emphatic insistence on the dichotomy of "orality *versus* textuality" (1983, 32, emphasis added) does
nothing to dispel the attribution of the so-called "great divide" to him. On the other
hand, Kelber is correct that "the attentive reader will observe that my understanding
of tradition and gospel is more nuanced than the label of the Great Divide gives it
credit for" (1997, xxi), since he often speaks of texts absorbing tradition (instead of
being completely "fixed"; 1983, 105) and of the blurring of the lines between orality
and textuality (1983, 23). In my view, Kelber's original study emphasized the complexity of early Christian media culture; further research has shown that it was even more
complex than he initially imagined.

11. Kelber's seminal work emphasized social identity as the key for understanding
transmission processes (1983, 24–25), but this insight was largely overlooked in subsequent research (see Horsley 2008, 47; Keith 2011b, 66).

according to *oral* conventions" (2008, 72, emphases added).[12] Further-more, and ironically, while disagreeing with Kelber's view on the precise effect of the introduction of the written medium, Dewey exhibits perfectly the oral-preference perspective that Kelber champions: "Whether com-posed in performance, by dictation, or in writing, the Gospel of Mark was composed in an oral style and performed orally. *The gospel remains fun-damentally on the oral side of the oral/written divide*" (2008, 86, emphasis added; see also 73). Such statements raise the obvious question, Why, then, did Mark produce a manuscript? Whatever it meant in terms of content and context, upon textualization the Gospel of Mark very clearly moved into the written medium. This fact does not require the further conclusion that the Gospel of Mark thereby left orality behind, but there is no point in denying its new media status.

Dewey and Kelber are far from alone in displaying the oral-preference perspective. Dunn consistently speaks of texts functioning *as if* they were oral tradition in claiming that Matthew and Luke could have written their Gospels, and copied Mark's—acts that were, if nothing else, textuality in action—in "oral mode" (Dunn 2005b, 50; similarly 2003, 212, 214, 218, 220, 221, 237, 254; 2005a, 110; 2005b, 53, 59; see critique in Keith 2011b, 57–61). Anne Wire also has placed the accent upon orality in arguing that Mark's Gospel was an oral composition (2011; see also Shiner 2003, 2006), and there are many other scholars who exhibit a preference for speaking of Mark's Gospel in terms of its dependence upon, reflection of, or affinity with orality (inter alia, Bryan 1993, 65–151; Hearon 2006, 3–20; Horsley 2008, 63–70; 2010, 155–56; Rhoads, Dewey, and Michie 2012, xii; Shiner 2003; see also Achtemeier 1990, 3–27; Hearon 2010, 379–92). On the one hand, these studies provide an important crosscurrent in a long stream of biblical scholarship that has ignored the oral environment of early Chris-tianity altogether. On the other hand, the oral-preference perspective has sometimes led to inaccurate statements or truncated lines of enquiry.[13] An

---

12. More broadly, Achtemeier claims that the New Testament writings as a whole "are oral to the core, both in their creation and in their performance" (1990, 19).

13. As another clear example, it is common to find unqualified statements that ancient manuscripts did not have spacing between words, paragraph divisions, or other helps to the reader (e.g., Horsley 2008, 51; Rhoads 2010, 181; Wire 2011, 42–43, 190; see also Achtemeier 1990, 10–11, 17, 26). The unqualified nature of these comments reflects a lack of familiarity with ancient texts. Even some of the earliest Christian manuscripts provide ekthesis, varying degrees of spacing, sense-unit and paragraph division, punctuation, and other readers' aids (e.g., 𝔓52, 𝔓46, 𝔓64, 𝔓66, 𝔓45, 𝔓75; see further Hurtado 2006, 177–85).

unfortunate side-effect of the oral-preference perspective in this regard has been a neglect of the Gospel of Mark's status as written text and its reflection of textual media dynamics. The time is thus ripe to complement these studies by considering the significance of what Mark added to the transmission process—a manuscript.

MARK AND THE *ZERDEHNTE SITUATION* OF MANUSCRIPT CULTURE

Whether in modern or ancient times, a book is itself an object whose physical and visual properties are significant, with the result that a manuscript's significance or "meaning" often extends beyond its content. This reality is perhaps most clear in the case of magical papyri or books used as amulets (Gamble 1995, 237–41) but often extends to other texts as well. The physical significance of writing is magnified in predominantly illiterate and oral cultures like the one in which Mark wrote his Gospel, where books held a numinous value (Carr 2005, 10; Thatcher 2006, 141). What, then, was the significance of manuscripts in such a media environment? Certainly, the content of the text, or at least a group's assumptions about that content, contributed to its significance to some degree. But "we fail to grasp a crucial aspect of the ancient function of texts if we focus exclusively on their contents" (Carr 2005, 10). Particularly relevant in this regard is the work of cultural memory theorist Jan Assmann on cultural texts, the *Traditionsbruch*, and the *zerdehnte Situation*.

CULTURAL MEMORY AND CULTURAL TEXTS

In a seminal 2005 article that argued for approaching the Jesus tradition as social memory, Alan Kirk and Tom Thatcher identify the topic of "Written Gospels as Commemorative Artifacts" as one of seven new directions for research based on the introduction of social/cultural memory into New Testament studies (2005a, 41). Kirk and Thatcher devote only one summary paragraph to the topic but point readers to Egyptologist and cultural memory theorist Jan Assmann, who distinguishes between the communicative memory (*kommunikative Gedächtnis*) of a living generation and the cultural memory (*kulturelle Gedächtnis*) that extends beyond that generation and into the authoritative cultural repertoire of a group (see further J. Assmann 2006b, 3–30; Kirk 2010, 1:838–42). For Assmann, memory/ tradition that becomes cultural memory thus becomes cultural texts (*kulturelle Texte*; see also A. Assmann 1995, 232–44) or what Carr, dependent upon Assmann, calls "long-duration texts" (Carr 2005, 10). These texts are institutionalized and carry both normative (What shall we do?) and formative (Who are we?) power for the construction of group identity (J. Assmann 2006b, 29, 104; see also Carr 2005, 10; Kirk 2005a, 201). In Assmann's words, "Cultural texts form the cement or connective backbone of a society that ensures its identity and coherence through the sequence of generations" (J. Assmann 2006a, 78).

As Kirk observes regarding the Gospels in particular, "the pertinence of social and cultural memory theory analysis for clarifying the phenomenology of the gospel tradition should be evident.... The Gospel tradition may be understood as *the artifact of memory*" (Kirk 2010, 1:819–20, emphasis original; see also Kirk and Thatcher 2005a, 25–42). Even more specifically, Assmann's theories are important for understanding Mark's textualization of the gospel, because a central feature of Assmann's understanding of the transmission of cultural memory involves the relationship between oral and written tradition and the transition between the two.

The *Traditionsbruch*

Heretofore in Gospels scholarship, the most significant aspect of Assmann's cultural memory program for theories of the textualization of Mark's Gospel has been his concept of *Traditionsbruch* (J. Assmann 1992, 32, 157, 218, 293–94; 2000, 87–89 // 2006b, 68–70). Assmann locates the *Traditionsbruch* in the shift between the communicative memory of interpersonal interaction and the cultural memory it must become if a group's identity is to survive the death of the generation that stands at its origins. In short, as an "emergent community" (Kirk 2010, 1:840–41; see 2005b, 6) slowly loses touch with its origins through the death of the first generation, the group has thrust upon it "eine Krise in der kollektiven Erinnerung" ("a crisis in the collective memory"; J. Assmann 1992, 218). Assmann consistently locates this crisis of memory at the forty-year mark from the originating event (1992, 11, 51, 217, 218) and contends that, "Wenn eine Erinnerung nicht verlorengehen soll, dann muß sie aus der biographischen in kulturelle Erinnerung transformiert werden" ("If a memory should not be lost, then it must be transformed from biographical memory into cultural memory"; 1992, 218). A crisis of memory can occur also in well-established cultures that undergo a traumatic experience that similarly threatens group identity (Kirk 2005b, 6). To illustrate, Assmann locates the textualization of Deuteronomy in the wake of the trauma associated with the Josianic reform, which redefined Israelite identity as monotheistic, and views Deut 28 in particular as a means of addressing the perception that idolatry led to the Assyrian and Babylonian exiles (J. Assmann 2006b, 55–57, 68–69; also 1992, 215–22).

Although for Assmann both oral and written tradition can transmit cultural memory (oral tradition through festival and ritual, written tradition through manuscripts; 2006b, 39–40, 105), writing is a particularly effective means of stabilizing group identity in the crisis of memory and therefore of transitioning collective memory into cultural memory. Writing, of course, involves the possibility of cultural forgetting of ritualized tradition that does not become institutionalized (2006b, 118). Importantly, however, it also offers "the possibility of preservation" (2006b, 39) because its more durable medium offers the opportunity of survival. "In such situations we find not only that new texts emerge, but also that already existing texts are given an enhanced normative value. Where the contact with living models is broken, people turn to the texts in their search for guidance" (2006b, 69). The perception of permanence contributes to the symbolic value of written cultural memory. As such, textualization is an important stage "along the road to canonization" (2006b, 71), and it is canonization that technically ensures the transition from communicative to cultural memory, not textualization alone (2006b, 39–40). The *Traditionsbruch* thereby establishes the move from oral to written tradition, from communicative to cultural memory, as a cultural coping mechanism that draws upon a manuscript's relative durability and symbolic value, an effort at identity (re)construction in the aftermath of a crisis of generational succession, violence, or other cultural threats (Kirk 2010, 1:842).

New Testament scholars have found Assmann's theory of the *Traditionsbruch* to be effective in explaining the textualization of biblical tradition, in some cases following Assmann's lead in applying the concept to the textualization of Deuteronomy. Most prominent here is Kelber: in his more recent work, Kelber's understanding of Mark's composition has shifted toward identity-construction, specifically in reference to Assmann's conception of the *Traditionsbruch* (Kelber 2005, 228–29, 243–44; see Thatcher 2008a, 12).

> If we date the Gospel [of Mark] some forty years after the death of the charismatic founding personality, and in all likelihood in the aftermath of the destruction of Jerusalem in 70 CE, one could conceivably understand the document [Mark's Gospel] as a narrative mediation of a threefold crisis: the death of Jesus, the devastation of Jerusalem culminat-

ing in the conflagration of the Temple, and the cessation of a generation of memories and memory carriers. Could we not be dealing here with an acute example of a *Traditionsbruch* that, following an initial trauma, was acutely compounded by a secondary dislocation some forty years later? (Kelber 2005, 244)

This lengthy quotation is justified in order to note the perfect storm of Assmann's *Traditionsbruch* model and Kelber's prior ideas, which combine into a seemingly formidable explanation for the textualization of Markan Jesus tradition. In particular, one may note the shared emphases of a crisis of communicative memory at the forty-year mark and an experience of violence that threatens group identity.[14] Remaining intact from Kelber's earlier work, then, is the general date of the composition of Mark as well as its function as a means of confronting an earlier crisis (the crucifixion) in light of a more recent crisis (destruction of the temple). Joanna Dewey follows Kelber in affirming, in regard to Mark's Gospel, "that there was some sort of *Traditionsbruch* (break in the tradition) post-70 CE, due both to the disruption caused by the war and to the passage of time and the death of the first generations" (2008, 73). Similarly, Kirk accounts for the textualization of Mark (and Q) in early Christianity in terms of the *Traditionsbruch*, as well as of the Torah in postexilic Judaism (Kirk 2010, 1:842; 2005a, 205–6, 205 n.12). With regard to Mark in particular, Kirk attributes textualization to a generational succession *Traditionsbruch* (2010, 1:842).

As indicated by the review above, the *Traditionsbruch* theory of Mark's composition has much to commend it. It fits firmly within the traditional dating of Mark between 60 and 80 CE and thus within circa forty years of Jesus' crucifixion. It also fits with the many proposals that Mark wrote in response to some trauma, whether the crucifixion (Gundry 1993, 1, 1026, 1044)[15] (although under Kelber's *Traditionsbruch* theory a much later

---

14. As Thatcher (2008a, 12) notes, even before the publiction of *Oral and Written Gospel* Kelber consistently located the writing of Mark's Gospel in a post-70 CE context, forty years after the crucifixion. See, e.g., Kelber 1979, 13, 70, 91–92.

15. Gundry denies that orality/writing lay at the base of Mark's writing. "The Gospel of Mark contains no ciphers, no hidden meanings, no sleight of hand: ... No freezing of Jesuanic tradition in writing" (1993, 1). He criticizes Kelber directly on this count later (1023 and 1044 on a separate issue). Following statements of Clement of Alexandria, inter alia, Gundry places the writing of Mark in Rome, based on Peter's preaching, and for the benefit of Caesar's knights: "Especially in Rome, the center of power and culture, and more especially among these knights, representing Roman power and culture, death by crucifixion would be repugnant and an apology for the

response to the crucifixion),[16] the Neronian pogroms in Rome (see Hengel 2000, 78–79; Lane 1974, 12–17; Spivey, Smith, and Black 2007, 60–61), or the destruction of Jerusalem,[17] to name only a few possibilities. Alternatively, the text as a response to a generational succession crisis of memory makes sense in the context of an early church that was obsessed with the first generation of leadership and identifying and maintaining living connections to it (e.g., John 21:24; Papias in Eusebius, *Hist. eccl.* 6.14.17; Irenaeus, *Haer.* 3.3.2–3). Furthermore, as noted earlier, a violence-inspired *Traditionsbruch* and a generational succession-inspired *Traditionsbruch* are not mutually exclusive possibilities, especially in the case of early Christianity, where both were occurring some forty years after Jesus' death. The *Traditionsbruch* theory of Markan composition thus provides a thoroughly plausible media-critical answer to the question of Mark's textualization that coheres with broader historical hypotheses in Markan scholarship.

But despite the *Traditionsbruch* theory's considerable help in offering plausible explanations, or plausible contexts, for Mark's production of a written Gospel, it remains incomplete as a theory of textualization. First, the model offers no guidelines for identifying the precise situation to which Mark might be responding. Several situations in early Christianity could, or even did, cause crises of memory. The written Gospel as response to the trauma of the crucifixion makes complete sense in this framework, but it also makes sense as a response to Neronian persecution, a response to 70 CE, a response to the death of the first generation of apostles, and a response to a number of similar possibilities.

Second, and more important, as Assmann's own work demonstrates, although written tradition can be a helpful means of managing a memory crisis, oral tradition is also capable of transferring communicative memory into cultural memory in the form of ritual and festival (2006a, 75–79; 2006b, 105). In other words, a *Traditionsbruch* does not always require a manuscript for the group's successful navigation of the crisis and is there-

---

Cross, such as Mark's, would be called for" (1993, 1045). Gundry does not explain why the knights needed a manuscript of the narrative rather than an oral presentation of it.

16. For an argument for the early formation of the Markan narrative (not necessarily text) as a response to the crucifixion, and in dialogue with Kelber, see Keith and Thatcher 2008a, 197–214.

17. Prior to *The Oral and the Written Gospel*, Kelber himself advocated this position and referred to it as "a scholarly consensus [that] is beginning to emerge" (1979, 13–14, 70, 91–92, quote 13). More recently, see Roskam 2004, 236. Edwards places the authorship of Mark's Gospel in Rome between the Neronian pogroms and the destruction of Jerusalem in 70 CE (2002, 9; cf. Yarbro Collins 2007, 14; Stein 2008, 14–15).

fore not an *automatic* explanation for the textualization of oral tradition. One must still explain what a manuscript contributed to the transference of memory that was not available in the form of early Christian rituals such as weekly worship meetings, the Eucharist, and baptism.

As should be clear, in making these observations, I am not rejecting the relevance of the *Traditionsbruch* for understanding the textualization of Mark. This model firmly establishes that the textualization of memory is at core related to the (re)construction of group identity, especially in violent contexts and/or contexts of cultures with an "emergent" identity. The aforementioned cautious criticisms are intended simply to underscore that a comprehensive understanding of Mark's textualization cannot rest on this concept alone.

MANUSCRIPTS AND THE *ZERDEHNTE SITUATION*

Building upon prior applications of the *Traditionsbruch* theory, I propose that the more significant aspect of Assmann's model for understanding the textualization of Mark's Gospel is his concept of the *zerdehnte Situation*. This concept is more important than the *Traditionsbruch* not only because it explains how a manuscript can aid the transformation of collective memory into cultural memory (and thus underlies the *Traditionsbruch* theory) but also, and primarily, because it foregrounds what a manuscript contributes to the transmission process that orality does not. This focus upon the distinctive contribution of a manuscript to the transmission process stands in contrast to the oral-preference perspective. It is perhaps unsurprising, then, that thus far New Testament scholars have overlooked the relevance of this concept (see Keith 2011b, 63–69).

For Assmann, *the* categorical distinction between oral tradition and written tradition is that writing does not demand the "co-presence" of the transmitter of the tradition and the audience that ritual and festival require: "What is decisive for the genesis of texts is the separation from the immediate speech situation" (2006b, 103). Thus, despite the fact that a textualized tradition runs "risks of being forgotten" if that particular text fails to become institutionalized (2006b, 105–6, quote 118), once institutionalized, the *zerdehnte Situation* opens the tradition up to a vista of transmission that ritual and festival cannot support.

> The two situations, speaker and messenger on the one hand, messenger and listener on the other, are separated in time and place and yet

in communication with each other through the text and the manner of its transmission. The *immediate* situation of co-presence is replaced by "the *expanded* context" [*zerdehnte Situation*], in which from two to virtually an infinite number of individual situations can unfold and limits of which are set only by the availability of the text and the manner of its transmission. (2006b, 103; see also 2006a, 75).

As indicated by the reference to a messenger who memorizes a text from one author/performer and travels to another locale to repeat it, Assmann acknowledges that oral communication, too, can create a form of the *zerdehnte Situation*. This form is, however, a restricted form that cannot match a written text's distinct ability to escape interpersonal communication (2006a, 75–76). Whereas a messenger may create a form of the *zerdehnte Situation* by connecting one text-generating context with a separate text-receiving context, this transmission is still dependent upon the physical presence of the messenger. In contrast, "literature [connects] virtually infinite concrete situations that may stretch in time" (2006a, 75). "Writing is just one form of transmission and re-enactment, albeit a very decisive one. The use of writing in the transmission of cultural texts changes fundamentally the time-structure of cultural memory. All the other forms of institutionalizing an extended situation [*zerdehnte Situation*] depend on time and place, on temporal recurrence and/or spatial translocation.... To reconnect with the meaning of written cultural texts, you do not have to wait for the next performance, you just have to read them" (2006a, 77).

The above point must be emphasized, for it is crucially important to understanding what a manuscript contributes to the transmission process. Writing opens cultural texts to a virtually limitless history of reception, so long as the papyrus or parchment of extant copies endures. Of course, there must also be a reader in order to actualize the tradition, and this is a form of limitation inherent to textuality. But this very constraint of textuality is also what allows it to break the constraints of orality, since the tradition's audience is no longer confined to those who are physically present before the author/performer/messenger. The reader can be anyone, anywhere, at any time. Manuscripts thus enable communicative memory to become cultural memory in a distinct way because they allow cultural texts to cross space and time, becoming long-duration texts that are received generation after generation.[18]

---

18. Written texts also enable a culture of interpretation and thus a class of interpreters (J. Assmann 2006b, 40–41; see also 69). Along these lines, Black observes that

Two further points on the significance of the *zerdehnte Situation* that a manuscript enables must be emphasized. First, within Assmann's concept of the *zerdehnte Situation* resides an important distinction between his view of the relationship between orality and textuality and Kelber's view. Technically, Assmann's theory is both similar to and dissimilar from Kelber's original perspective. Similar to Kelber, Assmann points out the distinction between oral and written media in terms of whether the author/speaker and audience/readers are co-present or separated. Dissimilar from Kelber, however, Assmann accounts for the continuity between oral and written tradition in their shared function as identity-forming memory in addition to the discontinuity between the media forms in their contexts of reception. In other words, Kelber's original thesis defined the distinction between orality and textuality as one of media and contexts, and thus suffered from the fall of the so-called great divide and the growing recognition that in antiquity manuscript tradition often functioned similarly to oral tradition. Kelber also saw the identity-construction of the written text as necessarily an attack on the identity-construction of the oral tradition. In contrast, Assmann's theory of the *zerdehnte Situation* defines the distinction between orality and textuality as one of communication.

> The concept of the expanded context [*zerdehnte Situation*] does not apply to the *storage*, but to the communication of a message. It refers to the majority of concrete communication situations in which the communication is uttered. Compared to this communication, the question of storage is superficial. The essential distinction between the oral and the written transmission of cultural texts consists, therefore, not in the storage medium or technology, but in the form in which the expanded context [*zerdehnte Situation*] is institutionalized. (J. Assmann 2006b, 105)

The institutionalization of memory in the *zerdehnte Situation* therefore points to the fact that textuality does not necessarily involve an alternative identity-construction process.[19] Although this is possible, it can also function as an extension or hardening of the identity-construction processes already underway in the oral tradition. In this way Assmann's theory is an improvement on Kelber's original theory because it highlights what

---

Mark's shift of the tradition from orality to textuality actively enabled the resultant focus upon the Gospel's authorship among patristic interpreters (1994, 200).

19. Achtemeier was therefore correct that Kelber's argument in this regard "would fall into the category of premature conclusions" (1990, 4 n. 7).

Kelber had correct (the introduction of a manuscript demands explanation), addresses what he ignored (how the introduction of a manuscript continued the transmission process), and provides warrant for dismissal of the less-persuasive aspects of his original thesis (the introduction of the manuscript was an attack on oral Christology).

The second important point is that Assmann identifies the creation of the *zerdehnte Situation* as the root cause of textualization. As noted above, he refers to it as "decisive for the genesis of texts" (2006b, 103). Although speculating on an ancient (or modern) person's intentions is dangerous business, the notion that an ancient person would place oral tradition/communicative memory into a manuscript (and thus create the possibility of cultural memory) because of the manuscript's ability to escape the confines of co-presence has the virtue of explaining the media transition in terms of what was added to the situation that was previously missing—the manuscript. Along these lines, I note again that the manuscript's ability to create a *zerdehnte Situation* that stretches through time and space is precisely why it is an attractive means of managing a *Traditionsbruch* and the reconstitution of group identity in its wake. In this sense, not only is the *zerdehnte Situation* theory of textualization compatible with the *Traditionsbruch* theory; the latter is intricately dependent upon the former.

Conclusion

Building on the above observations, I propose that, regardless of which *Traditionsbruch* in early Christianity Mark may have been responding to, he chose the written medium as a means of response that extended the audience of his Gospel beyond the limits of interpersonal communication. That is, he textualized the gospel tradition in order to create a *zerdehnte Situation*. I offer the preceding argument for this proposal in the guise of the title of this essay—prolegomena to a more comprehensive reassessment of Mark's textualization of the Jesus tradition. In anticipation of future discussion, I close with four further implications of my argument that Mark textualized the oral tradition in order to create a *zerdehnte Situation*.

First, my theory offers solid grounds for joining with those scholars who argue that we should not dismiss entirely the patristic evidence concerning Mark's textualization.[20] Indeed, Eusebius's citation of Clement of

---

20. Hengel in particular champions the reliability of the patristic testimony concerning the writing of Mark's Gospel (1984, 1–45; 1985, 47, 50; 2010, 36–37) against

Alexandria (late second/early third century CE) explains *why* Mark wrote with language that exhibits precisely what Assmann means by the replacement of the immediate situation with the extended situation (*zerdehnte Situation*) being the "genesis" of writing.

> But a great light of religion shone on the minds of the hearers of Peter, so that they were not satisfied with a single hearing or with the unwritten teaching [τῇ ἀγράφῳ ... διδασκαλίᾳ] of the divine proclamation, but with every kind of exhortation besought Mark, whose Gospel is extant, seeing that he was Peter's follower, to leave them a written statement of the teaching given them verbally, nor did they cease until they had persuaded him, and so became the cause of the Scripture called the Gospel according to Mark. (*Hist. eccl.* 2.15.1; trans. Lake, LCL)

Eusebius attributes this account to book 6 of Clement's *Hypotyposes* (2.15.2) and reproduces it later in book 6 of his *Ecclesiastical History*: "When Peter had publicly preached the word at Rome ... those present ... exhorted Mark, as one who had followed him for a long time and remembered what had been spoken, to make a record of what was said; and that he did this, and distributed the Gospel among those that asked him" (6.14.6; trans. Oulton, LCL). The same tradition appears in Clement's comments on 1 Pet 5:13 in his *Adumbrationes*, preserved in a sixth-century Latin translation, except here he identifies "those present" as "Caesar's equites" (Wilson, *ANF* 2:573; "equestrians," Black 1994, 139). Like the Clementine tradition, Irenaeus (second century CE) reports that Mark wrote the Gospel in Peter's absence, in this case the cause of his absence being his death (Irenaeus, *Haer.* 3.1.1). The anti-Marcionite Prologue to Mark makes a similar claim.

On the one hand, that some of the traditions claim Mark wrote before Peter died (Clement of Alexandria in Eusebius, *Hist. eccl.* 6.14.7; Eusebius, *Hist. eccl.* 2.15.2; Origen in Eusebius, *Hist. eccl.* 6.25.5) and others claim he wrote after Peter's death (Anti-Marcionite Prologue; Irenaeus, *Haer.* 3.1.1; see also Papias in Eusebius, *Hist. eccl.* 3.39.15) inspires legitimate questions concerning the historicity of these traditions. On the other hand, they all

---

a line of scholarship that is, in the words of Black, "so leery of patristic biases ... that the burden of proof tends to be shifted onto those who would give any credence whatever to the fathers' comments on the Gospels' authorship" (1994, 198). To cite a recent example, Roskam claims Papias is "of *no* use to us in dating or locating Mark's Gospel" due to his "apologetic character" (2004, 77, emphasis added). The issues here are complex (see Black 1994, 195–257), but in any case the discussion above pertains only to patristic comments on the shift from orality to textuality.

agree that Mark's Gospel entered the written medium as a means of overcoming the absence of the oral performer/proclaimer Peter. Regardless of the accuracy of the details, the discussion above supports the notion that manuscripts of Mark were intended to overcome the restrictions of oral performance. In fact, there may be no better examples of the *zerdehnte Situation* being "decisive for the genesis of texts" (J. Assmann 2006b, 103) in early Christianity.

Second, the preceding discussion cautions against any claim that one specific "occasion" is more likely to have prompted the writing of Mark's Gospel than another. The crucifixion, the Neronian pogroms, the destruction of the temple, or the death of the first generation of apostles were all *Traditionsbrüche* that could have called forth a textualized Gospel in order to stabilize the tradition into cultural memory. It may be just as likely that it was a combination of these factors, as Kelber originally proposed. For this reason, I have focused in this essay instead upon the role of the manuscript medium in this process.

Third, another neglected aspect of the manuscript medium's role in this process concerns its ability to reflect identity through the *zerdehnte Situation* distinctly as a material artifact. One cannot physically see and touch oral tradition. Oral tradition thus cannot play the visual and aesthetic roles in reading communities—in particular in liturgical settings—that a physical manuscript is capable of playing. Furthermore, one can craft a material artifact in order to reflect group identity, whereas one cannot (to state the obvious) physically shape oral tradition. Assmann elsewhere reflects on this aspect of decorated material culture: "A knife and a jar do not fulfill their function any better by being decorated with ornaments or figures, but they gain immensely in morphological features, or pregnancy, permitting their identification with regard to provenance, date, and cultural context" (2006a, 70). He therefore concludes that "in early times ... the aesthetic seems inseparably linked to the mnemonic" (2006a, 70).

Although observing the connection between manuscripts and society is not new in New Testament studies (Roberts 1979), this understanding of manuscripts' distinctive ability to reflect identity in contrast to oral tradition is a particularly fruitful line of future enquiry. This applies not only to the question of the textualization of Mark but also to further developments in early Christian book culture, especially early Christians' seizing upon the codex book form (see Stanton 2004, 165–91). Christian usage of the codex in practices that were instrumental to the expression of their identities as Christ-followers doubly reflected that identity as distinct from non-Christian Jews, on the one hand, and Greco-Roman pagans, on the other, both of whom demonstrably preferred bookrolls for their texts. Codices thus extended the *zerdehnte Situation* of identity-construction through cultural texts beyond the specific reading communities that used those texts and into broader contexts where the physical artifact represented Christian identity apart from (but related to) the content it transmitted. It was not by accident that the empire eventually attacked Christianity itself by destroying its books in the Diocletianic persecution of the early fourth century CE. Again, much work remains here.

Fourth and directly related to these points, contrary to the oral-preference perspective, scholarly assessment of Mark's textualization of the Jesus tradition must henceforth be capable of explaining, and thus include, the *Wirkungsgeschichte* of that act. This is not to claim that (we can know that) Mark intended everything that came in the wake of his media transition of the gospel tradition. It is, however, to claim that his act of writing contained within it potentialities that later became realities in early Christian manuscript culture, realities that were, therefore, in one form or another, dependent upon his initial impetus. Buttressing an oral-preference perspective with a *Wirkungsgeschichte* perspective on Mark's actions is particularly appropriate because the explosion of Gospel literature in the early church, along with its center-stage role in identity-construction processes, demonstrates that Mark's employment of textuality in order to transition the gospel tradition into cultural memory was overwhelmingly successful.

Works Cited

Achtemeier, Paul J. 1990. *Omne verbum sonat*: The New Testament and the Oral Environment of Late Antiquity. *JBL* 109:3–27.

Assmann, Aleida. 1995. Was sind kulturelle Texte? Pages 232–44 in *Literaturkanon—Medienereignis—Kultureller Text: Formen interkultureller Kommunikation und Übersetzung*. Edited by Andreas Poltermann. GBIU 10. Berlin: Schmidt.

Assmann, Jan. 1992. *Das kulturelle Gedächtnis: Schrift, Erinnerung und politische Identitiät in frühen Hochkulturen*. 6th ed. Munich: Beck.

———. 2000. *Religion und kulturelles Gedächtnis*. 3rd ed. Münich: Beck.

———. 2006a. Form as Mnemonic Device: Cultural Texts and Cultural Memory. Pages 67–82 in Horsley, Draper, and Foley 2006.

———. 2006b. *Religion and Cultural Memory: Ten Studies*. Translated by Rodney Livingstone. Stanford, CA: Stanford University Press.

Black, C. Clifton. 1994. *Mark: Images of an Apostolic Interpreter*. Studies on Personalities of the New Testament. Minneapolis: Fortress.

Bockmuehl, Markus. 2006. *Seeing the Word: Refocusing New Testament Study*. Grand Rapids: Baker Academic.

Bryan, Christopher. 1993. *A Preface to Mark: Notes on the Gospel in Its Literary and Cultural Settings*. New York: Oxford University Press.

Bultmann, Rudolf. 1963. *The History of the Synoptic Tradition*. Translated by John Marsh. Rev. ed. Peabody, MA: Hendrickson.

Carr, David M. 2005. *Writing on the Tablets of the Heart: Origins of Scripture and Literature*. Oxford: Oxford University Press.

Dewey, Joanna., ed. 1995. *Orality and Textuality in Early Christian Literature*. *Semeia* 65. Atlanta: Scholars Press.

———. 2008. The Gospel of Mark as Oral Hermeneutic. Pages 71–87 in *Jesus, the Voice, and the Text: Beyond* The Oral and the Written Gospel. Waco, TX: Baylor University Press.

Dibelius, Martin. 1934. *From Tradition to Gospel*. Translated by Bertram Lee Woolf. Scribner Library 124. New York: Charles Scribner's Sons.

Dunn, James D. G. 2003. *Jesus Remembered I. Christianity in the Making*. Grand Rapids: Eerdmans.

———. 2005a. Altering the Default Setting: Re-envisaging the Early Transmission of the Jesus Tradition. Pages 79–125 in *A New Perspective on Jesus: What the Quest for the Historical Jesus Missed*. London: SPCK.

———. 2005b. Q^1 as Oral Tradition. Pages 45–69 in *The Written Gospel*. Edited by Markus Bockmuehl and Donald A. Hagner. Cambridge: Cambridge University Press.

Edwards, James R. 2002. *The Gospel according to Mark*. Pillar New Testament Commentary. Grand Rapids: Eerdmans.

Gamble, Harry Y. 1995. *Books and Readers in the Early Church: A History of Early Christian Texts*. New Haven: Yale University Press.

Gundry, Robert H. 1993. *Mark: A Commentary on His Apology for the Cross*. Grand Rapids: Eerdmans.

Harris, William V. 1989. *Ancient Literacy*. Cambridge: Harvard University Press.

Hearon, Holly. 2006. The Implications of Orality for Studies of the Biblical Text. Pages 3–20 in Horsley, Draper, and Foley 2006.

———. 2010. Mapping Written and Spoken Word in the Gospel of Mark. Pages 379–92 in Weissenrieder and Coote 2010.

Hengel, Martin. 1984. Entstehungszeit und Situation des Markusevangeliums. Pages 1–47 in *Markus-Philologie: Historische, literargeschichtli-*

che und stilistische Untersuchungen zum zweiten Evangelium. Edited by Hubert Cancik. WUNT 33. Tübingen: Mohr Siebeck.

———. 1985. *Studies in the Gospel of Mark*. Translated by John Bowden. Philadelphia: Fortress.

———. 2000. *The Four Gospels and the One Gospel of Jesus Christ*. Translated by John Bowden. London: SCM.

———. 2010. *Saint Peter: The Underestimated Apostle*. Translated by Thomas Trapp. Grand Rapids: Eerdmans.

Hezser, Catherine. 2001. *Jewish Literacy in Roman Palestine*. TSAJ 81. Tübingen: Mohr Siebeck.

Horsley, Richard A. 2008. Oral Performance and Mark: Some Implications of *The Oral and the Written Gospel*, Twenty-Five Years Later. Pages 45–70 in Thatcher 2008b.

———. 2010. The Gospel of Mark in the Interface of Orality and Writing. Pages 144–65 in Weissenrieder and Coote 2010.

Horsley, Richard A., Jonathan A. Draper, and John Miles Foley, eds. 2006. *Performing the Gospel: Orality, Memory, and Mark*. Minneapolis: Fortress.

Hurtado, Larry W. 2006. *The Earliest Christian Artifacts: Manuscripts and Christian Origins*. Grand Rapids: Eerdmans.

Keith, Chris. 2009. *The Pericope Adulterae, the Gospel of John, and the Literacy of Jesus*. NTTSD 38. Leiden: Brill.

———. 2011a. *Jesus' Literacy: Scribal Culture and the Teacher from Galilee*. LHJS 8/LNTS 413. London: T&T Clark.

———. 2011b. A Performance of the Text: The Adulteress's Entrance into John's Gospel. Pages 49–69 in *The Fourth Gospel in First-Century Media Culture*. Edited by Anthony Le Donne and Tom Thatcher. ESCO/LNTS 426. London: Continuum/T&T Clark.

Keith, Chris, and Tom Thatcher. 2008. The Scar of the Cross: The Violence Ratio and the Earliest Memories of Jesus. Pages 197–214 in Thatcher 2008b.

Kelber, Werner H. 1979. *Mark's Story of Jesus*. Philadelphia: Fortress.

———. 1983. *The Oral and the Written Gospel: The Hermeneutics of Speaking and Writing in the Synoptic Tradition, Mark, Paul, and Q*. Voices in Performance and Text. Bloomington: Indiana University Press.

———. 1988. Die Fleischwerdung des Wortes in der Körperlichkeit des Textes. Pages 31–42 in *Materialität der Kommunikation*. Edited by Hans Ulrich Gumbrecht and K. Ludwig Pfeiffer. STW 750. Frankfurt: Suhrkamp.

———. 1995. Jesus and Tradition: Words in Time, Words in Space. *Semeia* 65:139–67.

———. 1997. Introduction to reprint of *The Oral and The Written Gospel: The Hermeneutics of Speaking and Writing in the Synoptic Tradition, Mark, Paul, and Q*. Voices in Performance and Text. Bloomington: Indiana University Press.

———. 2005. The Works of Memory: Christian Origins as Mnemo-History—A Response. Pages 221–48 in Kirk and Thatcher 2005b.

———. 2007. Orality and Biblical Studies: A Review Essay. *RBL* 12. Online: http://www.bookreviews.org/pdf/2107_6748.pdf.

———. 2008. The Oral-Scribal-Memorial Arts of Communication in Early Christianity. Pages 235–62 in Thatcher 2008b.

———. 2009. Conclusion: The Work of Birger Gerhardsson in Perspective. Pages 173–206 in *Jesus in Memory: Traditions in Oral and Scribal Perspectives*. Waco, TX: Baylor University Press.

———. 2010. The History of the Closure of Biblical Texts. Pages 71–99 in Weissenrieder and Coote 2010.

Kelber, Werner H., and Tom Thatcher. 2008. "It's Not Easy to Take a Fresh Approach": Reflections on *The Oral and the Written Gospel* (An Interview with Werner Kelber). Pages 27–43 in Thatcher 2008b.

Kirk, Alan. 2005a. The Memory of Violence and the Death of Jesus in Q. Pages 191–206 in Kirk and Thatcher 2005b.

———. 2005b. Social and Cultural Memory. Pages 1–24 in Kirk and Thatcher 2005b.

———. 2008. Manuscript Tradition as a *tertium quid*: Orality and Memory in Scribal Practices. Pages 215–34 in Thatcher 2008b.

———. 2010. Memory Theory and Jesus Research. Pages 809–42 in volume 1 of *Handbook for the Study of the Historical Jesus*. Edited by Tom Holmén and Stanley E. Porter. Leiden: Brill.

Kirk, Alan, and Tom Thatcher. 2005a. Jesus Tradition as Social Memory. Pages 25–42 in Kirk and Thatcher 2005b.

———, eds. 2005b. *Memory, Tradition, and Text: Uses of the Past in Early Christianity*. SemeiaSt 52. Atlanta: Society of Biblical Literature

Knight, Mark. 2010. *Wirkungsgeschichte*, Reception History, Reception Theory. *JSNT* 33:137–46.

Lane, William L. 1974. *The Gospel according to Mark*. NICNT. Grand Rapids: Eerdmans.

Le Donne, Anthony. 2009. *The Historiographical Jesus: Memory, Typology, and the Son of David*. Waco, TX: Baylor University Press.

Rhoads, David. 2010. Performance Events in Early Christianity: New Testament Writings in an Oral Context. Pages 166–93 in Weissenrieder and Coote 2010.

Rhoads, David, Joanna Dewey, and Donald Michie. 2012. *Mark as Story: An Introduction to the Narrative of a Gospel.* 3rd ed. Minneapolis: Fortress.

Ricoeur, Paul. 2004. *Memory, History, Forgetting.* Translated by Kathleen Blamey and David Pellauer. Chicago: University of Chicago Press.

Roberts, Colin H. 1979. *Manuscript, Society and Belief in Early Christian Egypt.* London: Oxford University Press.

Robinson, John A. T. 1976. *Redating the New Testament.* Philadelphia: Westminster.

Roskam, H. N. 2004. *The Purpose of the Gospel of Mark in Its Historical and Social Context.* NovTSup 114. Leiden: Brill.

Schröter, Jens. 2002. Von der Historizität der Evangelien: Ein Beitrag zur gegenwärtigen Diskussion um den historischen Jesus. Pages 163–212 in *Der historische Jesus: Tendenzen und Perspektiven der gegenwärtigen Forschung.* Edited by Jens Schröter and Ralph Brucker. BZNW 114. Berlin: de Gruyter.

Schwartz, Barry. 1982. The Social Context of Commemoration: A Study in Collective Memory. *Social Forces* 62:374–402.

———. 2005. Christian Origins: Historical Truth and Social Memory. Pages 43–56 in Kirk and Thatcher 2005b.

———. 2011. What Difference Does the Medium Make? Pages 225–38 in *The Fourth Gospel in First-Century Media Culture.* Edited by Anthony Le Donne and Tom Thatcher. ESCO/LNTS 426. London: T&T Clark.

Shiner, Whitney. 2003. *Proclaiming the Gospel: First-Century Performance of Mark.* Harrisburg, PA: Trinity Press International.

———. 2006. Memory Technology and the Composition of Mark. Pages 147–65 in Horsley, Draper, and Foley 2006.

Spivey, Robert A., D. Moody Smith, and C. Clifton Black. 2007. *Anatomy of the New Testament.* 6th ed. Minneapolis: Fortress.

Stanton, Graham. 1975. Form Criticism Revisited. Pages 13–27 in *What about the New Testament? Essays in Honour of Christopher Evans.* Edited by Morna Hooker and Colin Hickling. London: SCM.

———. 2004. *Jesus and Gospel.* Cambridge: Cambridge University Press.

Stein, Robert H. 2008. *Mark.* BECNT. Grand Rapids: Baker Academic.

Thatcher, Tom. 2006. *Why John Wrote a Gospel: Jesus—Memory—History.* Louisville: Westminster John Knox.

———. 2008a. Beyond Texts and Traditions: Werner Kelber's Media History of Christian Origins. Pages 1–26 in Thatcher 2008b.

———, ed. 2008b. *Jesus, the Voice, and the Text: Beyond The Oral and the Written Gospel*. Waco, TX: Baylor University Press.

Theissen, Gerd, and Dagmar Winter. 2002. *The Quest for the Plausible Jesus: The Question of Criteria*. Translated by by M. Eugene Boring. Louisville: Westminster John Knox.

Thiselton, Anthony C. 1992. *New Horizons in Hermeneutics: The Theory and Practice of Transforming Biblical Reading*. Grand Rapids: Zondervan.

Weissenrieder, Annette, and Robert B. Coote, eds. 2010. *The Interface of Orality and Writing*. WUNT 260. Tübingen: Mohr Siebeck.

Winn, Adam. 2008. *The Purpose of Mark's Gospel*. WUNT 2/245. Tübingen: Mohr Siebeck.

Wire, Antoinette Clark. 2011. *The Case for Mark Composed in Performance*. Biblical Performance Criticism 3. Eugene, OR: Cascade.

Yarbro Collins, Adela. 2007. *Mark*. Hermeneia. Minneapolis: Fortress.

Zhang, Tong, and Barry Schwartz. 1997. Confucius and the Cultural Revolution: A Study in Collective Memory. *International Journal of Politics, Culture and Society* 11.2:189–212.

Zimmermann, Ruben. 2010. Memory and Form Criticism: The Typicality of Memory as a Bridge between Orality and Literality in the Early Christian Remembering Process. Pages 130–43 in Weissenrieder and Coote 2010.

THE MEMORY OF THE BELOVED DISCIPLE: A POETICS OF JOHANNINE MEMORY

Jeffrey E. Brickle

Barry Schwartz's introduction to the present volume invites reflection on how social memory theory might illuminate the origins and context of the Johannine corpus. Conceiving of John as a cultural "memorian" (to borrow Jan Assmann's term; 1997, 21) contrasts sharply with a tenaciously held view that portrays the author of the Fourth Gospel as a solitary, mystical purveyor of largely independent and idiosyncratic traditions transmitted within a relatively closed sectarian community. Schwartz's provocative and insightful memory research compels one to reexamine John's plausible network of associations and attempt to explain how these associations might relate to the occasion and nature of John's literary project.

My contribution, which follows Schwartz's helpful lead in regarding ancient literature such as the Gospels as products of collective memory, suggests a modest paradigm shift. Although this essay will remain conversant with traditional categories ascribed to "John" (theologian, historian, storyteller), I will attempt to push beyond these categories. In the process, I will touch on a number of issues that are not particularly new to Johannine studies yet remain inextricably intertwined with a memory-focused analysis (e.g., canon consciousness; literary design; intertextuality; source, tradition, genre, and narrative-critical approaches; Christology). While constituting a discreet subdiscipline, the concerns of social memory theory thus intersect with a variety of critical approaches and methodologies. These concerns converge to bridge the frequently bifurcated aims of historical and literary analysis, serving to restore the vibrant relationship between the Fourth Gospel's underlying past and the text as it now stands.

As should become clear, the title of my essay ("The Memory of the Beloved Disciple") refers not only to the act of remembering the figure of the Beloved Disciple but also, and more particularly, to the nature of the way this individual remembered and expressed the past in his own present. The subtitle ("A Poetics of Johannine Memory") conveys that I am attempting to describe *a* (not *the*) poetics undergirding John's role and modus operandi as an early Christian memorian.

Fueled by Schwartz's concepts, this essay will explore the why, how, and what of Johannine memory dynamics—the inner workings driving John's recollection, shaping, and communication of the Jesus event. My analysis is more programmatic and suggestive in nature than detailed, more exploratory than conclusive. Resisting the temptation to extensively cite secondary research treating social memory and Johannine literature, I will instead focus upon the Fourth Gospel chiefly through the perspectives that Schwartz has provided, devoting little attention here to the Johannine Epistles and none to the Apocalypse. I propose that the Fourth Gospel represents a response to factors threatening the late first-century church by means of a collective and elevated vision of the past.

Situating Memories in the Unsettled Johannine Present

In seeking to re-create the nuts and bolts of John's social memory structure, it is necessary to attempt an overall reconstruction of the *Sitz im Leben* that gave rise to his particular exploitation of the past. Given the special focus of this volume, I will bypass the more extensive documentation and defense of this reconstruction that would be appropriate to a book dedicated to the Johannine literature. The following brief sketch of the situation behind the Fourth Gospel will serve here as a means by which to launch and spin my own Johannine "mnemohistory" (again, J. Assmann's term; 1997, 8).

An Aged Memorian in a Transitory Age

John represents what Schwartz would call an interested, "highly motivated" memorian confronting an intense, multifaceted memory crisis that came to a head during the waning years of the first century CE. While many issues likely contributed to this memory crisis, the following interrelated factors seem paramount.

(1) *An increasing remoteness in time and space from the actual Jesus event.* Memories are transient and tend to fade over time (Bauckham 2006, 319–20; Allison 2010, 1–10; McIver 2011, 143–61). Several decades separated John's constituents from the movement's beginnings. Furthermore, Jewish Christians who had emigrated from Palestine and settled in the diaspora—including Asia Minor, where the Fourth Gospel's recipients likely resided—not only experienced physical and cultural separation or

displacement from the "sacred," archetypal environs "where it all began," but Palestine itself had undergone a number of changes since the early first century.

(2) *The death of nearly all of the original participants in Jesus' ministry.* In his introduction to this volume, Schwartz (p. 16) notes that the writing of the Gospel narratives was prompted in part by "the dying of a generation of witnesses and a concern to secure their memories." The probable composition of the Fourth Gospel and Johannine Epistles during the mid-90s corresponded with the extreme limits of the threshold of direct testimony (see Kirk 2005, 5–6). By the twilight of the first century, the relatively few remaining eyewitnesses of the Jesus era would have been eagerly sought out, consulted, and prized as living links to the past.

(3) *The wake of the destruction of many of the tangible symbols of Judaism, the chief ideological wellspring of Christianity.* While viewed differently by outsiders, the Holy Land occupied a central presence within Jewish thought (Mendels 2004, 89–102). With the destruction of Jerusalem ("an exemplary place of memory"; A. Assmann 2011, 288) and the Herodian Temple in particular, Judaism suffered an irreversible, though not fatal, blow to its symbolic and theological world. Post-70 Judaism struggled to recapture its pre-70 essence, to effectively regroup in response to this calamity, and to recast its worship practices in the absence of the temple cult. Judaism's common memory had thus been in flux, and efforts had been underway to restore and reshape its collective identity in light of the destructive Jewish War.

(4) *Ongoing tensions between Jews and Christians.* While historically and theologically intertwined, differences between these groups had strained their relationship since the inception of Christianity (see Dunn 2006).

(5) *The changed face of Christianity from a predominantly Jewish to Gentile constituency.* While Palestine had long been impacted by Hellenism (Hengel 2003), the transition within the early church from a more Jewish- to Gentile-oriented ethos had further widened the gap between the movement's indebtedness to its Jewish roots and its embracing of a more Hellenistic identity.

(6) *Increasing pressure to conform to societal norms.* The encroachment of social opposition to the Jesus movement brought mounting coercion to relax distinctives and abandon the faith.

(7) *The delay of the parousia.* The promised imminent return of Christ had not (yet) occurred, forcing Christians to reevaluate the movement's

eschatological orientation (see further Schwartz 2011, 234–37). Some reinterpreted the delay as a summons to re-entrench in anticipation of a potentially long wait.

Together these multilayered factors swirled into a cloudy, unstable, and disturbing aggregate that necessitated the elevation of "the original portrayal of their [the early Christians'] subject [Jesus] through a reconfiguration of … recollections" (Schwartz, p. 8, above).

The seasoned memorian behind the Fourth Gospel and Johannine Epistles had been profoundly affected by these changes and addressed the crisis by means of a fresh, powerful, and authoritative memory articulation. As Mary Spaulding has suggested,

> during times of significant societal crisis and change, human beings do not readily and willingly accept the total transfiguration or elimination of all previous mnemonic associations. Instead they cling to familiar patterns of behavior in order to ward off threats to their corporate identity caused by the crisis. If the [Fourth] Gospel is portraying a historical group of people facing a verifiable crisis in identity … then the author of John may be responding to these traumatic issues with answers that will aid believers (and potential believers) in coping with the trauma and loss they are experiencing. (2009, 2)

John was able to offer a solution that was "familiar," yet innovative and arresting.

As is well known, the precise identity of the self-styled Beloved Disciple upon whom the overall witness of the Fourth Gospel appears to rest has been debated. If the Beloved Disciple was in any way associated with the historical Jesus and his movement, however, this figure evidently survived to an advanced age and would have been regarded by the church as a revered custodian of valuable Jesus traditions. John offered mature reflections on events that stemmed from the now-distant past. In the context of the sweeping changes described above that indelibly impacted Christians living during the first century's closing decade, he endured as an ideal candidate to address these challenges via the articulation of a rich and robust memory transaction—a sculpted version of the past that he imposed upon his shifting present. Through the media of a written Gospel and letters, John injected much-needed stability, renewed vitality, and far-reaching vision into a community located on the fringes of "communicative memory" (Kirk 2005, 5, employing Assmann's term).

Remembering in Concert

Schwartz's introduction rightly points out the situatedness of memories within groups. John's memory orientation was no different, and he deliberately identified himself with a number of other memory tradents, most of whom were already deceased by the time the Fourth Gospel was produced but who had in various ways participated in the Jesus events and shared their stories. John intentionally linked his personal memories of Jesus with a cadre of voices from the past and his present, revealing the collaborative nature of his project: "*we* have seen his glory" (John 1:14); "*we* know that his testimony is true" (John 21:24); "what *we* have seen and heard" (1 John 1:3).

Among other roles, late in his career John assumed in some measure the function of a scribe, affiliating with the ranks of the craft guild or network of Christian scribal memorians. Scribes played a unique and critical role in antiquity by transmitting cherished traditions, inculcating them on the hearts and minds of subsequent generations (Carr 2005). John came alongside those who transmitted their accounts of the early Christian legacy through the medium of writing, linking his inscribed voice to theirs.

We may also appreciate the complex ethos of the Beloved Disciple by regarding him symbolically as a library, librarian, and library patron, dynamically preserving, accessing, and ruminating upon a rich collection or network of internalized traditions and experiences. Such a depiction corresponds with Richard Hays's portrayal of Paul as a figure who processed Scripture internally (Hays 1989, 42–43). Like Paul, the Beloved Disciple kept a functioning internal "echo chamber" (Reis 2002), listening *within himself* to a symphony of texts—"a well-stocked memorial library" (Griffiths 1999, 53)—that he had committed to memory while weaving into his thoughts and compositions his own perspectives on the past. Like the medieval theologian Thomas Aquinas, John "communed with his memory constantly," meditating on a vast store of texts and experiences (see Carruthers 2008, 7). Schwartz's proposals are exceptionally relevant and applicable to a culture in which "[t]aking in a composition meant fully incorporating it in one's storehouse of knowledge in memory, and allowing oneself to be stamped and therefore changed by the process" (Lee and Scott 2009, 68). The seeds of John's contemplative lifestyle came to full fruition in his masterful literary works.

KEYS, FRAMES, AND DOORS: EVOKING A SACRED PAST

To borrow Schwartz's terminology, John employed the strategy of "keying" in calling forth "frames" that enclosed his particular portrait of Jesus. Schwartz suggests that keying involves "communicative movement—talk, writing, and ritual that publicly connects otherwise separate realms of memory" (Schwartz 2005, 250). In John's case, two primary matrices or frameworks were evoked through keying and then superimposed upon the memory of Jesus, forming the backdrop and chief conversation partners for his literary achievement. Yoon-Man Park points out that "it is in terms of an existing mental knowledge framework that people acquire incoming knowledge, experience, and events in stories, and are thus able to retrieve them from memory. Framed knowledge aids people to readily process what is happening in the real or story world by allowing them to make inferences" (2010, 23). Frames thus serve as a means to assist in the interpretation of a narrative through an established and remembered point of reference or cognitive structure. In short, we make sense of things through what we already know.

As I will maintain below, John employed a set of frames well known to his readers/hearers in order to assist their comprehension of his memory articulation. I suggest that these frames were not only familiar but deeply embedded within their internal mnemo-structures, rendering their reception of John's Gospel—especially after multiple oral performances—a rich, subtle, multivalent experience (see Thomas 2012, 1–11). The strategic devices of keying and framing afforded to John's audience particularized access to, and interpretation of, bygone yet still-much-alive figures and events, opening for "those who have not seen and yet have come to believe" (John 20:29) a door into a discrete sphere of the past. Several of the most significant frames that John evoked to key his Jesus story to familiar precedents will be briefly reviewed here.

THE NARRATIVE HISTORY OF ISRAEL

The "storied" nature of ancient Judaism is well known. As N. T. Wright notes, "[f]irst-century Judaism is an excellent example of a culture which quite obviously thrived on stories" (1992, 215). Stories are one of the most effective means by which to articulate a worldview and orient oneself in relation to one's past (Bartholomew and Goheen 2004), and they do so because narratives fundamentally shape identity and ethos (Gregory 2009).

While "every text triggers connections to other texts within its reader's memory" (Zumstein 2008, 121), John interfaced with the narrative of Israel in a distinctive fashion. More than simply drawing from Scripture in composing his Gospel, John seems to have assumed a form of hyper-, pan-, or even meta-metalepsis that effectively evoked the *entire narrative scope* of the sacred Jewish Scriptures as one of the backdrops or canvases for his Jesus story. "Metalepsis," a term coined by literary critic John Holland, works as follows: "When a literary echo links the text in which it occurs to an earlier text, the figurative effect of the echo can lie in the unstated or suppressed (transumed) points of resonance between the two texts" (Hays 1989, 20). Metalepsis corresponds closely with Schwartz's approach, offering what could be described as two sides of the same intertextual coin: metalepsis is aurality's version of collective memory's keying and framing.

By incorporating a heightened form of these techniques, John masterfully conveyed the dynamic sweep and living pastness of the Old Testament as an underlying and interactive setting in which to interpret the Jesus event. John does not merely comment ancillarily on certain passages he has culled from a textual database; rather, he grants admission to a dynamic, sensory-laden Old Testament memory theater inviting full audience participation (Thatcher 2011). Through a mimetic act of new creation, the Gospel of John evokes the very *presence* of the Jewish Scriptures—and by extension, the presence of the One who inhabits and speaks from these texts (see Steiner 1989).

The Prologue's opening clause (ἐν ἀρχῇ ἦν ὁ λόγος; "In the beginning was the Word"; John 1:1) keys the story to follow to the LXX Genesis creation account, thus reaching further back into the Old Testament narrative than the opening lines of the Synoptic Gospels. Whereas Mark's story opens with a portrayal of John the Baptist as a prophetic messenger fulfilling Mal 3:1 and Isa 40:3, Matthew's story begins with a stylized genealogy tracing Jesus' lineage back to Abraham and David, and Luke's Gospel (after a brief formal prologue) departs from a depiction of an elderly, barren priestly couple modeled after infertile couples of the patriarchal and later eras, John's starting point captures the essence of Jesus as God, present in and officiator of the creation of the cosmos.

Far from inferring a static or mechanical correspondence between text and subtext, the Fourth Gospel effectively launches or sets in motion the full compass of the Jewish Scriptures, which "play" like background music beneath the Johannine narrative structure. Through quotations, allusions, and thematic links, the Fourth Gospel artfully traces or weaves into its narrative tissue the substance of key Old Testament events, including the creation, the exodus, and the exile. The concentrated clustering of Old Testament citations in chapter 12 undergirding Jesus' triumphant ride into Jerusalem and the Jewish rejection of Jesus (see Köstenberger 2007, 467), for example, seems to suggest the conclusion of one "symphonic movement" of the Old Testament in John, which culminates in representative passages from the Psalms and Prophets.

In John's retelling of the story, then, Jesus was to be remembered upon the stage of primeval history and ancient Israel's iconic and tumultuous past. The Old Testament served as a veritable "framework of antecedent salvation history into which Jesus [was] placed" (Köstenberger 2009, 176). By means of this mnemonic staging technique, John implicitly addressed the problem of the theological and historical relationship of Christianity to the Old Testament Scriptures and Judaism. While not rejecting their Judaic roots, John's readers were to be a community centered around the One who had created the world and was the anticipated Jewish messiah and king.

FROM ΒΙΒΛΟΣ (MATTHEW 1:1) TO ΒΙΒΛΙΑ (JOHN 21:25): JOHN FOR REMEMBERERS OF THE SYNOPTICS

Rather than viewing John's relationship to the Synoptics primarily in terms of source (in)dependence (see Smith 2001; Brown 2003, 94–104; Sloyan 2006, 29–52), it may be more helpful to conceive of the historical, literary, and theological relationship between these texts in terms of associated memory tradents. Debates over Johannine dependence on the Synoptics have, in my opinion, obscured the symbiotic rapport that John shared with his predecessors who had also communicated particularized versions of the past. By limiting the discussion to whether or not John actually borrowed from the Synoptics, scholars overlook a key mnemo-framing device that John employed in crafting his narrative. What Park has perceptively observed regarding Mark's Gospel holds true as well for John's: "the main barrier to our appreciation as modern audiences/readers of the Markan oral-aural narrative is our ignorance of the background knowledge or frames on which the text is based" (2010, 23).

I submit that both John and his late first-century readers were well acquainted with the content of the Synoptic Gospels, which would have had more than sufficient time to circulate among the closely tied, socially networked Mediterranean church communities (see Bauckham 1998).

Furthermore, John keyed the Synoptics as another frame for his Gospel, albeit in ingenious and subtle ways. John wrote his Gospel to function as what might be termed a "reciprocal countermemory" to the influence of his long deceased comrade, Peter, whose presence and memory articulation seem to permeate and underlie the Synoptic tradition (Bauckham 2006, 155–82, 202–21).

The emergence of the Synoptic tradition had introduced "multiple versions" or "variations" (Schwartz's terms, p. 13, above) of the Gospel narrative reflecting in essence ternary points of origin. However, while not downplaying the distinctive emphases and complex literary achievements of Mark, Matthew, and Luke, the likelihood of Markan priority ties these Gospels to a shared reliance on the recollections of the apostle and eminent Christian memorian Peter. John added his voice to that of Peter and those indebted to Peter's memory formulation. He boldly departed, however, from Mark as a primary "source" and hence from a predominantly Petrine-based structuring of the Jesus story.

John was thus not simply trying to copy or imitate the Synoptic pattern with the intention of introducing a new flavor. In full awareness of the existence of the Synoptics, John skillfully crafted a contrasting yet mutually compatible version of the beginnings of the Jesus movement. He introduced a freshly minted template—consisting of recollections from his vantage point on the fringes of the apostolic era—upon which to impress his telling of the story. John had traversed the architectural topography of earlier traditions thoroughly and was thus "path-dependent" (Schwartz, p. 16, above) in his appropriation of the memory articulations of his now-deceased colleagues. John elected, however, to blaze a parallel side path, a path on which he never completely lost sight of their well-traveled route.

While John may not have been cognizant that he himself was writing "Scripture" in the formal sense, he was at least aware that he was contributing to a canon of memory underwritten by authorized and respected tradents. This would suggest that he espoused some form of "canonical consciousness" (Köstenberger 2009, 104) vis-à-vis Matthew, Mark, and Luke. With his own death pending, John reinforced the long-term stability inherent in multiple narrative versions that "transcend[ed] the limitations of any single individual's recollection" (Schwartz, p. 8, above).

How did John key his own memories of Jesus to the Synoptics? One way was by utilizing the same genre (essentially an adapted form of ancient *bioi*) that the Synoptic Evangelists had employed, a literary type that by John's era had long been established within the Christian communities (see

Aune 1987, 17–76; Burridge 2004). Like all genres, the conventional features of a Gospel aroused certain expectations on the part of the audience (Bauckham 2007, 17). John clearly evinced a "consciousness of genre"; in "his reflection upon it ... we can detect ... a very deep understanding of the complexities and paradoxes of what he was attempting" (Ashton 2007, 357–58). This is not to say, of course, that John did not engage in some modifications or "genre bending" (Attridge 2002). John's adoption of the narrative Gospel genre naturally invited reflective comparison between his memory communication and those of his Synoptic predecessors, whose literary productions had become, by the late first century, more or less boilerplates for expressing the Jesus story.

John also keyed significant Synoptic terminology. Forms of ἀρχή ("beginning") occur in the opening statements of Mark (1:1), Luke (1:2), and John (1:1–2). The first word of Matthew (βίβλος, "book") parallels the very last word of John (21:25), only the latter occurs in the plural form (βιβλία, "books"). The closing remarks in John (21:24–25) seem to imply that the author was aware of the existence of other "books" about Jesus. The fascinating link between Matthew's first word (βίβλος) and John's last (βιβλία) suggests John's signatory way of indicating that he considered closed or sealed by his testimony what now consisted of a collection of four "authorized" Gospels—a possibility rendered all the more intriguing by the leading role Matthew played as the favorite Gospel of the early church. These terminological correspondences not only indicated John's Synoptic-consciousness but also invited his readers to participate in a multilevel reading that dynamically compared and contrasted his account with the other three.

In various ways, John also assumed acquaintance with the *content* of the Synoptic tradition on the part of his readers. As Andreas Köstenberger has noted (1999, 36–37), the Fourth Gospel presupposes, for example, the reader's prior knowledge of Simon Peter (John 1:40), John the Baptist's imprisonment (3:24), a particular saying of Jesus (4:44), the Twelve (6:67, 71), and Mary and Martha (11:1–2). In addition, the account of the miraculous large catch of fish by the disciples in 21:1–14 suggests familiarity with the "corresponding" story of their calling in Luke 5:4–11. Many early Christian readers of John's Gospel would have been struck by John's retelling of the now-familiar Jesus tale. His readers made sense of the Fourth Gospel in part through their recollections of the Synoptic tradition with which they were thoroughly versed. The contours of the Synoptic itinerary and the individual pericopae had been deeply assimilated or mapped within readers' memories through what Elizabeth Minchin terms "episodic, or semantic, memory, that particular system which guides the comprehension and generation of narrative" (2001, 10). Like the Old Testament, the Synoptic tradition "played" beneath the Fourth Gospel's surface structure, forming a subdialogue for readers to ponder deeply. The interchange between the narrative and the keyed frames below the text resonated with rich counterpoint and generated a profoundly creative tension.

TABLES AND CHAIRS: ARRANGING NARRATIVE SURFACE STRUCTURES

As noted earlier, John stood jointly with his fellow memory tradents. As a type of mnemo-articulation, his literary achievement was the product of an "accumulated succession of commemorations" (Schwartz, p. 16, above, citing Olick 2007, 58). The activity of commemoration may be defined as "the selection, isolation, and celebration of historical events or figures that are deemed significant or in some way defining of a group's collective identity" (Le Donne 2011, 191). John submitted his commemorative text as a media artifact (see Kirk 2005, 9) or stabilizing instrument in response to a pressing memory crisis. Wolfgang Iser affirms the situatedness of texts such as the Fourth Gospel: "in general, literary texts constitute a reaction to contemporary situations, bringing attention to problems that are conditioned though not resolved by contemporary norms" (1978, 3).

Once again, narrative frameworks communicate worldviews and ideologies (Sternberg 1985), serving as the conceptual backbone of a society's or group's self-conception in relation to its past. These narrative frameworks are freighted with interpretive meaning. In contributing to a "grand narrative," "a master story that underlies and informs innumerable concrete tellings and retellings of the past" (J. Assmann 1997, 3), John chose to represent Christian origins through a similar-yet-contrasting narrative template that reenvisioned and heightened the story's mnemonic drama like "an eagle over more pedestrian depictions of the life of Christ" (Köstenberger 2004, 1).

Schwartz's general principle is surely correct in John's specific case: in the context of a later stage in relating the Jesus narrative, John presented a more intensified portrait of Jesus than Mark, just as Tarbell's portrait of Lincoln rose above Herndon's (Schwartz, p. 7–8, above). Along similar lines, Doron Mendels observes that "[i]n the Gospels we have evidence of how a community ... goes ... through a lengthy process of redefining its ... common collective memory" (2007, 151). From the composition of the Synoptics to the Fourth Gospel, one encounters an evolving series of portraits, each contributing to and further developing the remembered anthology of Jesus memories shared by the early Christians.

This exploration of John's mnemo-dynamics may be extended by considering ways in which his articulation of a socially oriented memory was expressed through the Fourth Gospel's *literary design* and *surface structures*. My comments under each of the following sections are admittedly fragmentary but are nonetheless intended to promote further thought and discussion. Raymond Brown's overall outline of the Fourth Gospel (1997, 337–61; 2003, 298–316) provides a workable and (to me) quite convincing structural hypothesis with which to organize this portion of our discussion, although I will add sectional subtitles. Given Papias's concern with order in the compositional arrangement of the Gospels, John's conformance to "literary order" as opposed to Mark (Bauckham 2006, 217) indicated his careful shaping and mnemonic repackaging of events in light of his own perspectives on the Jesus story.

The Prologue (John 1:1–18): Remembering before the Gospel

The Fourth Gospel's opening section, whose vocabulary, syntax, poetic nature, and themes evoke the creation account, conveys a sense of suspended timelessness and spacelessness. Readers are immediately introduced to a radical form of pastness that surpasses that communicated by the Synoptics, so much so that Alan Culpepper cites this past perspective in the Prologue as an example of "pre-historical" analepsis (1983, 56–57, 106).

According to John, Jesus was Yahweh—the God of the Old Testament—and as such preexisted the historical events narrated in the Gospel. While other Gospels had arguably set forth a high Christology by identifying Jesus as Yahweh (Beardsley 2012; Bauckham 2007, 239–52), John's memory crisis led him to express the agelessness and "antiquity" of his chief subject more immediately and directly by evoking the sensation of an extremely distant past. At the same time, "the prologue takes the audience into the perpetual present of the action" (Brant 2004, 26).

The Book of Signs (John 1:19–12:50): Remembering Jesus' Journeys and Encounters

Whereas the Synoptics depict a wide range of Jesus' miracles, the Fourth Gospel dramatically narrows the scope down to selected σημεῖα ("signs"), "acts with inherent christological symbolism" (Köstenberger 2007, 440). John's first readers would have been strongly impacted by the striking characters, discourses, images, and events that they encountered in the Book of Signs. Jesus' σημεῖα produce a range of responses from those who witness them, inviting introspection as well as clarifying and "reinforcing Christian faith" (Aune 1987, 59) in the context of intense political, religious, and social pressure.

In terms of characterization, John elevates not only his central figure but others around Jesus as well. Minor characters such as Philip, Nathanael (= the Synoptic Bartholomew?), and Thomas—all shrouded in relative obscurity in the Synoptics—could now be remembered not as names relegated to apostolic lists but as individual disciples who explicitly interact with Jesus and contribute to the narrative's plot. Other characters, such as Nicodemus and the Samaritan woman, were introduced for the first time (at least in the written medium) and likewise left indelible imprints on the church's collective memory. John's readers in the last decade of the first century could relate and (in some cases) aspire to emulate these figures of faith, assisted by John's fresh synthesis of various types of characterization (see Berlin 1994, 41–42).

Jesus' attendance at Jerusalem festivals would have accorded with "the Jews as the archetypal people of memory" for whom the "major festivals of the Jewish year … remember the historical narrative of a community" (Whitehead 2009, 136, referring to Yerushalmi's insights into Jewish commemorative rituals). Jesus' symbolic fulfillment of these festal celebrations, "a major structural and theological plank in John's gospel" (Köstenberger 2009, 412), exalted his role as the figurative aspiration behind these rituals of memory (see also Burge 2012).

As for John's viewpoint on eschatology, Schwartz has characterized his unique angle in this way: "a great achievement of John's Gospel, the only Gospel to portray Jesus as a non-apocalyptic prophet, is its distinctive approach to the delay of the Parousia, one that merges future into present eschatology while retaining belief in, although scarcely mentioning, the Parousia itself" (2011, 236–37). Stated differently, "in Jesus the distinction between [the future age to come] and [the present age] has collapsed, so that believers in Jesus are able to experience end-time blessings already in the here and now" (Köstenberger 2009, 297). Since the expected future had not arrived, the future was drawn into the present, with the result that until Christ's return the memory of the future became the symbolic and provisional reality of the present. Through his largely realized eschatological outlook, "John ... has elevated 'inaugurated' eschatology to a higher plane than the Synoptic presentation" (Köstenberger 2009, 297), a fitting mnemonic perspective for late first-century Christians experiencing a delayed parousia.

The Book of Signs also incorporates meaning-laden spatio-temporal frameworks that evoke collective memory. Alan Kirk notes that "[m]emory attaches to places and landscapes.... The space within which memory is plotted is a *social* framework because space is conceptualized, organized, and shaped by the group inhabiting it" (2005, 2–3, emphasis original). As an important aspect of memory, the socially constructed nature of sacred and secular spaces has often been overlooked in biblical studies, being overshadowed by geographical and historical approaches to the topic (Malbon 1986; George 2009; Stewart 2009). Jesus' various peregrinations in this section of the Fourth Gospel cover several locations in Palestine that would be familiar to Jewish families who may have emigrated from this region, those from a Jewish background who would have learned about many of these archetypal places as children, and readers of the Synoptics. In discussing the work of noted architect Wes Janz, Frances Downing observes that "[a]ncestral places often fix our own identities with the people and places of our developing years" (2000, 30). For Downing, "we all retain memories of places. They identity who we are as individuals. At the same time, they tie us to networks of people, culture, and society. Even through time, they reach into the past to people whose lives and experiences were as real as ours, and into the future to those who lives we can only imagine" (2000, 3).

The Fourth Gospel's spatial orientation tied John's readers to Jesus and the Christian community via a renewed feeling of "landedness" (to use Walter Brueggemann's term; 2002, xi), restoring a sense of shared identity and spiritual well-being for those experiencing isolation or distance. Brueggemann states that "land is never simply physical dirt but is always physical dirt freighted with social meaning derived from historical experience" (2002, 2). As they mentally traveled to the various Johannine *lieux de mémoire* featured in his account, John was able to anchor his readers more securely into his network of memory alliances.

As Shimon Bar-Efrat perceptively asserts, time is another critical dimension influencing narrative, because a "narrative cannot exist without time, to which it has a twofold relationship: it unfolds within time, and times passes within it" (1989, 141). Like space, time is also conceptually and culturally organized, since human beings tend to schematize their "visions of history" (Zerubavel 2003, 86). A great deal has been said elsewhere about the phenomenon of John's structuring of time, a prominent device in the Book of Signs. In a classic treatment of John's use of narrative time stemming from the research of Gérard Genette, for example, Alan Culpepper (1983, 51–75) helpfully examines and applies temporal elements such as order (anachronies, analepses, prolepses), duration (factoring in scenes, summaries, ellipses), and frequency (singulative, repetitious, repetitive, and iterative narrative structures). In the Fourth Gospel, time "moves, imperceptibly almost, from a flow of days to a flow of feasts to a flow of years" (Brant 2004, 37, quoting Thomas Brodie). It seems clear that John departed from many elements intrinsic to the Synoptic temporal framework and did not adhere to a rigid chronological time scheme but embraced a somewhat organic approach to time that permitted his narrative structure to breathe. His handling of time would have impacted "how the past [was] registered and organized *in* [his late first-century readers'] *minds*" (Zerubavel 2003, 2, emphasis original). This would have included a mental overlaying of John's temporal pattern upon the memory of the Synoptic framework, collectively resulting in a bilevel, multiplex relationship.

All in all, I suggest that John's approach to time resonated with Christians facing a memory crisis by vividly projecting a sophisticatedly rendered, temporally oriented vision of the past onto their present.

THE BOOK OF GLORY (JOHN 13:1–20:31): REMEMBERING JESUS' ENCOUNTERS WITH HIS OWN AND WITH DEATH

The first part of this section of the Fourth Gospel, which portrays "Jesus focused upon preparing his disciples for his forthcoming departure and their own role thereafter" (Cummins 2008, 68), features the Last Supper and the Farewell Discourse (the latter episode absent, of course, from the Synoptics). These are intensively formative scenes in the shaping of the mnemonic Jesus community, marking important Johannine textual sites of memory. In this intimate, instructive atmosphere with the core of the foundational memorians present, including Peter and the Beloved Disciple—whose proximity to Jesus will define and shape his role as a discerning memory articulator (John 13:23–25; 21:20)—the circle of apostles were to be remembered first and foremost as *disciples* of Jesus. It is here that Judas forfeits his ongoing role as a corroborating memorian. Craig Keener offers the intriguing possibility that the Farewell Discourse echoed Moses' final discourse (2003, 2:896), with the result that this Deuteronomic precursor may have served as an intrinsic memory frame. As I have suggested elsewhere, 1 John appropriated the memory and ethos of the Farewell Discourse in confronting the secessionist crisis (Brickle 2012).

In place of the physical, flesh-and-blood Jesus no longer accessible to late first-century Christians, his presence was soon to be mediated through the παράκλητος, a distinctive Johannine moniker for the Holy Spirit (John 14:16, 26; 15:26; 16:7; 1 John 2:1; see Burge 1987, 6–10). Fittingly, "the discourse underlines the theme of Jesus' continuing presence with his people. In place of an eschatological discourse preceding the passion, as in the Synoptic traditions and probably traditions known to the Johannine community ... John treats his audience to an emphasis on the present experience of Jesus' presence through his past return to them" (Keener 2003, 2:898). Among other roles, the παράκλητος served a vital mnemonic function (John 14:26). I take Jesus' statement, "But the advocate, the Holy Spirit ... will ... remind you of all that I have said to you," as assuring more than assistance in recalling Jesus' ipsissima verba, extending more broadly to include guidance in the disciples' processing, selection, and shaping of the remembered traditions (John 20:30–31; 21:24–25).

The closing portion of the Book of Glory culminates in a "climactic rendering" of the crucifixion and resurrection (Cummins 2008, 68). Significantly, "the temporal pacing [came] to an abrupt halt at the passion, death, and resurrection to focus the reader's complete attention on an ideological perspective: the 'lifting up' of Jesus" (Resseguie 2005, 188). This episode takes on a markedly paschal significance as John keys Jesus' death to the Israelite Passover (Köstenberger 2009, 419–20).

The Epilogue (John 21): Remembering a Resurrection Appearance

The final chapter of the Fourth Gospel, which looks back as well as forward, contrasts the fates of two key Christian memory tradents during a post-resurrection appearance along the Sea of Tiberias: Peter, whose influence again may underlie Mark and hence Matthew and Luke; and, the Beloved Disciple, who is closely related to, and perhaps identical with, the author of the Fourth Gospel (21:24–25). Bradford Blaine contends that "Peter and [the Beloved Disciple] should be seen as composite halves of the ideal Johannine Christian, with [the Beloved Disciple] representing insightful faith and Peter representing praxis" (2007, 128). Each figure was to take his respective position within Christian memory as exemplifying faith and discipleship for what Rekha Chennattu calls "the new covenant community" (2006, 176). Like Peter and Paul in Acts, Peter and the Beloved Disciple in the Fourth Gospel function as "prototypical" and "superordinate" agents for social identity formation "in the midst of diversity and conflict within the Christ movement" (Baker 2011, xv).

The closing section possibly represents an apologetic for the Beloved Disciple's unexpected longevity as compared to his comrade, who is destined to be martyred. Both were to serve until death or the parousia (John 21:18–23) as faithful witnesses of what they had seen, despite the consequences—a pointer to the readers faithfully to persist in the face of potential persecution. The Epilogue, which I take as an integral part of John's overall narrative structure, infers the imminent death of its author and thus the supreme urgency of publishing his memory articulation.

REMEMBERING THE MEMORY OF THE BELOVED DISCIPLE

Schwartz's research continually raises the question of how the past shapes the present and, inversely, how the present shapes perceptions of the past (see Kirk 2005, 15). Schwartz reminds us that modern notions of the past tend to contrast sharply with the ethos of memory stemming from Second Temple Judaism. The ancients clearly related to their past differently than we do to ours (Lowenthal 1985, xvii, 74–124). For many in antiquity, "[t]o remember was to live, to forget was to die. Memory became the essential link to the past" (Byrskog 2009, 2). During the span of time in which the Gospels were written, memory was even more "situation-dependent" than now and even more profoundly a "*social* phenomenon" (Schwartz, p. 7, above, emphasis original).

Schwartz's insights call for a reexamination of the underlying poetics of John's memory-oriented articulation. As suggested earlier, the Fourth Gospel entailed a work of "mediation" (Schwartz, p. 21, above) by a memorian fully suited to address the exigencies of the looming Christian memory crisis of the 90s CE. Through a variety of strategies, John's sophisticated mnemo-composition drew his audience into a unified collective identity. The composition of this written record by a venerated witness who survived into the twilight of the apostolic era was intended to infuse renewed intensity into what Eviatar Zerubavel calls the "sociomental topography of the past" (2003, 1). This process was enacted through a reschematization of the existing Synoptic exemplar that was largely dependent on Petrine testimony.

The long-standing misconception of the Fourth Gospel as essentially a Synoptic "supplement"—a view that can be traced back to Clement and

Origen—thus constitutes a gross oversimplification of this Gospel's rich and engaging dynamics. Following this view, John more or less filled in the missing gaps in the story left by his Synoptic counterparts. Yet the Fourth Gospel, for which memory was a complex interpretive affair (John 2:17, 22; 12:16), was far more sophisticated than this model would suggest. As argued earlier, John's artful use of keys, frames, and other mnemonic devices renders the experience of reading and remembering the Fourth Gospel anything but straightforward and one-dimensional.

Although sometimes dismissed as an illegitimate stepchild of the Synoptics, the author of the Fourth Gospel experienced Jesus in a manner that profoundly impacted the constitution of his memory and imagination in a distinctive and lasting way, equipping him to engage a crisis of memory that endangered his community's very survival. In concert with the testimonies of his fellow tradents, John drew from the past in order to address the present and pave the way for the future.

WORKS CITED

Allison, Dale C., Jr. 2010. *Constructing Jesus: Memory, Imagination, and History*. Grand Rapids: Baker Academic.

Ashton, John. 2007. *Understanding the Fourth Gospel*. 2nd ed. Oxford: Oxford University Press.

Assmann, Aleida. 2011. *Cultural Memory and Western Civilization: Functions, Media, Archives*. Cambridge: Cambridge University Press.

Assmann, Jan. 1997. *Moses the Egyptian: The Memory of Egypt in Western Monotheism*. Cambridge: Harvard University Press.

Aune, David E. 1987. *The New Testament in Its Literary Environment*. Library of Early Christianity 8. Philadelphia: Westminster.

Baker, Coleman. 2011. *Identity, Memory, and Narrative in Early Christianity: Peter, Paul, and Recategorization in the Book of Acts*. Eugene, OR: Pickwick.

Bar-Efrat, Shimon. 1989. *Narrative Art in the Bible*. JSOTSup 70. Sheffield: Sheffield Academic Press.

Bartholomew, Craig G., and Michael W. Goheen. 2004. *The Drama of Scripture: Finding Our Place in the Biblical Story*. Grand Rapids: Baker.

Bauckham, Richard, ed. 1998. *The Gospels for All Christians: Rethinking the Gospel Audiences*. Grand Rapids: Eerdmans.

———. 2006. *Jesus and the Eyewitnesses: The Gospels as Eyewitness Testimony*. Grand Rapids: Eerdmans.

———. 2007. *The Testimony of the Beloved Disciple: Narrative, History, and Theology in the Gospel of John*. Grand Rapids: Baker.

Beardsley, Steven J. 2012. Luke's Narrative Agenda: The Use of Κύριος within Luke-Acts to Proclaim the Identity of Jesus. Ph.D. diss., Temple University.

Berlin, Adele. 1994. *Poetics and Interpretation of Biblical Narrative*. Winona Lake, IN: Eisenbrauns. [orig. 1983]

Blaine, Bradford B. 2007. *Peter in the Gospel of John: The Making of an Authentic Disciple*. Academia Biblica 27. Atlanta: Society of Biblical Literature.

Brant, Jo-Ann A. 2004. *Dialogue and Drama: Elements of Greek Tragedy in the Fourth Gospel*. Peabody, MA: Hendrickson.

Brickle, Jeffrey E. 2012. Transacting Virtue within a Disrupted Community: The Negotiation of Ethics in the First Epistle of John. Pages 340–49 in *Rethinking the Ethics of John: Implicit Ethics in the Johannine Writings*. Edited by Jan G. van der Watt and Ruben Zimmermann. Kontexte und Normen neutestamentlicher Ethik 3; WUNT 291. Tübingen: Mohr Siebeck.

Brown, Raymond E. 1997. *An Introduction to the New Testament*. ABRL. New York: Doubleday.

———. 2003. *An Introduction to the Gospel of John*. Edited by Francis J. Moloney. ABRL. New York: Doubleday.

Brueggemann, Walter. 2002. *The Land: Place as Gift, Promise, and Challenge in Biblical Faith*. 2nd ed. Overtures to Biblical Theology. Minneapolis: Augsburg.

Burge, Gary M. 1987. *The Anointed Community: The Holy Spirit in the Johannine Tradition*. Grand Rapids: Eerdmans.

———. 2012. *Jesus and the Jewish Festivals: Ancient Context, Ancient Faith*. Grand Rapids, Zondervan.

Burridge, Richard A. 2004. *What Are the Gospels? A Comparison with Graeco-Roman Biography*. 2nd ed. Biblical Resource Series. Grand Rapids: Eerdmans.

Byrskog, Samuel. 2009. Introduction. Pages 1–20 in *Jesus in Memory: Traditions in Oral and Scribal Perspectives*. Edited by Werner H. Kelber and Samuel Byrskog. Waco, TX: Baylor University Press.

Carr, David M. 2005. *Writing on the Tablets of the Heart: Origins of Scripture and Literature*. Oxford: Oxford University Press.

Carruthers, Mary. 2008. *The Book of Memory: A Study of Memory in Medieval Culture*. 2nd ed. Cambridge: Cambridge University Press.

Chennattu, Rekha M. 2006. *Johannine Discipleship as a Covenant Relationship*. Peabody, MA: Hendrickson.

Culpepper R. Alan. 1983. *Anatomy of the Fourth Gospel: A Study in Literary Design*. Philadelphia: Fortress.

Cummins, S. A. 2008. John. Pages 60–73 in *Theological Interpretation of the New Testament: A Book-by-Book Survey*. Edited by Kevin Vanhoozer, Daniel J. Treier, and N. T. Wright. Grand Rapids: Baker.

Downing, Frances. 2000. *Remembrance and the Design of Place*. Sara and John Lindsey Series in the Arts and Humanities 6. College Station: Texas A&M University Press.

Dunn, James D. G. 2006. *The Partings of the Ways: Between Christianity and Judaism and Their Significance for the Character of Christianity*. 2nd ed. London: SCM.

George, Mark K. 2009. *Israel's Tabernacle as Social Space*. Ancient Israel and Its Literature 2. Atlanta: Society of Biblical Literature.

Gregory, Marshall. 2009. *Shaped by Stories: The Ethical Power of Narratives*. Notre Dame, IN: University of Notre Dame Press.

Griffiths, Paul J. 1999. *Religious Reading: The Place of Reading in the Practice of Religion*. Oxford: Oxford University Press.

Hays, Richard B. 1989. *Echoes of Scripture in the Letters of Paul*. New Haven: Yale University Press.

Hengel, Martin. 2003. *Judaism and Hellenism: Studies in Their Encounter in Palestine during the Early Hellenistic Period*. Translated by John Bowden. Eugene, OR: Wipf & Stock. [orig. 1974]

Iser, Wolfgang. 1978. *The Act of Reading: A Theory of Aesthetic Response*. Baltimore: Johns Hopkins University Press.

Keener, Craig S. 2003. *The Gospel of John: A Commentary*. 2 vols. Peabody, MA: Hendrickson.

Kirk, Alan. 2005. Social and Cultural Memory. Pages 1–24 in *Memory, Tradition, and Text: Uses of the Past in Early Christianity*. Edited by Alan Kirk and Tom Thatcher. SemeiaSt 52. Atlanta: Society of Biblical Literature.

Köstenberger, Andreas J. 1999. *Encountering John: The Gospel in Historical, Literary, and Theological Perspective*. Encountering Biblical Studies. Grand Rapids: Baker.

———. 2004. *John*. BECNT. Grand Rapids: Baker.

———. 2007. John. Pages 415–512 in *Commentary on the New Testament Use of the Old Testament*. Edited by G. K. Beale and D. A. Carson. Grand Rapids: Baker.

———. 2009. *A Theology of John's Gospel and Letters: The Word, the Christ, the Son of God.* Biblical Theology of the New Testament. Grand Rapids: Zondervan.

Le Donne, Anthony. 2011. Memory, Commemoration and History in John 2:19–22: A Critique and Application of Social Memory. Pages 186–204 in *The Fourth Gospel in First-Century Media Culture.* Edited by Anthony Le Donne and Tom Thatcher. ESCO/LNTS 426. London: T&T Clark.

Lee, Margaret E., and Brandon Bernard Scott. 2009. *Sound Mapping the New Testament.* Salem, OR: Polebridge.

Lowenthal, David. 1985. *The Past Is a Foreign Country.* Cambridge: Cambridge University Press.

Malbon, Elizabeth Struthers. 1986. *Narrative Space and Mythic Meaning in Mark.* New Voices in Biblical Studies. San Francisco: Harper & Row.

McIver, Robert K. 2011. *Memory, Jesus, and the Synoptic Gospels.* SBLRBS 59. Atlanta: Society of Biblical Literature.

Mendels, Doron. 2004. *Memory in Jewish, Pagan and Christian Societies of the Graeco-Roman World.* Library of Second Temple Studies 45. London: T&T Clark.

———. 2007. Societies of Memory in the Graeco-Roman World. Pages 143–62 in *Memory in the Bible and Antiquity.* Edited by Loren T. Stuckenbruck, Stephen C. Barton, and Benjamin G. Wold. WUNT 212. Tübingen: Mohr Siebeck.

Minchin, Elizabeth. 2001. *Homer and the Resources of Memory: Some Applications of Cognitive Theory to the* Iliad *and the* Odyssey. Oxford: Oxford University Press.

Olick, Jeffrey K. 2007. *The Politics of Regret: On Collective Memory and Historical Responsibility.* New York: Routledge.

Park, Yoon-Man. 2010. *Mark's Memory Resources and the Controversy Stories (Mark 2:1–3:6): An Application of the Frame Theory of Cognitive Science to the Markan Oral-Aural Narrative.* Leiden: Brill.

Reis, David M. 2002. The Areopagus as Echo Chamber: *Mimesis* and Intertextuality in Acts 17. *Journal of Higher Criticism* 9:259–77.

Resseguie, James L. 2005. *Narrative Criticism of the New Testament: An Introduction.* Grand Rapids: Baker.

Schwartz, Barry. 2005. Jesus in First-Century Memory—A Response. Pages 249–61 in *Memory, Tradition, and Text: Uses of the Past in Early Christianity.* Edited by Alan Kirk and Tom Thatcher. SemeiaSt 52. Atlanta: Society of Biblical Literature.

———. 2011. What Difference Does the Medium Make? Pages 225–38 in

The Fourth Gospel in First-Century Media Culture. Edited by Anthony Le Donne and Tom Thatcher. ESCO/LNTS 426. London: T&T Clark.

Sloyan, Gerard S. 2006. *What Are They Saying about John?* Rev. ed. Mahway, NJ: Paulist.

Smith, D. Moody. 2001. *John among the Gospels*. 2nd ed. Columbia: University of South Carolina Press.

Spaulding, Mary B. 2009. *Commemorative Identities: Jewish Social Memory and the Johannine Feast of Booths*. ESCO/LNTS 396. London: T&T Clark.

Steiner, George. 1989. *Real Presences*. Chicago: University of Chicago Press.

Sternberg, Meir. 1985. *The Poetics of Biblical Narrative: Ideological Literature and the Drama of Reading*. Indiana Studies in Biblical Literature. Bloomington: Indiana University Press.

Stewart, Eric C. 2009. *Gathered around Jesus: An Alternative Spatial Practice in the Gospel of Mark*. Matrix: The Bible in Mediterranean Context. Eugene, OR: Cascade.

Thatcher, Tom. 2011. John's Memory Theatre: A Study of Composition in Performance. Pages 73–91 in *The Fourth Gospel in First-Century Media Culture*. Edited by Anthony Le Donne and Tom Thatcher. ESCO/LNTS 426. London: T&T Clark.

Thomas, John Christopher. 2012. *The Apocalypse: A Literary and Theological Commentary*. Cleveland, TN: CPT.

Whitehead, Anne. 2009. *Memory: The New Critical Idiom*. London: Routledge.

Wright, N. T. 1992. *The New Testament and the People of God*. Minneapolis: Fortress.

Zerubavel, Eviatar. 2003. *Time Maps: Collective Memory and the Social Shape of the Past*. Chicago: University of Chicago Press.

Zumstein, Jean. 2008. Intratextuality and Intertextuality in the Gospel of John. Translated by Mike Gray. Pages 121–35 in *Anatomies of Narrative Criticism: The Past, Present, and Futures of the Fourth Gospel as Literature*. Edited by Tom Thatcher and Stephen D. Moore. SBLRBS 55. Atlanta: Society of Biblical Literature.

THE SHAPE OF JOHN'S STORY:
MEMORY-MAPPING THE FOURTH GOSPEL

Tom Thatcher

This essay will engage two foundational premises of Barry Schwartz's theoretical model to address the long-debated questions of the "outline" of the
Gospel of John and, secondarily, of the relationship between the structure
of John's narrative and the actual past of the world outside that text. In
view of the obvious differences in structure and presentation between the
Fourth Gospel (FG) and the Synoptics, and following Clement of Alexandria's well-worn theorem that John's is a "spiritual Gospel" (Eusebius,
Hist. eccl. 6.14.5–7), commentators have tended to assume that FG's outline is essentially a function/expression of its author's theology and/or
literary style: John tells his story the way he does in order to advance certain theological premises that are grounded in cosmic realities rather than
Jesus' context. The present essay will contend, in dialogue with Schwartz's
research, that the outline of FG is in fact a simple function of the real-world
spatio-temporal frame that John chose to organize his memory of Jesus'
activity, so that the sequence and flow of the Gospel's presentation is less a
reflection of its theological substructure and more a reflection of the map
and calendar of Roman Palestine.

Viewing FG as one early Christian community's collective memory of
Jesus raises two important points that have characterized all of Schwartz's
research on historical figures.[1] First, representations of the past, and particularly of the more recent past, are integrally linked to their originating
events in a cause–effect relationship. Stated differently, the way that the
actual past is remembered is constrained, to some degree, not only by its
prior and present commemorations but also by its content—an intentional,
programmatic, and massive political and/or economic effort is required
to fabricate the past from nothing or to erase all memory of what actu-

---

1. Primarily iconic figures and events from American history (e.g., George Washington, Abraham Lincoln, Rosa Parks) but also and more recently early Christian
conceptions of Jesus (see Schwartz 2005a, 2005b, 2011).

ally happened. Second, commemorations of the past are often organized by, and indeed crystallize around, sites or "frames" of memory: significant events, places, or figures who serve as convenient hooks for organizing recollection (see, e.g., Schwartz 2008, xi–xii). Taken together—as Schwartz often takes them in his own work—these two principles highlight the ways that elements of the actual past can provide frames or anchors for subsequent acts of commemoration, including historical narratives such as FG. Specifically here, the outline of FG appears to be a product not of John's ideology but of mnemonic techniques that structure narrative commemorations by tying them to extratextual anchors, in this case to the physical and calendrical landscape that formed the backdrop for Jesus' career.

To explore this claim, and the larger potential of Schwartz's model for understanding the narrative structure of the Gospels as reflections of Jesus' career, the present essay will first review what might be called the "consensus position" on the outline of the Fourth Gospel. As will be seen, scholars tend to view the distinctive elements of FG's narrative structure as a product of John's theological tendencies, to such an extent that the Gospel evidences no true "plot" in the sense that its events are not linked in any obvious cause–effect sequence or logical pattern but rather are held together by thematic and symbolic networks. In point of fact, however, the sequence of John's story seems to be driven by extratextual factors. Specifically, FG's plot follows the map and the calendar of early Roman Palestine, with major movements in the story marked by Jesus' travels from place to place over time and individual episodes often contextualized within sites of Israelite memory—places and occasions charged with significant symbolic value. John's organization of his story on the basis of physical and temporal markers further suggests that FG was composed using standard ancient "memory theater" techniques, with real-world times and locations serving as memory sites that facilitated John's recall and narration of significant events. Returning to Schwartz's particular concern about the problems and potentials of using collective memory as a source for history, the essay will close with brief observations on FG's potential value as a source for the scope of Jesus' career.

Signs, Discourses, and the Drama of Decision: Thematic Approaches to John's Story

Proceeding from the premise that the "meaning" of the Fourth Gospel is tied to the structure of the story and the reader's interactions with its internal elements, recent discussion has tended to define the "outline" of FG—the order and progression of the various parts of the narrative—in terms of the story's key *themes*. Viewed in this light, the structure of John's Gospel reflects the logic of its thematic development, with the individual episodes held together by the repetition of motifs, terms, and symbols that gradually enlarge the reader's understanding of Christ. Put another way, the current consensus tends to view the outline of the Gospel as a linear expression of its author's ideology, specifically of John's christological outlook, and this ideology serves as the text's primary organizational principle. Thus, with a few obvious exceptions, event B in the Gospel of John does not follow event A because it did so in the actual past of Jesus' career (or the actual past of the history of Johannine Christianity), nor because these two events are clearly united in a cause–effect relationship, but rather because John judged that the present sequence would best express his theological beliefs and thus better serve his ultimate rhetorical purposes. Put yet another way, recent research effectively views FG's narrative structure as asynchronous and unrelated to anything outside its author's theological agenda.

This approach to FG's narrative structure is reflected in two influential proposals on the outline or "plot" of the Gospel, both of which explain the story's sequence, movement, and patterns of conflict and resolution primarily in terms of its thematic/theological interests. The first of these proposals was advanced by C. H. Dodd and further refined and popularized by Raymond Brown, whose monumental commentary on FG for the Anchor Bible series (1966–1970) has substantially extended the theory's life. The second proposal, similar in certain key respects to the first, emerged from Alan Culpepper's *Anatomy of the Fourth Gospel* (1983), a groundbreaking narrative-critical analysis that set the tone for much subsequent discussion of the plot and structure of FG. A brief review of these familiar theories will provide a helpful context for the present discussion of the relationship between the shape of John's story and the actual past that it purports to describe.

C. H. Dodd's reading of the Fourth Gospel, and hence his understanding of the book's sequence and outline, was predicated on the thesis that John views all of Jesus' deeds and words—both deeds *and* words, and *all* of them—as revelatory "signs" of Christ's divine identity. Building on this premise, Dodd posited a close and, indeed, essential correlation between FG's narrative and discourse/dialogue sections, with the latter serving as the Evangelist's theological commentary on the significance of the former (see Dodd 1953, 384, 451–52; 1963, 54, 321, 354–55, 349–50 n. 1). Consistent with this approach, Dodd viewed Jesus' longest speech in FG, the lengthy Farewell Address delivered in the upper room on the last night of Christ's life (John 13–17), as an extended explanation of the implications of the passion story (1953, 390–423, esp. 390, 394–96, 399–400). Noting that the Farewell is offered to the disciples privately while Jesus' other discourses are delivered in more public venues, Dodd detected a simple, three-part outline in John's presentation.

1. Proem (John 1): the poetic Prologue (John 1:1–18) and the call of the disciples, together introducing the reader to key terms and themes.
2. Book of Signs (John 2–12): Jesus' public ministry, including his various miracles and teachings.
3. Book of the Passion (John 13–21): Christ's final, private instructions to his closest followers, immediately followed by his death and resurrection appearances.

Dodd's further subdivisions ("episodes") of the Gospel under these three larger headings represent distinct, thematically unified units of narrative + discourse (event + theological explication). Thus, for example, the first subunit within the Book of Signs (John 2:1–4:42) includes two "signs," the first Cana miracle (water to wine) and the temple incident, followed by two discourses/dialogues that unpack the thematic/symbolic significance of these events, the Nicodemus dialogue (John 3:1–36) and Jesus' extended discussion with the Samaritan Woman (4:1–42). Dodd titles this section "The New Beginning" in view of the focus of these stories and discourses on the new life that Jesus brings through his ministry (see Dodd 1953, 297–317). Similarly, Dodd labels John 6, which combines the signs of the feeding and the sea-crossing with the subsequent "bread from heaven" discourse, "The Bread of Life," a title that again summarizes the predominant symbolism of that sequence (Dodd 1953, 333–45).

Without question, the Fourth Gospel leads its reader down a path of understanding that takes the form of an upward spiral, with key terms and themes introduced, explored, and later revisited and expanded in light of new developments. For purposes of the present discussion, however, it is relevant to note that Dodd portrays this thematic development as the primary organizational principle in FG's narrative, to such an extent that the story's sequence of events becomes essentially a linear expression of its philosophical premises. Dodd thus asserts that the Fourth Gospel's narrative structure "does not move along the direct line of a logical progress"—specific events do not follow one another for any particular reason—but rather resembles "a musical fugue" in the sense that "a theme is introduced and developed up to a point; then a second theme is introduced and the two are interwoven; then a third, and so on" (Dodd 1953, 383; see also 386–89). Inasmuch as these themes include, primarily, "life, light and judgment, the passion and glory of the Christ," FG is ultimately the story not of Jesus' career but of "the manifestation of the eternal Logos ... to the world of human kind" (1953, 383, 351; see also 1963, 9–10). For Dodd, the Gospel of John is a philosophical essay disguised as a narrative and shaped by the logic of its argument; his trademark emphasis on the historical specificity of Christ's revelation thus extended only to individual episodes in FG, not to the totality of John's plot (see, e.g., 1953, 199–200, 422–23, 439, 444; 1963, 4, 7–8).

While Dodd's proposal was first published over sixty years ago, the genius of his theory has remained influential through its adaptation in Raymond Brown's monumental Anchor Bible commentary on John (1966–1970).[2] Affirming Dodd's basic observations that FG's discourses function as commentaries on their respective signs (with the Farewell again unpacking the passion) and that the narrative naturally divides between Jesus' public and private ministries, Brown offered a four-part outline of the Gospel that explicitly plays on the language of Dodd's major headings (1966–1970, 1:cxxxviii–cxxxix; 2:541–42).

1. Prologue (John 1:1–18)
2. The Book of Signs (1:19–12:50)
3. The Book of Glory (13:1–20:31)
4. Epilogue (21:1–15)

Significantly for the present study, while Brown concurred with Dodd's observation that FG's discourses interpret the signs, he judged Dodd's division of the public ministry into seven distinct "episodes" to be artificial, proposing instead four subheadings within the Book of Signs that reflect

---

2. The lasting influence of Dodd and Brown on English-speaking scholarship is evident in varying degrees in a number of more recent proposals for FG's outline, including proposals that reflect widely divergent theories of the composition history of the text. See, e.g., Carson 1991, 103–8; Culpepper 1998, 77–86; Keener 2003, 1:xi–xxiv; Köstenberger 2004, 9–13; Kysar 2007, 19–23; Smith 1999, 21–22; von Wahlde 2010, 1:353–56; van der Watt 2007, 11–20; Witherington 1995, 41–43, 372 n. 126; also Jeffrey Brickle, pp. 196–201 in the present volume.

obvious geographical and temporal breaks in the narrative: "The Opening Days of the Revelation of Jesus" (John 1:19–51); "From Cana to Cana" (2:1–4:54); "Jesus and the Principal Feasts of the Jews" (5:1–10:42); and "Jesus Moves toward the Hour of Death and Glory" (11:1–12:36; Brown 1966–1970, 1:cxl–cxli). Thus, part 2 of the Book of Signs encompasses the two Cana miracles and everything in between (John 2:1–4:54); part 3 is loosely organized around Jesus' actions and teachings at various festivals in Jerusalem (Passover, Tabernacles, Dedication; 5:1–10:42); part 4 serves as a segue into the passion story. Brown similarly divided the Book of Glory into three simple movements that reflect the obvious chronological sequence of the text: Last Supper (John 13–17); passion narrative proper (Jesus' arrest, trials, and death; 18–19); and resurrection appearances (20–21; Brown 1966–1970, 1:cxlii).

But while Brown's outline highlights organic breaks in FG's narrative, his use of the heading "Book of Glory," an obvious modification of Dodd's more neutral "Book of the Passion," reflects his view that the individual elements of John's story are ultimately united by theological themes. Put another way, FG's chronological and temporal markers operate within and beneath a larger thematic/symbolic network that dominates the structure of the book. Thus the episodes in part 1 of the Book of Signs are united by the theme of testimony/calling; part 2 develops the themes of "replacing Jewish institutions and religious views" and "the different reactions of individuals and groups to Jesus"; part 3 draws its energy from theological values associated with the various Jewish feasts; part 4, primarily the story of Lazarus's resurrection, is dominated by "the theme of life and death" (1966–1970, 1:cxliii–cxliv). Differing with Dodd, Brown was suspicious of proposals that posit a linear "development" of these various themes through the course of FG's narrative, preferring instead to focus on the theology and symbolism of individual units. This preference was, to some extent, a necessary corollary to Brown's conception of FG's composition history, which views the present text of the Gospel as the third edition of an earlier narrative that had been substantially revised and expanded, once by the Evangelist himself and then again, and more thoroughly, by one of his disciples (1966–1970, 1:xxxiv–xxxix; 2003, 64–69, 78–86). Of course, this editorial process produced a number of conspicuous theological discontinuities (aporias) that are now readily apparent in the text, making it impossible to speak of a consistent, linear development of themes across the narrative. At the same time, however, Brown's insightful readings of individual passages frequently emphasize the overall conceptual coherence of the story as it now stands, and his commentary's lengthy introduction and many helpful excurses explore key elements of Johannine theology that emerge in the course of John's account (see, e.g., Brown 1966–1970, 1:cv–cxxvii).

A second influential proposal on the outline/structure of FG was advanced by Alan Culpepper, whose *Anatomy of the Fourth Gospel* (1983)—arguably the most significant book in Johannine studies in the past thirty years—introduced Johannine scholars to narrative criticism. Applying an analytical model amalgamated from numerous interdisciplinary theories of literature, Culpepper addressed the outline/structure of the Fourth Gospel under the heading "plot" (see esp. ch. 4).

In Culpepper's view, the plot of John's Gospel is episodic (the individual scenes are relatively isolated and do not depend upon one another) and strategically repetitive. Unlike the Synoptics, John immediately discloses, through the poetic Prologue (John 1:1–18), Christ's identity and the tasks he must complete: redeeming the world and, especially, revealing the Father. Since Jesus is a static character—being God's Word in flesh (1:14) leaves little room for personal development—and, further, a hero who cannot fail to fulfill his purposes, all emphasis falls on the ways that other individuals in the story respond to him. Perhaps reflecting the inherently personal nature of faith, the conflict between belief and disbelief comes to its climax not at the end of John's story but numerous times throughout, as one character after another comes to a conclusion about Christ. Indeed, as Dodd had earlier observed (see, e.g., 1953, 379–89), "each episode [in FG] has essentially the same plot as the story as a whole.... The story is repeated over and over" as Jesus meets new people who struggle to understand his actions and radical claims. These many individual stories of faith(lessness), comprising the Gospel's distinctive scenes and movements, are tied together by their respective actors' initial ignorance of Jesus' true identity and by an expanding network of "metaphorical and symbolic images" that progressively disclose that identity to the reader (Culpepper 1983, 88–89). As a result, "plot and character ... blend almost inseparably in the Gospel of John," with each individual episode and the narrative as a whole inviting the reader to locate herself somewhere on the spectrum of decision (1983, 79). The sequence of the Gospel is a function of this larger rhetorical aim, and its "plot" is essentially the reader's own story of doubt and decision.

Taken together, the proposals of Dodd, Brown, and Culpepper illustrate four key premises of what might be called the current "consensus approach" to FG's structure/outline.

(1) The various individual scenes/episodes in FG, typically conceived as consisting of narrated signs and the related discourses/dialogues that unpack their significance, are each essentially epitomes of the whole. Thus the stories of the call of the disciples (John 1:19–51), Nicodemus (3:1–15), the Samaritan woman (4:7–42), and the blind man healed at Siloam (9:1–41) follow the same plot and make the same point with the same rhetorical affect as the entire Gospel.

(2) These individual episodes are loosely connected by common terms, themes, symbols, and narrative motifs and patterns, *not* by any obvious relationship of cause and effect. Thus while the Gospel's mode of presentation is sequential, the logic of that presentation is not linear: the events do not depend on one another but work together, largely through repetition, to build up a complex of meaning that makes the author's case.

(3) Because the movement of the Gospel is determined largely by its progress of ideas and its rhetorical aims, the actual order of events is essentially inconsequential. Theoretically, John could have connected these scenes in almost any order, provided, of course, that Jesus does not die until somewhere near the end (although John 21 may suggest that John's storytelling powers could overcome even that obstacle). The value of the whole story thus lies in the sum of its parts, and, like any sum, little would be lost by switching the sequence of the variables: 2 + 3 and 3 + 2 both come out to 5. John's location of the temple incident in chapter 2 of his story raises this hypothesis to the level of theory.

(4) In view of the first three points, for all practical purposes the outline of the Fourth Gospel has no direct connection to the real world in which Jesus lived or the actual past of his career—John is under no compulsion to sequence the events in his story in a way that might reflect anything Jesus did. This is not to say, of course, that John's presentation of Jesus' career, or of individual scenes from that career, is necessarily unhistorical, just that the total movement of the story is basically ahistorical. The Gospel often refers to, and draws symbolic value from, real-world times and places, but its outline follows Christ's campaign to reveal the Father before returning home to heaven.

Following Christ through the Fourth Gospel: Jesus' World and John's Outline

As noted above, most Johannine scholars today would likely explain the structure or "outline" of the Fourth Gospel with reference to the development of the text's major theological themes and/or the reader's experience of that development. Viewed in this light, one may say that the plot of the Gospel reflects its internal thematic development, while the characters in the story serve primarily to provide Christ with a audience for his self-revelations. The many and various physical and temporal settings mentioned in the Gospel, when discussed at all, are viewed either as staging for the individual episodes and/or as somehow further contributing to the christological symbolism of Jesus' discourses. The genius of this approach is twofold: on the one hand, it highlights the Gospel's key theological themes while also demonstrating how its various elements serve the ultimate goal of leading the reader to faith (John 20:30–31); on the other, it remains unburdened by any reference to the real world outside the text or the actual past of Jesus' career. The latter point, as an added bonus, eliminates any need to address the obvious differences between the course of Christ's ministry in John and the Synoptics or even to explain why the Johannine Jesus goes where he does and why it takes him so long (some three years total) to do what he does there. John shows these people doing these things at these times in these places in order to lead the reader down a path of decision, and that path largely determines the course of the story and the arrangement of its individual parts.

At the same time, however, a number of important proposals on FG's outline have drawn attention to John's strategic use of real-world *settings*, particularly references to space and time, as structuring devices. As noted above, Raymond Brown revised Dodd's outline of the Book of Signs (John 2–12) on the grounds that John's account of Jesus' public ministry seems to be loosely organized by geographical (Cana/Jerusalem/Samaria/Cana; 2:1–4:54) and chronological (the various Jewish festivals; chs. 5–10) markers. A similar proposal was advanced by Fernando Segovia, who, building on the narrative-critical work of Jeff Staley (1988, 58–73), argued that the Fourth Gospel's outline is driven by the motif of "the journey," a common theme in ancient historical/biographical writing. At a macro-level, the Gospel traces Christ's journey from heaven through the physical realm in a cosmic descent/ascent framework; within this larger movement, Jesus fulfills his revelatory mission in the context of "a series of geographical" journeys, the last of which culminates in his death (Segovia 1991, 31–35, 38–45, 50–51, quote 34). In Segovia's view, John's larger christological themes and rhetorical objectives are articulated within the framework of Jesus' (meta)physical travels, particularly through the repetition of patterns of revelation (by Christ) and response (by his audiences) in various settings.

For purposes of the present study, it will be helpful to take Segovia's seminal observation one step further: the outline of the Fourth Gospel does not, in fact, follow the development of its key themes but rather *Jesus' journeys across the map and the calendar.* Put another way, and stated in terms of narrative elements, John's story follows the course of its *settings,* not of its theology. Further, and significantly, the narrative world of FG is built on the topographical and temporal framework of the real world of Jesus, with the result that the Gospel's outline may be easily traced with reference to the Jewish festal calendar and the volume of the *Tabula Imperii Romani* dedicated to ancient Judea and Palestine, as indicated by the outline in the table below.

The Structure of the Fourth Gospel: Jesus in Space and Time

Note: **geographical markers** appear in bold; *temporal markers* appear in italics.

> **Bethany beyond Jordan** (1:28)
> > The interrogation of the Baptist (1:19–27)

> *"the next day"* (1:29)
> > John discusses Jesus' baptism (1:29–34)

> *"the next day"* (1:35)
> > two of John's disciples meet Jesus (1:35–39)

> > *"about the tenth hour"* (1:39)
> > > Andrew introduces Peter to Jesus (1:40–42)

> *"the next day"* (1:43)
> > **Galilee/Bethsaida** (1:43, 44)
> > Jesus meets Philip and Nathanael (1:43–51)

> *"the third day"* (2:1)
> > **Cana of Galilee** (2:1, 11)
> > the wine miracle at the wedding, Jesus' first "sign" (2:1–11)

> > **Capernaum** (2:12)
> > Jesus stays in Capernaum for a short time with his family and disciples (2:12)

> *"not many days" later, during "the Passover of the Judeans"* (2:12–13)
> > **The temple complex, Jerusalem**
> > The temple incident (2:13–22)
> > Jesus does many "signs" (2:23–25)

"at night" (3:2)
> Jesus' dialogue with Nicodemus, followed by the narrator's comment
> (3:1–21)

"after these things" (3:22; referring to the events in Jerusalem)
> **the countryside of Judea**
> Jesus and his disciples teach and baptize (3:22)

> **Aenon near Salim** (3:23)
> John the Baptist discusses Jesus' ministry with his own disciples, followed
> by the narrator's explication (3:23–36)

> **Jacob's well near Sychar, Samaria, on the way to Galilee** (4:1–6)
> *"about the sixth hour"*[3]
> Jesus' dialogue with the Samaritan Woman (4:7–27)

> > **Sychar in Samaria** (4:28)
> > The Samaritan woman tells the people of her village about Jesus (4:28–30)

> > **Jacob's Well** (4:31)
> > Jesus discusses the "harvest" with his disciples (4:31–38)
> > The Samaritans ask Jesus to remain with them (4:39–40)

> > **Sychar in Samaria** (4:40)
> > Jesus remains in Sychar two days, leading many Samaritans to believe
> > (4:40–43)

"after two days" (4:43; see 4:40)
> **Galilee** (4:43, 45)
> Jesus is well received by the Galileans because of the signs he had done at
> Passover (4:45)

> **Cana of Galilee** (4:46, 54)
> *"the seventh hour"* (4:52)[4]
> Jesus heals a royal official's son (who is in Capernaum) (4:47–54)

---

3. John does not indicate the duration of Jesus' journey through the countryside
of Judea. Enough time passes to arouse the suspicion of the Pharisees and the disciples
of John the Baptist (see John 3:23–26; 4:1–3).

4. John does not indicate how long Jesus has been in Galilee before the royal official approaches him; 4:47 suggests that the second Cana sign takes place soon after
Jesus' return to his home region.

"after these things" during "a Feast of the Judeans" (5:1)[5]
    Jerusalem (5:1)
        Jesus goes to Jerusalem for a festival (5:1)

    a Sabbath (5:9)
        the Pool of Bethesda (5:2)
        Jesus heals a lame man (5:1–9)
        "The Jews" confront the lame man for carrying his mat on Sabbath
        (5:10–13)

  "after these things" (5:14)
    the temple complex (5:14)
    Jesus confronts the healed man and is confronted by "the Judeans" (5:14–18)
    Jesus discusses the various "witnesses" who validate his actions (5:19–47)

"after these things," near the Passover season (6:1, 4)
    "the other side" of the Sea of Galilee (6:1)
    Jesus feeds a crowd miraculously; they seek to make him "king" (6:2–15)

    that evening (the evening of the day of the feeding; 6:16–17)
    on the Sea of Galilee on the way to Capernaum (6:16–17)
    Jesus walks on water (6:17–21)

"the next day" (the day following the feeding; 6:22)
    the place of the feeding miracle (6:22–24)
    The crowds search for Jesus and realize he is gone (6:22–24)

    a synagogue in Capernaum (6:17, 24, 59)
    The "Bread of Life" Dialogue (6:25–59)
    Many of Jesus' followers reject him (6:60–71)

"after these things," before the Feast of Tabernacles (7:1–2)
    Galilee (7:1, 9)
    Jesus' brothers encourage him to attend the festival (7:2–8)

"after his brothers went up to the festival (of Tabernacles)" (7:10)
    Jesus goes to the festival (in Jerusalem) "secretly" (7:10)
    "The Judeans" look for Jesus and discuss his identity (7:11–13)

---

5. The specific "feast" that John has in mind here cannot be determined, with the various proposals—Purim, Passover, Rosh Hoshanah, Tabernacles—reflecting differing conceptions of the most appropriate theological/thematic backdrop for the events and discourse of John 5. The vague nature of the reference suggests that John is less concerned with the symbolism of the unnamed festival than with explaining why Jesus happened to be in Jerusalem on this occasion. All emphasis is placed on the fact that the healing takes place on Sabbath at a large purification pool (Bethesda).

"the middle of the festival" (7:14)

The temple complex (7:14, 28)

Jesus debates with the crowd over the earlier Sabbath healing (7:14–36; cf. 5:1–9)

"the last day, the great day of the festival," a Sabbath (7:37; 9:13)[6]

the "treasury" in the temple complex (8:20)

Jesus offers "living water," creating a schism among the crowds (7:37–44)[7]

Debate over whether the Christ can come from Galilee (7:45–52)

Debate over Jesus' origins and attempted stoning (8:12–59)

leaving the temple complex (9:1)

Jesus tells a blind man to wash his eyes in the Pool of Siloam (9:1–7)

the Pool of Siloam (9:7)

The blind man is healed and interrogated by his neighbors (9:7–12)

? (a location in Jerusalem)[8]

The blind man is interrogated by Pharisees and put out of the synagogue (9:13–34)

---

6. John 9:1 indicates that the healing of the blind man took place "as Jesus was going out" (παράγων) of the temple complex after the dialogues of 7:37–8:59, thus suggesting that the events of 7:37–10:21 all took place on the same day—assuming, of course, that John 7:53–8:11 is not original to the composition (see 8:1–2, which would create a temporal break in the sequence). John 7:37 refers to this occasion as "the last day, the great [day] of the festival" (ἐν τῇ ἐσχάτῃ ἡμέρᾳ τῇ μεγάλῃ τῆς ἑορτῆς), while John 9:13 indicates that the healing took place on Sabbath.

7. The events of John 7:37–44 apparently take place in the temple complex, although John does not specify their location. The reference to the "last day of the feast," the presence of a public audience for Jesus' words, and the fact that Jesus' earlier teachings were also delivered in the temple complex suggest that he is still in this location for the "living water" discourse. The lack of a prior spatial reference may suggest that John envisions all of 7:37–8:59 taking place in the "treasury" area of the temple complex.

8. The events of John 9 clearly take place in several different locations, but John does not precisely identify them. Jesus meets the blind man while leaving the temple complex; the man is then healed at Siloam, down the hill to the south of the temple, and apparently interrogated first by the bystanders there or in his own neighborhood (9:8–12; note οἱ γείτονες at 9:8); these individuals then send him for a hearing before the Pharisees in an unspecified location (9:13). John may envision that the man's interrogation and Jesus' subsequent confrontation with the Pharisees take place somewhere in the temple complex, inasmuch as Jesus' other major discourses in Jerusalem are set in this location.

Jesus accuses the Pharisees of blindness and delivers the Good Shepherd discourse (9:40–10:18)

"The Judeans" are divided over Jesus (10:19–21)

Winter, at the Feast of Dedication (10:22)[9]

the Stoa of Solomon in the temple complex, Jerusalem (10:22–23)

Jesus debates with the crowds over his identity and escapes a stoning (10:24–39)

across the Jordan, where John had been baptizing (Bethany) (10:40)[10]

Many believe in Jesus on the basis of his signs (10:40–42)

Jesus receives word of Lazarus's illness and does not come to heal him (11:1–6)

two days later (two days after Jesus receives word of Lazarus' illness; 11:6)

Jesus and the disciples debate whether he should go to Lazarus (11:7–16)

four days after Lazarus' burial (11:17)

on the road outside Bethany (near Jerusalem) (11:1, 18, 30)

Jesus speaks with Martha about Lazarus' condition (11:19–37)

the home of Mary, Martha, and Lazarus (11:31)

Martha reports to Mary that Jesus has arrived (11:28–31)

on the road outside Bethany (near Jerusalem) (11:30)

Mary and the crowds meet Jesus (11:32–37)

Lazarus's tomb (11:38)

Jesus restores Lazarus to life (11:38–45)

? (a location in Jerusalem)[11]

The leading Judeans meet and determine that Jesus must die (11:46–53)

Ephraim, a village in the wilderness of Judea (11:54)

Jesus retreats to the countryside to avoid arrest (11:54)

---

9. While a number of weeks clearly pass between John 10:21 and 10:22, John does not reveal where Jesus went during the intervening period.

10. The duration of Jesus' sojourn at Bethany beyond Jordan is unclear. John envisions that Jesus arrived there in December (after Hanukkah), remained there long enough to gain a following, and left sometime before Passover the following spring (see John 10:40–42; 11:55).

11. The events of John 11:46–53 are clearly not set at Lazarus's tomb and likely not in Bethany, in view of the participants and John's use of ἀπῆλθον ("some of them went to the Pharisees") at 11:46.

during the period of purification before the Passover festival (11:55)
Jerusalem (11:55)
The Passover crowds look for Jesus at the festival (11:55–57)

six days before Passover (12:1)
Lazarus's house in Bethany (near Jerusalem) (12:1–2)
Mary anoints Jesus' feet at a banquet (12:2–11)

"the next day" (12:12)
on the road from Bethany to Jerusalem (12:12)
The triumphal entry (12:13–19)

Jerusalem (the temple complex?) [12]
Some "Greek" pilgrims ask to see Jesus; he says that his hour has come (12:20–36)
Narrator's summary of popular responses to Jesus (12:36–43)
Jesus' final call to faith (12:44–50)

? (a location in Jerusalem) [13]
night, after dinner has been served (the Passover meal?) (13:1–2, 30) [14]

Jesus washes the disciples' feet and gives them a "new command" (13:4–20)

---

12. John 12:20 locates the comments that follow at the Passover festival in Jerusalem; the venue for Jesus' remarks is clearly public, as evident from the presence of the crowd at 12:29. Parallels between this scene and earlier encounters between Jesus and the festival crowds suggest that John envisions this exchange taking place in the temple complex.

13. The specific location of the Farewell Discourse, though clearly not the temple complex, is not indicated. The context suggests that John envisions the dinner taking place in a private home in Jerusalem within convenient walking distance of the garden mentioned at 18:1. As an alternate possibility, John may be thinking that Christ has returned to Lazarus's house in Bethany (see 12:1), although this location would seem inconsistent with the subsequent reference to Jesus' movement "across the valley of the Kidron" (πέραν τοῦ χειμάρρου τοῦ Κεδρὼν; 18:1)—there would be no need to cross the Kidron on the way from Bethany to Olivet.

14. Literally: πρὸ δὲ τῆς ἑορτῆς τοῦ πάσχα (John 13:1). John's conception of the timing and nature of the Last Supper, particularly whether John viewed the Last Supper to be a Passover meal, is notoriously difficult. John 13:1 seems to refer to the same meal mentioned at 13:2—Jesus knew "before" the meal was served that his return to the Father was imminent and therefore, after the table had been laid, washed the disciples' feet and delivered the "new command." Whether or not this meal was a Passover is complicated by the fact that John subsequently states four times that Jesus died on the Day of Preparation, that the chief priests had not yet eaten the Passover meal when they brought Jesus to Pilate, and that the authorities requested that Jesus' legs be broken so that he would die before the festival began (18:28; 19:14, 31, 42). John refers to the Last Supper simply as a δεῖπνον (13:2, 4), the standard term for a group banquet.

Jesus identifies his betrayer (13:21–30)
Jesus predicts Peter's betrayal (13:31–38)
Jesus promises the disciples access to the Father (14:1–11)
Jesus promises that the disciples will do "greater works" through the
Paraclete (14:12–31)

on the way to the garden (14:31; 18:1)
The vine and the branches (15:1–17)
Jesus predicts that the disciples will be persecuted (15:18–16:11)
Jesus discloses his identity to the disciples (16:12–33)
Jesus prays for the disciples (17:1–26)

a garden across the Kidron Valley (18:1)
Jesus' arrest (18:2–14)
the courtyard of the house of Annas (18:13)[15]
Peter denies Jesus (18:15–18)

inside Annas's house (18:13, 19)
Jesus is questioned by Annas and sent on to Caiaphas (18:19–24)

the courtyard of the house of Annas, near a charcoal fire (18:18, 25)[16]
Peter denies Jesus (18:25–27)

"early" the next morning, the Day of Preparation for the Passover (18:28; 19:14, 31, 42)
Pilate's Praetorium (18:28)[17]
Jesus is led to trial (18:28)

outside the Praetorium (18:28–29)
Pilate asks the Jewish authorities about the charges against Jesus (18:29–32)

inside the Praetorium (18:33)
Pilate asks Jesus whether he is "king of the Jews" (18:33–38)

---

15. John indicates that the posse brought Jesus to Annas for questioning but does not specify where this interrogation occurred. The attached story of Peter's denial is situated in "the courtyard of the high priest" (ἡ αὐλή τοῦ ἀρχιερέως), presumably referring to Annas (18:13) in view of the fact that Jesus is later sent to Caiaphas (18:24). Jesus' initial hearing thus seems to take place in Annas's house.

16. After his interrogation by Annas, Jesus is "sent to Caiaphas" (ἀπέστειλεν ... πρὸς Καϊάφαν; 18:24) and from there taken to Pilate (18:28). The verb "sent" implies that Jesus leaves Annas's house; the actual site of the meeting with Caiaphas, and the events of that meeting, are not specified, perhaps because John has already indicated Caiaphas's interpretation of the situation (11:49–50).

17. As commentators have often noted, the narrative structure of the Roman hearing follows Pilate's movements in and out of the Praetorium. See, e.g., Brown 1994, 1:757–58; Moore 2006, 56–63; Thatcher 2009, 64–67, 70–84.

outside the Praetorium (18:38)
Pilate asks if Jesus should be freed; the crowd asks for Barabbas instead
(18:38–40)

inside the Praetorium (see 19:4)[18]
Jesus is scourged and mocked (19:1–3)

outside the Praetorium (19:4)
Pilate pronounces Jesus innocent; "the Judeans" reveal that Jesus claimed
to be "Son of God" (19:4–8)

inside the Praetorium (19:9)
Pilate asks Jesus where he is from; Jesus says that the one who handed
him over has the "greater sin" (19:9–11)

"about the sixth hour" (of the same day; 19:14)
    outside the Praetorium[19] (19:12–13)
    Pilate seeks to negotiate Jesus' release (19:12–15)
    Pilate sends Jesus for crucifixion (19:16)

Golgotha ("Place of the Skull") (19:17)
    Jesus is crucified (19:16–22)
    Soldiers divide Jesus' clothing (19:23–24)
    Jesus speaks to his mother and the Beloved Disciple (19:25–27)

"after this" (after the exchange between Jesus and the Beloved Disciple; 19:28)
    Jesus dies (19:28–30)
    Jesus' corpse is "pierced" with a spear (19:31–37)

"after these things" (after Jesus dies on the Day of Preparation; 19:38)
    Joseph and Nicodemus receive and prepare Jesus' body (19:38–40)

a garden near the site of the crucifixion (19:41)
    Jesus is buried (19:40–42)

---

18. John does not specifically indicate that Pilate reentered the Praetorium to scourge Jesus, but this movement may be inferred from the facts that (1) the preceding scene is set outside, whereas Jesus is clearly inside; and, especially, (2) 19:4 says that Pilate "went out again" (ἐξῆλθεν πάλιν ἔξω) after the scourging, thus implying that he must have reentered the building at some point after 18:38.

19. John does not specifically indicate that Pilate left the Praetorium to negotiate Jesus' release, but this movement may be inferred from the facts that (1) throughout the episode, the "Jews" remain outside the building in order to maintain their ritual purification for Passover (18:28); and, especially, (2) 19:13 indicates that Pilate "led Jesus out" (ἤγαγεν ἔξω) in the course of his final appeal, thus suggesting that Pilate himself must also have left the building at some point after 19:11.

early morning, the first day of the week (Sunday) (20:1)
   Mary Magdalene finds the tomb opened (20:1)

the place where the disciples are staying in or near Jerusalem[20]
   Mary reports that Jesus' body is missing (20:2)

Jesus' tomb (20:3)
   Peter and the Beloved Disciple discover that the tomb is empty (20:3–10)
   Mary Magdalene meets Jesus outside the tomb (20:11–17)

the place where the disciples are staying in or near Jerusalem
   Mary Magdalene reports that Jesus is alive (20:18)

evening of the same day, the first day of the week (Sunday) (20:19)
the place where the disciples are staying in or near Jerusalem[21]

   Jesus appears to the disciples and commissions them (20:19–23)
   Thomas refuses to believe that Jesus appeared to the others (20:24–25)[22]

eight days after Jesus' first appearance to the disciples (20:26)
   the place where the disciples are staying in Jerusalem (20:26)
   Jesus appears and invites Thomas to touch his wounds (20:26–29)
   Narrator's summary of the purpose of the book (20:30–31)

"after these things" (21:1)
   the Sea of Tiberias/Galilee (21:1)
   Peter persuades a number of disciples to go fishing with him (21:2–3)

"early" in the morning (21:4)
   Jesus appears to the disciples as they are fishing (21:2–8)

---

20. John does not specify the location of Mary Magdalene's meeting with Peter and the Beloved Disciple; the place is obviously somewhere in or near Jerusalem. John 20:10 indicates that Peter and the Beloved Disciple "went back again to their own [places]" (ἀπῆλθον οὖν πάλιν πρὸς αὐτούς; NRSV: "to their own homes," although the reference is clearly not to Galilee) after leaving the tomb, which must refer to the house(s) where the disciples were lodging, presumably the same location where Mary meets with them at 20:2 and again at 20:18.

21. John does not specify the location of Jesus' appearance to the disciples; the location is presumably the same as that of Mary Magdalene's earlier discussions with them (20:2, 10, 18).

22. The iterative imperfect verb ἔλεγον ("they were saying") at John 20:25 indicates that the discussions between Thomas and the other disciples, in which Thomas expresses doubt over their claims, took place over the eight-day period before Jesus' next appearance.

the shore by the Sea of Galilee (21:9, 11, 20)
Jesus eats a meal with the disciples (21:9–14)
Jesus predicts the fates of Peter and the Beloved Disciple (21:15–23)
Narrator's closing remarks (21:24–25)

The Shape of John's Story: Jesus in Space and Time

Even a cursory review of the table above will reveal that the structure of FG, the outline that organizes the development and flow of the story, is driven by references to times and places. Before proceeding to considerations of the potential significance of this fact for understanding the composition of FG and the relationship between that narrative and the actual past, it will be helpful to offer three general observations on the table above.

1. The World in the Text Is the World outside the Text

The first observation simply states the obvious: the movement of John's story is clearly marked by, and is in fact entirely dependent upon, references to the geographical and temporal settings of the action—by/upon references to real-world space and time.

On the former (space), John, unlike Mark and, especially, Luke and, even more especially, Thomas, consistently locates Jesus' words and deeds in precise locations, even when these settings appear to be relatively insignificant to the action. Thus, the Johannine Jesus is baptized in "Bethany beyond Jordan" and meets several of his first disciples in Bethsaida, a village he never visits again (John 1:28, 43–44); John the Baptist's famous "he must increase, I must decrease" speech is set at "Aenon near Salim," a hamlet so obscure that scholars cannot reach a consensus on its location (3:23); John (the Evangelist) goes out of his way to clarify that Jesus is in Cana when he heals the royal official's son in Capernaum and that this is the same place where Jesus had earlier turned water to wine (4:46, 54; see 2:1); the Bread of Life discourse is set, almost as an afterthought and for no obvious reason, in Capernaum (6:59); Martha and Mary meet Jesus, not in their house in Bethany, but rather on the road outside the town (11:20, 30); when the Sanhedrin seeks Jesus' life he withdraws, not simply to the wilderness, but specifically to the Judean village of Ephraim (11:55).

This topographical precision extends not only to regions and towns but occasionally even to specific buildings. Thus, the Bread of Life discourse did not take place on a hillside near the lake but rather in a synagogue (6:59), a note that makes no difference to the contents of that speech and that in fact obscures John's conception of the size of its audience—no first-century building in Galilee could hold anything like five thousand people indoors (perhaps suggesting that "synagogue" refers to an outdoor "assembly" of the people rather than to any specific place). John also notes that Jesus' Light of the World discourse was delivered, not merely in the temple complex at Tabernacles, but very specifically in the area where the offering urns were located (τό γαζοφυλάκιον; John 8:12–20). John similarly clarifies that Jesus' debate with the crowds at Hanukkah took place in the temple's Stoa of Solomon (10:22–23). During the Roman trial scene, Pontius Pilate goes in and out of the Praetorium seven different times (18:28–29, 33, 38; 19:4, 9, 12–13; implied at 19:1). Nothing happens nowhere in the Fourth Gospel.

A similar attention to detail characterizes John's notes on the timing of events, which together communicate a strong sense of sequence between one episode and the next, even in cases where there is no clear casual or thematic relationship between consecutive scenes. This chronological precision is evident not only in John's references to important dates on the religious calendar (Tabernacles, Passover, Dedication, Sabbath, etc.) but also, and perhaps more particularly, in the many incidental indications that a certain event took place on "the next day," "the third day," or "the eighth day" after the preceding, or "six days" before the following, or even simply "after these things" (μετὰ ταῦτα). To take one obvious example, John 1:19–2:11, the story of the first disciples, is carefully structured as a series of events that take place over the course of seven consecutive days (1:29, 35, 43; 2:1).

John sometimes marks not only the day/occasion on which an event occurred but also the specific time. Thus, Andrew introduces Peter to Jesus at "about the tenth hour" (John 1:39–40); Nicodemus comes to meet with Jesus "at night," the same time that Judas will later leave the upper room to betray Christ (3:2; 13:30); Jesus meets the Samaritan woman by the well at "about the sixth hour," the same time that Pilate will later hand him over for crucifixion (4:6; 19:14); Jesus meets the royal official and heals his son at "the seventh hour" (4:52); Jesus walks on water in "the evening," the same time he will later appear to the disciples for the first time after being raised (6:16; 20:19). In point of fact, John rarely moves from one major scene to the next without somehow marking the passage of time, even when he does not specify a change in location (see 3:2; 7:37; 13:1–2; 20:18–19, 26). Overall, references to time and space serve as the points or stations through which the Fourth Gospel moves in its course.

2. The Rhetoric of Time and Place

A second observation on FG's outline relates to the first: in the Gospel of John, references to time and place are notable not only for their sheer number but also for the fact that much of the action and dialogue is specifically contingent upon them—"contingent" in the sense that the significance, narrative logic, or dramatic intensity of many events and sayings is established primarily by their setting. To cite an obvious example, the events and dialogues of John 5–10 are unified by frequent references to the two Sabbath healings that dominate the action in these chapters (5:1–9; 9:6, 14). At least fourteen different times, the narrator, Jesus, and other characters allude to the fact that Jesus has healed on the Sabbath (5:9, 10, 16, 18; 6:2; 7:1, 19–23; 8:46; 9:14, 16, 24, 25, 31; 10:32–38), so that the several significant Jerusalem discourses/dialogues in this section are continually reframed in reference to the larger question of whether a "Christ" could also be a "sinner" (Sabbath-breaker).[23] A number of studies have highlighted the interplay between the theological values typically associated with the various Jewish festivals in these same chapters and the discourses of Christ that take place on these occasions, so that Jesus' Sabbath-breaking is tied to a larger complex of ideas that draws its energy from a deep well of Jewish memory (see, e.g., Guilding 1960; Yee 1989; Kerr 2002, 205–67; Schlund 2005; Burge 2012). Overall, John frequently refers to times and places not simply to mark the bare sequence of events but also to indicate why certain events are significant or/and why things must happen as and when they do.

3. FG's Outline Is Not a Function of Its Theology

A third observation pertains to the consensus approach to FG's structure/outline discussed earlier. As noted above, scholars have tended to outline the Fourth Gospel in terms of its significant themes—in fact, these themes are often used as section headings in both translations of the Gospel and

---

23. John 7:1 does not mention the Sabbath but refers explicitly to the events of 5:18 and in fact serves as a continuation of that narrative string; the references to Jesus as a "sinner" at John 8:46; 9:24, 25, 31 clearly refer to the "sin" of breaking Sabbath; the "works" to which Jesus alludes at 10:32–38, particularly in view of the close verbal and thematic parallels between 10:26–30 and the Good Shepherd discourse at 10:7–18, must be primarily the healing of the blind man at Siloam in the immediately preceding sequence.

commentaries on it. While outlines of this kind are helpful for highlighting key concepts in Johannine theology, they are beset by a common burden that is widely acknowledged simply because it must be: John does not develop his ideas in any obviously logical fashion. Of course, readers who read the entire Gospel from beginning to end will doubtless experience a sense of developing consciousness, as terms, concepts, images, and themes are repeated with variation again and again. But one could scarcely argue that the Christology of the Farewell Address (chs. 13–17) is somehow "more advanced" than, or in any way dependent upon, the content of the Bread of Life discourse (ch. 6), or that either of these passages would be any less sublime without the other. In fact, FG's Prologue (1:1–18) is arguably its theological highpoint, with the rest of the story largely unpacking and illustrating the profound claims that are articulated in the first eighteen verses of the book. Recognizing these realities, many scholars have stressed that the Fourth Gospel's thematic development is best viewed not as a line of progress but rather as a "spiral of thought" or, perhaps even better, as a complex web of interlocking themes and symbols, a labyrinth that can be entered at almost any point (van der Watt 2007, 28). Simply put, John does not save the best of his theology for last.

While the implications of the above observation for considerations of Johannine theology lie beyond the scope of the present study, it is relevant to note here that the widely recognized nonlinear development of themes and concepts in FG reflects the simple fact that *John's narrative is not structured by its thematic development*. Rather, the story is structured by geographical and temporal markers that correspond to real-world places and times outside the text. Put another way, no clear thematic "progression" can be traced in John's story simply because John's story does not follow a clear thematic progression; it follows, instead, Jesus' movements across the map and the calendar. Because the various topics, terms, and themes that John wishes to develop can only be addressed at appropriate points in that movement, the story's thematic matrix necessarily cannot follow any obvious path of linear development. As a result, the oft-noted "upward spiral" of themes in FG is best understood as an aspect of the phenomenology of reading, not as a structural element of the text.

To take an obvious example, John explores several significant theological points in his account of Christ's encounter with the Samaritan woman and her compatriots (John 4:7–42). These themes include, among others, Judean–Samaritan relations; the decentralization of cult, shifting the focus of worship from monumental sites of civic religion to expressions of personal piety; Jesus' ministry to marginalized individuals; and Christ's commissioning of his disciples to extend his own work. Since John clearly connects these themes to the episode at Jacob's well, he necessarily can discuss them only on an occasion when Jesus is present in that place. Further, inasmuch as Jesus is a Galilean who regularly travels to Judea and back, the basic topography of Roman Palestine dictates that Christ can only be at Jacob's well in the context of a journey from Galilee to Judea or, vice-versa, through Samaria. And since such a journey must take place after Jesus has been somewhere else and before he goes somewhere else, John must necessarily raise the issues and themes associated with the Samaritan woman *after* discussing the issues and themes associated with some other time/place in Galilee or Judea and *before* discussing themes associated with yet another time/place in Galilee or Judea. To take another example, the Johannine Jesus can only cleanse the temple and confront the brokers of the Judean great tradition in Jerusalem, and he is only in Jerusalem every so often and is always there after doing something else and before doing something else somewhere else. FG's sequence of themes, and the reader's expanding comprehension of those themes, is thus a function of the sequence of Jesus' movements across real-world time and space.

JESUS AT THE MEMORY THEATER: JOHN'S COMPOSITIONAL TECHNIQUE

As noted earlier, while the movement of the Fourth Gospel clearly leads the reader through an expanding comprehension of key themes and concepts, the story is built on the ground and the calendar. Stated in terms of ancient compositional techniques—the methods that John may have used to write a Gospel—one could say that FG is heavily dependent on *place* as an organizing principle. While this focus on place over thematic development and cause–effect sequencing has produced a plot that is, at times, puzzling to modern readers, it is nevertheless entirely explicable in terms of John's own communications culture. Specifically, the Gospel of John appears to have been produced through "memory theater" techniques of oral composition, techniques that in this case depend heavily on real-world sites of memory drawn from the actual past of Jesus' historical context.

In John's communications culture, lengthy oral performances such as political speeches, arguments in court, and philosophical discourses were typically prepared and rehearsed in advance. To facilitate recall of the prepared material before live audiences—recall both of the content and of the order of presentation—rhetors relied heavily on "place system" or "memory theater" mnemonic strategies (see Thatcher 2011).[24] The most significant of these strategies was widely associated with Simonides of Keos (550s–460s BCE), a legendary lyric poet famous for being the first to perform compositions publicly and for pay and, in his own time, for his ability to inflame the emotions of his audience when describing epic death scenes. According to popular lore, Simonides was once commissioned to compose and recite an honorary ode at a large banquet. After finishing the performance, he was called to the door for an urgent message; as he stood outside, the building suddenly collapsed behind him, killing the large gathering of guests. The weight of the stones crushed many of the corpses, and the friends and family of the deceased appealed to the lucky bard to identify the remains. Simonides realized that he could name the mangled victims by visualizing the seating arrangements at the dinner and mentally noting the position of each guest. This remarkable experience led him to conclude that "the best aid to clearness of memory consists in orderly arrangement," specifically arrangements based on familiar places (Cicero, *Orat.* 2.355; Quintilian, *Inst.* 11.2.11–16; see Yates 1966, 27).

Simonides proceeded to develop a performance memory system based on the mental visualization of two types of pictures, which Cicero, Quintilian, and other later Latin rhetoricians would call *loci* (places) and *imagines* (images). The latter, images, are visual representations of important facts or ideas that one might wish to recall when delivering a speech, similar to the modern custom of tying a string around one's finger to remember something. *Loci* are mental portraits of real or imaginary places, such as the rooms of a house or a familiar row of shops in a marketplace (see, e.g., *Rhet. Her.* 3.29ff.; Quintilian, *Inst.* 11.2.21). Following Simonides's system, rhetors and philosophers could prepare for a speech or debate by placing images that represented the relevant facts and arguments in a fixed *locus*. At the moment of delivery, one would simply picture the imagined space, review the symbolic images in the order in which they appeared to the mind's eye, and discuss the points associated with each.

For example, in preparing a long speech, one might associate each of the major points with a piece of exercise equipment, then situate each piece of equipment in a gymnasium. In performance, the orator would simply walk through the gym in his mind's eye and discuss the points associated

---

24. For a helpful overview of the utilization of place systems through the Renaissance period, with reflection of the influence of this memory technique on the Western theological tradition, see Spence 1983, 1–21.

with the objects he encountered in each area. Similarly, a lawyer preparing for trial might imagine the places and people he would typically encounter on a walk from home to the court; the course of this journey would serve as an outline for the argument, with each place and person along the way representing a relevant precedent or piece of evidence. Some performers apparently preferred to use imaginary *loci* that might allow them to catalogue larger and more complex bodies of data. Quintilian notes that Metrodorus of Scepsis (early first century BCE) developed a memory theater based on the signs of the zodiac (see *Inst.* 11.2.22), which he apparently envisioned as a massive cosmic arena that could hold a large number of representative images in its twelve sections. Thus, "the localities will preserve the order of the facts, and the images of the facts will designate the facts themselves" (Cicero, *Orat.* 2.355).

It is important to stress that the model described here in no way represents an esoteric or arcane performance tradition; it was rather the normal technique of public speaking in John's world. Quintilian's *Institutio oratoria*—produced at the same time (80s CE) that Christians were telling stories about Jesus to Greek audiences and Matthew, Mark, Luke, and John were writing Gospels—clearly presupposes that the reader is already aware of the basic details of the Simonides legend, and in fact seems more concerned with correcting misunderstandings and abuses of Simonides's memory system than with explaining how to use it (see 11.2.11–22).

Applied to the case at hand, the fact that FG's narrative sequence is heavily dependent on references to time and space suggests that Johannine Christians, including the Fourth Evangelist, told stories about Jesus by visualizing a place and/or an occasion, locating images of Jesus and other actors against this backdrop, then describing the interactions between those people in that context. Settings and characters would thus function together as memory prompts for significant events, dialogues, and themes. John might, for example, visualize Jesus and the disciples gathered for a private meal at a house in Jerusalem on the last night of Christ's life. As various disciples make comments or ask Jesus questions, John recalls certain themes and sayings of Jesus that he associates with each character. The images of Judas Iscariot and Peter evoke memories of Jesus' words about his betrayal (John 13:21–38); moving around the table in his mind's eye, comments by Thomas (14:5), Philip (14:8), and the other Judas (14:22) remind John of Christ's words concerning his departure and the coming of the Spirit. The road from the upper room to the garden (14:31; 18:1) then serves as the mental/mnemonic backdrop for the remainder of the

Farewell Discourse. To take another example, John might visualize the Jerusalem temple and the rituals of the Tabernacles festival, locate Jesus and other characters in that arena, then describe the transactions that he envisions between them, thus producing the series of dialogues that now appear in John 7–8. In the same way, the account of the temple incident at 2:13–20 would be the written version of a running commentary on what John saw in his mind's eye.

If the model described above reflects John's typical procedure for composing stories about Jesus in live performance—and in point of fact, we know of no other model from antiquity that he might have followed—one can readily understand why the Fourth Gospel (1) emphasizes real-world places and times as its primary organizational principle and also (2) tends to treat individual episodes as relatively isolated events. On point 1, John seems to have sequenced his story by envisioning Jesus' movement over the ground through time, locating Christ and other characters in specific places at specific moments and envisioning what they did and said in those places. Each of these settings, in turn, would serve as a memory prompt for the discussion of specific themes and theological principles—always, of course, as appropriate to the immediate context—with the result that the thematic development of the Gospel could not progress in any straight line. On point 2, John's narrations of these individual episodes seem to have followed a relatively small number of plotlines; put another way, John tells stories about Christ interacting with different people in different places in similar ways. Overall, in the Fourth Gospel, and in sharp contrast to the Synoptics, everything has to happen somewhere sometime, a fact that suggests that John's memory of Jesus' activity, and his sense of the overall course of Christ's career, were entirely bound to time and space. Shifts in scene thus serve as bookmarks in John's imagination.

THE PAST IN THE PRESENT IN JOHN'S GOSPEL

In dialogue with the narrower concerns of the present volume, and particularly in dialogue with Barry Schwartz's trademark emphasis on the relationship between the actual past and its subsequent representations, three brief remarks on the potential ramifications of the preceding discussion for understanding FG's value as a potential source for Jesus are in order.

First, as Schwartz stresses in the introduction to the present collection, while the actual past is always necessarily experienced as the remembered past, it nevertheless exerts formative pressure on its subsequent representations. This principle helpfully explains the phenomenon observed earlier here: even the most grandiose theological statements in the Fourth Gospel are framed by the everyday world in which Jesus and his first followers lived and, consequently, from which the Johannine tradition originated. While John states explicitly that he has written a careful and selective account that seeks to lead the reader to faith—that is, to accept his own view of Christ (20:30–31; 21:24)—his memories nevertheless appear to be constrained by or, perhaps better, built upon the real-world circumstances of Jesus' context. Specifically here, while the plot of John's Gospel on one level traces the revelatory career of Christ's descent and ascent, as per the consensus view outlined above, John does not present his theological claims in a particularly orderly fashion simply because his story is driven by the real-world limitations of the map and the calendar. To cite a relevant parallel, the world of the Fourth Gospel is the same world that provides the backdrop for Josephus's *Jewish War*, and this world has substantially shaped John's memory and, consequently, his story about Jesus.

The above observation leads to a second, and perhaps more significant, point: while the sequence and structure of John's Gospel obviously differ from those of the Synoptics in substantial ways, they never do so in service of the incredible. The structural differences between John and Mark, and even the differences in detail between the few common scenes they share, are best explained by the assumption that these two "authors" (= storytellers) have utilized different memory systems for organizing their respective presentations of Jesus' career. Mark's system is beyond the scope of the present study; John's is clearly grounded in recollections of Jesus' movements from place to place over time. The fact that these movements differ from Mark's portrait suggests only that John is drawing on different mnemonic resources in plotting his narrative—and note that the verb "plotting" is used here in the literal sense of marking a space on the ground.

Further to this point, and narrowing a previous comment: it was noted earlier that FG's outline may be traced on the map of Roman Palestine. In point of fact, maps as we know them today would not have been accessible to a person like the Fourth Evangelist. Most ancient "maps," at least the kind that informed and were articulated in historical narratives such as the Fourth Gospel, took the form of narrative descriptions of regions based on the notes of travelers (or on earlier works that were based on the notes of travelers), essentially travelogues that described the land as it might be experienced in the course of a journey. It would therefore be more accurate to say that the outline of the Fourth Gospel follows not the map but *the land*, reflecting the perspective of a person who, like Josephus, likely had never seen a detailed visual representation of Roman Palestine but had walked that ground often and thereby gained a sense of the geographical relationships between various places and the means of moving between them. The same would necessarily be true of FG's dependence on the calendar: for John, calendars did not hang on walls but rather were embedded in the everyday, cyclical flow of time that structures traditional lifeways.

These two observations lead to a third and final point: to the extent that Jesus' movements through time and space in FG "make sense"— "make sense" not only as the residue of John's visual memory techniques but also in the sense that they bear verisimilitude in terms of the places a person like Jesus may have gone and the times he may have gone to those places—one cannot simply assume that John's presentation of the scope and range of Jesus' ministry is an ideological construct. Of course, John portrays Jesus in terms that would both reflect and speak to the needs of his own churches, but in turn, and as Schwartz everywhere stresses, that portrait would also bear the marks of its earlier iterations and, ultimately, of its originating events. Stated simply, John may have used specific places and occasions as memory prompts just because Jesus himself had done and said significant things at those places.

This third observation helps to explain an element of FG that scholars have often overlooked: while many of the places and times that frame Jesus' actions tap into fixed sites of memory, others do not. There is no obvious reason why John the Baptist's "I must decrease" saying should be set in Aenon near Salim, wherever that is (John 3:23), nor why Jesus' Bread of Life discourse should have been delivered in/to a Capernaum synagogue (6:59), nor why John would feel the need to specify that Jesus withdrew to Ephraim after raising Lazarus (11:54). Even less significant, by simple virtue of their vagueness, are John's many indications that a certain event took place "on the next day" or simply "after these things," temporal notes that mark a change in setting but obviously carry no symbolic value. The fact that John often situates Jesus in highly symbolic sites of memory underscores the fact that he often does not. Schwartz's approach would suggest that the latter instances are best explained as the residue of the actual past, at the very least the physical impressions on memory of the landscape through which Jesus moved.

In conclusion, then, the outline of the Fourth Gospel, viewed through the lens of Schwartz's emphasis on the reciprocal relationship between past and present and the mnemonic power of sites of cultural memory, offers substantial insights on both the composition history of the text and of its potential value as a source for Jesus. On the former, the "plot" of John's story is not grounded in its theological claims but rather in Jesus' movements through space and time, with these occasions and places serving as mnemonic anchors both for narrating individual episodes and for stringing them together in longer sequences. On the latter, the fact that John uses Jesus' real world as his memory theater suggests that his presentation of the scope and movement of Christ's career at least reflects the world as it was and would have been.

Works Cited

Brown, Raymond E. 1966–1970. *The Gospel according to John*. AB 29–29A. 2 vols. New York: Doubleday.

———. 1994. *The Death of the Messiah: From Gethsemane to the Grave*. ABRL. 2 vols. New York: Doubleday.

———. 2003. *An Introduction to the Gospel of John*. Edited by Francis J. Moloney. ABRL. New York: Doubleday.

Burge, Gary M. 2012. *Jesus and the Jewish Festivals: Ancient Context, Ancient Faith*. Grand Rapids, Zondervan.

Carson, D. A. 1991. *The Gospel according to John*. Grand Rapids: Eerdmans.

Culpepper R. Alan. 1983. *Anatomy of the Fourth Gospel: A Study in Literary Design*. Philadelphia: Fortress.

———. 1998. *The Gospel and Letters of John*. Interpreting Biblical Texts. Nashville: Abingdon.

Dodd, C. H. 1953. *The Interpretation of the Fourth Gospel*. Cambridge: Cambridge University Press.

———. 1963. *Historical Tradition in the Fourth Gospel*. Cambridge: Cambridge University Press.

Guilding, Aileen. 1960. *The Fourth Gospel and Jewish Worship: A Study of the Relation of St. John's Gospel to the Ancient Jewish Lectionary System*. Oxford: Clarendon.

Keener, Craig S. 2003. *The Gospel of John: A Commentary*. 2 vols. Peabody, MA: Hendrickson.

Kerr, Alan. 2002. *The Temple of Jesus' Body: The Temple Theme in the Gospel of John*. JSNTSup 220. New York: Sheffield Academic Press.

Köstenberger, Andreas J. 2004. *John*. Baker Exegetical Commentary on the New Testament. Grand Rapids: Baker.

Kysar, Robert. 2007. *John: The Maverick Gospel*. 3rd ed. Louisville: Westminster John Knox.

Moore, Stephen. 2006. *Empire and Apocalypse: Postcolonialism and the New Testament*. The Bible in the Modern World 12. Sheffield: Sheffield Phoenix.

Schlund, Christine. 2005. *Kein Knochen soll gebrochen werden: Studien zu Bedeutung und Funktion des Pesachfests in Texten des frühen Judentums und im Johannesevangelium*. WUNT 107. Neukirchen-Vluyn: Neukirchener.

Schwartz, Barry. 2005a. Christian Origins: Historical Truth and Social Memory. Pages 43–56 in *Memory, Tradition, and Text: Uses of the Past in Early Christianity*. Edited by Alan Kirk and Tom Thatcher. SemeiaSt 52. Atlanta: Society of Biblical Literature.

———. 2005b. Jesus in First-Century Memory—A Response. Pages 249–61 in *Memory, Tradition, and Text: Uses of the Past in Early Christianity*. Edited by Alan Kirk and Tom Thatcher. SemeiaSt 52. Atlanta: Society of Biblical Literature.

———. 2008. *Abraham Lincoln in the Post-heroic Era: History and Memory in the Late Twentieth Century*. Chicago: University of Chicago Press.

———. 2011. What Difference Does the Medium Make? Pages 225–38 in *The Fourth Gospel in First-Century Media Culture*. Edited by Anthony Le Donne and Tom Thatcher. ESCO/LNTS 426. London: T&T Clark.

Segovia, Fernando F. 1991. The Journeys of the Word of God: A Reading of the Plot of the Fourth Gospel. *Semeia* 53:23–54.

Smith, D. Moody. 1999. *John*. Abingdon New Testament Commentaries. Nashville: Abingdon.

Spence, Jonathan D. 1983. *The Memory Palace of Matteo Ricci*. New York: Penguin.

Staley, Jeffrey L. 1988. *The Print's First Kiss: A Rhetorical Investigation of the Implied Reader in the Fourth Gospel*. SBLDS 82. Atlanta: Scholars Press.

Thatcher, Tom. 2009. *Greater Than Caesar: Christology and Empire in the Fourth Gospel* Minneapolis: Fortress.

———. 2011. John's Memory Theatre: A Study of Composition in Performance. Pages 73–91 in *The Fourth Gospel in First-Century Media Culture*. Edited by Anthony Le Donne and Tom Thatcher. ESCO/LNTS 426. London: T&T Clark.

Tsafrir, Yoram, Leah Di Segni, and Judith Green. 1994. *Tabula Imperii Romani Iudaea-Palestina: Eretz Israel in the Hellenistic, Roman, and*

Byzantine Periods. Jerusalem: Israel Academy of Humanities and Sciences

Wahlde, Urban von. 2010. *The Gospel and Letters of John*. 3 vols. Eerdmans Critical Commentary. Grand Rapids: Eerdmans.

Watt, Jan G. van der. 2007. *An Introduction to the Johannine Gospel and Letters*. T&T Clark Approaches to Biblical Studies. New York: T&T Clark.

Witherington, Ben. 1995. *John's Wisdom: A Commentary on the Fourth Gospel*. Louisville: Westminster John Knox.

Yates, Francis. 1966. *The Art of Memory*. Chicago: University of Chicago Press.

Yee, Gale. 1989. *Jewish Feasts and the Gospel of John*. Wilmington, DE: Glazier.

"According to the Scriptures":
Suffering and the Psalms in the Speeches in Acts

Rafael Rodríguez

Analysis, then, is sorting out the structures of signification ... and determining their social ground and import. (Clifford Geertz, 1973, 9)

It is as if suffering itself survives as a visceral memory, while its explanation, still deeply felt, is more a result of ideological work, the work of
framing remembrance in categories of victim/oppressor. For the people
involved, what they went through is all too real, but it is also open to
changes in definition. (Iwona Irwin-Zarecka, 1994, 60)

The shifting significance of Abraham Lincoln in American memory since
his assassination in 1865 (see Schwartz 2000, 2008) is analogous to the
varying—and so variable—interpretations of Jesus' suffering throughout
the last two millennia. The present essay surveys how the author of Luke-
Acts employs traditions from the Psalms to provide an appropriate interpretation of Jesus' crucifixion. First, we will briefly survey Barry Schwartz's
model of social memory as "keying," in which the past is matched to the
present. Second, we will examine the function of quotations, allusions,
and/or echoes of the Psalms within the speeches of Acts that help contex-
tualize Jesus' suffering. Finally, we will address three questions in light of
the data from Acts: *Why* do people bother to remember the past? *How* do
they pursue remembering? And, *What consequences* in (and for) the present result from remembering?

From the very beginning, Jesus' followers found themselves confronted
with the problem of interpreting Jesus' suffering, especially his crucifixion
as a messianic pretender by a Roman prefect. All four canonical Gospels
explicitly portray Jesus' crucifixion in ways that render the event meaningful and mitigate its challenge to the early Christian estimation of him
as "the Son of God." The Emmaus pericope (Luke 24:13–35) provides a
striking example of this portrayal. Cleopas describes Jesus as "a man, a

prophet powerful in deed and word" (ἀνὴρ προφήτης δυνατὸς ἐν ἔργῳ καὶ λόγῳ; 24:19).[1] This is the only time Luke attributes the adjective δυνατός (powerful) to Jesus, though his Gospel repeatedly associates Jesus with the related noun δύναμις (power). So when the otherwise unknown Cleopas[2] describes Jesus as powerful in deed and word, readers already understand the substance undergirding the adjective. Nevertheless, Luke bumps up against the limits of his ability to remember Jesus in terms of power in the very next verse: "our chief priests and rulers handed him over εἰς κρίμα θανάτου [lit. "unto judgment of death"] and ἐσταύρωσαν αὐτόν [they crucified him]" (Luke 24:20). Whatever else Jesus' earliest followers wished to say about Jesus, they could not avoid the fact that he ended up nailed to a Roman cross.

Let the memory work begin.[3] According to Luke, Jesus responds to Cleopas's portrayal of recent events as follows: "And he said to them, 'O, you foolish and slow of heart to believe everything the prophets said. Was it not necessary for the Christ to suffer these things [οὐχὶ ταῦτα ἔδει παθεῖν τὸν Χριστόν] and then to enter into his glory?' And beginning with Moses and all of the prophets, he explained to them by means of all the scriptures the things concerning himself [τὰ περὶ ἑαυτοῦ]" (Luke 24:25–27). Throughout his Gospel, Luke has provided various hints (e.g., 2:34–35) and outright predictions (e.g., 9:22, 44) of Jesus' impending suffering, but he has refrained from appealing to biblical traditions to frame that suffering, with one exception. In the third passion–resurrection prediction, Luke refers to πάντα τὰ γεγραμμένα διὰ τῶν προφητῶν ("all the things written

---

1. See the similar description of the young Moses in Acts 7:22: καὶ ἐπαιδεύθη Μωϋσῆς [ἐν] πάσῃ σοφίᾳ Αἰγυπτίων, ἦν δὲ δυνατὸς ἐν λόγοις καὶ ἔργοις αὐτοῦ ("Moses was educated in all the wisdom of the Egyptians, and he was powerful in his words as well as his deeds"). In light of the link Luke makes between Jesus and the promised "prophet like Moses" (Deut 18:15–19; see Acts 3:21–24; 7:37–39), the echo must be intentional.

2. Bauckham (2002, 206–10) identifies Luke's Cleopas with the Clopas mentioned in John 19:25.

3. The term "memory work" comes from Iwona Irwin-Zarecka, who uses it to refer to the effort and expense involved in producing texts, objects, rituals, and the like associated with collective memory. Memory work produces "the 'infrastructure' of collective memory, all the different spaces, objects, 'texts' that make an engagement with the past possible" (1994, 13). Applied to the present study, the memory work began, at the latest, when the Evangelist decided to put together an account of Jesus' life and teachings for Theophilus (see Luke 1:1–4). My reference to the memory work "beginning" in Luke 24:25 assumes a perspective *within* (rather than *of*) Luke's narrative.

through the prophets"; see 18:31–34).[4] The Emmaus pericope, however, turns squarely to Hebrew biblical tradition, *qua* tradition, to provide the necessary context for interpreting Jesus' suffering.

As this example illustrates, the early Christians—including the Third Evangelist—explicitly and emphatically rooted the innovative image of the suffering Messiah in Israel's biblical tradition. This essay turns to the work of Barry Schwartz (and other social memory theorists) to provide a theoretical model and vocabulary for understanding the role of one specific corpus—the book of Psalms—in the development of early Christian interpretations of Messiah's suffering. Specifically, Schwartz speaks of "the matching of past and present" (2000, passim) or, to highlight the theme of the present volume, "keying" and "framing." For the present discussion, this "matching" refers to mapping the connections between established and publicly available patterns of discourse for Jews in the late Second Temple era with early Christian christological ideas, specifically here the idea of the "suffering Messiah."

Toward a Model of Social Memory (and Remembering)

Social memory theory raises the following questions: *Why* do people bother to remember the past? *How* do they pursue remembering? *What consequences* in (and for) the present result from remembering?[5] The emphasis among historians, particularly historians of Jesus, on assessing a tradition's authenticity often obscures these questions, apparently following the logic that, once we doubt a tradition's authenticity, its social significances—its motivations (why?), means (how?), and effects (what consequences?)—no longer matter.[6] For social memory theorists, *wie es eigentlich gewesen* is

---

4. For the language of "passion–resurrection predictions" instead of the standard "passion predictions" (and, relatedly, "passion–resurrection narrative"), see Carey 2009, 46–48.

5. Schwartz complains that ideological approaches to memory illumine the first and third of these questions but completely neglect the second. "The politics of memory produces little understanding of collective memory as such—only of its causes and consequences. How the past is symbolized and how it functions as a mediator of meaning are questions that go to the heart of collective memory, but they have been skirted" (Schwartz 2000, 17).

6. For example, Maurice Casey rejects the notion that the historical Jesus had any interest in or concern for Gentiles: "The Gentile mission does not have any setting in the teaching of Jesus—he expected the kingdom to come too soon for it take place" (2010, 374). However, all four Gospels—and certainly Paul's letters, also—credit "the

only one part of the problem; in addition to "what actually happened," the images and patterns that render the past culturally meaningful also require explanation. In this vein, Barry Schwartz addresses the "matching" of past to present: "Keying defines social memory's function, matching the past to the present as (1) a model *of* society, reflecting its needs, interests, fears, and aspirations; (2) a model *for* society, a template for thought, sentiment, morality, and conduct; and, (3) a *frame* within which people find meaning for their experience" (p. 16, above). Social memory theory affirms the reality and autonomy of the past, whose features and existence transcend the ideological interests of the present.[7] Simultaneously, it emphasizes the present as the ever-shifting context in which images of the past are configured and employed.[8]

The semiotic (= meaning-making) function of memory, what Schwartz calls "memory as a cultural system" (2000, 17–20), is an important feature of this "matching" of past and present. Memory provides significant and effective discursive resources for legitimating certain beliefs, values, and/or courses of action in the present. "But this is half the truth, at best, and a particularly cynical half-truth, at that" (Schudson 1989, 113). Memory also functions as "an organization of symbolic patterns on which people rely to make sense of their experience.... [M]emory becomes a meaning-conferring cultural system" (Schwartz 2000, 17–18). Human beings, as "meaning-seeking subjects" (Shore 1991, 10), navigate reality by means of symbolic patterns and cultural conventions that render the inchoate experiences of reality meaningful.[9] We do not perceive reality and then,

---

teaching of Jesus" with the origin of the early Christian concern for proclamation to and inclusion of Gentiles. This does not authenticate the Gentile mission as a feature of the life of the historical Jesus. But Casey exhibits no concern whatsoever to explain why, how, or to what effect our extant sources unanimously remember Jesus exhibiting an interest in Gentiles.

7. Iwona Irwin-Zarecka (1994) explores this transcendence—the reality of the past itself—and the problems it presents to any efforts to develop intelligible and satisfying accounts of the past of the Holocaust.

8. Kirk and Thatcher explain the potential contribution of social memory to "the problem of the Gospel traditioning processes" in terms of the observation that "Jesus was represented through multiple acts of remembering that semantically fused the present situations of the respective communities with their memory of the past as worked out in commemorative practices, *with neither factor swallowed up by, or made epiphenomenal of, the other*" (2005, 33, emphasis added). See also Fentress and Wickham 1992, 24.

9. Bradd Shore refers to "culturally motivated practices as *meaning-creating activities*" (1991, 10, emphasis added). See also Berger and Luckmann's famous monograph, *The Social Construction of Reality* (1966).

subsequent to and separate from the act of perception, search for patterns and precedents that enable us to comprehend and talk about our perceptions. *Perception and interpretation take place simultaneously.* Subsequent reflection—alone and with others—alternatively extends, modifies, challenges, transforms, and/or confirms earlier interpretations. Whether or not human beings are *capable* of observing reality without simultaneously interpreting it (and I do not think we are), we certainly do not *normally* do so. And all this talk of perception and interpretation takes as its starting point the reality that is there to be perceived and interpreted in the first place. "Reality sets limits to perception.… No one can live in a real world if we see only what suits us" (Lindesmith, Strauss, and Denzin 1988, 124). To return to Schwartz's introduction to the present collection, "interpretation is more often forced upon the observer of an event by its inherent quality than imposed by the observer's worldview and interests. Put another way, *reality counts more than bias in the remembering of most events most of the time*" (pp. 20–21, emphasis original).

Thus the utility of Barry Schwartz's argument that "[t]he past is matched to the present as a model *of* society and a model *for* society" (2000, 18). Constructionist approaches—what Schwartz refers to as "presentist" models of memory (e.g., 2005a, 44–45)—provide helpful insight into the dynamics of the past-as-model-*of*-society, in which ideologically motivated actors in the present (re)configure images of the past "in terms of the needs, interests, fears, and aspirations of the present." Such approaches, however, do not address the dynamics of the past-as-model-*for*-society, in which ideologically motivated actors are themselves configured by past events and established representations of those events.[10] Schwartz's double-sided model reminds us to account for both the variability of the past in the ever-shifting present and the continuity of memory across successive generations. Our analyses must account for *both* the way memories are modified as they are expressed through time and across space *as well as* how they preserve their connection to "the essence of the events to which they refer" (Schwartz, p. 9; see also 1991b).

---

10. Subramanian recognizes the dialectic between past (= text) and present at Qumran: "It is evident that Psalm 37 is interpreted in light of the community's situation, on the one hand, and that the community's crisis is seen in light of Psalm 37, on the other" (2007, 34).

Jesus' Suffering and the Book of Psalms
in the Acts of the Apostles

The early Christians clearly perceived Jesus as the hermeneutical key that unlocked the true significance of Israel's scriptures. Without contesting this observation, I would like to counterbalance it with another: the Emmaus pericope reverses this direction of influence. Cleopas and his companion have misunderstood the events of Jesus' death, which has brought into question their hope that Jesus would redeem Israel (Luke 24:21).[11] This misunderstanding has prevented the disciples from grasping the significance of the women's report of the empty tomb and the angelic vision, even after they have confirmed the facts of that report (24:22–24). In order to frame these events properly, the hitherto unrecognized Jesus walks them through "Moses and all the prophets" and διερμήνευσεν αὐτοῖς ("he explained to them") by means of all the Scriptures the things about himself (24:27). The *what* that Jesus explains to the disciples, the unknown factor, is τὰ περὶ ἑαυτοῦ ("the things concerning himself"), and he turns to πάσαις ταῖς γραφαῖς ("all the Scriptures"), the known factor, to explain that unknown factor. In other words, Luke turns to Moses and all the prophets, even to "all the Scriptures," to illumine the proper significance of Jesus' suffering, his death, and the women's unsettling reports.

Unfortunately, nowhere in Luke 24 does Luke explain the content of Jesus' exposition of "all the Scriptures."[12] Luke thereby privileges the *fact* of biblical tradition's epexegetical function vis-à-vis Jesus' suffering over the specific *mechanisms* of that function. The speeches in Acts may provide some explanation of Luke's understanding of the relation between the Bible and Jesus' suffering.[13] The remainder of this section will briefly sketch the

---

11. Thus the significance of the imperfect tense of ἠλπίζομεν ("we were hoping"; Luke 24:21; see BDF §330).

12. Luke reverses the known and unknown terms at the end of Luke 24. Whether or not any confusion remained about the significance of the events of Jesus' passion (vv. 44–49 provide no hint, unless the apostles' commission as Jesus' witnesses in v. 48 implies they have finally caught on), he clearly says that Jesus διήνοιξεν αὐτῶν τὸν νοῦν τοῦ συνιέναι τὰς γραφάς ("opened their minds to understand the Scriptures"; 24:45).

13. "[T]he speeches [in Acts] construct the framework through interpretation of biblical texts. They flesh out Jesus' thematic statement in Luke 24:44–47 that his death and resurrection as Christ, as well as the preaching of repentance and forgiveness to all nations, 'has been written.' *In the speeches we see the biblical proof*" (Juel 1988, 82–83, emphasis added).

function of quotations, allusions, and/or echoes of the Psalms within the biblical framework that Luke employs to make sense of Jesus' suffering.[14]

The first reference to the Psalms occurs early in Acts. Prior to the unusual events of Pentecost, Peter turns to "the Scripture [τὴν γραφήν] in which the Holy Spirit spoke beforehand through the mouth of David concerning Judas" (Acts 1:16). Luke does not mention which specific scripture he might have in mind, though NA[27] suggests Ps 41:10 in a marginal note.[15] Four verses later, Peter refers explicitly to the book of Psalms (βίβλῳ ψαλμῶν) and cites two different texts from this "book."

Acts 1:20	**Psalms 68:26; 108:8 (LXX)**
²⁰ γέγραπται γὰρ ἐν βίβλῳ ψαλμῶν·	
<u>γενηθήτω ἡ ἔπαυλις αὐτοῦ</u> ἔρημος	²⁶ <u>γενηθήτω ἡ ἔπαυλις αὐτῶν</u> ἠρημωμένη,
<u>καὶ μὴ ἔστω ὁ κατοικῶν ἐν</u> αὐτῇ,	<u>καὶ ἐν</u> τοῖς σκηνώμασιν αὐτῶν <u>μὴ ἔστω</u>
καί·	<u>ὁ κατοικῶν.</u>
	⁸ γενηθήτωσαν αἱ ἡμέραι αὐτοῦ ὀλίγαι,
<u>τὴν ἐπισκοπὴν αὐτοῦ</u> λαβέτω <u>ἕτερος.</u>	καὶ <u>τὴν ἐπισκοπὴν αὐτοῦ λάβοι ἕτερος.</u>
²⁰ For it is written in the Book of Psalms,	
"<u>Let his residence become</u> desolate,	²⁶ <u>Let their residence become</u> desolated,
<u>and let there be no one who</u> <u>dwells in</u> it,"	<u>and let there be no one who dwells in</u> their tents.
and,	⁸ Let his days become few,
<u>Let another person take his position.</u>	and <u>may another person take his position.</u>

---

14. The language of "quotations, allusions, and echoes" has become standard among students of the connections between Hebrew biblical traditions and New Testament texts. The precise distinctions between these three phenomena, as well as standard methods for detecting them, are complicated questions that lie beyond the scope of the current essay.

15. *Sic.* Psalm 41:9 (LXX 40:10) reads, "For even my close companion [ὁ ἄνθρωπος τῆς εἰρήνης μου], upon whom I placed my hope, who ate my loaves of bread, has magnified treachery against me."

Peter's citation from Ps 69 (LXX 68) reflects a broader Christian tradition of reciting this psalm in connection with the events (and aftermath) of Jesus' execution.[16] John cites Ps 69:9 in his account of the temple incident (John 2:17), which he then immediately associates with Jesus' death (see 2:18–22). Moreover, all four canonical Gospels echo Ps 69:21 in their accounts of the crucifixion (see Mark 15:36 par.; John 19:29). Paul identifies the part of Israel that rejected the gospel with the psalmist's opponents (Rom 11:9–10; Ps 69:22–23). Four chapters later, Paul employs the language of Ps 69:9 to explain Jesus' attitude of self-sacrifice (Rom 15:3).[17] When Peter identifies Judas with David's adversaries in Ps 69, he participates in an established tradition among early Christians for making sense of Jesus' suffering.[18]

The same can be said of Peter's quotation of Ps 109 (LXX 108). Mark 15:29–32 (par. Matt 27:38–44) alludes to Ps 109:25, in that the passers-by "shake their head" at Jesus[19] while the two bandits revile him.[20] Luke draws from two different psalms to explain Judas's fate and the apostles' response to it, suggesting that, when he refers to τὴν γραφήν ("the Scripture"; Acts 1:16), he has in view *a larger, encompassing tradition embodied in particular*

---

16. Tate (1990, 192) refers to the "prayer of the suffering servant in this psalm." Such language is not inappropriate, given the psalmist's self-identification as ὁ παῖς σου ("your servant") and his cry of suffering (θλίβομαι; "I am afflicted") in v. 18 (LXX); see also v. 37 (τὸ σπέρμα τῶν δούλων αὐτῶν; "the offspring of their slaves").

17. In so doing, however, Paul transforms the psalmist's commitment to God, such that he receives the reproaches intended for God, into a prediction of Christ's service of others. Although a number of commentators argue that Paul applies the verse from the psalm to Jesus' relationship to God (e.g., Dunn 1988, 839; Moo 1996, 868; Schreiner 1998, 747), the context of Paul's argument in Rom 14:1–15:13 makes this exceedingly unlikely. Rather, "[i]n the context of Rom 15, the selection of this quotation serves perfectly to sustain a mutually accepting attitude between the 'weak' and the 'strong'" (see Jewett 2007, 879–80, quote 880).

18. In addition, we should note Ps 69's thematic similarities with Ps 22, especially given the latter's considerable influence over the earliest accounts of Jesus' passion (see Carey 2009). Among other things, Ps 69 expresses a sense of abandonment by God (cf. Ps 69:3 with 22:1) and yet preserves a confidence in God's ultimate deliverance (cf. Ps 69:33 with 22:24). In their commentary on Ps 69, Hossfeld and Zenger (2005, 172–74) identify a three-part structure of lament (vv. 2–14b), petition (vv. 14c–30), and praise (vv. 31–37).

19. Mark 15:29//Matt 27:38 = κινοῦντες τὰς κεφαλὰς αὐτῶν ("shaking their heads"); Ps 108:25 (LXX) = ἐσάλευσαν κεφαλὰς αὐτῶν ("they shook their heads").

20. Mark 15:32//Matt 27:44 = ὠνείδιζον αὐτόν ("they insulted him"); Ps 108:25 (LXX) = ἐγενήθην ὄνειδος αὐτοῖς ("I became an insult to them").

texts rather than a single specific text.[21] That is, Luke *keys* Judas to already existing cultural scripts, which are evident in multiple and various texts and which give Judas's actions a particular significance (see Bock 2007, 87). "*Keying*," Schwartz explains, "transforms the meaning of activities understood in terms of one event by comparing them with activities understood in terms of another" (Schwartz 2000, 226). In his introduction to the present volume, Schwartz explains that "keying (perhaps most familiar to biblical and rabbinics scholars as an aspect of typology) transforms the meaning of activities understood in terms of one reference frame by comparing them with activities understood in terms of another" (Schwartz, p. 15, above). By holding Judas's role in Jesus' arrest up against the publicly accessible model of treachery embodied in biblical tradition, and specifically in the Psalms, Luke renders Judas "a traitor." Further, by keying Judas to the Psalm's insider-traitor, Luke reinforces the interpretation of Jesus as the faithful (= righteous) sufferer, the victim of the traitor's treachery.

In the next chapter of Acts, Peter expands on God's act of raising Jesus from the dead, adding that God "loosened τὰς ὠδῖνας τοῦ θανάτου ("the pains of death") because he was not able to be restrained by death" (2:24). In the New Testament, the phrase "pains of death" occurs only here; it occurs three times in the LXX, always within a psalm.[22] In all three instances, the pains of death are "encircling" (κυκλόω) and/or "encompassing" (περιέχω) the victim. Luke goes on to explain God's "breaking-through" by quoting verbatim from Ps 16.

Acts 2:25–28	Psalm 15:8–11 (LXX)
[25] Δαυὶδ γὰρ λέγει εἰς αὐτόν·	
<u>προορώμην τὸν κύριον ἐνώπιόν μου διὰ παντός,</u>	[8] <u>προωρώμην τὸν κύριον ἐνώπιόν μου διὰ παντός,</u>
<u>ὅτι ἐκ δεξιῶν μού ἐστιν ἵνα μὴ σαλευθῶ.</u>	<u>ὅτι ἐκ δεξιῶν μού ἐστιν, ἵνα μὴ σαλευθῶ.</u>

---

21. This usage may differ from other early Christian texts. See, for example, Michaels 2010, 170 n. 56.

22. See 2 Kgs 22:6 (a psalm of David); Pss 17:5; 114:3 (LXX). Similarly, the psalmist refers to ὠδῖνες ᾅδου (Ps 17:6 LXX), which parallel παγίδες θανάτου and which are said to encircle (περικυκλόω) the psalmist (see also Polycarp, *Phil.* 1.2; Acts 2:24). See also 1QH 11.26–28, which expands the image of death's traps, climaxing with "and the ropes of death enclose with no escape" (וחבלי מות אפפו לאין פלט‎), 11.28; García Martínez and Tigchelaar 1998, 2:166, 167).

²⁶ <u>διὰ τοῦτο ηὐφράνθη ἡ καρδία μου</u>
   <u>καὶ ἠγαλλιάσατο ἡ γλῶσσά μου,</u>
   <u>ἔτι δὲ καὶ ἡ σάρξ μου κατασκηνώσει</u>
   <u>ἐπ᾽ ἐλπίδι,</u>
²⁷ <u>ὅτι οὐκ ἐγκαταλείψεις τὴν ψυχήν μου</u>
   <u>εἰς ᾅδην</u>
   <u>οὐδὲ δώσεις τὸν ὅσιόν σου ἰδεῖν</u>
   <u>διαφθοράν.</u>
²⁸ <u>ἐγνώρισάς μοι ὁδοὺς ζωῆς,</u>
   <u>πληρώσεις με εὐφροσύνης μετὰ τοῦ</u>
   <u>προσώπου σου.</u>

⁹ <u>διὰ τοῦτο ηὐφράνθη ἡ καρδία μου,</u>
   <u>καὶ ἠγαλλιάσατο ἡ γλῶσσά μου,</u>
   <u>ἔτι δὲ καὶ ἡ σάρξ μου κατασκηνώσει</u>
   <u>ἐπ᾽ ἐλπίδι,</u>
¹⁰ <u>ὅτι οὐκ ἐγκαταλείψεις τὴν ψυχήν μου</u>
   <u>εἰς ᾅδην</u>
   <u>οὐδὲ δώσεις τὸν ὅσιόν σου ἰδεῖν</u>
   <u>διαφθοράν.</u>
¹¹ <u>ἐγνώρισάς μοι ὁδοὺς ζωῆς,</u>
   <u>πληρώσεις με εὐφροσύνης μετὰ τοῦ</u>
   <u>προσώπου σου,</u>
   τερπνότητες ἐν τῇ δεξιᾷ σου εἰς τέλος.

[25] For David says to him·

<u>I foresaw the Lord before more</u>
   <u>through everything,</u>
   <u>because he is at my right hand, so</u>
     <u>that I may not be shaken.</u>
[26] <u>For this reason my heart is gladdened,</u>
   <u>and my tongue rejoices greatly,</u>
   <u>and my flesh also will dwell in hope,</u>
[27] <u>because you shall not abandon my</u>
   <u>soul to Hades,</u>
   <u>nor will you give your holy one to</u>
     <u>see corruption.</u>
[28] <u>You made known to me the paths of</u>
   <u>life;</u>
<u>with your presence you shall fill me</u>
   <u>with gladness.</u>

[8] <u>I foresaw the Lord before more</u>
   <u>through everything,</u>
   <u>because he is at my right hand, so</u>
     <u>that I may not be shaken.</u>
[9] <u>For this reason my heart is gladdened,</u>
   <u>and my tongue rejoices greatly,</u>
   <u>and my flesh also will dwell in hope,</u>
[10] <u>because you shall not abandon my</u>
   <u>soul to Hades,</u>
   <u>nor will you give your holy one to</u>
     <u>see corruption.</u>
[11] <u>You made known to me the paths of</u>
   <u>life;</u>
<u>with your presence you shall fill me</u>
   <u>with gladness;</u>
   there are delights in your right hand
   to the very end.

Surprisingly, the New Testament does not quote, allude to, or echo Ps 16 very often; Loci Citati vel Allegati (NA[27]) mentions Acts 2:25–28, 31 and

13:35.[23] The psalmist speaks of ἡ σάρξ μου ("my flesh") dwelling in hope because the Lord will not abandon τὴν ψυχήν μου ("my soul") to Hades (Ps 15:9–10 LXX). Luke certainly found this language useful for his insistence that the apostles' encounters with the risen Lord were more than visionary experiences (see Luke 24:37–43; Acts 1:3; cf. Luke 24:23), despite Christ's strange ability to disappear suddenly (Luke 24:31), to appear suddenly in the midst of a crowd (Luke 24:36), and even to ascend up into the clouds (Luke 24:51; Acts 1:9).[24] More important, as noted earlier, this "psalm of confidence" (Craigie 1983, 155; Bock 2007, 123) provides a response to the mortal suffering connoted in the psalmic language (viz. ὠδῖνες θανάτου; "pains of death") in Acts 2:24.

Luke has Peter read this useful language literally (Bock 2007, 126), so that David's death and burial preclude the promise of Ps 16 from applying to him (Acts 2:29). Later Luke will have Paul read Ps 16 just as literally (Acts 13:35). Immediately after quoting Ps 15:10 (LXX), which shares key terminology with the immediately preceding reference to Isa 55:3,[25] Paul makes the same case as Peter: David served his generation, died, was buried, and saw decay (Acts 13:36); Ps 16, therefore, cannot refer to David and must refer to someone else. The innovative element of Luke's memory work here focuses on the psalmist's confidence that he would be delivered *from* death, which in Acts becomes Jesus' victory/deliverance *through* death: "whereas from the psalmist's theological perspective, death would end it all, in the experience of Jesus, death became a door. The psalmist rose up in confidence against the danger of death: Jesus rose up in confidence from the actual stronghold of death" (Craigie 1983, 158). Ironically, this innova-

---

23. The use of Ps 16 specifically appears to be Luke's own unique contribution to the tradition of appealing to the Psalter to place Jesus' suffering (and vindication) in biblical perspective (unless this use stems from Peter's and/or Paul's preaching, as the narrative suggests). Bruce (1988, 65) makes an interesting reference to Midrash Tehillim on Ps 16:9 ("'my glory rejoices over the Lord Messiah, who will rise from me,' that is, from David"), but this text is too late (eleventh century?) to shed any light on Ps 16 in the first century (even if Midrash Tehillim preserves older material).

24. Contrast Raphael's admission at the denouement of the story of Tobit: "All the days I appeared to you, I neither ate nor drank anything; instead, you were seeing a vision" (12:19; GI). The verse reads differently in GII but makes the same point: "You saw me, that I never ate anything; instead, a vision appeared to you."

25. As Luke cites them, the adjective ὅσιος ("holy, hallowed") and the future active indicative form of the verb δίδωμι ("I give") occur in both Isa 55:3 and Ps 15:10 (LXX); Isa 55:3 LXX uses διαθήσομαι ("I will make") instead of Luke's δώσω ("I will give"). Moreover, both share a connection with Δαυίδ ("David"; see Ps 15:1 LXX).

tive interpretation results from a literal construal of the psalmist's words. The same literal hermeneutic applies to Luke's reading of Ps 110:1 in Acts 2:34–35.

Two chapters later, as Peter explains the healing of a lame man to the temple authorities, he reads the events of Jesus' suffering—and especially the Sanhedrin's role in handing him over to Pilate—into the implied narrative of Ps 118.

Acts 4:11	Psalm 117:22 (LXX)
[11] οὗτός ἐστιν ὁ λίθος, ὁ ἐξουθενηθεὶς ὑφ᾽ ὑμῶν τῶν οἰκοδόμων, ὁ γενόμενος εἰς κεφαλὴν γωνίας.	[22] λίθον, ὃν ἀπεδοκίμασαν οἱ οἰκοδομοῦντες, οὗτος ἐγενήθη εἰς κεφαλὴν γωνίας.
[11] This is the stone, the one who was rejected by you the builders, the one who became the cornerstone.	[22] A stone, which the builders rejected, this one became the cornerstone.

The New Testament includes numerous references to Ps 118. All three Synoptic Gospels and the Gospel of Thomas quote Ps 118:22 in the conclusion of the parable of the Wicked Tenants (Mark 12:10–11 par.; Thomas 65–66). In addition, 1 Pet 2:4, 7 alludes to Ps 118:22 even as it quotes directly from Isa 28:16. All four canonical Gospels, the undisputed Pauline letters, Hebrews, and Revelation all make references—direct quotations as well as allusions—to other parts of Ps 118. Again, Luke participates in a larger tradition of keying Jesus' suffering (and vindication) to the words of Ps 118. The proverbial image in Ps 118:22 provides the people an opportunity to "discern divine providence in the unlikely royal reversal" (Allen 2002, 167), which reversal, in its application to Jesus, refers not just to his resurrection but also to his defeat of the enemies of God's people and his enthronement at God's right hand. Interestingly, Ps 118 makes two references to the psalmist's commitment to heed God's word rather than his opponents' threats or the rulers' decrees (Ps 118:6, 9; see Acts 4:19–20; 5:29).

After the Sanhedrin dismisses them, Peter and John return to the rest of the disciples and report what has happened. The apostles then turn to God in prayer, and in the process they key their experiences with the Sanhedrin to the complaint of Ps 2.

Acts 4:25–26	Psalm 2:1–2 (lxx)
²⁵ ὁ τοῦ πατρὸς ἡμῶν διὰ πνεύματος ἁγίου στόματος Δαυὶδ παιδός σου εἰπών·	
ἱνατί ἐφρύαξαν ἔθνη	¹ Ἵνα τί ἐφρύαξαν ἔθνη
καὶ λαοὶ ἐμελέτησαν κενά;	καὶ λαοὶ ἐμελέτησαν κενά;
²⁶ παρέστησαν οἱ βασιλεῖς τῆς γῆς	² παρέστησαν οἱ βασιλεῖς τῆς γῆς,
καὶ οἱ ἄρχοντες συνήχθησαν ἐπὶ τὸ αὐτὸ	καὶ οἱ ἄρχοντες συνήχθησαν ἐπὶ τὸ αὐτὸ
κατὰ τοῦ κυρίου καὶ κατὰ τοῦ χριστοῦ αὐτοῦ.	κατὰ τοῦ κυρίου καὶ κατὰ τοῦ χριστοῦ αὐτοῦ.

²⁵ The one who said through the mouth of our father, David, your servant, through the Holy Spirit,	
"Why do the nations rage,	¹ Why do the nations rage,
and the peoples plot empty schemes?	and the peoples plot empty schemes?
²⁶ The kings of the earth have taken their stand,	² The kings of the earth have taken their stand,
and the rulers gathered together	and the rulers gathered together
against the Lord and against his messiah."	against the Lord and against his messiah.

The New Testament makes a number of references to Ps 2.[26] In light of the psalm's victorious tenor (see Craigie 1983, 62–69), the New Testament primarily refers to Ps 2 in the context of Jesus' exaltation over his enemies.[27]

---

26. According to a minority of witnesses (Bezae, many Old Latin manuscripts, and a number of early fathers), the theophanic voice in Luke 3:22 quotes Ps 2:7. Given the popularity of Ps 2:7 among the early Christians and the comparative paucity of this variant among the extant evidence, the NA[27] and UBS committees rightly print Luke 3:22 in agreement with Mark 1:11 (Metzger 1994, 112–13; *pace* Ehrman 1993, 62–67).

27. Acts 13 associates Jesus' resurrection with his enthronement (citing Ps 2:7) and his reception of the holy and sure promises of David (see Bock 2007, 457; also Juel 1988, 59–88, esp. 77–87). The opening chapter of Hebrews exalts Jesus above the prophets (Heb 1:1), noting that he is heir of all things (1:2). This Jesus sits to the right of the Majesty (1:3), and the latter has declared Jesus his own Son (Heb 1:5, quoting Ps 2:7). Four chapters later the author tells his readers that Jesus did not exalt himself

Jesus' exaltation is evident also in Acts 4. He is God's holy servant, anointed by God, and those who opposed him—Herod and Pilate, along with the Gentiles and the peoples of Israel—could only act according to God's plan (4:27–28). Even so, the element of suffering is notable in Acts 4, not of Jesus himself but of the apostles. The Sanhedrin, who will soon execute Stephen (Acts 7), directly opposes Peter and John (4:17–18, 21), and the gathered group of disciples understands the danger of their position (4:29; see also 5:17, 33). Psalm 2, which does not appear to have participated in the tradition of messiah's suffering but rather expressed his exaltation over his enemies, now provides the apostles a proper orientation toward their own suffering and suggests their appropriate response. Since other New Testament references to Ps 2 do not share these overtones of danger and suffering, this appears to be an innovative use of the psalm.

Paul's references to the Psalms in Acts 13 were mentioned earlier; he directly quotes from Ps 2:7 (see 13:33) and Psalm 16:10 (see 13:35).

Acts 13:33, 35	Psalms 2:7; 15:10 (LXX)
³³ ὅτι ταύτην ὁ θεὸς ἐκπεπλήρωκεν τοῖς τέκνοις [αὐτῶν] ἡμῖν ἀναστήσας Ἰησοῦν ὡς καὶ ἐν τῷ ψαλμῷ γέγραπται τῷ δευτέρῳ·	⁷ διαγγέλλων τὸ πρόσταγμα κυρίου
<u>υἱός μου εἶ σύ,</u>	Κύριος εἶπεν πρός με <u>Υἱός μου εἶ σύ,</u>
<u>ἐγὼ σήμερον γεγέννηκά σε.</u>	<u>ἐγὼ σήμερον γεγέννηκά σε.</u>
	¹⁰ ὅτι οὐκ ἐγκαταλείψεις τὴν ψυχήν μου εἰς ᾅδην
³⁵ διότι καὶ ἐν ἑτέρῳ λέγει· <u>οὐ δώσεις τὸν ὅσιόν σου ἰδεῖν διαφθοράν.</u>	<u>οὐδὲ δώσεις τὸν ὅσιόν σου ἰδεῖν διαφθοράν.</u>
³³ That God brought this to fulfillment for us, their children, by raising Jesus, as also it is written in the second psalm:	⁷ when I proclaimed the command of the Lord,
"You are my son,	"The Lord said to me, '<u>You are my son;</u>
<u>Today I have begotten you.</u>"	<u>Today I have begotten you.</u>'"

---

to the position of high priest; God himself declared Jesus his Son (Heb 5:5 = Ps 2:7) and appointed him to be a Melchizedekian priest (Heb 5:6 = Ps 110:4). See also Rev 2:26–27 (= Ps 2:8–9).

[35] Therefore he says in another place, "You will not give your holy one to see corruption."

[10] Because you shall not abandon my soul to Hades,

nor will you give your holy one to see corruption.

Both of Paul's references to the Psalms reproduce the conditions noted in the discussion of Acts 2:25–28 (= Ps 16:8–11) above. When Jesus experiences rejection and suffering, he stands in a long line of figures from Israel's history, especially the illustrious King David. Like David, Jesus trusts in God's faithfulness to those who trust in him, and Jesus, more than David, was vindicated by God for his faithfulness.

Acts includes many other allusions to the Psalms; the discussion here has highlighted references that function as what Schwartz calls "frames" that oriented early Christians toward the desired understanding of and response to Jesus' suffering in particular. Moreover, Acts makes myriad references to Hebrew biblical tradition outside the Psalms—and to other written traditions besides. Again, the discussion here has focused narrowly on the role the Psalms played in early Christian attempts to make sense of, and communicate to others about, the events of Jesus' passion. Two summary observations may be made before proceeding.

First, Luke sits firmly within larger social and cultural patterns of traditioning, rhetoric, and hermeneutics as he reads the Psalms and maps them onto Jesus' suffering (and vindication), but he does so as an innovative and original contributor to that tradition. Luke refers to many of the same texts other Christians found useful for talking about Jesus (Pss 69; 110; 118; etc.), and he refers to them in many of the same ways. Even so, whatever impression Luke's preface (Luke 1:1–4) may give, he does not merely pass on what he has received from eyewitnesses and servants of the word. This fact is evident in his references to Ps 16 in Acts 2:25–28, 31 and 13:35. Luke's distinctive emphasis on the corporeality of Jesus' resurrection may have evoked the memory of this psalm, which explicitly mentions both the psalmist's "flesh" (ἡ σάρξ μου; 15:9 LXX) and his "soul" (τὴν ψυχήν μου; 15:10 LXX). Luke, however, is the only New Testament author to draw this connection.[28] Similarly, Luke's distinctive reference to Ps 2 in Acts

---

28. See here Bock 2007, 124, who surprisingly suggests, on the basis of the references to Ps 16 in Acts 2 and 13, that "this psalm may well have been a part of church tradition explaining Jesus' resurrection." Perhaps, but Bock neglects to note that refer-

4:25–26 was noted above. Despite the popularity of this psalm elsewhere in the New Testament, only Acts 4 refers to Ps 2 in the context of suffering. So while Luke certainly stands within the broad stream of Second Temple Jewish and early Christian exegetical tradition, he also handles that tradition innovatively and creatively.

Second, Luke uses γραφή ("Scripture"; note the capitalization) in reference to *a larger encompassing tradition* rather than a specific written text ("scripture").[29] This is most clearly evident in Acts 1:16, 20, where Peter speaks of Judas's actions and fate as a fulfillment of "the Scripture," by which he means (at least) Pss 69:25; 109:8. Of course, Peter (= Luke) could have cited other specific written texts had he wished, but he has sufficiently made his point.[30] The same dynamic is at work in Paul's references to Ps 16 (and Isa 55:3) in Pisidian Antioch: the *tradition* of the Davidic "eternal covenant" (Isa 55:3)—and not merely the words δίδωμι ("I give," in Paul's quotation; cf. the LXX διαθήσομαι; "I will make"), ὅσιος ("holy one"), and Δαυίδ ("David")—brought these texts together.[31] This larger tradition also explains the quotation from Ps 2:7 in Acts 13:33. *Scripture*, rather than scripture(s), provided the "enabling referent" (Foley 1995) that allowed Jesus' followers to locate Jesus' sufferings within the history of Israel and

---

ences to Ps 16 *occur only in Acts*. This is hardly a sufficient basis to posit a wider "church tradition."

29. Bruce (1988, 44–45) speaks of "messianic 'testimonies' from the Old Testament … compiled and circulated at an early date for ready reference" by the early Christians. Luke, however, gives no indication of any written collection of messianic prooftexts at work in Acts 1.

30. For a similar conclusion regarding the Gospel of Luke (and the Synoptic tradition more generally), see my discussion of the phrase "traditions of Israel's restoration" in Rodríguez 2010, 214–15 and passim.

31. See here Bruce 1988, 260; Witherington 1998, 412; Bock 2007, 457. Pervo (2009, 339) calls the reference to Isa 55:3 "superfluous and confusing" (see also Kistemaker 1990, 485), though nothing in the text suggests that either Luke or his audience (as he imagined it) would have found it such. Interestingly, the Middle Egyptian expands Acts 13:34: "He has raised him up from the dead in such a way as never again to return to decay, that all the people may know [it] and repent. For thus it is written in the prophet Isaiah, '*I will make with you an everlasting covenant, the holy things of David*'" (cited in Pervo 2009, 339, emphasis added; see also Petersen 1964, 240). The change from τὰ πιστά ("the faithful things") to "everlasting covenant" is hardly a significant move, especially given the reference to "an eternal covenant" (MT= ברית עולם; LXX = διαθήκην αἰώνιον] in Isa 55:3. So Bock, despite overstating his case and not providing any historical or textual argument, rightly notes, "It is often said that Luke's version lacks a reference to the covenant, but this overstates the difference. Any Jew would be aware that the 'holy things of David' alludes to the covenant" (2007, 457).

Israel's relationship with God, to communicate that understanding to others, and to formulate responses they considered culturally and socially (and theologically) appropriate.

CONCLUSIONS: WHY? HOW? AND SO WHAT?

How does Luke's appropriation of the Psalms inform the questions raised earlier in this essay: *Why* do people bother to remember the past? *How* do they pursue remembering? *What consequences* in (and for) the present result from remembering?

On the first question above (Why remember?), the publicity and cultural significance of Jesus' crucifixion meant that Jesus could not have functioned plausibly as an object of memory without incorporating (or countering) explanations of his suffering. But why should *Jesus* have been an object of memory in the first place? Why did Jesus not fade into little more than a name in a passage in a book on a shelf? This question is larger than the extant evidence that might point us toward the beginnings of answers. Potential factors might include, among other things, his anticipation and explanation of his suffering beforehand (especially on the basis of the Baptist's encounter with Herod Antipas) and/or his followers' success in convincing themselves and others that they encountered Jesus alive after his execution. Other options notwithstanding, one reason this particular victim of crucifixion became an object (and a vehicle) of memory is the early Christians' ability to construct plausible readings of Israel's scriptures in light of Jesus' suffering and vice versa. Factors such as these provided Jesus' followers, in the aftermath of his public and shameful execution, an option other than retreat from their enthusiasm for Jesus and understanding of his role in Israel's hoped-for redemption.[32]

On the second question above (How do groups remember?), the discussion here has highlighted the role of biblical tradition (specifically the Psalms) in framing the salient experience of suffering in Jesus' biography. This framing is only one aspect of Luke's memory work as he narrates and explains the story of Messiah's suffering. Another aspect must be his deci-

---

32. Schwartz raises a similar issue with respect to the (near-)complete dismissal of the supernatural from our reconstructions of Jesus: "If such stories ... are dismissed entirely from our understanding of Jesus, where are we to find his charisma? And if we cannot find that charisma, how are we to explain Jesus' extraordinary place in his generation's memory? If Jesus did nothing out of the ordinary, why did his contemporaries remember him at all?" (p. 30, above).

sion to *write* Luke-Acts, to put pen (or quill) to parchment and write out by hand a two-volume διήγησις ("account") of Jesus and the apostles.[33] Luke positions his written text alongside other γραφαί ("writings or scriptures") as part of ἡ γραφή ("the Scripture"). Jesus may have appealed to Moses and all the prophets and to all the Scriptures as he explained his suffering to Cleopas and the unnamed disciple, but Luke moves in the other direction. The Third Evangelist establishes the ἀσφάλεια ("certainty";[34] see Luke 1:1–4) of the gospel message as well as of his interpretation of Israel's Scriptures by producing his own written text. As a written text, Luke delimits appropriate readings of Israel's written Scriptures from inappropriate readings. Loveday Alexander has positioned the ἀσφάλεια offered by Luke-Acts not against other written Gospels but against the oral instruction (κατήχησις) Theophilus has received (1993, 140–41). I would expand this point: Luke-Acts does not simply provide orientation toward oral catechetical material but toward biblical tradition itself. Luke, by writing his text, installs the gospel tradition—and especially his expression of that tradition—among ἡ γραφή (*Scripture*, in the sense discussed above).[35]

On the third question above (What are the consequences of remembering?), in appealing to biblical traditions to frame Jesus' suffering, Luke effectively reframed Israel's scriptural tradition in terms of the suffering Messiah. Luke-Acts does not give the impression that Luke thought he was writing Scripture (texts whose authority approximated the authority of Moses or David or the prophets)—it would misrepresent Luke's intention to approach his books as an "expansion" of the biblical corpus. Quite the opposite: Luke has *restricted* the scope of Scripture by narrowing the range of interpretive possibilities down to one: τὰ περὶ ἑαυτοῦ ("the things concerning himself" = Jesus). Or, to use Martin Jaffee's language of "text-interpretive tradition" (2001, 7–8), the Lukan presentation of Jesus' life

---

33. To the best of my knowledge, why Luke wrote Luke-Acts has not received sustained or thorough examination. Loveday Alexander (1993, 211–12) raises this question ("When and why are texts written down?") at the end of her study, but I am not aware that anyone has specifically set out to propose an answer. Thatcher 2006 considers this issue—why someone would *write* a Gospel—with respect to John's Gospel and compares some aspects of John's strategy with that of Luke but does not extend his examination to the Synoptics.

34. Alexander (1993, 187) renders ἵνα ἐπιγνῷς ... ἀσφάλειαν, "so that you (that is, Theophilus) may have assured knowledge."

35. Interpreters of Luke-Acts have long observed the biblical style of Luke's language and rhetoric, which observation coheres well with the point I am making here (see Alexander 1993, 201; Bovon 2002, 3, 4–5; Bock 2007, 13; Pervo 2009, 7–8).

and teachings, including or perhaps even *especially* his suffering, "come[s] to be so closely associated with public renderings of a text [= the Hebrew Bible] as to constitute its self-evident meaning."[36] As a result, certain distinctions (e.g., between psalms of the righteous sufferer and messianic psalms) become blurred, since ultimately both concern, again, τὰ περὶ ἑαυτοῦ—Jesus.[37]

But most important, certainly for disciples like Cleopas and his companion, Luke has deflated the narrative attending the act of crucifixion. This is a common observation, but its common-ness ought not discount its importance: crucifixion was a public spectacle that reinscribed Rome's power and made a mockery of alternatives to that power.[38] The act of crucifixion, *rather than its victims*, defined the experience for the onlooking public. The early Christians managed, ultimately very successfully indeed, to extricate Jesus from the anonymizing experience of crucifixion and, moreover, to insinuate his crucifixion into the tradition of the suffering of God's (righteous) people.[39] Jews had been crucified by the thousands, both before and after Jesus (and two alongside him!), but none of them came to represent or be representative of the suffering of Israel. Jesus' followers

---

36. Jaffee continues: "As a tradition, the text-interpretive material exists in the memories of both the textual performers and their auditors. The public readers deploy the text selectively in light of their judgment of their audiences' capacities, while audiences supply it in their reception of the reading" (2001, 8).

37. With respect to Ps 2, Peter Craigie notes, "Here, the reference of the term [*anointed one* or *Messiah* (Ps 2:2)] in the context of the psalm's initial use is simply to the *human* king, for whom the coronation was conducted. It was only from a more distant perspective in history that the messianic implications of the psalm could be discerned" (1983, 66). It could only have helped that, even before the Christian era, the righteous sufferer was often, if not usually, a royal (= messianic) figure. Similarly, see Bruce 1988, 44–45.

38. "[T]his strangely 'exalting' mode of execution was designed to mimic, parody, and puncture the pretensions of insubordinate transgressors by displaying a deliberately horrible mirror of their self-elevation" (Marcus 2006, 78).

39. It would be interesting to explore this observation in light of Schwartz's argument, in the current volume, that social memory "plays out within existing social networks, namely, clusters of people who are likely to share the beliefs and values of the storytellers.... Clustering thus enhances the receptivity to the stories while it limits their variation to a range compatible with the recipients' culture" (p. 12). Specifically, how did existing Jewish social structures (the temple, synagogues, families, the diaspora, etc.) facilitate the "variation" in the explanation of Jesus' crucifixion from "execution" toward "righteous suffering"? Crossley 2006 applies sociological research on social networks to issues of Christian origins (particularly the rise of the Gentile mission).

developed an alternative memory that framed Jesus' suffering differently by keying that suffering to preexisting symbolic patterns. This essay has highlighted, within a very small sample of texts (the speeches in Acts), how one tradent (the author of Luke-Acts) keyed Jesus' suffering to Israel's biblical tradition (the book of Psalms).

Works Cited

Alexander, Loveday. 1993. *The Preface to Luke's Gospel: Literary Convention and Social Context in Luke 1.1–4 and Acts 1.1*. SNTSMS 78. Cambridge: Cambridge University Press.

Allen, Leslie C. 2002 *Psalms 101–150*. WBC 21. Nashville: Thomas Nelson.

Bauckham, Richard. 2002. *Gospel Women: Studies of the Named Women in the Gospels*. Grand Rapids: Eerdmans.

Berger, Peter L., and Thomas Luckmann. 1966. *The Social Construction of Reality: A Treatise in the Sociology of Knowledge*. New York: Doubleday.

Bock, Darrell L. 2007. *Acts*. BECNT. Grand Rapids: Baker Academic.

Bovon, François. 2002. *Luke 1: A Commentary on the Gospel of Luke 1:1–9:50*. Hermeneia. Minneapolis: Fortress.

Bruce, F. F. 1988. *The Book of the Acts*. Rev. ed. NICNT. Grand Rapids: Eerdmans.

Carey, Holly J. 2009. *Jesus' Cry from the Cross: Towards a First-Century Understanding of the Intertextual Relationship between Psalm 22 and the Narrative of Mark's Gospel*. LNTS 398. London: T&T Clark.

Casey, Maurice. 2010. *Jesus of Nazareth: An Independent Historian's Account of His Life and Teaching*. London: T&T Clark.

Craigie, Peter C. 1983. *Psalms 1–50*. WBC 19. Waco, TX: Word Books.

Crossley, James G. 2006. *Why Christianity Happened: A Sociohistorical Account of Christian Origins (26–50 CE)*. Louisville: Westminster John Knox.

Dunn, James D. G. 1988. *Romans*. 2 vols. WBC 38A–B. Nashville: Thomas Nelson.

Ehrman, Bart. 1993. *The Orthodox Corruption of Scripture: The Effect of Early Christological Controversies on the Text of the New Testament*. Oxford: Oxford University Press.

Fentress, James, and Chris Wickham. 1992. *Social Memory*. New Perspectives on the Past. Oxford: Blackwell.

Foley, John Miles. 1995. *The Singer of Tales in Performance*. Bloomington: Indiana University Press.

García Martínez, Florentino, and Eibert J. C. Tigchelaar. 1998. *The Dead Sea Scrolls Study Edition*. 2 vols. Leiden: Brill.

Geertz, Clifford. 1973. *The Interpretation of Cultures: Selected Essays*. New York, NY: Basic Books.

Hossfeld, Frank-Lothar, and Erich Zenger. 2005. *Psalms 2: A Commentary on Psalms 51–100*. Hermeneia. Minneapolis: Fortress.

Irwin-Zarecka, Iwona. 1994. *Frames of Remembrance: The Dynamics of Collective Memory*. New Brunswick: Transaction.

Jaffee, Martin S. 2001. *Torah in the Mouth: Writing and Oral Tradition in Palestinian Judaism 200 BCE–400 CE*. Oxford: Oxford University Press.

Jewett, Robert. 2007. *Romans*. Hermeneia. Minneapolis: Fortress.

Juel, Donald. 1988. *Messianic Exegesis: Christological Interpretation of the Old Testament in Early Christianity*. Philadelphia: Fortress.

Kirk, Alan, and Tom Thatcher. 2005. Jesus Tradition as Social Memory. Pages 25–42 in *Memory, Tradition, and Text: Uses of the Past in Early Christianity*. SemeiaSt 52. Atlanta: Society of Biblical Literature.

Kistemaker, Simon J. 1990. *Exposition of the Acts of the Apostles*. New Testament Commentary. Grand Rapids: Baker.

Lindesmith, Alfred R., Anselm L. Strauss, and Norman K. Denzin. 1988. *Social Psychology*. Englewood Cliffs, NJ: Prentice Hall.

Marcus, Joel. 2006. Crucifixion as Parodic Exaltation. *JBL* 125:73–87.

Metzger, Bruce M. 1994. *A Textual Commentary on the Greek New Testament*. 2nd ed. Stuttgart: German Bible Society.

Michaels, J. Ramsey. 2010. *The Gospel of John*. NICNT. Grand Rapids: Eerdmans.

Moo, Douglas J. 1996. *The Epistle to the Romans*. NICNT. Grand Rapids: Eerdmans.

Pervo, Richard I. 2009. *Acts: A Commentary*. Hermeneia. Minneapolis: Fortress.

Petersen, Theodore C. 1964. An Early Coptic Manuscript of Acts: An Unrevised Version of the Ancient So-called Western Text. *CBQ* 26:225–41.

Rodríguez, Rafael. 2010. *Structuring Early Christian Memory: Jesus in Tradition, Performance, and Text*. ESCO/LNTS 407. London: T&T Clark.

Schreiner, Thomas R. 1998. *Romans*. BECNT. Grand Rapids: Baker.

Schudson, Michael. 1989. The Present in the Past versus the Past in the Present. *Communication* 11:105–13.

Schwartz, Barry. 2000. *Abraham Lincoln and the Forge of American Memory*. Chicago: University of Chicago Press.

———. 2008. *Abraham Lincoln in the Post-Heroic Era: History and Memory in the Late Twentieth Century.* Chicago: University of Chicago Press.

Shore, Bradd. 1991. Twice-Born, Once Conceived: Meaning Construction and Cultural Cognition. *American Anthropologist* 93:9–27.

Subramanian, J. Samuel. 2007. *The Synoptic Gospels and the Psalms as Prophecy.* LNTS 351. London: T&T Clark.

Tate, Marvin E. 1990. *Psalms 51–100.* WBC 20. Dallas: Word Books.

Thatcher, Tom. 2006. *Why John Wrote a Gospel: Jesus—Memory—History.* Louisville: Westminster John Knox.

Witherington, Ben. 1998. *The Acts of the Apostles: A Socio-rhetorical Commentary.* Grand Rapids: Eerdmans.

ON THE DIFFICULTY OF MOLDING A ROCK: THE NEGOTIATION OF PETER'S REPUTATION IN EARLY CHRISTIAN MEMORY[*]

Frederick S. Tappenden

[Strong social constructivists] see the past as precarious, its contents hostage to the conditions of the present. They set forth an atemporal conception of collective memory that relates things remembered to the beliefs, aspirations, and fears of the here and now. While well-grounded empirically, they offer a one-sided perspective. As [Michael] Schudson (1989) put it: "The present shapes our understanding of the past, yes. But this is half the truth, at best, and a particularly cynical half-truth, at that." (Schwartz 1991, 222)

As with his apostolic counterparts, the reputation of Peter in the early centuries of the Christian movement is described best as "mixed." One need look no further than the undisputed Pauline epistles, the earliest Christian writings, to see that Peter is portrayed in both negative and positive ways. On the one hand, Paul portrays Peter as both the first to see the risen Christ (1 Cor 15:3) and as one of three "pillars" in the Jerusalem church (Gal 2:9). On the other hand, these positive descriptions are tempered by the image of Peter retained in Paul's account of the dispute at Antioch (Gal 2:11–14). Here Peter is said to have stood condemned (2:11) for having detracted from inclusive table fellowship with Gentiles (2:12); he is portrayed as one who acts out of fear (2:12) and not in accordance with the gospel (2:14); he leads others in his hypocrisy (2:13) and thus warrants Paul's rebuke (2:14).

The reception of this early and quite difficult Petrine depiction was varied in early Christian literature (for recent discussions, see Leppä 2011, 109–11; Mitchell 2012, 220–21). Within the Petrine pseudepigrapha, for instance, the dispute at Antioch is never mentioned (Smith 1985, 210), the only exception perhaps being the (now-disputed) Kerygmata Petrou, which seeks to justify Peter's actions at Antioch in light of Matt 16:17 (*Ps.-Clem.*

_____

[*] The author gratefully acknowledges the Social Sciences and Humanities Research Council of Canada and the Fonds de recherche du Québec—société et culture, whose generous support enabled the research reported here.

17.19). Other early Christians found in the Antioch incident evidence for
Paul's superiority among the apostles—according to Tertullian, Marcion
saw Paul's rebuke of Peter as a sign of the latter's ignorance (*Praescr.* 23).
Tertullian specifically disagreed with Marcion on this point, preferring to
speak of Paul and Peter as complementing one another rather than representing any fixed opposition (*Praescr.* 23; see also Irenaeus, *Haer.* 3.13.1).
Three later receptions are also worth noting: (1) Eusebius (*Hist. eccl.* 1.12.2)
reports Clement's insistence that the "Cephas" mentioned in Gal 2:11 is
not Peter but another disciple; (2) Jerome argues that, out of concern for
the salvation of those who still held to the law, Peter only pretended to side
with those from James so as to allow Paul's rebuke to correct the hypocrisy of observing the law (*Comm. Gal.* 1.2.11–13, 14a); and, (3) Augustine,
concerned with the truthfulness of the Scriptures, understands Peter as
genuinely erring and humbly receiving Paul's rebuke (*Ep.* 40.3–7 [esp. §5];
82.4–30 [esp. §§8, 22]; see also 28.3–5).

These diverse texts attest to the difficulty that Gal 2:11–14 produced
for Peter's reputation in the early Christian movement. One textual tradition that is noticeably missing from the above overview is the canonical
Acts of the Apostles. Despite the fact that both Peter and Paul dominate the
Acts narrative, the Lukan author (hereafter referred to as "Luke" for con-
venience) neither mentions the incident at Antioch nor gives any hint that
a dispute ever existed between the two apostles. For many, the silence of
Acts is construed as evidence either that Luke was *unaware* of Paul's letters
or that he *freely reworked or replaced* the Pauline account. Addressing both
of these interpretive tendencies, the present study argues that Luke was in
fact aware of Gal 2:11–14 and that he took conscious though restrained
steps toward improving the image of Peter codified therein. That is to say,
I hope to demonstrate that Paul's Epistle to the Galatians exerted pressure
upon Luke such that the image of Peter in Acts was both *formed* in relation
to and *informed* by the earlier Pauline letter.

Luke and the Epistles of Paul

I begin by laying a finger on the key historical—indeed, hermeneutical—
issue that this paper addresses: the extent to which Luke both knew and
made use of Paul's epistles. The silence of Acts on the incident at Antioch
has not gone unnoticed in discussions of the relationship between the
Pauline and Lukan writings. On the one hand, the Tübingen school of the
nineteenth century took it for granted that Luke constructed much of his

narrative from the Pauline epistles; accordingly, Luke's portrayal of Peter and Paul becomes a "synthesis" within F. C. Baur's dialectical reading of early Christian history. On the other hand, in contrast to Baur's polarization of early Christian diversity (Smith 1985, 211; Bockmuehl 2010, 62–68), the majority of twentieth-century scholars expressly denied any connection between Luke's writings and the Pauline letters (e.g., Vielhauer 1966; Barrett 1976). As is often noted, Luke's Paul is not a letter writer, nor is there any mention of epistolary communications between Paul and any of the churches. The only possible exception is Acts 15:22–35, though Pervo (2006, 54) rightly notes that here Paul does nothing more than accompany the letter carriers from Jerusalem. The pervasiveness of this scholarly consensus still lingers today and is evinced in John Riches's (2008) commentary on the reception history of Galatians. Treating Acts as an early reception of the figure of Paul, Riches (2008, 97) does not examine the extent to which Luke may have appropriated Paul's Epistle to the Galatians.

One could insist, of course, that Riches not be faulted on this point. The Lukan narrative is much more conciliatory than Paul's letters, and Luke not only contradicts the epistles at many points but also omits many details—theological or otherwise—that modern scholars might expect him to include. As always, the burden of proof lies with the exegete. Over the past century a minority of scholars have persistently judged Luke's knowledge of—and perhaps use of—Paul's letters in the positive (e.g., Enslin 1938, 1970; Knox 1966). Particularly important for many such scholars are the compelling historical considerations. So, for example, despite his conclusion that "no convincing case can be made for Luke's reliance on the letters of Paul," John Knox asks,

> How could he [Luke] have escaped knowing them? ... I agree with Enslin [1938, 83] that it is all but incredible that such a man as Luke ... should have been "totally unaware that this hero of his had ever written letters" and quite as hard to believe that he would have found it impossible, or even difficult, to get access to these letters if he had wanted to. Paul had been too central and too controversial a figure in his own time to have been forgotten so soon. Too many important churches owed their existence to him for his name not to have been held in reverence in many areas and his work remembered. (Knox 1966, 282–83)

More recently Lars Aejmelaeus (2011, 56–57) articulates a similar point by appealing to four historical considerations drawn from Christoph

Burchard (1970): (1) Paul's various letters are written to churches scattered across Asia Minor, Macedonia, Achaia, and Italy, and from the letters we can deduce Paul's presence in many other cities and regions across the Mediterranean; (2) from the letters we know that they were discussed and argued and even that Paul's letters were known by others outside his communities (2 Cor 10:9–11); (3) 1 Clement provides evidence that at least 1 Corinthians was copied and circulated beyond Corinth, a practice that may have happened for other letters, too; and, (4) the Deutero-Paulines indicate that Paul's letters were both known and imitated quite early on (certainly prior to Acts). Taken together, these points suggest to Aejmelaeus (2011, 57) that "it is futile for the exegete to try 'to kick against the pricks': some kind of positive relationship between Luke's and Paul's texts becomes a necessary assumption."

Despite these historical considerations, demarcating Luke's reception of Paul is a complex historical and hermeneutical task. The evidence customarily amassed spans both the Gospel and Acts and is usually of the following six kinds: (1) scattered and usually small instances of verbal agreement, where Luke demonstrates familiarity with Paul's letters as aural/written texts (e.g., the parallels between Galatians and Acts examined in Leppä 2011); (2) scattered and usually small instances of conceptual and/or contextual alignment (e.g., see Pervo's [2006, 70–73] comparison of the Ananias and Sapphira narrative [Acts 5:1–11] with Paul's instructions concerning the immoral brother in Corinth [1 Cor 5:3–5]); (3) overlap between the content and scope of Pauline geography and company as sketched in both the letters and Acts (Enslin 1938, 84–86, 89–90; Pervo 2006, 96–100, 102–4); (4) instances where events noted by Paul are plausibly construed as occasioning Luke's narrative depictions (e.g., the account of Paul being lowered through a Damascus window in a basket [2 Cor 11:32–33 and Acts 9:23–25]; see Aejmelaeus 2011, 65–69; Pervo 2006, 60–64); (5) instances where Luke can be seen to adopt and interpret Paul's thought (e.g., the notion of justification by faith; see Pervo 2006, 58–60); and, (6) instances where the Paul of Acts speaks in the way that the epistolary Paul writes (e.g., Paul's farewell speech in Miletus [Acts 20:17–35]; see Aejmelaeus 2011, 69–71; Pervo 2006, 111–33).[1]

Part of the problem, as Richard Pervo admits, is that much of the evidence outlined above takes the form of nothing more than small bundles

---

1. The most thorough recent examination of the evidence is offered by Pervo (2006, 51–147).

of scattered sticks, and most scholars are generally "suspicious … [of arguments that] create a forest by accumulating twigs" (2006, 136). The present study takes heed of Pervo's sober warning but suggests that the problem lies not in the nature of the evidence but rather in the methods employed in assessing the source- and reception-critical relationship between the Lukan narrative and the Pauline epistles. That is to say, what we are facing may not be a problem of textual paucity but rather of narrowly construed theoretical predispositions.

Lars Aejmelaeus (2011, 62, 74) suggests that the relationship between the Lukan and Pauline writings can only be determined via "detailed textual comparison," which he later demarcates as "literary-critical and reception-critical examinations." This may well be true, but giving theoretical definition to what constitutes credible data is surely a contested point. Such credible data is often narrowly construed as concrete linguistic or textual evidence (i.e., the presence of a specific word or phrase in two or more traditions); so, for example, Heikki Leppä (2011, 92 and 95) points to instances of "verbal agreement" as the "fingerprint[s] of Paul" in the text of Acts. Similarly, many of the scattered twigs that Pervo (2006, 51–147) points to are instances of linguistic agreement between Luke and Paul. While Pervo's (2006, 135–36) overall argument is compelling, many of his individual conclusions lack the robust character that critical scholarship demands (as he himself seems aware). In this light, Paul Elbert (2006, 226) rightly points to the need for "the construction of a credible text-critical hypothesis or a serious *wissenschaftliche Exegese*, hopefully satisfying methodologically rigorous criteria," though even he understands such an enterprise largely in relation to near-verbatim correlation. The present study suggests that this methodological program would benefit greatly from the expansion of theoretical horizons (and so also methodological tools) to envision not only ways in which written texts interlace but also ways in which authors and audiences obtain and engage such texts.

One important expansion of our theoretical horizon is to focus on what Thomas Brodie (2001, 104 n. 1) calls the "literary aspect" of a text, which he insists is "more tangible and verifiable [than either history or theology]." Helpfully pointing to three criteria for determining literary dependence,[2]

---

2. Brodie's (2001, 105–10) three criteria for determining literary dependence are (1) external plausibility, (2) similarities significant beyond the range of coincidence, and (3) intelligible differences. In Brodie's estimation, all three are reasonably met in identifying Luke's knowledge and use of the Pauline epistles.

Brodie insists this "literary aspect" includes "similarities of theme, motif, plot/action, detail (including linguistic details), order, and completeness" (2001, 109). Brodie's model is helpful in that it offers a broader framework, with a larger number of potential contact points, within which to assess how texts interlace one another. Nonetheless, attendance to literary dimensions does not go far enough. At issue are the problems that emerge when a text is divorced from reading contexts that are not historically and culturally grounded. On the one hand, "meaning" is not just a matter of literary devices (themes, motifs, plot, etc.) but is always actualized by real human subjects reading texts within real social contexts and historical situations. Accordingly, it is problematic to assert that a text's literary dimensions can be identified independent of such reading contexts (whether those be ancient or modern contexts). On the other hand, and more to the focus of this study, is the importance of recognizing that texts often assert influence upon other texts. That is to say, established traditions not only exist as part of the intertextual web of meaning but actually serve to give shape and form to the web itself (at least for authors and perhaps also their targeted readers).[3] Though a text's meaning is never limited to the author and/or any one reading community—a point that is in step with the poststructuralist foundations of intertextuality proper (Hatina 1999)—texts are meaningfully indebted to established traditions that exert social and cultural influence from inception to composition to reception. Accordingly, Brodie's literary model must be supplemented with a greater attention to social and cultural factors (what he seems to bracket out as "historical" and therefore more conjectural).

In attempting to expand our models of textual reception, the present study draws on theoretical concerns related to collective memory and reputation construction, models that provide resources for grounding the narrative worlds of written texts within differing reading communities. More specifically, I will explore how Gal 2:11–14 functions as a *lieu de mémoire*, a site of memory, that exerts superpersonal effects on the present to such a degree that reputational entrepreneurs[4] (such as Luke) were not able simply to "rewrite" the past but rather forced to creatively interact with

---

3. Much depends on one's methodological focus. For this study I am interested in the extent to which Luke functions as a reputational entrepreneur who is aware of texts such as Paul's letters and the Gospel of Mark. Quite consciously, then, I do not explore the various ways the Lukan narratives are themselves read by later communities.

4. The term "reputational entrepreneur" is adopted in part from Barry Schwartz (2000, 67) but more so from Gary Alan Fine (2001, 11–13).

it, thus putting forth commemorative images that stand alongside of, and worked together with, their already-established counterparts. In my view, this theoretical apparatus yields a richer and more robust understanding of reception-critical dynamics than models that focus solely on textual and/ or literary correlations, simply because it envisions textual reception as an aspect of collective memory whereby reputational entrepreneurs encode and construct memories in relation to both established pasts and changing presents. I am not insisting that the scope of a text's meaning be limited to intentionally encoded structures but rather suggesting that textual dependence—in this case, Luke's knowledge and use of Paul's letters—requires a more robust framework than merely identifying textual citations and literary correspondence.

Building upon a number of recent studies, my working assumption from the outset is that Luke was both aware of and used Paul's letters, especially Galatians, in formulating the Acts narrative (see esp. Leppä 2002, 2011; Pervo 2006; Marguerat 2009; Liljeström 2011). Evidence for this assumption will be presented and evaluated through close analysis of the presentation of Peter in Acts 10–11 and 15. It is important to note that much of the data examined in this paper has already been well documented elsewhere. Of particular note is the work of William O. Walker Jr. (1985, 1998), who focuses primarily on the image of Paul as conveyed in the Acts narrative. Working with an eye toward second-century disputes about Paul, Walker argues that Luke uses the *Peter* figure in an effort to rehabilitate the image of *Paul*. Not only does Walker (1985, 16–17; 1998, 82, 85) reject out of hand the possibility that Luke is rehabilitating Peter's image; he also places an undue emphasis upon the formative power of the present. Indeed, the two go hand in hand in Walker's analysis: he portrays Luke's commemorative efforts as conditioned largely by the social pressures of the second century while accounting little for the (in)formative power of established traditions. It is on these points—the rehabilitation of Paul rather than Peter and the primacy of the present—that the present study stands as a necessary counterpoint to Walker.

While it cannot be denied that the image of Paul was contested in the second century, Peter's image was just as much in need of revision; indeed, it is not Paul but Peter who, in Gal 2:11–14, causes division and hypocrisy while also being implicated in a quasi anti-Gentile ideology (themes that stand in sharp contrast to Luke's *Tendenz*). By focusing on the reputation of Peter rather than Paul, this study explores the extent to which the past is not just *rewritten* but rather creatively *retained* and *re-presented*. The potential value of this approach is highlighted by Pervo's observation that "Luke's appropriation of Paul demonstrates that he did not employ primary sources to discover 'what actually happened,' but *as aids in imposing his own construction of the past*" (2006, 52, emphasis added). For Pervo, and Walker, too, the past is malleable, flexible, and subservient to the social pressures and demands of the present. Within this strong constructionist framework, Luke adapts and alters his sources with very little restraint from those sources. As a counterpoint, and in dialogue with Barry Schwartz's more balanced approached to the relationship between past and present, the present study examines how Luke not only reworks his source texts but also how those very source texts impose certain restrictions and limitations on what Luke is able to do.

In light of the foregoing, I argue in this study that Luke portrays Peter in such a way as to mnemonically negotiate an apostolic reputation that had already been established and codified in Paul's letter to the Galatians. Accordingly, the following analysis serves as a case study that addresses the broader hermeneutical issues that surround Luke's use of Paul's letters. I contend that collective memory theory provides a framework within which to envision alternative ways—ways that both include and move beyond textual citations and literary correspondence—in which Luke can be seen to creatively make use of Paul's letters. The following analysis will elaborate this point by specifically highlighting commemorative reputations and the dynamism of mnemonic construction and negotiation, both of which are discussed with respect to Luke's use of the Gospel of Mark and Paul's Epistle to the Galatians.

REPUTATIONAL STABILITY, MNEMONIC TENSION, AND THE LUKAN PETER

To introduce the question of commemorative reputations more fully, it will be helpful first to examine Luke's attitude toward his sources in light of collective memory theory. We are fortunate in that we can examine how Luke uses one of his undisputed sources (the Gospel of Mark) specifically with respect to the portrayal of Peter therein. Of particular interest is the relationship between these texts when examined not from a source-critical perspective (that is, Luke's appropriation and/or alteration of the Markan *text*) but rather from a reputational point of view. Put another way, the present study is interested in the relative descriptions of Peter in these two texts, in the alterations and/or retentions that characterize his commemoration, and in the contours that define his figure. Accordingly, the examination of both the Markan and Lukan Peters will bring into clearer focus the way Luke negotiates already-established reputations.

PETER IN THE GOSPEL OF MARK

How societies or subcultural communities both perceive and remember significant figures is directly related to the way such communities engage their present world. Sociologist Gary Fine (2001) notes that the reputations of historical figures provide communities a shared public space wherein to discuss issues of pressing concern. "[E]ven when we recognize the thinness of our knowledge of these figures, their celebrity [or reputation] serves to connect us to each other and provides us with an unthreatening space to converse about vital social matters" (2001, 4). In this way, the reputations of key figures take on superpersonal dimensions such that historical personalities are commemorated not necessarily for their own sake but because their image enables the commemorative community to engage the present world.

In an important respect, this is the kind of commemorative activity that seems to be taking place in the Gospel of Mark, where Peter functions as a figure with whom the Markan audience can identify. This is particularly evident in the many positive and negative depictions of the apostle in the Markan narrative, which several scholars have taken as a sign of Peter's "every-person" image (Best 1981, 12; Ehrman 2006, 21; Cassidy 2007, 115–17; contra Weeden 1971; Smith 1985, 162–90). There can be little doubt that Peter is a prominent figure in Mark—he is the first disciple called by Jesus (along with his brother; 1:16–18), he is listed first in the group of the Twelve (3:13–19), and his voice is heard more often than any other disciple (8:29; 9:5; 10:28; 11:21; 14:29–31, 66–72). Nonetheless, the image of Peter in Mark is also met with strikingly negative depictions: Peter is rebuked by Jesus and even addressed as "Satan" (8:27–31), he falls asleep in the garden of Gethsemane (14:32–42), and he denies Jesus three times after insisting that he will not do so (14:26–31, 53–72). These positive and negative depictions point to what Timothy Wiarda (1999, 34) calls the "distinctive" rather than "static" characterization of Peter in the Gospel of Mark. Accordingly, the Markan narrative seems to commemorate Peter as a kind of "every-person," a figure with whom the Markan audience can identify and in whom they can find themselves. This portrayal comes into clearer focus at those points in the narrative where Peter's words and/or actions direct the audience's attention toward social and political realities that appear to be sources of stress to the Markan community. Two examples will suffice to illustrate this phenomenon.

Peter's pedestrian, "every-person" image is clear in the Markan account of Peter's confession of Jesus as "Christ" (Mark 8:27–33). In this passage Jesus' identity is brought to the fore through the depiction of Peter as a Galilean with a particular understanding of what the Messiah would be like: someone who would overthrow, rather than suffer at the hands of, Rome. Peter is here portrayed as a person caught up in the midst of those messianic expectations that likely pressured the Markan community itself in the midst of the Jewish Revolt of 66–70 CE (for the Markan context, see Marcus 1992; 2000, 25–39). Against Peter's misperception, Jesus' messianic identity is laid bare; Peter the "every-person" thus functions as a cultural symbol through whom the Markan community can grapple with the notion of a suffering Messiah within the context of heightened sociopolitical conflict.

To cite another example, Peter's "every-person" image can also be seen in the account of his denial (Mark 14:26–72), especially when examined in conjunction with the larger Markan theme of persecution (see 4:16–17; 13:9–13; esp. 13:19). The prevalence of this latter theme points beyond the narrative world to suggest a social reality stressing the Markan community. While Jesus is presented as the model par excellence of one who endures trials (Marcus 2000, 29), it is Peter (and the disciples) who typifies the opposite position. This is seen particularly in Jesus' prophetic pronouncement that the disciples will desert him (14:26–31), to which Peter responds twice with exorbitant zeal, "even if all become deserters, I will not" (14:29). By emphasizing Peter's zeal, the Markan Gospel commemorates an apostle who, despite his good intentions, succumbs to the pressures of desertion. Peter's "every-person" image thus enables the community to grapple with the socioreligious reality of persecution; indeed, just as Jesus prophesied the disciples' desertion (14:26–31), so he predicted the Markan community's impinging persecution (13:9–13). Accordingly, Peter stands as a cultural symbol for the community, and his reputation as one who denied Christ becomes a kind of social space for conversing about what it means to remain faithful to Christ amidst trials. The commemoration of Peter enables the Markan audience to evaluate their own response so as to ensure that they, unlike Peter, will not be overcome with good intentions and no action (see 14:32–42, esp. 37–38). The Markan Peter is remembered not as an idyllic disciple who is to be emulated but as an example of how one ought not to act. Peter embodies discipleship gone awry.

To suggest that the Markan Peter is an "every-person" is not to suggest that he is simply a universalized archetype or trope but rather to insist that the figure of Peter performs a social function within the world of the Markan community. The Markan Peter is not *just* a normal disciple; rather, *because of* his normality, Peter rises above the story world of the narrative and becomes a cultural symbol in the real world of the Markan community. Peter's reputation as an "every-person" thus enables the Markan audience to grapple with those issues that characterize their present social world.

Peter in the Lukan Narrative

In an important respect, the past is always recalled and refashioned in relation to the social impulses of the present. This does not mean, however, that the past is entirely rewritten with each new remembrance. In his introduction to the present volume, and consistent with the general tone of his research, Barry Schwartz compellingly argues that mnemonic images established in *lieux de mémoire* function as cultural voices that shape the mnemonic activity of the present as much as social impulses do. Examining the commemoration of George Washington in post–Civil War America, Schwartz demonstrates that the memory of Washington was in a state of mnemonic tension in the later nineteenth century. The older, stable image of an "idealized" hero lost cultural resonance in a postwar society that focused more on "realism" and a desire to "know what George Washington 'was really like' in his everyday life" (Schwartz 1991, 226). Schwartz demonstrates that, while the image of Washington changed to reflect the present social climate, the older image was never lost in the process.

> Post–Civil War America spoke about Washington in two languages. The new language evoked images of a democratic Washington, an ordinary man acquainted with hardship, warm in his affections, and approachable. The older language evoked images of a pre-democratic Washington—a hero unconquerable and incorruptible, dignified and remote. *As postwar Americans contemplated the new Washington, they never forgot his original image or rejected what it stood for.* (Schwartz 1991, 229, emphasis added)

Far from being a passive object that is continually rewritten, the past is a dynamic voice that exerts pressure on the present, simultaneously forming and informing one's recollections. As Schwartz stresses, mnemonic stability is as much a part of the commemorative process as mnemonic alteration.

In various ways the Markan image of Peter functioned as a stable *lieu de mémoire* that Matthew and Luke were forced to negotiate rather than simply replace. Matthew, for instance, retains virtually every Markan episode in which Peter appears while also retaining (and enhancing) the basic positive/negative structure of Peter's reputation.[5] Similarly, though Luke's Gospel reflects a freer commemorative approach,[6] it would be wrong to assert that Luke has completely recast the figure of Peter. Indeed, in a number of instances it seems clear that the prior Markan depiction of Peter restrained Luke's mnemonic liberties. Again, two examples will suffice to illustrate this trend.

The Lukan versions of the transfiguration (Luke 9:28–36) and the Mount of Olives/Gethsemane episode (22:39–46) provide interesting test cases. In the former passage, Luke highlights Peter's "every-person" image by noting that Peter, James, and John were very tired (9:32); the reference is unique to the Lukan version and seems to function in relation to the parallel reference to drowsiness in the Mount of Olives pericope of 22:39–46 (//Mark 14:32–42). In the latter episode, whereas Mark remembers *only* Peter, James, and John as falling asleep while Jesus is praying, Luke instead insists that *all* twelve disciples were present on the mount and that they *all* fell asleep (thus, Peter is not singled out). Removing the emphasis solely from Peter and placing it instead on the Twelve as a group, Luke omits the

---

5. The sole exception is Mark 1:35–39, which Matthew has not carried over into his Gospel. See also Mark 5:31, 35–43; 11:20–26; 13:3–5; 16:7, all of which Matthew incorporates without specific reference to Peter. At the same time, Matthew adds Peter to one Markan narrative (Matt 14:22–33//Mark 6:45–52), infuses Peter (to varying degrees) into two Q sayings (Matt 15:14//Q 6:39; Matt 18:21//Q 17:4), and includes one reference to Peter not found elsewhere in the Synoptics (Matt 17:24–27). The overall structure of Peter's image in Matthew is again centred around positives and negatives, though now heightened—e.g., positive: Peter as the foundation of the *ekklēsia* (Matt 16:17–19); negative: rather than narrating the postresurrection redemption of Peter, Matthew instead leaves the apostle as an apostate who "went out and wept bitterly" (Matt 26:75).

6. This is most clearly seen in passages such as Jesus' visit to Peter's house (which Luke places before the calling of Peter [4:38–41, contra Mark 1:29–34//Matt 8:14–17]); the calling of Peter (where Luke presents a new and different account [5:1–11, contra Mark 1:16–18//Matt 4:18–20]); Jesus' rebuke of Peter (which Luke completely omits [9:18–27, contra Mark 8:27–9:1//Matt 16:13–28]); and Peter's postresurrection activities (where Luke diverges from both Mark and Matthew and accords more with Paul [cf. Luke 24:34 with 1 Cor 15:5]).

Markan stress upon Peter's weaknesses. Interestingly, however, Luke has not forgotten the memory of *Peter's* drowsiness, though he has transplanted it into his account of the transfiguration. Here the Lukan Peter is not overcome by fatigue; rather, Peter is remembered as one who, in the midst of a revelatory moment, perseveres through exhaustion and is rewarded for it (a point that Luke makes explicit in 9:32). Contra the Markan narrative, the Lukan Peter is memorable not *because* his weaknesses are something with which to be identified but rather because of his ability to persevere through such weaknesses and exhibit an ideal response to Jesus.

A similar mnemonic process may be observed in the Lukan accounts of Peter's confession and later denial. On the one hand, Luke completely omits Jesus' rebuke of Peter (see Luke 9:18–20)—of all the Markan texts that present Peter in a difficult light, the direct association with Satan was doubtless one of the more troublesome. Yet Luke has not totally abandoned this adversarial association, though he has refocused it. In Luke's account of Peter's denial, Jesus specifically attributes the apostle's betrayal to the work of Satan (22:31), and Jesus further prays that Peter's faith will not fail (22:32). Here Luke downplays Peter's inability to persevere by implicating the adversarial figure as the cause behind the apostle's denial. Just as with Peter's drowsiness, Luke has not so much omitted the difficult aspects of Peter's reputation as he has redirected them toward a more positive, idyllic understanding of the apostle. Thus Luke displays a high degree of mnemonic freedom within the constraints of a stabilized reputation.

Both of the examples just noted suggest that Luke recognizes and accepts the Markan text as a stable *lieu de mémoire*—to return to Schwartz's paradigm, Mark's source text exerts a certain gravitational pull that sets limits on Luke's commemorative work. In composing his Gospel, though Luke gravitates toward an idyllic depiction of Peter, he must do so in ways that are clearly restrained by the prior Markan account. Accordingly, where Mark remembers Peter as an "every-person" who exemplifies discipleship gone awry, Luke remembers Peter as an "every-person" who, in the midst of weakness, models exemplary intentions and actions. Here the characteristics and nuances of Peter's reputation in Luke's Gospel are (in)formed by the prior tradition.

That Luke's commemoratives liberties were restrained by the Markan precedent can be further seen in Luke's second volume, where the image of Peter is exclusively positive and explicitly tends toward the idyllic. Only in Acts does an image of Peter emerge that is absent of embarrassment, unintelligence, and apostasy (contra even to Luke's Gospel). The Peter of

Acts is a decisive and steadfast leader (e.g., Acts 1:15–26) whose surprising oratory skills bring many to faith (e.g., 2:14–42; 3:11–4:4) and who is dramatically empowered by the Spirit (e.g., 3:1–10; 5:15; 9:36–42). Perhaps the most noteworthy difference between the Peter of Acts and the Peter of Luke's Gospel has to do with the frame in which the apostle is cast: the Peter of Acts is characterized by his exceedingly Jesus-esque qualities. Far from being a mere literary device, the various Peter–Jesus parallels that extend across the Lukan narrative function as the mnemonic frame within which Peter is keyed.[7] Though the Peter of Luke's Gospel is mnemonically framed vis-à-vis the Markan Peter, the Peter of Acts is mnemonically framed vis-à-vis the Lukan Jesus (Baker 2011, 119). To this end, Peter is remembered as a charismatic leader who functions as the prominent voice and actor of the church in an extremely Jesus-esque way.

Overall, then, compared to Luke's Gospel, Acts betrays a compositional situation that appears less restrained by stabilized *lieux de mémoire*, or at least by sites of memory that depicted Peter negatively. While the question of the sources of Acts remains shrouded in historical fog, even those who propose an underlying tradition for Luke's Petrine material insist that such a source likely regarded Peter quite favorably (e.g., Pervo 2009, 13). Evidence will be considered below that suggests at least some of Peter's image in Acts is constructed in relation to a stabilized *lieu de mémoire* that is more negative; nevertheless, the larger contours of Peter's reputation in Acts reflects a more positive outlook which, even if dependent on a prior source, certainly reflects Luke's own positive perception of Peter. Even across the Lukan narrative, the Peter of the Gospel stands in contrast to the Peter of Acts: generally speaking, the former is mnemonically negotiated while the latter is mnemonically idyllic.

In summary, the preceding analysis has suggested that, although Luke has a much more positive perspective on the figure of Peter than Mark, his commemorative practices were nonetheless constrained by the image

---

7. On intra-textual Lukan parallels between Jesus and Peter, Paul, and other apostolic figures, see, e.g., Praeder 1984. By way of specific examples, Luke Timothy Johnson (1992, 71–72) notes that Peter's acts of healing parallel Jesus' in many key respects (e.g., cf. Luke 5:17–26 with Acts 3:1–10); this is especially evident in the accounts of Jarius's daughter and Tabitha (cf. Luke 8:40–56 and Acts 9:36–43). Similarly, Peter's exit from the narrative in Acts 12:1–17 is especially evocative of Jesus' resurrection appearances in Luke 24 (Pervo 2009, 307–12). More to the topical focus of the present study is the correlation of Jesus eating with sinners in Luke 15:1–3 and Peter eating with Gentiles in Acts 11:3 (Leppä 2011, 97).

of the apostle codified in the earlier Markan source text. Luke could not just forget certain aspects of Peter's image (e.g., drowsiness, association with Satan, and the "every-person" persona), but he could rearticulate these features so as to fit his own commemorative climate. In this way, the Markan narrative functioned as a stable *lieu de mémoire* for Luke, one that both *formed* and *informed* the general image of Peter that Luke was able to put forth. In essence, Luke was confronted with two divergent mnemonic expressions: the stable though difficult Markan image of Peter, on the one hand, and the contemporary and positive image of Peter that ultimately found expression in Acts, on the other. The portrayal of Peter in Luke's Gospel stands in the tension between these two extremes and shows Luke negotiating Peter's reputation so as to accommodate both images.

Reputational Rehabilitation in Acts

As just noted, the image of Peter in Acts is exceedingly positive and primarily static: Peter is portrayed as an idyllic figure who speaks and acts decisively, insightfully, and authoritatively. While this image persists across the majority of the Acts narrative, depictions of Peter's interactions with Gentiles is another matter. In these episodes Peter undergoes a transformation: although initially hesitant toward ethnic intermixing within the communities of the Way, by Acts 15 Peter ultimately stands at the vanguard of the Gentile mission. Although this aspect of Peter's image remains overwhelmingly positive, the contours of his relationship to Gentiles is by far the most dynamic aspect of Luke's reputational entrepreneurship. This shift in focus, where Peter's image seems negotiated toward the idyllic, suggests that Luke may be working in relation to a more stabilized *lieu de mémoire*. In the following I consider three aspects of Acts 10–11 and 15 that suggest that Gal 2:11–14 functioned as just such a memory site. Put differently, in Acts we find a commemorative image of Peter that was both *formed* in relation to and *informed* by Paul's earlier Epistle to the Galatians.

Geography and Memory: The Itinerant Peter

Perhaps the most subtle aspect of the Lukan (re)commemoration of Peter relates to the geographical locales with which the apostle is associated. Luke isolates Peter's itinerant ministry to the geographical area of Roman Palestine, primarily Jerusalem (Acts 1–9:11, 15) but also Samaria (8:14–24), Lydda (9:32–25), Joppa (9:36–43), Caesarea (10:1–48), and a few unnamed Samarian and Judean locales (8:25; 9:32). This picture stands in sharp contrast to the presentation of Peter's travels in other early Christian sources. Paul and a few other traditions connect Peter with both Corinth (1 Cor 1:12; 3:22; see also 9:5) and Antioch of Syria (Gal 2:11–14; see Ignatius, *Romans* 4.1–3; Origen, *Hom. Luc.* 6.4). Additionally, several sources from the late first century onward connect Peter with Rome (1 Pet 5:13; Papias, frag. 21.2 [Holmes 2007]; Acts of Peter 30–41; see also John 21:18–19; 1 Clem 5.1–7; 2 Clem 5.1–4) and even the northern and central regions of Asia Minor (1 Pet 1:1). Determining the extent of Peter's presence and activity in these regions is difficult. What is certain, as Markus Bockmuehl (2010, 77) rightly notes, is that most of the New Testament sites associated with Peter (e.g., Galilee, Jerusalem, Caesarea) do not seem to have retained or produced any form of localized Petrine traditions/memories; the only exceptions are Syria and Rome, neither of which cohere with Luke's emphasis on Roman Palestine. Within this broader commemorative landscape, Luke presents a geographically truncated image of Peter.

It is perhaps not insignificant that Luke explicitly keeps Peter away from Antioch, despite the fact that this Syrian city is otherwise prominent in the Acts narrative (11:19–26; 13:1–3; 14:26–15:2, 22–35; 18:22–23). Of particular note is the cryptic reference to Peter's exit from the narrative at 12:17: "then he left and went to another place." Despite overtones that point to Peter's martyrdom and parallels with the resurrection appearances of Luke 24 (Pervo 2009, 307–12), Luke seems to offer here a not-so-subtle nod toward Peter's non-Judean ministry without stressing its content in any great detail. Seen within the theoretical framework adopted in this essay, it is plausible to suggest that Luke was compelled by his source text (Gal 2:11–14) to create room for an Antiochan Petrine ministry, while at the same time taking steps to reframe that very source text. Put another way, Luke may have been uncomfortable with Paul's account of Peter's actions in Antioch (Gal 2:11–14) but nevertheless felt compelled to create narrative space in which to accommodate Peter's Syrian ministry. To this end, it is not insignificant that Luke does not explicitly deny Peter's presence in Antioch, as if to refute any Petrine connection with that city; rather, Luke leaves the issue open-ended. Based on the assessment of Luke's use of Mark offered earlier, this is precisely the way Luke both acknowledges and adapts a stable *lieu de mémoire*. Just as Luke was unable wholly to rewrite the Markan portrayal of Peter, neither is he able wholly to replace the Petrine image codified in Galatians.

TRANSFORMATION AND MEMORY: THE INCLUSIVE PETER

If Luke's geography creates a mnemonic world in which Peter's actions at Antioch are implicitly granted without being explicitly emphasized, the account of Peter's interaction with Cornelius (Acts 10:1–11:18) completely reframes the image of Peter enshrined in Gal 2:11–14. Here the commemorative artistry of Acts comes into clearer focus, as Luke functions as a reputational entrepreneur in the most acute sense. This reframing is achieved largely through the establishment of various Peter–Paul parallels that exist not within the narrative world of Acts (though these are important, too; see Praeder 1984) but rather between the literary worlds of both Acts and Galatians: that is, Luke creates *cross*-textual parallels that complement and stand alongside the various *intra*-textual Peter–Paul parallels within the Acts narrative. By keying Peter's interaction with Cornelius into a (specifically) Galatian image of Paul, Luke evokes certain aspects of the epistolary Paul as a frame for Peter's reputation.[8] Considering the narrative of Acts 10–11 in light of Gal 2, three observations are particularly significant.

First, in both Acts 10 and Gal 2 Peter is portrayed as having undergone a transformation on issues of Jewish–Gentile interaction within the church. While the Galatian Peter undergoes a negative transformation from an inclusivist to an exclusivist posture, the Lukan Peter undergoes the opposite alteration. Contrary to Galatians, Luke portrays Peter as one who was once inclined toward the law but comes to embrace the open call of the gospel to all humanity. Similar to Paul in Galatians (Gal 2:6; 3:27–28), the Peter of Acts insists that God does not show partiality nor distinguish between Jew and Gentile (Acts 10:28, 34–35). In this cross-textual parallel, it is more Peter's image than Paul's that is altered; the former apostle is brought into closer alignment with the latter, thus alleviating any sense of the difficulty between Peter's reputation at Antioch and Luke's broader, inclusive themes.

Second, both Paul and Luke link issues of mixed table fellowship and divine revelation to what they take as the ideal apostolic image. Although the exact nature of the Antioch dispute is not clear from Gal 2:11–14, Paul mentions the incident because it stands, in his view, as a microcosm of the

---

8. The cross-textual and intra-textual layers of Acts are rich, as the Peter figure is framed not only in relation to the Lukan Jesus (as noted earlier) but also in relation to both the Lukan and the epistolary Pauls. For Luke, the three figures of Jesus, Peter, and Paul mnemonically interlace each other in ways that extend beyond the narrative world of Luke-Acts and thus require grounding within an oral/aural performative context in which the Lukan and Pauline writings are read alongside one another.

situation in Galatia. The main issue for Paul is not so much the observance of the Torah (either at Antioch or in Galatia) as the concern that ethnic particulars not divide the inclusive *ekklēsia*. A similar concern is found in Acts, where Luke also focuses on the issue of mixed table fellowship. Similar to Paul, Luke is less concerned with the legality of ethnic intermixing and instead frames dietary restrictions as a metaphor for Jewish–Gentile interaction in the *ekklēsia*. This point is underscored in Acts 10, where even though the divine voice to Peter insists on the cleanliness of all *food* (10:9–16), the Lukan author makes clear that *ethnic distinctions* are actually in view (10:27–29). The key concern for both Luke and Paul, then, is ethnic intermixing within the church, and for both authors the Peter figure stands squarely in the middle of this social issue.

Most important, and perhaps not by coincidence, both Luke and Paul further cohere in their insistence that issues of Jewish–Gentile intermixing functioned as the catalyst for Peter's transformation. According to Paul, Peter undergoes a negative transformation because he adheres to the requests of those from James (Gal 2:12), therefore concerning himself with human rather than divine approval (see Gal 1:10). Luke, on the other hand, directly links Peter's positive transformation to a divine revelation. Rather than dubiously retreating from ethnically mixed company (as in Galatians), the Peter of Acts receives divine visions and acts upon them (Acts 10). In this way, Peter (Acts 10:9–16), like Paul (Gal 1:11–12), receives his nondiscriminatory gospel by means of divine revelation. Not only are the two apostles brought into cross-textual alignment such that they jointly proclaim an inclusive gospel that is rooted in divine revelation, but they do so in a way that specifically rehabilitates the contours of Peter's image as codified in Galatians.

Third and finally, in a number of ways the Peter of Acts stands as the mirror image of the Peter of Galatians. The mirror metaphor is apt; though reversed, the Lukan Peter is identical to its Galatian counterpart. Where Paul presents Peter as more concerned with human than divine approval, Luke portrays Peter as conversely more concerned with Christ's revelation than with the opinions of those in Jerusalem (see esp. Acts 11:1–18). Similarly, where Paul portrays Peter as a fickle apostle who retreats from Gentiles, Luke remembers him as confidently entering Cornelius's house "without raising an objection" (10:29; also 10:20). More significantly, where Paul remembers Peter "not acting ... in accordance with the truth of the gospel" (Gal 2:14), Luke remembers him as the authoritative advocate of the gospel to the Gentiles (Acts 15:7). Of particular note is the gospel that Peter proclaims: as scholars have long recognized, by stressing themes such as the "forgiveness of sins" (10:43), "faith" (10:43; 15:9), and "salvation through grace" (15:11), Peter's message has a markedly Pauline flavor—an *epistolary*, specifically *Galatian*, Pauline flavor (see, e.g., Weizsäcker 1894, 1:211–12; Walker 1985, 12; 1998, 78–85; Pervo 2006, 92; Lëppa 2002, 119–25). Here, then, the Peter of Acts is cross-textually keyed into the Paul of Galatians, a conflation that rehabilitates Peter's earlier and more difficult image while also underscoring Luke's vision of Peter and Paul as co-workers in the Gentile mission.

In summary, there are a number of important cross-textual Peter–Paul parallels that emerge when Acts and Galatians are read together. These parallels complement those embedded within the Acts narrative itself and create a mnemonic framework in which the Lukan Peter is keyed into the epistolary Paul, thus bringing the two figures into closer alignment. As noted earlier, however, these commemorative activities are fashioned in such a way that the Lukan Peter stands as the mirror image of its Galatian counterpart. Both the contours of the Lukan Peter and the specifics of his transformation find their catalyst in Gal 2:11–14. Similar to Luke's use of the Gospel of Mark, the commemoration of Peter in Acts is both restrained and informed by the Pauline text.

ADVOCACY AND MEMORY: THE STEADFAST PETER

Luke's image of Peter as one who embodies the inclusive nature of the gospel is most explicit in the portrayal of Peter as the defender and advocate of the Gentile mission. These roles are explicitly attributed to Peter in Acts 11, and it is perhaps not coincidental that this chapter includes explicit textual evidence—in the form of verbal agreement—for Luke's use of Gal 2:11–14. Heikki Leppä points particularly to the combination of the terms οἱ ἐκ περιτομῆς (Acts 11:2; cf. Gal 2:12), συνεσθίω (Acts 11:3; cf. Gal 2:12), and ἀκροβυστία (Acts 11:3; cf. Gal 2:7) as concrete source-critical evidence for what he calls the "quite clear fingerprint[s] of Paul" (2011, 94–98, quote 95; 2002, 35–61). Just as in Galatians, Peter is confronted by a group of circumcised Jerusalemites (οἱ ἐκ περιτομῆς) who take issue with his participation in mixed table fellowship. In contrast to Galatians, however, Luke sets Peter apart from his Jerusalem counterparts: he who went to the Gentiles without "discrimination" (διακρίνω; Acts 10:20; 11:12; see also 15:9) is now "criticized" (διακρίνω; 11:2) for having done so. As noted earlier, the Peter of Acts does not submit to the wishes of these circumcised believers but rather withstands their criticism and insists upon the importance of the Gentile mission (11:1–18). Ultimately, all of Paul's criticisms of Peter in Gal 2:11–14 are answered in Acts 10–11 and 15, as Peter becomes the exemplified inclusivist who, in the face of human pressures, remains faithful to the revelation of Christ.

This point becomes clearer in Acts 15:1–21, where Luke has Peter make a surprise return to the narrative for the sole purpose of defending Paul's Gentile mission at the Jerusalem Council. Here Luke's efforts as a reputational entrepreneur are laid bare, as not only Peter but also James and even Barnabas—those most negatively portrayed in Gal 2:11–14—are brought into the Evangelist's rehabilitative crosshairs. In a key passage, Acts 15:7–21, Peter's voice silences the otherwise lively debate of the council (15:7) and becomes the foundation upon which James's decision is constructed (15:14). Although Paul also plays an explicit role here (15:12), Luke places the bulk of the council's decision on Peter and James. Moreover, the content of Peter's address is particularly worth noting. While Paul rebukes Peter for having compelled the Gentiles to "live like Jews" (ἰουδαΐζω; Gal 2:14), in Acts Peter explicitly insists that the council not "put on the neck of the disciples a yoke that neither our fathers nor we have been able to bear" (Acts 15:10). Here again Luke's commemorative activities are restrained by the earlier tradition: although the prior Pauline depiction set the agenda of Peter's reputation, Luke turns the negative elements on their head and thus commemorates a more favorable, inclusivist Petrine image.

In summary, the preceding analysis has suggested that Luke takes specific steps toward rehabilitating the image of Peter that had been codified in Paul's account of the incident at Antioch in Gal 2. Just as Luke's Gospel was unable to dispense completely with the Markan Peter, so Acts was unable to ignore the image of Peter codified in Gal 2:11–14. In light of his exceedingly positive outlook on Peter, Luke faced the challenge of explaining how an idyllic hero of the faith could also be a disunifying hypocrite (as per Paul's account). Luke achieves such reputational rehabilitation by creatively refashioning all the difficult contours of Peter's image codified in Galatians. While Paul's Epistle to the Galatians does much to diminish the reputation of Peter, Luke's Acts does much to revive it.

Conclusions and Implications

This study has taken its point of departure from Barry Schwartz's insistence on the stability of memory. I have argued that Schwartz's theorem helpfully illuminates certain aspects of Luke's commemorative artistry while also providing a theoretical framework that brings to light certain ways in which Luke can be seen to draw on the Pauline epistles. To summarize my main point: Luke did not construct an image of Peter independent from previous commemorative expressions but rather sought to negotiate his much more positive Petrine image with the more negative images that had already been established in various *lieux de mémoire* (the Gospel of Mark and Paul's Epistle to the Galatians). This points to what Schwartz calls, in the introduction to this volume, the "path-dependency" of memory: texts are "affected not only by their social contexts but also by previous representations of their content" (p. 16). Accordingly, it is not enough simply to insist that Luke, working under the impulses of the early second century, sought to rehabilitate Paul's image by freely reshaping Peter's (so Walker 1985, 1998). Such an assertion places undue emphasis on the formative power of the present without giving proper attention to the carrying power of the past. This is not to deny any commemorative rehabilitation of Paul's image, although it is to acknowledge Luke's acute interest in the Petrine image and his practice of constructing that image in ways that are mnemonically indebted to established memory sites.

To insist that Peter's image was in need of repair is to presume that Luke understood the Pauline account of the incident at Antioch to have gained enough cultural cachet as to warrant reframing. This assertion is surely a contested point, one that raises the question of the status of Paul's letters, at least Galatians, at the time of Luke's writing. The findings reported here invite us to consider with renewed eyes not only the extent to which Paul's letters were known in the early second century (e.g., see Pervo 2010, 23–61) but also Luke's attitude toward such writings. As a corollary to the "path-dependency" of memory, the stress that many New Testament scholars place on points of *difference* or even *antagonism* between Luke and Paul seems potentially misguided. So, for example, Leppä (2011, 101) argues that "Luke criticizes Gal 2" so as to "correct" Paul's account of the incident at Antioch such that Acts is "almost directly antithetical" to Galatians. On the one hand, there can be little doubt that Luke is at least partially opposing his Pauline source—such is the nature of reputational *rehabilitation*. On the other hand, Luke need not be construed with such an antithetical predisposition. Returning to Schwartz (1991), the key point to stress is the recognition that divergent mnemonic reputations can exist simultaneously. Pointing to the multifarious nature of collective memory, Schwartz insists that strong social constructivists err by "underestimat[ing] the present's carrying power. They fail to see that the same present can sustain different memories and that different presents can sustain the same memory" (1991, 234, see also 226). When applied to Peter's reputation, and specifically with an eye on Luke's attitude toward the Pauline epistles, Luke may not be replacing or even contradicting Galatians so much as offering a contemporary and relevant account that stands *alongside* Galatians. Indeed, the fact that Peter is keyed into the Galatian Paul suggests Luke sees Galatians not as a text to be refuted but rather *retained*, even if it requires *reframing*. To this end, despite Pervo's insistence that Luke seeks to "submerge" or "refute Gal 2, or at least some implications of it," he more constructively points to Acts as a "hermeneutical key" for Paul's epistles (2006, 94–96, 138). Schwartz's theorem of the stability of *lieux de mémoire* provides a compelling theoretical context in which to explore Acts as an interpretive framework for, rather than definitive correction of, Paul's letters.

On this point of theoretical contexts, one further implication of this study concerns the nature of what we identify as "credible data" when examining Luke's potential knowledge and use of Paul's letters. The foregoing has proceeded from the conviction that one must not unduly prioritize certain kinds of knowledge over others. That is to say, while instances of verbal agreement and literary correspondence are important in evaluating Luke's use of Paul, such data is only mistakenly self-evident and must be self-critically evaluated within explicit theoretical frameworks. With respect to the Peter figure, I have demonstrated that *both* verbal agreement *and* literary correspondence are reception-critically meaningful when they are placed *within* the dynamic context of mnemonic construction and negotiation. This underscores the importance—and potentiality—of exploring alternative ways of envisioning and identifying Luke's use of Paul. In addition to Luke's commemorative sensibilities and the (in)formative nature of mnemonic construction and negotiation, I have elsewhere examined the potential of cognitive linguistics for shedding light on ritual meals in both Luke and Paul (Tappenden 2012). A further avenue of exploration would relate to oral/aural performance as the context in which the Lukan and Pauline writings were read alongside one another. For now, this study has demonstrated that the social dynamics of collective memory offer a promising theoretical framework in which to evaluate Luke's use of his sources, one that I have here established on the grounds of Luke's use of Mark and further elaborated as a way of illuminating Luke's use of Galatians. By focusing on Luke's reputational entrepreneurship, I hope this study has contributed to our understanding of how Luke's use of Paul's epistles can be plausibly construed in new and credible ways.

Works Cited

Aejmelaeus, Lars. 2011. The Pauline Letters as Source Material in Luke-Acts. Pages 54–75 in *The Early Reception of Paul*. Edited by Kenneth Liljeström. Publications of the Finnish Exegetical Society 99. Helsinki: Finnish Exegetical Society.

Baker, Coleman. 2011. *Identity, Memory, and Narrative in Early Christianity: Peter, Paul, and Recategorization in the Book of Acts*. Eugene, OR: Pickwick.

Barrett, C. K. 1976. Acts and the Pauline Corpus. *ExpT* 88:2–5.

Best, Ernest. 1981. *Following Jesus: Discipleship in the Gospel of Mark*. JSNTSup 4. Sheffield: JSOT Press.

Bockmuehl, Markus. 2010. *The Remembered Peter: In Ancient Reception and Modern Debate*. WUNT 262. Tübingen: Mohr Siebeck.

Brodie, Thomas L. 2001. Towards Tracing the Gospels' Literary Indebtedness to the Epistles. Pages 104–16 in *Mimesis and Intertextuality in Antiquity and Christianity*. Edited by Dennis R. MacDonald. Studies in Antiquity and Christianity. Harrisburg, PA.: Trinity Press International.

Burchard, Christoph. 1970. *Der Dreizehnte Zeuge*. FRLANT 103. Göttingen: Vandenhoeck & Ruprecht.

Cassidy, Richard J. 2007. *Four Times Peter: Portrayals of Peter in the Four Gospels and at Philippi*. Interfaces. Collegeville, MN: Liturgical Press.

Ehrman, Bart. 2006. *Peter, Paul, and Mary Magdalene: The Followers of Jesus in History and Legend*. Oxford: Oxford University Press.

Elbert, Paul. 2006. Possible Literary Links between Luke-Acts and Pauline Letters Regarding Spirit-Language. Pages 226–54 in *The Intertextuality of the Epistles: Explorations of Theory and Practice*. Edited by Thomas L. Brodie, Dennis R. MacDonald, and Stanley E. Porter. New Testament Monographs 16. Sheffield: Sheffield Phoenix.

Enslin, Morton S. 1938. Luke and Paul. *JAOS* 58:81–91.

———. 1970. Once Again, Luke and Paul. *ZNTW* 61:253–71.

Fine, Gary Alan. 2001. *Difficult Reputations: Collective Memories of the Evil, Inept, and Controversial*. Chicago: University of Chicago Press.

Hatina, Thomas R. 1999. Intertextuality and Historical Criticism in New Testament Studies: Is there a Relationship? *BibInt* 7:28–43.

Holmes, Michael W. 2007. *The Apostolic Fathers: Greek Texts and English Translations*. Grand Rapids: Baker Academic.

Johnson, Luke Timothy. 1992. *The Acts of the Apostles*. SacPag 5. Collegeville, MN: Liturgical Press.

Knox, John. 1966. Acts and the Pauline Letter Corpus. Pages 279–87 in *Studies in Luke-Acts: Essays Presented in Honor of Paul Schubert, Buckingham Professor of New Testament Criticism and Interpretation at Yale University*. Edited by Leander E. Keck and J. Louis Martyn. Philadelphia: Fortress.

Leppä, Heikki. 2002. Luke's Critical Use of Galatians. Ph.D. diss., University of Helsinki.

———. 2011. Luke's Selective Use of Gal 1 and 2. Pages 91–124 in *The Early Reception of Paul*. Edited by Kenneth Liljeström. Publications of the Finnish Exegetical Society 99. Helsinki: Finnish Exegetical Society.

Liljeström, Kenneth, ed. 2011. *The Early Reception of Paul*. Publications of the Finish Exegetical Society 99. Helsinki: Finish Exegetical Society.

Marcus, Joel. 1992. The Jewish War and the Sitz im Leben of Mark. *JBL* 111:441–62.

———. 2006.Crucifixion as Parodic Exaltation. *JBL* 125:73–87.

Marguerat, Daniel, ed. 2009. *Réception du Paulinisme dans les Actes des apôtres/Reception of Paulinism in the Acts of the Apostles*. BETL 229. Leuven: Peeters.

Mitchell, Margaret. 2012. Peter's "Hypocrisy" and Paul's: Two "Hypocrites" at the Foundation of Earliest Christianity. *NTS* 58:231–34.

Pervo, Richard I. 2006. *Dating Acts: Between the Evangelists and the Apologists*. Santa Rosa, CA: Polebridge.

———. 2009. *Acts: A Commentary*. Hermeneia. Minneapolis: Fortress.

———. 2010. *The Making of Paul: Constructions of the Apostle in Early Christianity*. Minneapolis: Fortress.

Praeder, Susan Marie. 1984. Jesus–Paul, Peter–Paul, and Jesus–Peter Parallelisms in Luke-Acts: A History of Reader Response. Pages 23–39 in *SBL Seminar Papers, 1984*. SBL Seminar Papers 23. Missoula, MT: Scholars Press.

Riches, John. 2008. *Galatians through the Centuries*. Blackwell Bible Commentaries. Oxford: Blackwell.

Schwartz, Barry. 1991. Social Change and Collective Memory: The Democratization of George Washington. *American Sociological Review* 56:221–26.

———. 2000. *Abraham Lincoln and the Forge of National Memory.* Chicago: University of Chicago Press.

Smith, Terence V. 1985. *Petrine Controversies in Early Christianity: Attitudes Towards Peter in Christian Writings of the First Two Centuries.* WUNT 2/15. Tübingen: Mohr Siebeck.

Tappenden, Frederick S. 2012. Luke and Paul in Dialogue: Ritual Meals and Risen Bodies as Instances of Embodied Cognition. Pages 203–28 in *Resurrection of the Dead: Biblical Traditions in Dialogue.* Edited by Geert Van Oyen and Tom Shepherd. BETL 249. Leuven: Peeters.

Vielhauer, Philipp. 1966. On the "Paulinism" of Acts. Translated by William. C. Robinson Jr., and Victor Paul Furnish. Pages 33–50 in *Studies in Luke-Acts: Essays Presented in Honor of Paul Schubert, Buckingham Professor of New Testament Criticism and Interpretation at Yale University.* Edited by Leander E. Keck and J. Louis Martyn. Philadelphia: Fortress.

Walker, William O., Jr. 1985. Acts and the Pauline Corpus Reconsidered. *JSNT* 24:3–23.

———. 1998. Acts and the Pauline Corpus Revisited: Peter's Speech at the Jerusalem Conference. Pages 77–86 in *Literary Studies in Luke-Acts: Essays in Honor of Joseph B. Tyson.* Edited by Richard P. Thompson and Thomas E. Phillips. Macon, GA: Mercer University Press.

Weeden, Theodore J. 1971. *Mark: Traditions in Conflict.* Philadelphia: Fortress.

Weizsäcker, Carl. 1894. *The Apostolic Age of the Christian Church.* Translated by James Millar. 2 vols. London: Williams & Norgate.

Wiarda, Timothy. 1999. Peter as Peter in the Gospel of Mark. *NTS* 45:19–37.

Social Memory and Commemoration of the Death of "the Lord": Paul's Response to the Lord's Supper Factions at Corinth

Dennis C. Duling

Paul's attempt to resolve factions related to the Lord's Supper meal at Corinth (1 Cor 11) poses a series of questions. Were the divisions based on ethnic divisions between Judeans and Gentiles, for example, differences in dietary restrictions? Were the factions reflective of social stratification in the Greco-Roman world? Did they mirror tensions in banquet customs in the broader culture? Did the usual living and dining spaces in which Christians gathered contribute to the divisions? What was Paul's approach for resolving the differences, and was he successful in resolving them? Particularly for the purposes of the present volume, how did he use commemorative ritual strategies to address the situation, and how did these strategies tie into his key message and its moral implications?

This essay will approach these questions by coordinating several proposals in current research on Paul, his social context, and his rhetorical strategy. These proposals will be summarized and related to insights derived from Barry Schwartz's view of social memory: specifically, Schwartz's thesis that a stable essence persists within the fluidity of social memory and that this stable essence is reinforced by ritual commemorations that, in turn, contribute to a community's social identity. The discussion may be outlined as follows:

1. The Corinthian Lord's Supper Context: Social Conflict and Social Spaces
2. "The Strong" and "the Weak" in 1 Cor 8–10
3. Stratification and Equality in Ancient Banquets and Commemorative Rituals
4. Insights from Barry Schwartz's Views of Social Memory
5. Commemoration and Ritual Theory: Schwartz and New Testament Scholarship

6. Social Memory and Social Morality in Paul's Letters
7. Paul's Response to the Factions: Keying the Banquet Commemoration to the Memory of "the Lord's" Traumatic Death

The Corinthian Lord's Supper Context: Social Conflict and Social Spaces

Wayne Meeks emphasizes that for Paul "the complementary terms which define what the [Corinthian] community's character ought to be are its 'holiness' and its unity" (1986, 130–31). But as Paul had learned from both oral reports (1 Cor 1:11; 16:17; 5:1; 11:18?) and a letter (7:1), the Corinthian church was anything but holy and unified. It was, rather, plagued by immorality and divisive factions, and one dispute centered on the Lord's Supper.

> 11:17 Now in the following instructions I do not commend you, because when you come together it is not for the better but for the worse. 18 For, to begin with, when you come together as a church, I hear that there are divisions [σχίσματα] among you; and to some extent I believe it. 19 Indeed, there have to be factions [αἱρέσεις] among you, for only so will it become clear who among you are genuine [οἱ δόκιμοι]. 20 When you come together, it is not really to eat the Lord's Supper [οὐκ ἔστιν κυριακὸν δεῖπνον φαγεῖν]. 21 For when the time comes to eat, each of you goes ahead with [προλαμβάνει] your own supper [τὸ ἴδιον δεῖπνον], and one goes hungry and another becomes drunk. 22 What! Do you [pl. throughout v. 22] not have houses to eat and drink in? Or do you show contempt for the church of God and humiliate those who have nothing? What should I say to you? Should I commend you? In this matter I do not commend you! ...
>
> 33 So then, my brothers and sisters, when you come together to eat, wait for one another. 34a If you are hungry, eat at home [ἐν οἴκῳ], so that when you come together, it will not be for your condemnation. (nrsv, changing "homes" to "houses" in v. 22)

Three major interpretations of the situation behind Paul's comments in the above passage have surfaced, all related to spaces where separate churches or "the whole church" met. The first theory derives from Gerd Theissen and Jerome Murphy O'Connor. They note that 1 Cor 11:20–21 states that "each of you goes ahead with your own supper, and one goes hungry and another becomes drunk"; these are singular forms that suggest individual behavior. However, verse 22 shifts to plural forms, a change that leads Theissen to suggest that Paul is referring to a group, the wealthy few (cf. 1 Cor 1:26) who own "houses" (οἰκίας; 11:22), dine early (11:21, 33) and separately, and feast on more and better quality food and drink (11:21, 34). A second group is composed of "those who have nothing" (11:22) and are "hungry" (11:21). Theissen's interpretation is socioeconomic: "It can be assumed that the conflict over the Lord's Supper is a conflict between poor and rich Christians" (1982a, 151).

Subsequent interpreters have tried to clarify the Corinthian factions in relation to spaces where church members assembled together and also to gatherings of "the whole church," in particular at Corinth. Although the semantic range of οἶκος can be very broad (Klauck 1981, 15–20), a common interpretation is a self-standing "house," which has contributed to an extensive discussion of Corinthian "house churches." Murphy-O'Connor thinks that a gathering of "the whole church" (1 Cor 14:23; see also Rom 16:23) of about forty to fifty persons, as contrasted with a gathering in the "church in your (or their) *oikos*" (Phlm 2; 1 Cor 16:19; Rom 16:3–5a), would have required a large house such as the "sumptuous" villa excavated in the Anaploga district of Corinth, which, judging from its elaborate floor mosaic, seems to have been owned by a wealthy patron (Murphy-O'Connor 1983, 78–85; 2004; 2009; see Jongkind 2001, 143–44; Romano 2005, 58). In such a house, the host and a very few wealthy upper strata guests could have eaten more and better quality food earlier and separately while reclining in a large dining room (*triclinium*). The overflow, the majority poor (1 Cor 1:26), could have eaten some time later, while "sitting" (1 Cor 14:30) out in the atrium (Murphy-O'Connor 1983, 153–62; 2004, 133; 2009, 189–93). Murphy-O'Connor's proposal is consistent with widespread views (the "new consensus") that Paul's churches consisted of a cross-section of social strata distributed into two major social ranks: a few elite and many nonelite. Theissen accepted Murphy-O'Connor's archaeological proposal as evidence for his socioeconomic interpretation of the Lord's Supper factions in terms of a conflict between the rich and the poor (2001, 83).

Many scholars respond positively to Murphy-O'Connor's proposal. However, a second spatial theory is associated especially with Robert Jewett and Peter Lampe (Jewett 1993; see also Lampe 1991). Urban Christ believers were very poor and would have lived in tiny, upper-level apartments of large overcrowded apartment buildings on a city block (*insula*). In this scenario, "the whole church" could have gathered in one of the shops at ground level or perhaps in one of the larger apartments just above them. Thus, the "house church" concept should be replaced by a "tenement church" concept. If this model is applied to Corinth, the factions would have arisen within the poor, more "egalitarian," members of the church, not between an upper and lower stratum. A similar theory has been proposed in relation to Ephesus (Billings 2011, 568). Such interpretations shift the cross-section of social strata in the churches to poverty, a focus that has been vigorously argued by other scholars (Meggitt 1998; Friesen 2004).

The "tenement church" theory is attractive for Rome. How does it fit smaller cities such as Corinth? The third spatial possibility for interpreting factions is related to studies by Andrew Wallace-Hadrill, David Balch, and Peter Oakes. Wallace-Hadrill's research (1994, 2003) shows that at Pompeii and Herculaneum the same city block (*insula*) might host not only a large apartment building but also houses of various sizes, including larger ones that contained "housefuls" of people from different social levels, including slaves, and shops. David Balch agrees and suggests that "the whole church" at Herculaneum could have consisted mainly of different ranks of people at the *lower end* of the social hierarchy, including successful artisans, impoverished artisans, freedmen, freedwomen, slaves, and the very poor (2008, 49–58). Peter Oakes offers a similar interpretation for the Insula of Menander at Pompeii, a block on which there is not only a spacious mansion but also mid-sized to small "houses" and shops (2009a; 2009b; 2010, 180). Oakes creatively analyzes four different-sized houses and four different social ranks of persons living in them, again at the lower end of the socioeconomic spectrum, and suggests that the medium-sized craftworker's house was large enough to host a large church gathering. He coins the expression "craftworker house church" as an alternative to the villa-type "house church" and the "tenement church" but adds that his model makes the contrast between house churches and tenement churches unnecessary (Oakes 2009b, 70, 91).

Do any of these three alternative spatial theories help to explain the factions at *Corinth*? Large, multistory apartment buildings like those at Rome, Ostia, and Ephesus have not yet been excavated in the first-century layers at Corinth (so Jongkind 2001, 143–44; Romano 2005, 58). However, several two-story buildings with shops and second-story flats have been excavated on Corinth's East Theater Street (Jongkind 2001, 142–43). In a critique of Murphy-O'Connor's large villa theory, David Horrell argues that the upstairs rooms of the East Theater Street buildings had enough space for multistratified, lower-strata church members to meet, citing as an illustration the story of Eutychus, who, while listening to Paul's lengthy speech in Ephesus, dozed off and fell three stories to his death (Acts 20:9; Horrell

2004, 354–68; see Schowalter 2010). Murphy-O'Connor accepts some of Horrell's critique and responds that it is plausible that smaller subgroups met in such spaces, but not "the whole church" (Murphy-O'Connor 2009, 190–93; also Smith 2012, 7–8). Oakes thinks that the Pompeii *insula* with its various houses and corresponding lower social strata can be a model for understanding other cities, including Corinth and, with appropriate modifications, even Rome (Oakes 2009a, 2009b, 2010).

Finally, there are other proposals, such as that the Corinthians did not gather in "households" at all (cf. v. 22), but rather in other, possibly rented quarters, for example, a synagogue, clubhouse (Malina and Pilch 2006, 110), or "Roman cellar building" (Adams 2012, 22–37). These are interesting proposals but do not offer more powerful alternatives for interpreting the factions.

In sum, scholars are now divided about the nature of "household" spaces as a way to solve the Lord's Supper factions at Corinth. The large apartment "tenement church" context for the large meal gatherings should await further excavations at Corinth, although Oakes thinks that a nonelite house theory such as his "breaks down the main social contrast usually drawn between churches based in houses and those based in apartments" (Oakes 2009b, 70). This means that socioeconomic conflict between the wealthy elite stratum and the poor nonelite stratum must now take into account a more variegated social stratification *at the lower levels*, as in the *insulae* studies of Pompeii and Herculaneum and as suggested by the East Theater Street buildings at Corinth. At the same time, while some "new consensus" writers may have too easily passed over widespread poverty and mixed social strata at the lower end of the social hierarchy, there still could also have been tensions between lower strata and a highly ranked patron/host and his or her friends. The reasons for not abandoning this possibility totally are at least twofold: (1) Paul's comments about meal factions elsewhere in 1 Cor 8–10; and (2) social status tensions at upper-end Mediterranean banquets in general. These reasons need to be considered.

"The Strong" and "the Weak" in 1 Corinthians 8–10

Dennis Smith, among others, thinks that the meal factions in 1 Cor 11 are related to the dietary conflict in 1 Cor 8–10 between "the weak" Corinthians who will not eat "food offered to idols" and "the strong" who will (2003, 183; Theissen 1982b). Ellen Bradshaw Aitken illumines this thesis by arguing that an early homily (Paul's?) lies behind 1 Cor 10:1–22, a sermon that articulated a familiar "cult legend" about the exodus saga, including the wilderness wanderings, the Sinai covenant, the worship of the golden calf, and the entry into the promised land (Aitken 1997, 360–64; cf. esp. Meeks 1982; 1983, 99). Paul wrote that the scriptural account contained two "types" of Israelites (1 Cor 10:6): "all our ancestors" who shared in cloud, sea, baptism into Moses, spiritual food, and spiritual drink (1 Cor 10:1–4); and "some [of our ancestors]" who desired evil, that is, idol worship, sexual immorality, testing Christ, and murmuring (1 Cor 10:7–10). These two "types" corresponded to "a cultic meal properly performed and one gone awry," and the latter set the stage for Paul's interpretation of the Corinthian factions in chapter 11 (Aitken 1997, 360). This explains why Paul quotes Exod 32:6 ("The people sat down to eat and drink, and they rose up to play" at 1 Cor 10:7 and then suggests that these things were "written down to instruct us" (1 Cor 10:11b). This means that Paul drew on social memory to give moral instructions to the Corinthians about the meal, then proceeded to offer his own "instructions" (1 Cor 11:17). I shall return to the specifics of the connection later; for the moment I concentrate on the social-contextual conflict between the weak and the strong that informs it.

The weak–strong conflict in 1 Cor 8–10 is not simply "ethnic," that is, that Judean ritual purists were rejecting Gentile dietary practices (Gal 2:11–14); food objections were being posed presumably by *Gentiles* (former synagogue "God-fearers"? 1 Cor 8:7, 10:32; see Theissen 1982b, 123–24). In the case of private banquets, Paul tends to side with "the strong" who have "knowledge" that idols do not really exist. Yet, Paul criticizes "the strong" who dine in pagan temples by saying that they eat at "the table of demons," an act incompatible with consuming the bread/body and cup/blood of Christ (see 1 Cor 10:14–22). To preserve unity, he warns that "the strong" should restrict their freedom if it causes a brother with a "weak conscience" "for whom Christ died" to stumble (8:9–11; 10:25–29).

A choice between dietary and socioeconomic explanations may not be necessary, since, as some scholars think, "the strong" were probably also wealthier Corinthians (Theissen 1982b, 124–28; Meeks 1986, 133). The question is whether a conflict between strong and weak could also occur at lower social levels among mixed social strata, as suggested by the above alternative space considerations. If so, both dietary and spatially based socioeconomic conflicts could have threatened the "equality" at the meal, and thus the purity/unity of "the body" (see 1 Cor 10:17; 12; 13). The key moral norm for Paul was freedom within the bounds of love. From this discussion, Murphy O'Connor's suggestion that "the whole church" met in a larger house and that smaller gatherings met in smaller houses, seconded by Dennis Smith (2012), remains at least an option.

The second reason noted above for viewing the Lord's Supper conflict as an expression of tensions between various social strata at banquets—the general climate of ancient Mediterranean banquets—also deserves some discussion.

STRATIFICATION AND EQUALITY IN ANCIENT BANQUETS AND (OTHER) COMMEMORATIVE RITUALS

Matthias Klinghardt, Dennis Smith, and Hal Taussig maintain that formal meals among ancient Mediterranean peoples should not be interpreted in isolation from each other as separate types but rather viewed as variations of a single, generic meal pattern: the Greco-Roman (Mediterranean) banquet model. Thus, "sacred" and "secular" meals should be analyzed together (Klinghardt 1996; Smith 2003; Taussig 2009, 26, 68–69). They discuss bodily positions (reclining) and participants at meals ("president"/*symposiarch*, servants, invited guests, "entertainers," and dogs) and emphasize that the ancient banquet pattern involved two sequential acts: (1) the *deipnon*, or "supper," which was the main meal in the evening, followed by a libation to the gods; and (2) the *symposium*, which featured drinking, entertainment, music, games, philosophical discussion, storytelling, or teaching.

For Klinghardt, Mediterranean banquets expressed social values. Dennis Smith uses different language, a "social code" that has "a pattern of social relations" (see Douglas 1966, 1972, 1984), and offers a helpful five-point summary (Smith 2003, 9–12; see also Taussig 2009). I have added brief descriptions.

1. Social boundaries (who receives an invitation; who dines with whom, when, and where)
2. Social bonding (solidification of previous and new social networks, "propinquity" and "homophily" in social network analysis)
3. Social obligation (meal "etiquette" grounded in ideas about friendship, joy, pleasure, and the like)
4. Social stratification (ranking of reclining guests according to their perceived status)
5. Social equality (tendencies to equal treatment of guests; sense of community)

As the list above indicates, the Mediterranean social code for banquets contained a built-in tension. On the one hand, social obligation based on cultural norms of friendship and community (point 3) contributed to an ideal of social "equality" at meals (point 5). On the other hand, full social "equality" did not exist in antiquity (Elliott 2002, 2003); indeed, this ideal was in contradiction with traditional cultural norms believed to preserve the natural moral order: social boundaries (point 1), social stratification (point 4), and inner-stratum social bonding (point 2). A telling example of this built-in tension between social stratification and social "equality" is that all invited banquet guests were ideally considered to have "equal status," yet in reality the host or *symposiarch* usually positioned them around the table according to their social rank, and, on occasion, the more honored guests of higher rank received more and better quality food and drink (Pliny the Younger, *Letters* 2.6; Martial, *Epigrams* 3.60).

The sacred meal of the Passover, first-century elements of which are preserved in the third-to-seventh-century CE Tosephta (Smith 2003, 144–50), fits the Mediterranean banquet model. It needs to be highlighted here not only because of its importance in some interpretations for the background of the Lord's Supper meal but because it commemorates Israel's escape from slavery to freedom in a promised land and is therefore foundational for Israel's social memory and ethnic identity. Indeed, Josephus calls special attention to its *memorial* significance (*War* 4.402; see also 2.10) and often locates dramatic social, political, and military events at the time of the Jerusalem Passover (Goldberg 2012). Social memory will be very important for Paul's attempt to resolve the factions at Corinth as well. For a brief look at social memory and commemorative ritual theory, I turn to the theories of Barry Schwartz.

Insights from Barry Schwartz's Views of Social Memory

Barry Schwartz contrasts two theoretical approaches to collective memory (1991b). In *constructionism*, the past is a construct that serves the needs of the present, "a fabrication that present circumstances shape." Scholars who take this approach view the past as "precarious," "a foreign country" (Schwartz 1991b, 222; see Lowenthal 1985). The most influential representative of this approach is Maurice Halbwachs, widely recognized as the "father of collective memory" studies. In *essentialism*, however, the past "shapes our understanding of the present rather than the other way around," although of course this can produce "a distortion in a different direction"

(Schwartz1991b, 222). Schwartz seeks to steer a middle course between these two extremes (see 1982, 376–77), offering a synthetic, "contrapuntal" theory of memory (1991b, 231–32, 234a). Still, he thinks that the construc-tionist view has been too dominant: social change *affects* social memory, but it does not *determine* it. Indeed, there persists "an existing structure of assumptions about the past—an 'available past' … that people accept as given and that possesses a self-sustaining inertia" (1991b, 222b). While variant and contested versions of the past seem to suggest that memory is not stable, in reality there is a stable historical core, a stability within insta-bility, a continuity within discontinuity (1991b, 234). In the introduction to the present volume, Schwartz reiterates this principle emphatically. "As these memories were passed on, they were modified, but the essence of the events to which they refer remained unchanged. This essence, and the ways and reasons it is maintained, are the principal subjects of my research into social memory" (p. 9).

Schwartz illustrates his theory by showing, for example, how historically sequential images of George Washington—the earlier presenting Washing-ton as the dignified and aristocratic "ideological spokesmen" of the upper classes, the later imagining him as a "democratized" and "Lincolnesque" common man and "ideological spokesmen" of the lower classes—together preserved the inherent "essence" of Washington (1991b, 234). In a similar study, Schwartz shows how competing statues of Abraham Lincoln—one elegant and distinguished (supported by conservative elitists), the other plain and simple (supported by progressive egalitarians)—interacted and constrained each other to shape America's collective memory of Lincoln, the essential Lincoln (1991a). "The past, then, is a familiar rather than a foreign country; its people different, but not strangers to the present" (1991b, 234b).

In the introduction to his essay in this volume, Schwartz applies his essentialist-leaning contrapuntal theory to the New Testament Gospels. He admits that oral tradition changes the image of Jesus but cautiously argues for a historical realism in which a "central tendency," an "objective existence," a "real historical core," a "stable essence" is preserved across generations.

> In many cases, this essence is itself exaggerated, underemphasized, falsi-fied, misrepresented, and misunderstood, but it would be a mistake to take these distortions as social memory's paradigm. Nor may we assume that memories are usually, let alone always, valid. Realism's assumption is more modest: interpretation is more often forced upon the observer of an event by its inherent quality than imposed by the observer's world-

view and interests. Put another way, *reality counts more than bias in the remembering of most events most of the time.* (Schwartz, pp. 20–21, emphasis original).

Schwartz thinks that memory in the "four partially independent Gospels" is not simply a "repository of distortions, which ... do little more than make the present meaningful"; the Gospels are rather "a repository of both authentic and inauthentic information" (pp. 14, 20, above). While avoiding the risk of essentialism (see Duling 2011), I shall attempt to incorporate aspects of Schwartz's perspective, where relevant, in what follows.

Commemoration and Ritual Theory: Schwartz and New Testament Scholars

Schwartz says that commemoration, "the evaluative aspect of *chronicling*," celebrates and safeguards "the ideal" by extracting "those extraordinary events which embody our deepest and most fundamental values" (1982, 377). Commemoration selects salient persons and events of the past for their significance for the present and centers on the moral significance of the past for the community that remembers. Drawing on Alan Kirk's survey of ritual theories (Kirk 2005b, 7–10, 15), Schwartz writes that commemorative ritual, "as a standardized, repetitive, and symbolic activity that allows participants to define their relation to the past, ... fixes in mind the events of the past, a process facilitated by the emotional assembling of the community itself" (Schwartz, p. 10, above; see also Connerton 1989, 4; Keightley 2005).

Ritual commemorative perspectives like those of Schwartz are also found among biblical scholars who analyze ancient banquet practices, including the Lord's Supper. Hal Taussig, building on the banquet model of Klinghardt and Smith, derives ritual theories from a number of specialists and urges that rituals are the primary way groups in safe places at special times (I oversimplify a complex analysis here) "reflect," "reproduce," "communicate," "focus," "perform," "reframe," "integrate," "structure," or "perfect" seemingly contradictory "intractable issues" of the larger society. However, says Taussig, rituals do not always achieve such social integration (2009, 55–67). Similarly, Richard DeMaris argues that rituals usually arise in times of social conflict, and, while they may help to resolve conflict and unify groups, they can also generate conflict because they can be inadequate, misapplied, have unintended consequences, or simply not work as expected.

Ultimately, "the social context of a rite will determine whether it increases or lessens social conflict" (DeMaris 2008, 33; see also Kirk 2010, 62).

Applied to the study at hand, ritual meals echoed the social tensions inherent in ancient Mediterranean banquets. They offered catharsis, community, friendship, and reduction of status-laden social boundaries, but they also maintained social inequities. In Taussig's terms, meals "*simultaneously enabled social bonding and social boundaries (or social stratification and social equality)*" (2009, 63, emphasis original). These issues are important for Paul's response to the factions in 1 Corinthians, a response that centers on social memory and social morality.

Social Memory and Social Morality in Paul's Letters

In 1946, decades before the "collective memory boom," Nils Dahl gave a University of Oslo inaugural professorship lecture titled "*Anamnesis*: Memory and Commemoration in Early Christianity" (Dahl 1976 [1946]). Dahl's discussion of New Testament memory terms (Greek *mnē*-root terms) and their roots in Judean (ancient "Jewish") literature emphasized three points. First, language about memory in the New Testament is not new or distinctive but rather derived from the surrounding culture (also Verhey 1992). Second, therefore, New Testament writers do not offer a sophisticated philosophical analysis of "memory" and "recollection," as does, for example, Aristotle's *De memoria et reminiscencia* (see Ricoeur 2004, 15–21). Third, whereas Aristotle restricts the sense of μνημονεύω ("I remember") to the past (*Mem. rem.* 449b), New Testament usage adds the importance of memory and commemoration for the present and future or, in terms of contemporary memory theory, how past events and persons key and frame present and future behavior. In short, in the New Testament social memory is used rhetorically to develop and maintain social morality.

Dahl emphasized the term *zākar*, "he remembers," which is prominent in Hebrew Bible covenant passages. Yahweh reminds his people that, in response to his liberating them from bondage and giving them the promised land, they must keep his commandments (Ps 103:18). They must remember by means of mnemonic signs such as fringes, phylacteries, and mezuzahs (Num 15:37–41; Deut 6:5–9; 11:18–21) and continually perform memorial acts: rituals, words, psalms, hymns, daily prayers, sacrifices, and blowing of trumpets at the Jerusalem temple (Dahl 1976, 11–14). This convergence of past, present, and future is perpetuated in the later Mishnaic Passover commemoration: "in every generation a man must regard himself as if he came forth himself out of Egypt" (m. Pesaḥ. 10.4). Furthermore, the rabbis preserved social memory by memorizing, interpreting, and debating Yahweh's commands and applying them to behavior in everyday life.

In Paul's letters there is a tension between social memory and social morality. Paul remembers his recruits' fine moral qualities and actions collectively but then reminds them of his gospel and admonishes them to correct behavior. An excellent illustration of this tension is the contrast between the "thanksgiving" sections of Paul's letters and later exhortations. The customary thanksgiving in Greco-Roman letters included three interrelated elements: (1) a traditional "health wish"; (2) a prayer to the gods on behalf of someone (usually the recipient[s]); and (3) a "memory motif," that is, "making remembrance" (μνείαν ποιούμενοι) of a person or persons to the gods (O'Brien 1974; Arzt 1994). In Paul's thanksgivings, the prayer-memory combination incorporates his famous faith, hope, and love triad (1 Cor 13) to rhetorically complement and reinforce his readers/hearers' positive moral attributes and actions.

> We [Paul and his co-writers] always give thanks to God for all of you [readers/hearers], constantly making remembrance of [μνείαν ποιούμενοι] you in our prayers, remembering [μνημονεύοντες] before our God and Father your work of faith and labor of love and steadfastness of hope in our Lord Jesus Christ. (1 Thess 1:2–3; see also Phlm 4–6; Phil 1:3–5)

Yet despite his apparent confidence in his readers'/hearers' spiritual progress, Paul eventually reminds them of his gospel's moral requirements (Mitchell 2005, 210–11). As proclamation is followed by parenesis, social memory is followed by social morality. As noted, this memory/morality rhetorical strategy is used when Paul "instructs" the Corinthians about the Lord's Supper in 1 Cor 11 by introducing it in chapter 10 with proper and improper cult meals.

Dahl observed that in Paul's new gospel, "knowledge" (γνῶσις) is correlated with memory. The Thessalonian believers *remember*—they *already* "know"—but Paul proceeds to *remind* them anyhow. "The first obligation of the apostle vis-à-vis a community is to make the faithful remember what they have received and already know—or *should* know.... It is only a question of doing still more perfectly" (Dahl 1976, 15). Dahl then generalized, "I would say that for the early Christians, knowledge was an ἀνάμνησις ("memory"), a recollection of the γνῶσις ("knowledge") given to all those who have believed in the gospel, received baptism, and been incorporated into the church" (1976, 16). Dahl did not emphasize *collective* memory—its rediscovery by scholars came years later—but it is clearly implied.

Having attempted to understand some possible reasons for banquet factions at Corinth on the basis of spatial contexts and purity issues, having looked at the conflict between "equalitarian" ideology and social stratification reality at such meals, as well as ritual commemoration, and having looked at the interplay between social memory and social morality, we are in a better position to understand Paul's response to the Corinthian banquet factions: remembering the Lord's Supper and keying it to the Lord's traumatic death.

PAUL'S RESPONSE TO THE FACTIONS: KEYING THE BANQUET COMMEMORATION TO THE MEMORY OF "THE LORD'S" TRAUMATIC DEATH

In 1 Cor 11:23–32 Paul responds to the Lord's Supper factions as follows:

> 23 For I received [παρέλαβον] from the Lord what I also handed on [παρέδωκα] to you, that the Lord Jesus on the night when he was handed over [παρεδίδετο] took a loaf of bread, 24 and when he had given thanks [εὐχαριστήσας], he broke it, and said, "This is my body [τὸ σῶμα] that is for you. Do this in remembrance [τὴν ἀνάμνησιν] of me." 25 In the same way he took the cup also, after supper [μετὰ τὸ δειπνῆσαι], saying, "This cup is the new covenant [ἡ καινὴ διαθήκη] in my blood [ἐν τῷ ἐμῷ αἵματε]. Do this, as often as you drink it, in remembrance [τὴν ἀνάμνησιν] of me." 26 For as often as you eat this bread and drink the cup, you proclaim the Lord's death until he comes. 27 Whoever, therefore, eats the bread or drinks the cup of the Lord in an unworthy manner will be answerable for the body and blood [τοῦ σώματος καὶ τοῦ αἵματος] of the Lord. 28 Examine yourselves, and only then eat of the bread and drink of the cup. 29 For all who eat and drink without discerning the body eat and drink judgment against themselves. 30 For this reason many of you are weak and ill, and some have died. 31 But if we judged ourselves, we would not be judged. 32 But when we are judged by the Lord, we are disciplined so that we may not be condemned along with the world. (NRSV, changing "betrayed" to "handed over" in v. 23)

Scholars agree that Paul's information about the commemoration of Jesus' last meal was not from Paul's individual memory. The terms "received" (παρέλαβον) and "delivered" (παρέδωκα) in 11:23 are technical terms for handing on oral tradition (see Pirqe 'Abot 1.1; 1 Cor 15:3b; Jeremias 1966, 101–4), which suggests a "Christian collective memory"

(Keightley 2005; Kelber 2005, 238; 2006; Kirk and Thatcher 2005a, 40; Kirk 2010, 61–62). Yet, Paul says that he received it "from the Lord" (11:23), and Schwartz and Schuman write, "[j]ust as history reflects the values commemoration sustains, commemoration is rooted in historical knowledge" (2005, 185). Did Paul preserve "historical knowledge," a "central tendency," an "objective existence," a "stable essence" from Jesus himself?

Paul was not one of the Twelve and presumably had never even met Jesus. To be sure, he knew and cited a few details about Jesus' life and teachings, but he did not place his emphasis there: "even though we once knew Christ 'according to the flesh' [κατὰ σάρκα], we no longer know him that way" (2 Cor 5:16). What "we" *do* "know"—what "we" *should* remember together—is that the one who was "in the form of God" took "the form of a servant," was "born in the likeness of men," and was crucified, died for "our" sins, was buried, was resurrected, and was exalted to heaven, to save those who believe (Phil 2:6–11; 1 Cor 15:3–5a; Rom 1:3–4). In critical terms, Paul's "stable essence" would seem to be what modern scholars would call a "Christ myth." But is there more?

Paul's major moral solution to the Corinthian divisive factions was to reframe the deviant Corinthian banquet practices by keying the meal to a salient, "primal," emotion-provoking, covenant-forming, traumatic, historical, but idealized, historical event: "Jesus Christ crucified" (1 Cor 1:2; 2:2; see 1:18; Mitchell 2005, 308–9). This event evoked not only the redemptive power of a heroic martyr's death but the trauma of its violence (Hengel 1977). As Alan Kirk says,

> The invoking of an existing cultural script—for example martyrdom—to fix the meaning of, and give narrative coherence to, the specific experience of violence brings us in touch with the central dynamic of social memory: its interpretative "keying" (Schwartz 2000, 225–32) or "analogic mapping" (Malkki 1995, 121) of the experiences of the present with salient events of the past that exist as semantically dense *Erinnerungsfiguren* (Assmann 1992, 52), or "frame images" (Schwartz 1998a [1998]). (Kirk 2005a:194)

In rejecting the late formation of the passion narrative, Chris Keith and Tom Thatcher write, "Violent events, like Jesus' crucifixion, traumatize group memory to such an extent that memorialization is necessary almost immediately, and the development of commemorative narratives is a typical mnemonic strategy for the maintenance of group identity" (2008, 204). Paul lifted up *the* salient event, the violent death of a hero-martyr, as a redemptive act that both replicated yet replaced the atoning significance of sacrifice in the temple (Rom 3:23–25: "'expiation' [ἰλαστήριον] by his blood").

The Lord's Supper banquet is "from the Lord" and is rooted in a historical core that persists: Jesus' traumatic, violent death. "For as often as you eat this bread and drink the cup, you proclaim *the Lord's death* until he comes" (1 Cor 11:26). The section 1 Cor 11:23–32 is full of parenetic language: "unworthy manner" (v. 27), "answerable" (v. 27), "examine" (v. 28), "judgment" (v. 29), "disciplined" (v. 32), and "condemned" (v. 32). But Paul himself wants to say more about the commemoration: it contains "the Lord's" own moral imperative in word and deed, evident in the traditional saying, "Do this in remembrance [ἀνάμνησιν] of me." Dahl put it this way:

> Historians of liturgy belonging to diverse confessions agree in seeing in *anamnēsis*, commemoration, a fundamental theme of, one can justifiably say, *the* fundamental theme of celebration of the Lord's Supper in the early church. The commemoration was not something that took place essentially within individual believers, in the subjective memory. The celebration itself, i.e., thanksgiving, sacrifice, and sacrament (*mystērion*), was a commemoration, an *anamnēsis* of the death and resurrection of Jesus where the history of salvation was re-presented by the sacrament commemoration. (Dahl 1976, 21)

As previously noted, Paul combined memory and morality. He anticipated the ritual act of eating bread together with "body" language (1 Cor 10:16–17) and reminded the Corinthians that they should not abuse the practice, as some Israelites had (10:21). He had anticipated the cup that is passed around with an instructive Sinai covenant ritual that contained the expression "the blood of the covenant" (Exod 24:8; cf. Zech 9:11), spoke of "a sharing in the blood of Christ" (1 Cor 10:16), and followed it with a warning, "You cannot drink the cup of the Lord and the cup of demons" (1 Cor 10:21a). Similarly, in 1 Cor 11 the language "my body for you" (1 Cor 11:24), which shaded off into the *corporate* body (Koester 2005, 348), and the cup that is "the new covenant in my blood" is coupled with warnings. "Whoever, therefore, eats the bread or drinks the cup of the Lord in an unworthy manner will be guilty of profaning the body and blood of the Lord…. For anyone who eats and drinks without discerning *the body* eats and drinks judgment upon himself" (1 Cor 11:27, 29).

In short, divisive factions at Corinth degrade the ritual banquet and do not "build up" the church. They profane what is sacred—the body of

Christ, which is the body social. Indeed, in Paul's view profaning the body has physical consequences: weakness, illness, and death (1 Cor 11:30).

Hal Taussig, referring to libations that were "poured out" and drunk to honor the gods or the emperor's genius at the beginning of the *symposium*, thinks that a circulating cup of wine symbolized the crucifixion of "the Lord" (1 Cor 11:25). In its *pre-Pauline context* it had sociopolitical bonding power, for it was a "meal of resistance to Roman imperial power" (Taussig 2009, 130–35). Was this also true for Paul?

Given the problematic of "hidden transcripts" in ancient texts, this question may not be answerable, yet given Israel's collective memory of the Passover, the question begs answering. To be sure, 1 Cor 11 makes no mention of the Passover meal, and there are good historical arguments that Jesus did not really celebrate a Passover meal (Mark 14:2; John 13:1; 19:31; Did. 10.1; b. Sanh. 43a [Jesus was hanged on the eve of Passover]; see Duling 2003, 530–31, 546–47). However, the non-Passover memory is contested by the Gospel traditions themselves (e.g., Mark 14:10–16). It is also generally accepted that the "new covenant in my blood" language echoes the "new covenant" language of Jer 31:31–34, which clearly draws the contrast with the old Mosaic covenant and the exodus commemorated by Judeans in the Passover/Feast of Unleavened Bread. Paul certainly recalls the Passover at times (1 Cor 5:6–8; 8:1; 10:16; 16:5–8). Thus, whether Jesus historically ate the Passover or not, it may well be that Passover overtones were implicit for Paul's tradition and perhaps Paul's own understanding of the Lord's Supper tradition (see Walters 2012). Whatever the case, the confession that Jesus is "Lord" (1 Cor 12:3; Rom 10:9; Phil 2:11; see also Rom 1:3–4), a title that not only translated "Yahweh" in the Septuagint but also was given to the Roman emperor, could have been a hidden transcript.

As a response to the factions at the Corinthian meal, Paul explicitly appeals to the moral authority of Jesus' command to commemorate the Lord's Supper—"Do this in remembrance of me" (1 Cor 11:24, 25)—and keys the ritual to the memory of Jesus' violent death, apparently hoping that Jesus' words, actions, and death would induce the Corinthians to "correct" their banquet behavior. He hopes that social morality will be induced by social memory. In terms of Mediterranean banquet etiquette, his focus would have countered traditional social bonding and social boundaries based on social stratification, including ethnic/dietary and socioeconomic conflicts, with obligation based on social "equality." As Taussig says, Paul "placed [structurally] marginalized persons together and asked them to learn to relate to one another … [an instruction that] challenged the honor shame codes by enacting in a semipublic space the giving of honor to those considered 'shameful'" (2009, 150). In Paul's view, exhortation to correct practice would hopefully serve his paramount concern to "build up" the "body of Christ" and preserve the purity and unity of the church (Koester 2005, 347–49).

The Synoptic Gospels contest the Pauline Lord's Supper memory by explicitly representing Jesus as celebrating the Passover with his disciples. Also, they portray Judas Iscariot not simply as one who "handed over" Jesus according to God's plan (1 Cor 11:23; see also Rom 8:32–33) but as one who "betrayed" Jesus (Mark 14:17–21 par.; contrast the Gospel of Judas). Moreover, only the Lukan version has a cup "after supper" that is "poured out for you," including the words "the new covenant in my blood" and "do this in remembrance of me" (Luke 22:19b–20). Scholars generally recognize that this "second cup" in the Lukan Gospel is somewhat awkward and that Luke (or a later editor?) has amended his version to conform to a Pauline-type tradition. From the perspective of contrapuntal memory, it is interesting that the two versions are literarily combined, certainly another way to preserve stability and continuity, whether historical or not.

Finally, reflecting on the variations in social memory of the banquet/Lord's Supper leads to the observation that eucharistic divisions have perpetually cropped up in the Western church. They were not only theological but contextual in the sense that they were related to social factors that included social stratification (e.g., Niebuhr 1962). These debates illustrate that fact that commemorative ritual helps to resolve "intractable" problems but is not always up to the task. The different meal rituals in the various Christian denominations, some of which try to (re)establish links with the Passover, illustrate in their own way the multiple social contexts and multiple forms of social memory, as well as an essential core rooted in a historical fact, the crucifixion. Paul's hope for a purity and unity based on the memory of Jesus' traumatic death and the right form of commemoration is a hope not yet fulfilled.

WORKS CITED

Adams, Edward. 2012. Placing the Christian Communal Meal. Pages 22–37 in *Text, Image, and Christians in the Graeco-Roman World. A Festschrift in Honor of David Lee Balch.* Edited by Aliou Cissé Niang and Carolyn Osiek. Eugene, OR: Pickwick.

Aitken, Ellen Brandshaw. 1997. Τὰ δρώμενα καὶ τὰ λεγόμενα: The Eucharistic Memory of Jesus' Words in First Corinthians. *HTR* 90:359–70.

Arzt, Peter. 1994. The Epistolary Introductory Thanksgiving in the Papyri and in Paul. *NovT* 36:29–46.

Assmann, Jan. 1992. *Das kulturelle Gedächtnis: Schrift, Erinnerung und politische Identitiät in frühen Hochkulturen.* 6th ed. Munich: Beck.

Balch, David L. 2008. Rich Pompeian Houses (*domus*), Shops for Rent, and the Large, Multi-story Building (*Insula*) in Herculaneum as Typical Spaces for Pauline House Churches. Pages 42–58 in *Roman Domestic Art and Early House Churches.* Edited by David Balch. WUNT 228. Tübingen: Mohr Siebeck.

Billings, Bradley S. 2011. From House Church to Tenement Church: Domestic Space and the Development of Early Urban Christianity— The Example of Ephesus. *JTS* 62:541–69.

Connerton, Paul. 1989. *How Societies Remember.* Themes in the Social Sciences. Cambridge: Cambridge University Press.

Dahl, Nils Alstrup. 1976. Anamnesis: Memory and Commemoration in Early Christianity. Pages 11–29 in *Jesus in the Memory of the Early Church: Essays.* Minneapolis: Augsburg. [orig. 1946]

DeMaris, Richard E. 2008. *The New Testament in Its Ritual World.* New York: Routledge.

Douglas, Mary. 1966. *Purity and Danger: Analysis of Pollution and Taboo.* New York: Praeger.

———. 1972. Deciphering a Meal. *Daedalus* 101:61–81.

———. 1984. *Food in the Social Order. Studies of Food and Festivities in Three American Communities.* New York: Russell Sage Foundation.

Duling, Dennis C. 2003. *The New Testament. History, Literature, and Social Context.* Belmont, CA: Wadsworth.

———. 2006. Presenting the Issue: Social Memory and Biblical Studies: Theory, Method, and Application. *BTB* 36:2–4.

———. 2011. Memory, Collective Memory, Orality, and the Gospels. *HTS Teologiese Studies/Theological Studies* 67:103–13.

———. 2012. *A Marginal Scribe: Studies of the Gospel of Matthew in Social-Scientific Perspective.* Matrix 7. Eugene, OR: Wipf & Stock.

Elliott, John H. 2002. Jesus Was Not an Egalitarian. A Critique of an Anachronistic and Idealist Theory. *BTB* 32.2:75–91.

———. 2003. The Jesus Movement Was Not Egalitarian but Family-Oriented. *BibInt* 11.2:1–38.

Friesen, Stephen J. 2004. Poverty in Pauline Studies: Beyond the So-Called New Consensus. *JSNT* 26:323–61.

Goldberg, G. J. 2012. Passover: An Assemblage of All Occurrences of Passover Descriptions in the Works of Josephus. *Thematic Concordance to the Works of Josephus.* Online: http://www.josephus.org/Passover .htm.

Hengel, Martin. 1977. *Crucifixion in the Ancient World and The Folly of the Message of the Cross.* Translated by John Bowden. Philadelphia: Fortress.

Horrell, David G. 2004. Domestic Space and Christian Meetings at Corinth: Imagining New Contexts and the Buildings East of the Theatre. *NTS* 150:349–69.

Jeremias, Joachim. 1966. *The Eucharistic Words of Jesus.* New Testament Library. London: SCM.

Jewett, Robert. 1993. Tenement Churches and Community Meals in the Early Church: The Implications of a Form Critical Analysis of 2 Thessalonians 4:10. *BR* 38:23–43.

Jongkind, Dirk. 2001. Corinth in the First Century AD: The Search for Another Class. *TynB* 52:139–48.

Keightley, Georgia Masters. 2005. Christian Collective Memory and Paul's Knowledge of Jesus. Pages 129–50 in Kirk and Thatcher 2005b.

Keith, Chris, and Tom Thatcher. 2008. The Scar of the Cross: The Violence Ratio and the Earliest Christian Memories of Jesus. Pages 197–214 in *Jesus, the Voice, and the Text: Beyond The Oral and the Written Gospel.* Edited by Tom Thatcher. Waco, Tex.: Baylor University Press.

Kelber, Werner H. 2005. The Works of Memory: Christian Origins as Mnemo-History—A Response. Pages 221–48 in Kirk and Thatcher 2005b.

———. 2006. The Generative Force of Memory: Early Christian Traditions as Processes of Remembering. *BTB* 36.1:15–22.

Kirk, Alan. 2005a. The Memory of Violence and the Death of Jesus in Q. Pages 191–206 in Kirk and Thatcher 2005b.

———. 2005b. Social and Cultural Memory. Pages 1–24 in Kirk and Thatcher 2005b.

———. 2010. Memory Theory: Cultural and Cognitive Approaches to the Gospel Tradition. Pages 57–67 in *Understanding the Social World of the New Testament.* Edited by Dietmar Neufeld and Richard E. DeMaris. New York: Routledge.

Kirk, Alan, and Tom Thatcher. 2005a. Jesus Tradition as Social Memory.

Pages 25–42 in Kirk and Thatcher 2005b.

———, eds. 2005b. *Memory, Tradition, and Text: Uses of the Past in Early Christianity*. SemeiaSt 52. Atlanta: Society of Biblical Literature.

Klauck, Hans-Josef. 1981. *Hausgemeinde und Hauskirche in frühen Christendom*. SBS 103. Stuttgart: Katholisches Bibelwerk.

Klinghardt, Matthias. 1996. *Gemeinschaftsmahl und Mahlgemeinschaft: Soziologie und Liturgie Frühchristlicher Mahlfeiern*. Tübingen: Francke.

Koester, Helmut. 2005. The Silence of the Apostle. Pages 339–49 in *Urban Religion in Roman Corinth*. Edited by Daniel N. Schowalter and Steven J. Friesen. Cambridge: Harvard University Press.

Lampe, Peter. 1991. The Roman Christians of Romans 16. Pp. 216–30 in *The Romans Debate*. Rev. ed. Edited by Karl P. Donfried. Peabody, MA: Hendrickson.

Lowenthal, David. 1985. *The Past Is a Foreign Country*. Cambridge: Cambridge University Press.

Malina, Bruce J., and John J. Pilch. 2006. *Social-Science Commentary on the Letters of Paul*. Minneapolis: Fortress.

Malkki, Liisa H. 1995. *Purity and Exile: Violence, Memory, and National Cosmology among Hutu Refugees in Tanzania*. Chicago: University of Chicago Press.

Meeks, Wayne A. 1982. "And Rose Up to Play": Midrash and Paraenesis in 1 Corinthians 10:1–22. *JSNT* 16:64–78.

———. 1983. *The First Urban Christians. The Social World of the Apostle Paul*. New Haven: Yale University Press.

———. 1986. *The Moral World of the First Christians*. Philadelphia: Westminster.

Meggitt, Justin J. 1998. *Paul, Poverty, and Survival*. Studies of the New Testament and Its World. Edinburgh: T&T Clark.

Mitchell, Margaret. 2005. Paul's Letters to Corinth: The Interpretative Intertwining of Literary and Historical Reconstruction. Pages 307–38 in *Urban Religion in Roman Corinth*. Edited by Daniel N. Schowalter and Steven J. Friesen. Cambridge: Harvard University Press.

Murphy O'Connor, Jerome. 1983. *St. Paul's Corinth. Texts and Archaeology*. Good News Studies 6. Wilmington, DE: Glazier.

———. 2004. House Churches and the Eucharist. Pages 129–38 in *Christianity at Corinth: The Quest for the Pauline Church*. Edited by Edward Adams and David G. Horrell. Louisville: Westminster John Knox.

———. 2009. *Keys to First Corinthians. Revisiting the Major Issues*. Oxford: Oxford University Press.

Niebuhr, H. Richard. 1962. *The Social Sources of Denominationalism*. 2nd ed. New York: Holt.

Oakes, Peter. 2009a. Contours of the Urban Environment. Pages 21–35 in *After the First Urban Christians. The Social-Scientific Study of Pauline Christianity Twenty-Five Years Later*. Edited by Todd D. Still and David G. Horrell. 2009. New York: T&T Clark.

———. 2009b. *Reading Romans in Pompeii*. Minneapolis: Fortress.

———. 2010. Urban Structure and Patronage. Christ Followers in Corinth. Pages 178–91 in *Understanding the Social World of the New Testament*. Edited by Dietmar Neufeld and Richard E. DeMaris. New York: Routledge.

O'Brien, Peter T. 1974. Thanksgiving and the Gospel in Paul. *NTS* 21:144–55.

Ricoeur, Paul. 2004. *Memory, History, Forgetting*. Translated by Kathleen Blamey and David Pellauer. Chicago: University of Chicago Press.

Romano, David Gilman. 2005. Urban and Rural Planning in Roman Corinth. Pages 25–59 in *Urban Religion in Roman Corinth*. Edited by Daniel N. Schowalter and Steven J. Friesen. Cambridge: Harvard University Press.

Schowalter, Daniel N. 2010. Seeking Shelter in Roman Corinth: Archaeology and the Placement of Paul's Communities. Pages 327–41 in *Corinth in Context: Comparative Studies on Religion and Society*. Edited by Steven Friesen, Dan Schowalter, and James Walters. NovTSup 134. Leiden: Brill.

Schudson, Michael. 1989. The Present in the Past versus the Past in the Present. *Communication* 11:105–13.

Schwartz, Barry. 1982. The Social Context of Commemoration: A Study in Collective Memory. *Social Forces* 62:374–402.

———. 1991a. Iconography and Collective Memory: Lincoln's Image in the American Mind. *The Sociological Quarterly* 32:301–19.

———. 1991b. Social Change and Collective Memory: The Democratization of George Washington. *American Sociological Review* 56:221–26.

———. 1998. Frame Image: Toward a Semiotics of Collective Memory. *Semiotica* 121:1–38.

———. 2000. *Abraham Lincoln and the Forge of American Memory*. Chicago: University of Chicago Press.

Schwartz, Barry, and Howard Schuman. 2005. History, Commemoration, and Belief: Abraham Lincoln in American Memory, 1945–2001. *American Sociological Review* 70:183–203.

Smith, Dennis E. 2003. *From Symposium to Eucharist. The Banquet in the Early Christian World*. Minneapolis: Fortress.

———. 2012. The House Church as Social Environment. Pages 3–21 in *Text, Image, and Christians in the Graeco-Roman World: A Festschrift in Honor of David Lee Balch*. Edited by Aliou Cissé Niang and Carolyn Osiek. Eugene, OR: Pickwick.

Taussig, Hal. 2009. *In the Beginning Was the Meal: Social Experimentation and Early Christian Identity*. Minneapolis: Fortress.

Thatcher, Tom. 2008. Beyond Texts and Traditions: Werner Kelber's Media History of Christian Origins. Pages 1–26 in *Jesus, the Voice, and the Text: Beyond* The Oral and the Written Gospel. Edited by Tom Thatcher. Waco, TX: Baylor University Press.

Theissen, Gerd. 1982a. Social Integration and Sacramental Activity: An Analysis of 1 Cor. 11:17–34. Pages 145–74 in *The Social Setting of Pauline Christianity*. Edited and translated by John H. Schütz. Philadelphia: Fortress.

———. 1982b. The Strong and the Weak in Corinth: A Sociological Analysis of a Theological Quarrel. Pages 121–43 in *The Social Setting of Pauline Christianity*. Edited and translated by John H. Schütz. Philadelphia: Fortress.

———. 2001. The Social Structure of Pauline Communities: Some Critical Remarks on J. J. Meggitt, *Paul, Poverty, and Survival*. *JSNT* 84:65–84.

Verhey, Allan. 1992. Remember, Remembrance. *ABD* 5:667–69.

Wallace-Hadrill, Andrew. 1994. *Houses and Society in Pompeii and Herculaneum*. Princeton: Princeton University Press.

———. 2003. *Domus* and *Insulae* in Rome: Families and Housefuls. Pages 3–18 in *Early Christian Families in Context: An Interdisciplinary Dialogue*. Edited by David L. Balch and Carolyn Osiek. Grand Rapids: Eerdmans.

PART 3
REFLECTIONS ON A COMING CONVERSATION

HARVEST

Barry Schwartz

Memory's fallibility is well documented; its powers, less so. Acknowledging the evidential traces that all significant events leave behind, the preceding essays in this volume make memory's credibility more evident. How ironic it is that so much ink has been spilled on social memory's incidental functions—the forgetting or ignoring of wrongdoing, legitimating and challenging power, exaggerating and underestimating beneficent acts, giving voice to the marginalized—while its major function, to bring us into more direct contact with the past, the very capacity that gives memory its survival value, has led to nothing significant in the way of theoretical explication. Social memory's contribution to humanity's survival is not its malleability; memory enhances our ability to survive because it permits us to retain and retrieve so much of the past. Memory does not and cannot work perfectly, but if it does not work well enough for the practical purposes that make Homo sapiens unique, then human *society* becomes impossible.

In this chapter I say nothing about the substance of the preceding essays in this volume but read them solely for the light they throw on ancient and first-century memory, as well as twenty-first-century social memory theory. My discussion will follow the sequence of the earlier chapters, beginning with the essays on the Old Testament.

I

The properties of narrative provide the basis of Carol Newsom's "Selective Recall and Ghost Memories." Narrative distills meaning from chronology; it also filters irrelevant information as it organizes what is pertinent. But the reader must be warned that "narrative" is a loaded concept because reality's leavings affect different authors differently. The early Hayden White (1987), for example, captured many intellectual hearts by declaring that the reality behind a narrative and the narrative itself are identical. But what are we to make of "ghost narratives," which are meaningless unless certain realities are assumed?

Psalms 105 and 106, Newsom shows, transmit contrasting messages: the former a story of God's protection; the latter of the people's sins against him. For Newsom, the juxtapositioning of these psalms clarifies the nature of the master narrative: "it is not a single, fixed story but a set of cultural memories that offers both constraint and the possibility to tell and retell the tale in an inexhaustible variety of ways" (pp. 45–46). By "inexhaustible," Newsom refers not to an inexhaustible number of themes but to inexhaustible variations on a theme. Or so it seems. As linguist Ferdinand de Saussure (1986) might put it, the master narrative is roughly analogous to *langue* (language); its variations, to *parole* (speech), such that different versions of the narrative transmit the same underlying story in different ways—just as an infinite variety of sentences may be assembled within the same language. If Newsom's master narrative (an analog of Kroeber's [1957] concept of *basic pattern*) is actually plural, composed of memories that combine into an infinite variety of stories, then one must wonder about the stable *langue* or "basic pattern" beneath this variation.

Newsom's topic concerns the role of "ghost memories" in the story of Nebuchadnezzar. The controversial Babylonian king Nabonidus in this regard figures into multiple narratives without being mentioned in any one of them. The practice is universal among fiction writers who immortalize enemies, friends, acquaintances, family members, and themselves in their novels, plays, and stories. Political orators, too, introduce historical persons who cannot be expressly identified but are clearly stand-ins for unmentionable contemporaries. How these "ghost memories" work, how they articulate the story of Nabonidus through that of Nebuchadnezzar, is problematic, yet what people believe they contain is expressed in the social memory. Why some historical characters can only be remembered when disguised in the form of another is the problem.

In making her argument, Newsom draws on Aleida Assmann's conviction that "stored" (archived) memory lacks meaning until removed and structured by the genius of the investigator. This is necessarily true. An unread document differs from a document already read and interpreted. But many unread documents must be partially meaningful, for many are eager to learn what they contain. Did the significance of the captured Nazi archives depend on the reader's constructive act? Are archives not revelatory as well as constructed? And what if different investigators construct different meanings from the same document? Are we then faced with multiple truths, unreliability, or a rank order of validity? If Ezekiel, in this regard, deliberately invented an alternative history, as Newsom believes, would "his deliberate distortion" not cause his own audience to at least hesitate before accepting it?

Although Newsom asks why Ezekiel's history differed markedly from Israel's master narrative, she never defines the latter's content, which may or may not be related to her belief in plural master narratives. Instead, she draws on Collingswood's dictum that "every present has a past of its own," with Ezekiel invoking both the former and the latter in order to make sense of both.

Newsom's main point concerns selective recall and deployment of Nebuchadnezzar as a screen on which memories of Nabonidus's reign are projected. As to Nebuchadnezzar's destruction of the First Temple: whether a foreign conqueror saves or destroys the temple is less important than his personifying and realizing God's will in doing so. Such is the mnemonic jujitsu Newsom discerns. Her chapter, too fascinating for words, gives us plenty to brood over.

II

"Old Memories, New Identities" shifts focus from ghost memories to "postmemories." Tim Langille begins with the discovery of the Damascus Document and Pesher Habakkuk, produced within the Qumran community sometime between the end of the first century BCE and the early decades of the first century CE. His argument, in barest outline, is that the First Temple's destruction and the subsequent exile left a strain of mourning that endured into and beyond the Second Temple period. The First Temple fell because of its iniquity and corruption. Qumran rejectionists considered the Kittim's (Romans') control over Jerusalem a reenactment of the Chaldeans' conquest half a millennium earlier. Only in a desert diaspora could an elect properly interpret the Scriptures and distinguish their peers from spiritual traitors. Once accomplished, the virtuous could return to cleanse a polluted Jerusalem and its temple and prepare the people for the end of days. The preexilic community and identity could then be found and restored.

Traumatic memories, according to Langille's informant, Marianne Hirsch, endure the longest and affect identity most powerfully because they mutate into "postmemories," which include the memory of traumas that precede the birth of an individual but are "transmitted so deeply as to seem to constitute memories in their own right." Because this statement is generally true, I take the liberty of offering a variation on the rule of parsimony: concepts must not be multiplied beyond necessity. Hirsch's concept of postmemory refers to no more than what people *know* about the past, what they *believe* and *feel* about it, how they *judge* it morally, and how closely they *identify* with it. To revisit my comments in the introduction to this volume, to a large degree what Hirsch says of postmemories is true of any past event, whether it occurred during or before the lifetime of the individual who thinks about it. Because the vividness with which such a "remembered" event is variable, instances of traumatic memory are cases of memory in general.

The point is worth stressing. "Social memory" refers not to the direct experiences that individuals store in their brains but how they think, feel about, and judge the knowledge they acquire—which means that *memory* is a metaphor, a way of thinking about complex, collective facts by reference to a familiar, individual faculty. To dismiss social memory as no more than a metaphor, however, does not tell us what social memory is, what it does, and how it relates to individual memory. Hirsch's concept of postmemory is not only metaphorical but also performs less work than the present volume's definition of social memory. As far as her idea of social memory's *sources* is concerned, no one denies that "imagination," "projection," and "creation" affect what we know, but memories are also established by their objects' reality.

That preexilic remorse remained after the rebuilding of the temple is an idea worth clarification. "New collective identities," Langille observes, "emerge out of ruptures or cultural crises..., more specifically through memories and *representations of ruptures or cultural crises*" (p. 62, emphasis added). I do not infer from this pivotal statement, nor do I think the author expects any reader to infer, that collective identities resulting from critical events are independent of the properties of the events themselves.

Langille does the reader a favor by attending to the relation between traumatic and originating events. Many writers have discussed the importance of founding eras because they powerfully affect all events that follow. Yet these founding eras need not necessarily entail trauma. The (1949) Basic Law in Germany, with its overwhelming emphasis on human rights, is commemorated annually, as is the case in many of the new states emerging from colonialism. In contrast, the assertion of another Langille informant, Bruno Latour, in whose view "pure beginnings and original unity are illusory," must be put in context. The context is Latour himself. He finds everything illusory, including the scientific practices he and Steve Woolgar (1974) "unmasked" in the Salk Laboratory. That such practices earned

Roger Guillemin a Nobel Prize in Medicine is simply part of a process to be "demystified." Accordingly, if Latour means by "pure beginnings" that all events have precedents and consequences, he is right; however, originating events, as understood by Mircea Eliade (1961), Edward Shils (1981), and Plato (Tudor 1972), refer to real turning points—the dismantling of existing laws and social structures and the creation of new ones.

Langille's argument raises another fascinating question, one that involves a kind of "latency period" between an event and its memory. He declares that traumas are remembered across generations and reshaped *after a long passage of time*. But is there always a waiting period for post-trauma damage assessments to be made? Such are the social memory issues raised by this ambitious and well-wrought essay.

III

Tim Langille's "Old Memories, New Identities" and Gabrielle Gelardini's "Cult's Death in Scripture" overlap partially in their pursuit of responsibility for the Second Temple's destruction. Appearing in proximity to 70 CE, Mark's Gospel tells of Jesus' predicting the Second Temple's fall, with the moral decline of the people and their leaders prompting Jesus' prophecy. Josephus, writing at about the same time, offers a different account, one that attributes responsibility for the temple's fall to the Jewish Zealots. Gelardini makes a direct comparison of Josephus and Mark, then assesses the differences between them.

When one compares Mark and Josephus in terms of "entrepreneurship," the capacity to sell one version of history over another, the winner must be Josephus. Three elements, according to Gary Fine (1996), determine one's ability to establish favored claims about historical events and persons: the claimant must be highly motivated and find it to be in her interest to attribute a certain reputation to another; she must know how to do so; finally, she must occupy a position in the social structure that makes her opinions matter beyond her inner circle of friends and acquaintances. Applied to the case at hand, Josephus was motivated to give a biased, pro-Roman view of the Jewish War—he was, after all, an officer in charge of the defense of the Galilee when Roman arms overran his unit. It is well known that Josephus saved himself after inducing his men to commit suicide. Turning himself over to the Romans, he became one of their most effective agents. He condemned the Jews for initiating hostilities against one another, against his Roman patrons, and for defiling the temple by

turning it into a military camp, thereby depriving God of his due obse-
quies and sacrifices. Josephus made no secret that he favored the Romans.
In Rome's service, Josephus the priest conducted himself shamelessly: the
Jewish God, he claimed openly, made the Roman army a holy instrument
to purify the temple and rid it of troublemakers.

Given this information, one must wonder how far Josephus must have
distorted the story of the fall of Jerusalem and the sacking of its temple. Yet,
he was an eyewitness, and a good historian can distinguish the truth of his
narrative from the biases that accompany it. Moreover, Josephus's accounts
did not depend solely on his own dispositions. He interviewed Jewish
deserters and consulted later the commentaries of Vespasian and Titus.
He was himself an expert in biblical texts and their interpretation. What
we have here is an eyewitness aware of the war's every aspect and able to
convert his observations into written testimony. Besides being motivated
and well-informed, Josephus's testimony was affirmed by the power of the
Roman Empire. Whoever mattered in Roman Judea read Josephus's version of events, or at least would affirm his version if they did.

In contrast, Mark offers no eyewitness testimony; rather, he interprets
the temple's fall by keying it to Jesus' prophecy. Granting Gelardini's premise
that temple and prophecy are somehow correlated in Mark's presentation,
I would restate her proposal by reversing the variables: Jesus' words could
not be keyed to the Jewish War simply because Jesus was dead while the war
was being fought; it was the War that was keyed to Jesus' prophecy, "Not
one stone shall stand upon another." But a key point is that Mark wrote his
Gospel between the mid 60s and early 70s, which means that the years of
Jewish-Roman fighting would be its context. *If* Mark wrote his Gospel, as
tradition and some modern scholars would suggest, *before* the War, then his
account of Jesus' prophecy gains so much the more force. Whether Mark's
Gospel preceded, accompanied, or followed the temple's destruction, however, he would have found its meaning in Jesus' words.

More directly to the theme of history and memory is Mark's use of
keying, which I wish to supplement with a few references to its counterpart, framing. Once historical situations and persons are "keyed into," they
become frames in terms of which current events are interpreted. For Christians in general, Jesus had become a point of normative reference, a frame
infusing meaning into their every significant act. In my introductory essay I
noted that the concept of "typology" is limited to biblical studies, while the
twin concepts of keying and framing apply more broadly. In this regard, it
is worth noting the difference between keying U.S. President John F. Ken-

nedy's assassination and funeral to those of Abraham Lincoln, on the one hand (with the latter simultaneously framing the former) and, on the other hand, the keying of the temple's fall to Jesus' words. The difference is that, at least in Mark's memory, Jesus' words seal the temple's fate, while no causal connection of any kind is attributed to the Lincoln-Kennedy parallel. The latter connection is purely semiotic, showing social memory to be less a force that makes things happen than a scaffold that shapes the meaning of events.

IV

As Langille's and Gelardini's chapters concern the causes of the Second Temple's fall, Steven Fraade's "Memory and Loss in Early Rabbinic Text and Ritual" concerns the adaptation of Jewish institutions to the temple's destruction. As soon as Fraade's topic became apparent to me, I expected to see a reference to "trauma and memory." No one has stated the premise of trauma research better than Jeffrey Alexander (2004). Trauma, he tells us, is a way of seeing things. It involves a sense of shock and fear, but "it is the meanings that provide the sense of shock and fear, not the events in themselves." Unfortunately, Alexander never gets around to asking whether these meanings have anything to do with traumatic *reality*. If meanings were in fact independent of reality, if reality were dependent on the meanings attributed to it, then we would live in a world in which one person's account of any situation is no better than anyone else's—an anarchical world in which nothing decisive can be said about anything.

Fraade fortunately has little in common with his constructionist Yale colleague. He believes that the Jewish people mourned the loss of the temple, deemed it traumatic because the holy place was pillaged, desecrated, and demolished. His question, however, is pivotal: What do we do when the object to be remembered is loss itself? The question is fascinating but unanswerable. One cannot remember a "loss," only a loss of *something*, and that lost something must be adapted to. How memory and commemoration facilitate or, more precisely, constitute adaptation is Fraade's actual issue. He discovered its irony: the destruction and loss of the temple caused it to play a stronger and more central role in Jewish culture. How so? Mundane commemoration made the temple's memory a conspicuous part of everyday life. The altering of familiar objects—allowing part of the ceiling of a house to remain unplastered in order to bring to mind the temple whenever one looked up, setting aside some food before beginning a meal, or removing part of a personal ornament as signs of reverence for the temple—by self-deprivation or omission the temple can be mourned properly while life goes on.

In addition, new beliefs about God's preferences emerged, especially that God is pleased more by prayer and Torah study than by the sacrifice of animals, which had been a major temple practice. Novel conceptions of proper worship are readily traced to Rabban Yohanan ben Zakkai, leader of the Jewish recovery movement. He energetically formulated scores of new rules to get around the temple's loss, rules that God favored. Nevertheless, the fate of Jerusalem and the temple left him personally adrift in a sea of deep and ceaseless mourning. Such is the nature of posttemple remembrance: sentiments of despair accompanied by the covenant's preservation through new practices relating the faithful to God.

To dismiss ben Zakkai's revisions as "rationalizations," "expedients," or "inventions" would be indolent, for such discrediting concepts are silent about *why* certain practices were selected and established and *how* they transformed Judaism. The transition from a temple-based Judaism to a Judaism based on decentralized synagogues required inestimable zeal and was the core of a literal cultural revolution. But Fraade is right to say that Jewish memory expresses continuity and rupture alike, although neither is ever complete. The radically new always contains within it a residue of the old order and the basis of its own replacement.

Fraade's essay provides a perfect transition from the Old Testament chapters in the present volume to those focused on early Christianity. Yohanan ben Zakkai was, after all, the youngest of the students of Hillel, one of Judea's most revered first-century holy men. Tension between the liberal, relatively open-minded house of Hillel and the dogmatic rigidity of the house of Shammai was the fundamental schism within Judaism during Jesus' lifetime. That Jesus was unaware of this division, did not knowingly identify with Hillel, is improbable. The opposite must be said for the Sanhedrin, which condemned Jesus. Its majority, although no longer represented by Shammai himself, contained his followers. To propose that Jesus identified with Judaism through his attachment to the Hillel tradition is a reasonable speculation.

V

Alan Kirk's theoretical statement on "The Memory–Tradition Nexus in the Synoptic Tradition" is relevant to the role of memory in all traditions. He is concerned to know where, and precisely how, memory and tradition intersect—a problem stemming from the scholarly tendency to analyze memory and tradition separately or, at best, to define tradition as a product of memory. Kirk's first step is to see what seven prominent biblical scholars— Richard Bauckham, Robert McIver, Alexander Wedderburn, Dale Allison, Samuel Byrskog, James Dunn, and Markus Bockmuehl—have to say about the problem. He finds them all instructive but deficient. All recognize the relation between memory and tradition to be problematic, but none can properly state, let alone explain, this relationship.

Kirk defines "tradition" as "an aggregate of cultural genres publicly cultivated in various media and apt to follow its own autonomous, often highly kinetic course of development" (p. 145). Comprising information and practices transmitted from the past, tradition is a manifestation of memory and always realized in one medium or another. Memory, on the other hand, "amounts to the abstraction of salient elements and patterns of meaning from the flux of experience and the configuration of these elements and patterns in mnemonically efficient, symbolically concentrated memory scripts that are mediated in various genres and schemas" (p. 151). Memory is not a vessel of *passive* recall but an active *faculty* that organizes experience into irreducible "engrams," which reorganize themselves into representations based on culture-specific schemata, cognitive frames enabling one to condense complicated events into a meaningfully simple representation.

Kirk gives us much to consider and admire; however, some of his assertions cover too much ground. First, consider a distinction that Kirk ignores. Some agents, like chroniclers, archivists, students preparing for a test, or machine operators memorizing complicated instructions, are not abstracting "salient elements and patterns of meaning"; they are concerned to memorize exactly. They are motivated tacticians, in contrast to cognitive misers who are content merely to remember a sequence of selected highpoints (Fiske and Taylor 1991). Thus, to say that memory is articulated in "culturally preformed genres and narrative scripts" (Kirk, p. 147) may be true, but some genres and scripts are based on more detailed and accurate information than others.

Personal memories, as Kirk correctly puts it, are shaped and processed into reminiscences—elementary units of oral traditions that rapidly stabilize before being transmitted. That which is transmitted is, to repeat, embedded in schematic forms. That these forms are preexisting, Kirk seems to be saying, makes them traditional.

The relation between memory and tradition is so vitally important that I would like to try to contribute to Kirk's conception. In this regard, something can be gained from Edward Shils's magisterial *Tradition* (1981). Tradition is any thing or way of doing things handed down from one generation to another; this includes books, images of people and events, machines, tools, monuments, instructional manuals, bank management practices, military strategies and tactics, regimental flags, and so on. In every case that which is handed down is something that existed before recipients used or even contemplated it. As a beneficiary of tradition, the individual inherits this thing; he does not invent it from scratch.

Every tradition, moreover, has custodians and exemplars. "As a temporal chain," Shils says, "a tradition is a sequence of variations on received and transmitted themes." Synonyms of "theme" include "basic pattern," "master narrative," "*langue*," and "schema." Shils calls these sequences "traditional" because observers find their essential elements to be recognizable and approximately similar in successive generations. The George Washington that we find in a biography written in 1800, for example, is easily recognizable in a book published in 2000, for expert custodians prevent the Washington biography from being unduly modified. Here we face a paradox: traditions are collective representations, but only individuals can protect and/or modify them. When traditions evolve, it is because their adherents wish to know more about them—make them more rational, truer, richer, broader. Or these same custodians may find other beliefs and practices more acceptable, causing the old tradition to diminish or even vanish. On the one hand, if "scripts" and "schemata" are *latent* concepts, meaningful to theoreticians but unknown to everyone else, including those who lived before the concepts were formulated, who are their custodians? The question is awkward because these twentieth- and twenty-first-century concepts are observers' tools, not subjects' self-conscious strategies of remembrance. On the other hand, memories are evanescent if there is no one to interpret them before transmitting them to a new generation. The schemata that guide these interpretations, however, are not consciously realized or deliberately transmitted *as tradition*; they are inferred from the interpretations themselves.

This is the issue I submit for discussion: Is tradition the source of social memory, as Kirk concludes? Is memory the source of tradition? Are they constituents of one another? Or are tradition and memory independent? I may define my own standpoint: without tradition, memories and their schematic infrastructure are isolated and meaningless; without memory, tradition lacks the content from which cultural scripts and schemata are apprehended in the first place.

VI

Although Chris Keith's "Prolegomena on the Textualization of Mark's Gospel" concerns itself with the First Evangelist's chosen medium, writing, it touches on the themes laid down by Kirk. Keith's question is why Mark abandoned an oral tradition in favor of converting his knowledge into a written Gospel and what were the consequences of his doing so.

The massive effects of writing and print cannot be ignored. As Keith puts it, "Writing opens cultural texts to a virtually limitless history of reception" (p. 176). But he is alive to the fact that the written tradition never replaced the oral but rather superimposed itself upon it. Given this premise, Keith takes on Werner Kelber. He starts with the observation that Kelber privileged the oral aspects of Mark's written Gospel. Kelber himself sees the written and oral traditions to be utterly different means of communication, the former permanent and fixed, the latter performative and, therefore, impermanent. Keith, too, recognizes the difference between the written and the spoken word, but he believes that Kelber overstates it.

Since the early 1980s, biblical scholars have placed new emphasis on the role of memory in the recording of historical events, but they have not satisfactorily described the relation between memory, literacy, and orality. As an instrument of cultural as opposed to communicative memory, Mark's text forms "the cement or connective backbone of a society that ensures its identity and coherence through the sequence of generations" (p. 171, quoting J. Assmann 2006, 78). Oral societies, by contrast, cannot survive their own origin. When a founding generation passes away, the only way its religious narrative can survive is for someone to record it in writing. Societies in which writing is unknown thus face a *Traditionsbruch*. Such is Jan Assmann's claim, which Keith deems inconclusive but nonetheless pivotal.

Keith lets Assmann off too easily, for one may ask whether any Middle Eastern society in the first century lacked a literate elite that recorded information about itself and its people. This is not to deny the existence of a *Tradition Krise* that directs the living generation's attention to the dying. For instance, the complete disappearance of America's founding leaders by 1830 was noted by many Americans, including intellectuals who condemned the mediocre obsession with commerce that had followed the heroic years of the Revolution. In the late twentieth century, the erection of the World War II and Korean War memorials in Washington, DC, was accelerated to allow surviving veterans to visit them. Indirectly related to Jan Assmann's claim, however, is Steven Fraade's suggestion that the Jewish community that survived the Second Temple's fall was no more nor less literate than the communities existing while the temple was intact. Jews maintained themselves not by the sudden diffusion of the written word but by the adopting of a decentralized synagogue system.

Assmann's notion of the *zerdehnte Situation*, in the current jargon, is "reified." Every generation produces variations—some slight, some significant—on the narratives it inherits, whether written or oral. Our present generation, which has perfected the mechanics of suspicion, goes even further by dissecting that pattern in order to "unmask" the hidden interests and ideological sources associated with it. As far as *la longue durée* is concerned, one need only read Gary Taylor's (1989) account of Shakespeare across generations or Jaroslav Pelikan's *Jesus through the Centuries* (1985). The text as such may be fixed, but its interpretation is not; however, that interpretation is itself restrained by the text's credibility. A statement's credibility, on the other hand, is not typically determined by its medium.

Nevertheless, Keith tells us that Mark's contemporaries expressly asked him to set down the Savior's life in writing so as to perpetuate it. Why Mark submitted to their pleadings is beside the point of the significance of his doing so. The transition from oral to written medium was not inevitable: before one writes, one must decide to write, and Mark deliberated in the context of the pressures and currents of the day—which were certainly more numerous than the *Traditionsbruch* theory asserts. As to the *Traditionsbruch* itself, which in Keith's opinion could have been activated by any number of pressures and currents, it is difficult to understand why it drew Mark to a written medium. True, the crucifixion, destruction of the temple, and persecution of Christians in Rome and elsewhere were all part of the world in which Mark wrote, but context must not be mistaken for cause. More convincing is Keith's last conclusion, that writing constituted a new source of power and of personal and collective identity. And who can doubt his conclusion that Mark's setting down Jesus' life in permanent script set in motion a Christian cultural revolution, one that appeared in many ways, including the eruption of a literature that was to surround the Gospels from the first to the twenty-first century?

VII

Jeffrey Brickle's "The Memory of the Beloved Disciple" challenges the conventional view that John's is an outlier Gospel based on idiosyncratic traditions. Living under conditions similar to those of the earlier Evangelists, John recognized the lengthening time gap separating the life of Jesus from the faithful of his own time, the death of most participants in Jesus' ministry, Rome's annihilation of many of the material symbols of Judaism, the failure of Jesus' apocalyptic prophecy, continuation of the conflict between Jews and Christians, competition among Christian communities for hegemony, and pressure to find an authoritative doctrine to unify the growing and rapidly diversifying Christian population. John's response to these conditions was unconventional, but he never alienated himself from the Tanak (Hebrew Bible), let alone the first three Gospels; rather, he deployed these as frames within which to interpret Jesus' ministry. The "foreknowledge" afforded by these writings resulted from John's keying his present predicament to antiquity. Brickle can therefore compare the Fourth Gospel to a symphony in which Jewish Scripture is harmony to John's new melody. "The interchange between the narrative and the keyed frames below the text resonated with the rich counterpoint and generated a profoundly creative tension" (p. 197). Simply put, John's Jesus personifies the whole of the Old Testament.

John's Gospel starts out with a bang: "In the beginning was the Word," which reflects a new conception of the creation of the universe that Jesus *as God* superintends. Having made this claim, John is compelled to compare his narrative to those of Mark, Matthew, and Luke. Instead of challenging them, he retains their *underlying* themes, to which his Book of Signs, Book of Glory, and Epilogue conform.

To my mind, the most salient part of the Book of Glory and Epilogue is John's handling of the delayed parousia, which constituted a critical challenge to those who took for granted Jesus' prophecy of an imminent apocalypse. Brickle's is the only chapter in the present volume to address this crisis, a crisis of belief and faith. In my view, the greatest crisis of the first century was not the imminent death of eyewitnesses to Jesus' life and death, the destruction of the temple, or Nero's massacres; it was the failure of Jesus' prophecy of a coming kingdom of God. That such a colossal event failed to occur must have had the deepest and most painful effect on his followers. Far from trying to explain away the failure of prophecy, Mark emphasizes Jesus' declaration of its imminence. With or without a written tradition, he must have known that failure of the expected apocalypse to materialize would be central to Christian consciousness. Moreover, even when we limit our attention to changes within the Christian culture of writing, we find a regular decline from Mark to John in references to an impending end of days. Based on a prophecy that failed, this crisis of belief tormented late first-century Christianity, and writing in itself did nothing to comfort the faithful.

In place of the prepassion eschatological discourse of the Synoptics, John emphasizes the saturation of the present with Jesus' spirit. Present and future are collapsed, "so that believers in Jesus are able to experience end-time blessings already in the here and now" (p. 199, quoting Kösten-berger 2009, 297). John thus reinforces his claim that Jesus' teachings, death, and resurrection constitute only the first stage in God's coming king-dom. To overestimate what this discovery meant to the Christian world is impossible. Brickle's last paragraph begins with the observation that John's Gospel is sometimes dismissed as an illegitimate stepchild of the Synoptic tradition; he then reiterates John's strong attachment to and knowledge of history, which raises an important point. One must acknowledge that John deviates from his three predecessors in significant ways, but if the Fourth Gospel derived exclusively from the recesses of John's imagination, no one would understand what he was saying—perhaps not even recognize it to be an authentic story about Jesus. Indeed, no one's mind is so free that one can construe a story unprecedented in all detail. Here is one of the reasons why the grip of the past is so powerful: not only does it allow one to move along lines anticipated by past experience; it also incorporates new experi-ence, including that of the Fourth Evangelist, into that which is so familiar as to seem traditional.

VIII

Tom Thatcher's "The Shape of John's Story" also recognizes the idiosyn-crasies of the Fourth Gospel, and he goes about its analysis in a way that complements Brickle's. Thatcher, too, is alive to the symphonic character of John's Gospel; like Brickle, he appreciates its poetic character and the spiraling of themes around one another. He reaffirms John's attachment to tradition while recognizing his Gospel's unique qualities.

For Thatcher, the plot of John's story "is not grounded in its theological claims but rather in Jesus' movements through space and time" (p. 237). Modern observers recognize the utility of John's methodical emplotment.

"The religious group," Halbwachs observed (1980), "more than any other, needs the support of some object, of some enduring part of reality, because it claims to be unchanging while every other institution and custom is being modified." The very permanence of the *physical* location, assuming the group is attached to it, carries the guarantee of *social* continuity. Distances among physical places also shape and fix religious narratives. The Synoptics, too, recognize Halbwachs's "localizations," but John emphasizes these more than any predecessor.

One can think about the problem from a different perspective. In the "extrinsic theory of cognition" (Geertz 1973), thinking is more than an occurrence in the individual mind; it is a matching of symbolic models to the makeup of the empirical world. The pilgrim is thinking when he runs his finger across a map: the finger representing himself, the map, a model of the way. Frederic Jameson's (1984) account of the Bonaventura Hotel and Kevin Lynch's (1960) theory of cognitive maps demonstrate that people cannot orient themselves in space and time without physical reference points. Such "localizations" enable people to know where they are and prevent themselves from getting lost.

Every memory, Thatcher seems to be telling us, involves two independent series, a series of external objects and a series of internal thoughts. This distinction is important because it bears on the question of whether John's places are fictional or real. Does he choose arbitrarily the places with which he associates Jesus' actions, or is he determined to identify place and time orderings because they stand for external information about when and where Jesus acted and of what he did?

I would like to put Thatcher's characterization into different words. All know that John's culture differed from that of his predecessors and that he interpreted it perceptively. He was sensitive to the persecution of Christian communities everywhere—including Rome. In the last decades of the century, persecutions continued under Domitian, while the Jewish-Christian split widened. The principal problem, however, was dissension within Christianity itself. John intended to subdue the many variant forms of Christian belief, including the heresies of Docetism and Gnosticism, whose "antichrist" leaders threatened the churches under his care. John's world was fragmented, but *fragmented commemoration* of Jesus must be distinguished from its *multivocal* forms (see Vinitzky-Seroussi 2009). Men and women who share the same beliefs but interpret them in different ways commemorate multivocally. For example, some Americans regard Abraham Lincoln primarily as savior of the Union; others, as a great emancipator; still others as man of the people and self-made man. But few Americans dispute Lincoln's being all these things. In contrast, fragmented commemoration includes multiple beliefs and the conduct of ritual in separate places where unique interpretations are expressed by dissociated communities of believers.

As John's religious world fragmented, he endeavored to reveal to Christendom the one true Jesus. He did so not by theological disquisition but by a concrete recounting of the Savior's life, compulsively following him from one place to another and putting his movements in chronological order. In Thatcher's words, "John uses Jesus' real world as his memory theater, [suggesting] that his presentation of the scope and movement of Christ's career at least reflects the world as it was and would have been" (p. 237). Hence the structure of Thatcher's own argument: almost a third of his chapter is devoted to John's articulating his Gospel by mapping the locations and the temporal order of Jesus' acts. His purpose: to win back the heretics and apostates by giving them an authentically concrete narrative of the Messiah's life.

IX

Rafael Rodriguez's "According to Scriptures" demonstrates the interdependency of tradition and memory in its discussion of Psalms. Rodriguez shows how established and publicly available patterns of Jewish discourse reveal what is behind the notion of the "suffering Messiah." The chapter is profoundly insightful, but its points about the simultaneity of perception and interpretation get us off to an unnecessarily rough start.

Rodriguez presents us with a variation on an old theme. Many decades ago Walter Lippmann (1922) declared that the average person defines an event before he sees it. Interpretation, he thought, precedes perception. For Lippmann to know this, he must have been one of the lucky few able to see an event *before* defining it. A venerable body of social psychological research, some described in this volume's introductory chapter, shows the truth of Lippmann's statement but in doing so reveals how limited that truth is. Imagine interpretation following and being influenced by perception, which is in turn affected by reality. Imagine, by contrast, perception and interpretation occurring concurrently. In the latter case, historical analysis, typology, keying, and framing are literally impossible—so impossible that Rodriguez never applies or returns to the point.

Luke's references to Jesus' suffering and the book of Psalms in the Acts of the Apostles are the real cases in point. Jesus' place in the world, his relation to God, the Jews, the coming kingdom—all these things, and others, make for a complicated picture worthy of Rodriguez's analytic skills. Luke tries to simplify the picture of Jesus' suffering by keying it to selected parts of the Old Testament. The psalmist, as Rodriguez sees Luke reading him, refers to God's protection of the righteous, their delight in following his ways, the coming triumph of the meek, God's announcing Jesus to be his only Son, the world's conspiring against God and his Chosen One. The section is as fascinating as it is instructive, showing as it does how thickly the web of the Old Testament surrounds Jesus' crucifixion and suffering. Luke knits Jesus' torment into the very fabric of Jewish history. Doing so, he makes plausible a scenario that would otherwise contradict itself, namely, a messiah being mocked, scourged, and executed among thieves. Few expected such a demise, but when prefigured in the ancient Testament it becomes at once comprehensible and inevitable.

The general problem, in Rodriquez's view, is to identify how Luke drew his parallels. Why is Jesus' suffering keyed to certain psalms and not others? If we only knew about Jesus' final hours before the four Gospels appeared, would we be able to predict from which psalms, and the verses within those psalms, Luke would draw? Could we do the same for every Gospel reference to the Old Testament?

Consider a scribe whose job is to set down in writing his own witnessing of Jesus' betrayal, suffering, and crucifixion. How would he go about doing so? Assume that he is looking at his task not as a reporter but as one who seeks to make Jesus' death meaningful. Cognitive psychologists would refer to the scribe's task as one of "pattern recognition," the mapping of a specific sequence of events in the present (including the passion) to a more general pattern seemingly prefigured in the Old Testament. An animal will react to an event by mapping it to an inborn schema (a bull will attack a red cloth); a human may do the same by mapping a familiar narrative, such as Jesus' prediction of the coming kingdom of God, to Noah saving God's virtuous from the flood (as portrayed iconically in the Church of the Holy Sepulcher). The Noah story would exist in the scribe's mind as a stored schematic pattern, and he would generalize this pattern to Jesus' saving the world.

Many Old Testament stories can be thus structured and stored. The scribe's recognition of the story pattern enables his readers and listeners to grasp the meaning of Jesus' suffering. Salvation as a reward for obedience to God, however inconvenient or even painful, is the pattern that links recent to old events.

These statements about pattern recognition are simplistic, but Rodri-guez's essay explores the issue, sensitizing us to "keying" and "framing" as special cases of "pattern recognition." Doing so, he addresses one of the deepest problems of Jesus scholarship. Matthew 27:12 serves as a representative case. Jesus says nothing in response to the Sanhedrin's accusations against him, "in order to fulfill prophecy" (Isa 53:7). Given the hundreds of events in Jesus' life keyed to Old Testament prophecy, often in such peculiar grammatical constructions as his doing this or that "in fulfillment of scripture" or "to fulfill" what some prophet or other had said, Rodriguez implicitly questions the precise nature of keying and framing in the first century. Because "fulfilling prophecy" and simi-lar constructions are rarely if ever found in the Old Testament itself, we ask (1) whether Jesus himself believed he was fulfilling Isaiah's proph-ecy by remaining silent; (2) whether Jews had reason to expect that the words and actions of their Messiah, whoever he might be, would con-form to Scripture; (3) whether this expectation occurred mainly to the four Gospel writers; and (4) why Scripture *frames* the events of Jesus' life mainly by *predicting* them.

X

Frederick Tappenden's "On the Difficulty of Molding a Rock" describes the negotiation of Peter's reputation in the process of revealing problems that attended Christianity's institutionalization. Peter was first to see the risen Christ, but he was also condemned by Paul for his determination to Juda-ize the Gentiles. That Paul, a latecomer who never knew Jesus, had the effrontery to criticize the Messiah's own apostle tells how rapidly the Chris-tian cultural and social landscape had changed. Paul's letter to the Gala-tians therefore affected Luke's portrayal of Peter in Acts. After reviewing the debate on this issue, Tappenden states: "[W]hat we are facing may not be a problem of textual paucity but rather of narrowly constructed theo-retical predispositions" (p. 265). The latter exclude the relation between a text's production and reception, which is the very issue Tappenden seeks to address.

Among the most useful approaches to the relationship between authors, reader reactions, and authors' reactions to their readers is that of German literary critic Hans Robert Jauss (1982). When the reader opens a book, Jauss explains, he or she locates it along a "horizon of expecta-tions" affected by previous experience. How far a text affirms or challenges readers' expectations affects the way they react to it. Tappenden, however, asserts that writers are not free to depict the past any way they please, while the range of readers' interpretations is equally limited. Writers and readers therefore "interact" with and influence one another. Accordingly, the substance of Tappenden's argument is that Luke's portrayal of Peter reflects Luke's own reading of Paul's letter to the Galatians. Galatians does not determine but rather imposes limits on what Luke can say about Peter, while Luke's portrayal of Peter affects the interpretation of Paul.

Bringing Mark as well as Luke into the picture, Tappenden takes a comparative approach reminiscent of Wendy Griswold's (1987) work on reviewer reactions to a single novel in different nations. Mark's Peter is one with whom his audience can identify: Peter demonstrates virtue, understanding, and faith, but he is also rebuked by Jesus, falls asleep in the garden during his time of watch, and, in the end, denies his Savior. Peter is an imperfect "every-person" whose image can be at once rejected and embraced. In Luke's Gospel we see an unmistakable residue of Mark's Peter; however, Peter is memorable here not because of his human imperfections but his determination to rise above them. Although restrained by Mark's prior conception of an imperfect disciple, Luke's portrayal is doubtlessly the more positive. Thus, as we move from Paul through Mark to Luke's Acts, we move from a relatively negative figure to a two-dimensional one, then to a positive figure worthy of reverence.

What, then, is one to make of Luke's reaction to Paul's bitter criticism of Peter's aversion to Galatian Gentiles? Luke could not ignore Paul any more than he could ignore Mark; therefore, he managed his readers' "horizon of expectations" by downplaying Peter's connection to Antioch, where his wrongdoing against Gentiles was most evident. In Acts, he declares that Peter actually subordinated his own views to Paul's. Describing Peter as a loyal and moderate inclusionist, Luke rehabilitates him.

An element of cognitive dissonance theory (Festinger 1957), which demonstrates and explains why the mind tends toward the maintenance of consonant or "balanced" states (Heider 1958), imposes itself on Tappenden's chapter. Unbalanced situations, including reputations involving positive and negative elements, are always unstable and susceptible to the mind's tendency toward certainty and conviction, which it achieves by revaluating a given reputation's individual elements. Tappenden's concept of reputational "rehabilitation" is a special case of cognitive dissonance theory. That Luke admires Paul and Peter alike makes Paul's condemnation of Peter a source of dissonance that Luke cannot abide; accordingly, his narrative subtracts weight from Paul's negative statements while adding weight to Mark's positive ones.

Tappenden's account of Luke's reframing of Galatians is an important addition to New Testament studies. He also puts his finger on cognitive balance, the "mechanism," as it were, which makes social memory work.

XI

The final New Testament essay in our collection, Dennis Duling's "Social Memory and Commemoration of the Death of 'the Lord,'" concerns a crisis for Christianity revolving around banquet practices. It is generally known that Jewish law prohibited the partaking of a meal with Gentiles and that, among Jews themselves, elites and commoners dined differently and separately. This same division appeared within the early Christian churches, including those with which Paul had contact, but some churches were more polarized than others. In his letter to the Corinthians, for instance, Paul expresses displeasure with affluent members' excluding the hungry poor as they feasted.

Banquets, even more than regular meals, reflect a community's status differences and attending tensions. Duling's analytic reference points therefore include social boundaries (who dines with whom), bonding (reflecting social networks), obligation (meal etiquette and the ideals on which they are based), social stratification (seating of guests according to their social rank), and social equality (equal treatment of guests). To conform to the last two norms at one and the same time is impossible and therefore a prescription for trouble.

Duling's theoretical model is semiotic: the ritual aspects of an ancient banquet, including the Lord's Supper, give a Christian reading of Christian society, expressing its moral values and predicaments. Banquets are not only good places to eat; they are good places with which to think—and to remember. The banquet, after all, is a constituent of commemoration and, as such, prominent among what Maurice Halbwachs called the "social frames of memory." This last statement is central to Duling's essay. "If food is treated as a code," Mary Douglas (1972) once remarked, "the messages it encodes will be found in the pattern of social relations being expressed. The message is about different degrees of hierarchy, inclusion and exclusion, boundaries, and transactions across the boundaries." The closeness of the match between the banquet's boundaries and the social structure is a good measure of its message's validity. Such is the implicit premise of Duling's analysis of Paul's response to the Corinthian factions—a project that bears on the intertwining of social memory and social status.

Jewish tradition submerges its adherents in history. The relentless readings of Psalms, the performances of ritual, the wearing of fringes, phylacteries, and mezuzahs, the blowing of the ram's horn—all these are reminders of the sacred past, as is the Passover obligation for all men and women to believe that they themselves came forth from Egypt. Among Christians, too, "The first obligation of the apostle vis-à-vis a community is to make the faithful remember what they have received and already know or should know" (p. 298, quoting Dahl 1976, 15).

For Paul, sharing meals and remembering together is essential to overcoming social discord. The act of sharing frames the banquet by keying it to the covenant-forming event itself, namely, the Lord's Supper, wherein each participant partakes symbolically and equally of the blood and body of Jesus. When wine and bread are taken by the affluent and the poor together, social differences become irrelevant. As Jesus' Passover death foreshadowed the Passover banquet, his Last Supper became an encompassing frame within which all people from all social niches gathered to eat and drink "in remembrance of me." To eat and drink "in remembrance of me" was impossible in a church where an elite celebrated itself. What Corinthian men and women believed in common, however, regularly subordinated their distinctions. Commemorative meals symbolized and reinforced the church's inclusiveness and unity.

XII

In this closing chapter, I have emphasized the use of social memory concepts in the expansion of biblical knowledge and, reciprocally, biblical knowledge's contribution to the more general problems of social memory. In the process, I detected a number of fresh themes and questions, which I briefly summarize here in closing.

> ▶ When memory is structured as a narrative, it takes the form of a core story and its variations. Ferdinand de Saussure comes analogically to mind. *Langue* is to *parole* what the story's "basic pattern" is to its variations. To bring Saussure into the picture gives us a fresh way to articulate the content of biblical narratives, one that *makes imperative* the recognition of agreement and variation, permanence and change.

- The phenomenon of the "ghost narrative," which is found not only in the biblical literature but also in novels, short stories, and political rhetoric, raises the question of why some historical persons and events are memorable only in the guise of others.

- Social memory is a metaphor, a way of thinking about a complex phenomenon by reference to a simpler and more familiar one. Many critics conclude with this assertion. To define social memory as a metaphor, however, tells nothing about the distribution of individual ideas and commemorative sentiments about the past or how these work through selection, exaggeration and muting, keying and framing. Above all, the consequence of ignoring the realities to which the metaphor of social memory refers, notwithstanding those who believe that the metaphoric character of thought determines what we make of reality, are critical but unexplored problems.

- References to religious origins are rarely arbitrary. Origins refer to distinct and intrinsically memorable turning points that consist of the rejection of existing religious modes and creation of new ones. Origins are also memorable because they contain the precedents of succeeding practices and events. This definition is contradicted by the discovery of an origin's source. Whether the discovery of a founding period's *causes* negate its being conceived as an *origin* is a theoretical problem, but the reality and consequences of founding eras is an empirical one.

- Serious questions about the keying/framing process are raised by claims that Jesus performed or refrained from performing certain actions "in order to fulfill" a prophecy of some kind. To do something in order to make a prediction come true makes the prediction itself meaningless. The invocation of a past event to frame a present situation, a common commemorative tactic, differs from biblical typologies, which relate Jesus' actions (and, apparently, Jesus' actions alone) to prophecies recorded in the Hebrew Scriptures.

- Hillel's and Jesus' lives partially overlapped, and the extraordinary similarity of their liberal interpretation of the law is well known. Hillel and his students were prominent in Jesus' days, and it is difficult to imagine his not knowing them. In what sense, then, might Hillel be a "ghost memory" in the four Gospels?

► The relationship between memory and tradition is here extenuated for the first time. At question is whether one is a cause of the other, whether they are independent or interdependent, or whether one is a constituent of the other.

► Among the key questions for social memory scholarship is how to formulate the temporal sequence of perception, memory, and interpretation. The issue, framed as it is by Kantian rationalism and Lockean empiricism, is perennial. The research task is now to distinguish events that are inherently memorable from those remembered mainly in terms of the foreknowledge presumed by typology and framing.

► *Traditionsbruch* is a crutch concept allowing those who invoke it to avoid the bother of ruling out alternatives to a theory that aligns certain events to the passing of generations. So far as it applies to social memory, *Traditionsbruch* presumes what it must demonstrate, namely, that no other factor accounts for what it purports to explain.

► The analysis of prophecy is essential to an understanding of first-century memory. How a community adapts to prophecy's failure is, to this end, equally essential.

► Subsumed under "the extrinsic theory of cognition," remembering is a matching of past events and current symbolic models. Matching event and model defines all thinking, religious and secular, and requires us to know precisely what we are doing when analyzing the contrasting cognitive dynamics shaping *typology*, on the one hand, and *keys and frames* on the other.

► Every memory is organized according to the principles of pattern recognition and cognitive dissonance.

► When historical works fall outside one's "horizon of expectations," their claims are often rejected in favor of new historical propositions. New propositions, however, are often less valid than the ones they replace. Biblical and social memory scholarship must therefore distinguish (1) the contexts within which historical claims are justifiably refuted yet remain unchanged, from (2) those within which such claims are amended to satisfy unjustified challenges.

▶ Analysis of first-century Christian banquets must draw attention to traditional Jewish dietary law, with its fierce distinctions
between Jews and Gentiles. Banquets also mark the significant
anniversaries they dramatize; accordingly, the ritual meal
encodes social memory as well as social boundaries.

I have tried to exclude from the above summary all significant issues
in social memory studies and the existing biblical literature. The result is
a sharper focus on what our authors have added to their fields. For me,
the preceding chapters bring existing theories of memory down to earth,
modifying them with new precision, clearer concepts, and fresh perspective. In turn, the application of social memory models to specific biblical
cases, including those addressed in the present volume, cannot have left
the body of biblical knowledge unchanged.

Works Cited

Alexander, Jeffrey C. 2004. On the Social Construction of Moral Universals:
The "Holocaust" from War Crime to Trauma Drama. Pages 196–263 in
Cultural Trauma and Collective Identity. Edited by Jeffrey Alexander,
Ron Eyerman, Bernhard Giesen, and Piotr Sztompka. Berkeley: Uni-
versity of California Press.

Assmann, Jan. 2006. Form as Mnemonic Device: Cultural Texts and Cultural Memory. Pages 67–82 in *Performing the Gospel: Orality, Memory,
and Mark.* Edited by Richard A. Horsley, Jonathan Draper, and John
Miles Foley. Minneapolis: Fortress.

Dahl, Nils Alstrup. 1976. Anamnesis: Memory and Commemoration in
Early Christianity. Pages 11–29 in *Jesus in the Memory of the Early
Church: Essays.* Minneapolis: Augsburg. [orig. 1946]

Douglas, Mary. 1972. "Deciphering a Meal." *Daedalus* 101:61–81.

Eliade, Mircea. 1961. *Images and Symbols.* New York: Sheed & Ward.

Festinger, Leon. 1957. *Theory of Cognitive Dissonance.* Evanston, IL: Row,
Peterson.

Fine, Gary A. 1996. Reputational Entrepreneurs and the Memory of
Incompetence: Melting Supporters, Partisan Warriors, and Images of
President Harding. *American Journal of Sociology* 101:1159–93.

Fiske, Susan T., and Shelley E. Taylor. 1991. *Social Cognition.* 2nd ed. New
York: McGraw-Hill.

Geertz, Clifford. 1973. *The Interpretation of Cultures: Selected Essays.* New

York: Basic Books.

Griswold, Wendy. 1987. The Fabrication of Meaning: Literary Interpretation in the United States, Great Britain, and the West Indies. *American Journal of Sociology* 92:1077–1117.

Halbwachs, Maurice. 1980. *The Collective Memory*. Translated by Francis Ditter and Vida Yazdi Ditter. New York: Harper & Row. [orig. 1950]

Heider, Fritz. 1958. *The Psychology of Interpersonal Relations*. Hillside, NJ: Erlbaum.

Jameson, Frederic. 1984. Postmodernism, or The Cultural Logic of Late Capitalism. *New Left Review* 146:53–92.

Jauss, Hans Robert. 1982. *Toward an Aesthetic of Reception*. Translated by Timothy Bahti. Minneapolis: University of Minnesota Press.

Kroeber, Alfred L. 1957. *Styles and Civilization*. Ithaca, NY: Cornell University Press.

Latour, Bruno, and Steve Woolgar. 1979. *Laboratory Life: The Social Construction of Scientific Facts*. Beverly Hills, CA: Sage.

Lippmann, Walter. 1922. *Public Opinion*. New York: Macmillan.

Lynch, Kevin. 1960. *The Image of the City*. Cambridge: MIT Press.

Pelikan, Jaroslav. 1985. *Jesus through the Centuries: His Place in the History of Culture*. New Haven: Yale University Press.

Saussure, Ferdinand de. 1986. *Course in General Linguistics*. Edited by Charles Bally, Albert Sechehaye, and Albert Riedlinger. Translated by Roy Harris. LaSalle, IL: Open Court. [orig. 1916]

Shils, Edward A. 1981. *Tradition*. Chicago: University of Chicago Press.

Taylor, Gary. 1989. *Reinventing Shakespeare: A Cultural History from the Restoration to the Present*. New York: Weidenfield & Nicholson.

Vinitzky-Seroussi, Vered. 2009. *Yitzhak Rabin's Assassination and the Dilemmas of Commemoration*. Albany: State University of New York Press.

White, Hayden. 1987. *The Content of the Form: Narrative Discourse and Historical Representation*. Baltimore: Johns Hopkins University Press.

CONTRIBUTORS

Jeffrey E. Brickle serves as Professor of Biblical Studies at Urshan Graduate School of Theology. His research interests focus on the convergence of the Johannine literature with ancient media culture. Along with contributing chapters to *The Fourth Gospel in First-Century Media Culture* and *Rethinking the Ethics of John*, Jeff is the author of *Aural Design and Coherence in the Prologue of First John*.

Dennis Duling is Professor Emeritus at Canisius College and a long-time leader in the application of social-science models and methods to problems in Christian origins. He is the author of numerous books and articles, including the influential textbook *The New Testament: An Introduction* (with Norman Perrin). A number of his most influential essays have recently been republished in *A Marginal Scribe: Studies in Matthew in Social-Scientific Perspective*.

Steven Fraade is the Mark Taper Professor of the History of Judaism at Yale University, where he teaches in the Department of Religious Studies and the Program in Judaic Studies. His books include *Enosh and His Generation: Pre-Israelite Hero and History in Post-biblical Interpretation*; *From Tradition to Commentary: Torah and Its Interpretation in the Midrash Sifre to Deuteronomy*; and *Legal Fictions: Studies of Law and Narrative in the Discursive Worlds of Ancient Jewish Sectarians and Sages*. His most recent research focuses on multilingualism in ancient Jewish culture and society.

Gabriella Gelardini is Adjunct Professor in New Testament at the University of Basel. She is the author/editor of numerous books and articles in German and English, particularly on the Gospel of Mark and the book of Hebrews, and is also the founder and co-chair of the Book of Hebrews in Context Group in the Society of Biblical Literature. Her works include *Christus militans: Studien zur politisch-militärischen Semantik im Markusevangelium vor dem Hintergrund des ersten jüdisch-römischen Krieges*; *"Verhärtet eure Herzen nicht": Der Hebräer, eine Synagogenhomi-*

lie zu Tischa be-Aw; and, *Hebrews: Contemporary Methods—New Insights* (editor).

Chris Keith is Professor of New Testament and Early Christianity at St Mary's University College, Twickenham, where he also serves as Director of the Centre for the Social-Scientific Study of the Bible. He is the author of *The* Pericope Adulterae, *the Gospel of John, and the Literacy of Jesus*; *Jesus' Literacy: Scribal Culture and the Teacher from Galilee*, and co-editor of *Jesus among Friends and Enemies: A Historical and Literary Introduction to Jesus in the Gospels*; and *Jesus, Criteria, and the Demise of Authenticity*. Chris is a member of the Memoria Romana project and currently serves as co-chair of the Bible in Ancient and Modern Media Section in the Society of Biblical Literature.

Alan Kirk is Professor of Early Christianity in the Department of Philosophy and Religion at James Madison University. In addition to memory and tradition, he has published on the Synoptic Problem, Q, and other topics in the history of Gospel literature. Alan is the author of numerous essays on the place of memory and writing in early Christian media culture and also of *The Composition of the Sayings Source: Genre, Synchrony, and Wisdom Redaction in Q*, and he is co-editor of *Memory, Tradition, and Text: Uses of the Past in Early Christianity*. He is currently working on a monograph on the double tradition in the Gospel of Matthew.

Tim Langille is a Visiting Lecturer in Religious Studies and Jewish Studies at the University of Pittsburgh. His research focuses on collective trauma and memory. Tim is in the process of turning his PhD dissertation, "Reshaping the Persistent Past: A Study of Collective Trauma and Memory in Second Temple Judaism," into a book. His current project, *The Jerusalem Temple as a Sacralized Landscape of Violence*, examines the relationship between trauma, violence, memory, and place in Josephus's *Judean War*.

Carol Newsom is Charles Howard Candler Professor of Old Testament and Director of the Graduate Division of Religion at Emory University. Widely recognized for her expertise in ancient Jewish wisdom traditions and the Dead Sea Scrolls, Carol is the author of seven books and numerous articles and is a former President of the Society of Biblical Literature. She is co-editor of both the *New Oxford Annotated Bible* and *The Women's Bible Commentary*.

Rafael Rodríguez is Professor of New Testament at Johnson University. His works include numerous papers and presentations on the origins of the Gospels, and he is author of *Structuring Early Christian Memory: Jesus in Tradition, Performance, and Text* and *Oral Tradition and the New Testament: A Guide for the Perplexed.*

Barry Schwartz is Professor Emeritus in the Department of Sociology at the University of Georgia. Schwartz is a leading voice on the study of collective memory and social psychology and is the author/editor of numerous books and essays. His publications include significant applications of social-science models to iconic figures and events in world and American history, along with (more recently) a number of papers and essays on problems in Christian origins. His most influential works include *Abraham Lincoln and the Forge of National Memory*; *Abraham Lincoln in the Post-heroic Era*; and *George Washington: The Making of an American Symbol*, along with many theoretical and applied studies in collective memory.

Frederick S. Tappenden is an FRQSC Postdoctoral Research Fellow at McGill University working in areas related to Paul and his reception. His works include his PhD dissertation, "Embodying Resurrection: Conceptualisations of this Life and the Next in the Undisputed Pauline Epistles," and the forthcoming *Language, Cognition, and Biblical Studies: Papers from the 2011 SBL International Meeting in London, England* (ed. with Tamás Biró). His current research project is entitled, "Embodying Hermeneutics: Early Christian Creativity and the Post-Pauline Construction of Hope."

Tom Thatcher is Professor of Biblical Studies at Cincinnati Christian University and the author/editor of numerous books and articles on the Johannine literature and ancient media culture. Tom is the founder of the John, Jesus, and History research unit in the Society of Biblical Literature and also serves as co-chair of the Bible in Ancient and Modern Media Section. His works on early Christian media culture include *Memory, Tradition, and Text: Uses of the Past in Early Christianity* (editor), *Why John Wrote a Gospel: Jesus–Memory–History*; *Jesus, the Voice, and the Text: Beyond* The Oral and the Written Gospel (editor); and, *The Fourth Gospel in First-Century Media Culture* (editor with Anthony Le Donne).

Author Index

SUBJECT INDEX

sectarian texts (Qumran), 67–68
selective recall, 2, 18, 19, 22, 42, 149, 150, 315
Sepphoris, 103, 105
Shammai (ancient rabbi), 320
Shishak (Egyptian general), 97
Shoah/Holocaust, 58 n. 2, 59 n. 4, 60, 244
shofar (ritual trumpet), 115–16, 118–19
"signs" (miracles in Gospel of John), 198–200, 211–16
Simon ben Giora (Jewish rebel leader), 92, 106, 107
Simon Peter. *See* Peter (biblical character)
Sim(e)on the Righteous (high priest), 120–21
Simonides of Keos, 232–33
Sin (Babylonian moon god), 49, 50
Sinai (site of memory), 77, 79, 82, 83, 294, 303
sites of memory, 15, 16, 31, 57, 58, 58 n. 3, 60–64, 67–70, 72, 73, 74, 76, 82, 83, 151, 189, 200–203, 210, 231, 236, 237, 268–69, 273–74, 276–77, 283
    calendars as, 76, 99, 109, 116, 209–10, 218, 228, 230, 231, 234, 235, 236, 327–28
    maps/land as, 210, 218, 230, 234–36, 327–28
    texts as, 268–69, 273–74, 275–77, 278, 283
social class divisions (early church), 291–93, 294–95, 295–96
social facts, 10
social memory. *See* collective/social memory
social morality, 299–301, 303–5. *See also* collective memory, normative force of
Socrates, 148, 151
Solomon (biblical character), 95
stored memory, 46–47, 312–13, 329
Suetonius (ancient historian), 104
Sukkot/Tabernacles (Jewish festival), 115–16, 117, 214, 220, 228, 234
symposium (ancient), 295–96, 304. *See also* meals

synagogue(s), 118, 227–28, 236, 259 n. 39, 293, 294, 320, 324
Synoptic tradition, 132, 132–34, 135–45, 147, 152 n. 24, 153–54, 195, 196, 256 n. 30. *See also* Jesus tradition
Syria (Roman province), 102–3, 278
Syrian Antioch, 263–64, 278, 279–80, 282, 283, 331

Tabernacles/Sukkot (Jewish festival), 115–16, 117, 214, 220, 228, 234
Tacitus, 104, 109
Teacher of Righteousness (Dead Sea Scrolls), 70–72, 75–76, 77, 77 n. 11, 79, 80–81
"telephone" game (model of oral tradition), 12–13, 134 n. 2
telescoping (compression of time), 70, 79, 80–81, 82
temple (Jerusalem) (site of memory/identity), 71, 73, 75, 76, 87, 95–97, 99–100, 102, 110, 299, 303, 315–16
    First Temple (destruction of), 52–53, 57, 58, 60–61, 68–70, 72, 73, 81, 82, 315
    Gospel of John and destruction of, 189, 325
    Gospel of Mark and destruction of, 89–90, 100–101, 104–10, 166–67, 172–74, 180, 317–19, 324
    Second Temple (destruction of), 16, 57, 60, 68–70, 89–90, 91–92, 93, 98, 106, 114, 115–19, 119–25, 166–67, 180, 315–17, 317–19, 319–20, 324
temple incident (John 2//Mark 11), 212, 216, 231, 234, 248
temporality (structural aspect of memory), 43–45, 58, 69, 77
tenement churches (ancient), 291–93
Tenth Legion (Roman), 103, 103 n. 4
Tertullian (church father), 264
texts (written). *See* documents
The American Slave (oral history collection), 8
Theudas, 26, 142

CPSIA information can be obtained at www.ICGtesting.com
Printed in the USA
BVOW07s0810030914

364596BV00002B/8/P